GRIEF AND THE HEALING ARTS:
Creativity as Therapy

Edited by
Sandra L. Bertman

Death, Value and Meaning Series
Series Editor: John D. Morgan

Baywood Publishing Company, Inc.
AMITYVILLE, NEW YORK

Library of Congress Catalog Number: 97-48681
ISBN: 0-89503-189-2 (Cloth)
ISBN: 0-89503-198-1 (Paper)

Library of Congress Cataloging-in-Publication Data

Grief and the healing arts : creativity as therapy / edited by Sandra
  L. Bertman.
      p.   cm. - - (Death, value, and meaning series)
   Includes bibliographical references and index.
   ISBN 0-89503-189-2 (cloth). - - ISBN 0-89503-198-1 (paper)
   1. Grief.   2. Counseling.   3. Arts- -Therapeutic use.   4. Death-
-Psychological aspects.   I. Bertman, Sandra L.   II. Series.
   BF575.G7G726 1999   97-48681
   155.9- -dc21   CIP

Dedication

– To all my medical, nursing, and psychology students at the University of Massachusetts, and at all the places I have been fortunate enough to teach;

– To my colleagues at ADEC (Association of Death Education and Counseling), IWG (International Work Group on Death, Dying and Bereavement), WIT (Women in Thanatology), NE AIDS/ETC (New England AIDS/Education and Training Center), and ASBH (American Society for Bioethics and Humanities) for their spirited participation in discussions and seminars and for their commitment to this work we hold sacred;

– To Tom Manning, Mary Handley, Lillian Goodman, Mary Kay Alexander, Sandy Marks, Jr., Marjorie Clay, Jean Edmonds, Bill Damon, Gerald Haidak, Brownell Wheeler, and the rest of the faculty at the University of Massachusetts Medical School who never lost their faith in the precepts of Hospice, the philosophy of Palliative Care, and the Program of Medical Humanities;

– To the individuals, families, and groups who have allowed me to be close to them in moments of isolation, suffering, grief, and joy;

– To those who died before this manuscript was completed: Bessie and Edward Bertman, Donald Paulson, Yoram BenPorath, Michael Bruno, Marilyn Lipsky, Sally Phillips, Mickey Miller, Katherine Becker, J. Havelka, Jessie Kesson, Judith English, Anthony Francis Yarnell Gamino, Jacqueline Lazare, Peter Lehner, and the Borkum family;

– To my grandson, Max Musial Bertman, who was in gestation and born while this book came to fruition;

– To the artists whose works are quoted, cited, and reproduced within these pages, and finally this book is dedicated

– To the artist within us all.

> It is something to be able to paint a picture, or to carve a statue, and so to make a few objects beautiful. But it is far more glorious to carve and paint the atmosphere in which we work, to effect the quality of the day—this is the highest of the arts.
>
> —Thoreau

Acknowledgments

I would like to acknowledge my enormous joy in creating this anthology of techniques, resources, and inspiration for practicing clinicians and educators.

I also want to thank those who worked along with me during the many years this volume was in the making for their enthusiasm, patience, attention to detail, and for their sleuth work in tracking sources and securing permission letters: Kathy Olmsted, Cathy O'Har, Sally Daugherty, Jenny Altschuler, Hanieh Vahidi, Jennifer Murphy, Nancy Perkins, and Ann Huculak.

I am deeply indebted to my sounding boards, Jack Morgan, Roberta Halporn, and Mary Costanza, for their seasoned guidance and supportive presence from my initial envisioning of this book throughout its many reincarnations; and most especially to my design consultant, Digitalclay Interactive Ltd., and my editors Judith Leet and Bobbi Olszewski whose expertise with the publishing process shaped this manuscript into polished form.

Finally, I am deeply indebted to the Charitable Trust, the Dana Project, and the grant endowment for the Program of Humanities and Palliative Care for their generous support.

*　　*　　*

The following acknowledgments are gratefully made to publishers, authors, artists, museums, and galleries in addition to those otherwise specifically mentioned within the text:

Cortney Davis,"The Body Flute," © 1994, originally published in *Hudson Review;* "What the Nurse Likes," "Becoming the Patient," © 1994, originally published in *The Body Flute.*

Elsa Dorfman, all photographs used in "The M(ortality) Word and the L(ove) Word," and in the Introduction, © 1998 by Elsa Dorfman. Used by permission of Elsa Dorfman.

Elsevier Science Ltd., The Boulevard, Langford Lane, Kidlington OX5 1GB, UK, "To Know of Suffering and the Teaching of Empathy," from *Social Science & Medicine,* © 1977 with kind permission.

Dusty (pseudonym of author), "Hello, David," © 1987. Used by permission.

Brenda Eng, "Puppets," © 1998. Photographs taken by author used with permission.

Paule French for photograph "A Silver Cross Made by Mrs. O," used in Regina Kelley's "Transformations: Visual Arts and Hospice Care," © 1998. Used with permission.

Galerie St. Etienne, NY, for permission to reprint Kaethe Kollwitz's "Ruf des Todes," © 1935, and "Abschied," © 1940.

Mindy Gough for photographs used in "Remembrance Photographs" from her personal collection, © 1998. Used with permission of author.

Roberta Halporn, "Gravestone Rubbing: Epitaph," © 1998. Used with permission.

Hamburger Kuntshalle. Co. Elke Walford, Hamburg, for permission to reprint Kaethe Kollwitz's "Die Eltem," © 1923.

C. Regina Kelley for photographs used in "Transformations: Visual Arts and Hospice Care," "Annie and Her Medicine Shield," "Annie and the Owl," "Column with Bell," © 1988. Used with permission.

William Lamers, for "The Grief Cycle," © 1978 by Wm. Lamers, Jr., MD.

DC Moore gallery for permission to reprint photographs of Nancy Fried's sculpture: "Self-Portrait," 1994, "Marking the Pain," 1995, "Cradling Her Sorrow," 1989, "The Nightmare," 1987, "Hanging Out," 1987, "Breast Flap," 1987, "The Flirt," 1986, Courtesy DC Moore Gallery, New York City.

Musées royaux des Beaux Arts, Brussels, for permission to reproduce Breughel's "La Chute D'Icare."

Museum of Fine Arts, Boston, Frederick Brown Fund, for permission to reprint Kaethe Kollwitz's "Self-Portrait," © 1921.

W.W. Norton & Company, Inc., for permission to reprint "The Five Stages of Grief" from *The Five Stages of Grief* by Linda Pastan. © 1978 by Linda Pastan.

National Gallery, Oslo, for permission to reprint Edvard Munch's "The Scream," 1895, "The Dance of Life," 1900, "The Dead Mother and Child," 1899, "The Sick Child," 1896, and "Fever," 1894.

© The New Yorker Collection 1977. Lee Lorenz from cartoonbank.com. for "The Closure Fairy." Reprinted with permission.

Carol Picard, "Songlines," © 1992, "Seeing Fred on a Respirator," © 1992, "Meditation on the Vietnam Women's Memorial," © 1994. Used by permission.

Christina Schlesinger, "Yusuf Hawkins" (mural), © 1998. Used by permission of the author.

Hannah Sherabin for drawing "Keriah," © 1998. Used by permission of the author.

Wilma Bulkin Siegel for "The Faces of AIDS: AIDS Quilt," © 1994. By permission of the artist.

Target Theatre, Victoria, B.C., Canada, for "Wake for Dying," © 1998. Script and photographs used with permission.

Vietnam Women's Memorial Project, Inc., for photograph of "Vietnam Women's Memorial," Washington, DC, Glenna Goodacre, sculptor (photo by Gregory Staley), © 1993. Used with permission.

Virago Press Ltd., for "Dear Edith," reprinted from *Where the Apple Ripens* by Jessie Ke sson. © The Estate of Jessie Kesson, 1985.

Contents

Grief and the Healing Arts: Introduction   1
Sandra L. Bertman

The Five Stages of Grief   2
Linda Pastan

THE ARTS, PERSONAL GRIEFS,
PROFESSIONAL ROLES

On the Psychology of Loss   21
William M. Lamers, Jr.

What the Nurse Likes   39
Cortney Davis

Preventing Harm in the Name of Help: Ensuring Ethical Care
Through the Concept of "Preserving Own Integrity"   43
Lynn Cummings

Becoming the Patient   51
Cortney Davis

Music—A Companion for the Journey from Mourning to Morning . . .   53
Sally S. Bailey

Night Nurse   59
Cortney Davis

Comfort Care   61
L. J. Schneiderman

To Know of Suffering and the Teaching of Empathy   71
Sandra Bertman and Melvin J. Krant

The Body Flute   85
Cortney Davis

Reflections on Suffering 89
Aaron Lazare

Hope and Millie 93
David Hatem

The Faces of AIDS: An AIDS Quilt 95
Wilma Bulkin Siegel

Seeing Fred on a Respirator 96
Carol Picard

SOME WAYS CAREGIVERS USE THE ARTS
FOR THEMSELVES AND FOR THOSE
THEY COMPANION

Using Art Therapy with Pediatric Oncology Patients 99
Linda G. Nicholas and Suzanne Lister

Art Techniques for Children with Cancer 119
Barbara M. Sourkes

**Puppets: Bridging the Communication Gap Between Caregivers
and Children About Death and Dying** 127
Brenda Eng

Transformations: Visual Arts and Hospice Care 139
C. Regina Kelley

Sound and Silence: Music Therapy in Palliative Care 145
Kevin Kirkland

Songlines 149
Carol Picard

Movies as Movement: Films as Catharsis in Grief Therapy 151
Lynne Martins

Forum Theatre: *A Wake for Dying* 173
Kate Wilkinson and Judith McDowell

Crisis in the Cafeteria 187
Maria Trozzi

The Life and Death of Yusuf Hawkins 199
Christina Schlesinger

Gravestone Rubbing: Epitaph 203
Roberta Halporn

**Remembrance Photographs: A Caregiver's Gift for Families
of Infants Who Die** 205
Mindy L. K. Gough

LESSONS FROM CULTURES OLD AND NEW

Culture, Creativity and Death 217
J. Havelka

Visible Words: Ritual in the Pastoral Care of the Sick and Dying 225
Kurt Stasiak

**The Role of the Visual Image in Psychodynamics of Grief Resolution
(Viewed Through Jewish Law and Tradition)** 237
Hannah Sherebrin

**Pathological Grief—A Problem in Search of a Definition:
The Tragedy of Hamlet as a Model** 253
Roberta Halporn

Keeping Emotional Time: Music and the Grief Process 265
Lesleigh Forsyth

A Study in Grief: The Life and Art of Kaethe Kollwitz 277
Louis A. Gamino

Death and Grief Made Visible: The Life and Work of Edvard Munch . . 289
Judith M. Stillion

Against Daily Insignificance: Writing Through Grief 303
Martha K. Davis

Sculpting Through Grief 313
Nancy Fried

AIDS Time: A Passage Through Cawthra Park 317
James Miller

Social Support "Internetworks," Caskets for Sale, and More:
Thanatology and the Information Superhighway 331
Carla J. Sofka

Healing and the Internet 343
Thomas R. Golden

BASIC NEEDS OF GRIEVING PEOPLE

Therapeutic Touch: For Those Who Accompany the Dying 351
Mary J. Simpson

The Nurse and the Art Are One
(Meditation on the Vietnam Women's Memorial, 1994) 367
Carol Picard

Hello, David 369
*Anonymous (written by a nurse recalling her
experiences in Vietnam)*

My Mother's Hands 371
Elaine Freed Lindenblatt

The Sourdough Father 373
Lesleigh Forsyth

The M(ortality) Word and the L(ove) Word 377
Elsa Dorfman

Dear Edith 393
Jessie Kesson

Silent Conversations 403
Leigh Westerfield

List of Contributors 409
Index 415

Grief and the Healing Arts: Creativity as Therapy

Introduction

Introduction

I want to write rage but all that comes is sadness. *A. Lourde*

My story is broke. Can you help me fix it? *H. Brody*

What an amazing life's work we therapists have chosen. To accompany fellow human beings to the depths of their suffering, for as long as it takes, until they find their own way back to an inner balance, a sense of oneness with themselves. And for us? How do we keep ourselves whole, so that the next person, "client," "patient" whom we hope to "help"[1] is not being served by a depleted therapist?

Multiple loss is our steadfast companion. How many times—and for how long at any one time—can we hold another's pain without needing to flee or resort to the very natural self-protective maneuvers that grief reflexively (and, at times, thankfully) triggers? Even more to the point, in both our personal and professional lives, how do we maintain our sanity? Our composure? Our intactness? Our authenticity?

This book is meant to refuel therapists, counselors, social workers, physicians, nurses, clergy, and all others who are committed to providing support to those in grief. My thesis is that if we let the artist residing deeply within us emerge, even the most seasoned therapist can become a more creative, more self-sustaining one. Each of us needs periodic re-inspiration, booster shots to invigorate our imaginations and souls.

*   *   *

We are all familiar with grief theory. All categorizations—stage, phase, helix-like, or task-based—address the following: 1) the realities of adjusting to a changed life; 2) the fact that we are meaning-making creatures; and 3) the idea of a healing trajectory. Many of our colleagues have fleshed out the nuts and bolts of grief therapy in "normal" (whatever *that* means since the term includes just about every manifested reaction) and special circumstances, such as traumatic, disenfranchised, and complicated mourning.[2] Though useful from descriptive "snapshot" points of view, stage theories tend to be oversimplified, lead to false expectations (too much of a recipe or "cookbook" approach, too rigidly sequential), and are often misunderstood. We must be careful not to trivialize or minimize the profundity and uniqueness of a personal or communal grief by reducing it to mere explanation or method. We must curtail our reliance on jargon: not everyone needs to "work through" or achieve "closure" or even express anger. Linda Pastan's poem "The Five Stages of Grief" is an appropriate response to our wishful attempts to categorize an age-old experience:

The Five Stages of Grief

Linda Pastan

The night I lost you
someone pointed me towards
the Five Stages of Grief.
Go that way, they said,
it's easy, like learning to climb
stairs after the amputation.
And so I climbed.
Denial was first.
I sat down at breakfast
carefully setting the table
for two. I passed you the toast—
you sat there. I passed
you the paper—you hid
behind it.
Anger seemed more familiar.
I burned the toast, snatched
the paper and read the headlines myself.
But they mentioned your departure,
and so I moved on to
Bargaining. What can I exchange
for you? The silence
after storms? My typing fingers?
Before I could decide, *Depression*
came puffing up, a poor relation
its suitcase tied together
with string. In the suitcase
were bandages for the eyes
and bottles of sleep. I slid
all the way down the stairs
feeling nothing.
And all the time Hope
flashed on and off
in defective neon.
Hope was a signpost pointing
straight in the air.
Hope was my uncle's middle name,
he died of it.
After a year I am still climbing,
though my feet slip
on your stone face.
The treeline
has long since disappeared;
green is a color
I have forgotten.
But now I see what I am climbing
towards: *Acceptance*
written in capital letters,
a special headline:
Acceptance,
its name is in lights.
I struggle on,
waving and shouting.
Below, my whole life spreads its surf,
all the landscapes I've ever known
or dreamed of. Below
a fish jumps: the pulse
in your neck.
Acceptance. I finally
reach it.
But something is wrong.
Grief is a circular staircase.
I have lost you.

Those who are in grief—and *they* are our teachers—remind us of the many selves contained within each of us. We are kaleidoscopic creatures. "Personhoods," a term coined by physician Eric Cassell, are made up of past life experiences, family, kinship, culture, roles, secret lives, perceived futures, and transcendent dimensions.[3] What Anatole Broyard writes in his essay "The Patient Examines the Doctor"[4] about patients' expectations of their physicians is telling, and it is equally applicable to grieving people and their therapists: they desire us to combine the roles of priest, philosopher, poet, lover, and I would perhaps add friend—and shaman.

Jungian theory postulates that what the therapist does is less a question of treatment than of developing the creative possibilities latent within the patient. In seeking us out, those in pain are looking for a safe place where they can be listened to, or perhaps even more important, a sanctuary where they can learn to listen to themselves. We are talking about sacred relationships that allow the baring of souls and acquaintance with inmost thoughts.

We need to remind ourselves that:

- when we create an atmosphere conducive to learning, healing can take place
- meaning must be discovered, not imposed
- the seeds of healing lie dormant within each one of us—"client" and therapist alike
- grief is not a pathologic but a life-cycle event
- grief is crazy-making, feels like a psychosis, is implosive, explosive, arbitrary, unjust, but is as basic to the human condition as love and joy
- the body has its own ways of grieving, manifested in physical symptoms (Freud, Bowlby, Lindemann, and Parkes speak of the "pangs" and "wounds" of grief)
- as caregivers our personal losses require attention: we must constantly monitor our own bodies, minds, and spirits and be brave enough to invite the spotlight within, as well as outward on those we attend.

When we practitioners engage in the arts as initiators or observers, our openness to clients' creative acts is often catalyst enough to enable grieving, to stimulate the search for meaning, and to initiate change—or at least negotiate a truce with the status quo. With the mediation of the arts (poetry, drawing, psychodrama, music and so forth), we and our clients become involved, to varying degrees, in heightened identification, catharsis, and insight. The beauty of the process is its openness to interpretations, jogging both us and those entrusted to our care out of our old ruts of perception toward enlarged understandings and possibilities (Figure 1). The readings I have included in *Grief and the Healing Arts: Creativity as Therapy* are designed and arranged to refresh, inspire, remind, and upon occasion, to jolt.

THE ARTS, PERSONAL GRIEFS, PROFESSIONAL ROLES

Many readings in the opening section are focused deliberately on the tension— the balancing act—between personal and professional involvement. How much should the therapist become involved is the thorniest of questions for practitioners in

Figure 1. "It's the Closure Fairy."

this field. Several therapists here speak of their own hands-on experience and efforts to maintain a healthy equipoise.

Synthesizing the traditional theories of grief, psychiatrist William Lamers provides the reader with a general overview in his essay "On the Psychology of Loss" and shows us the role of a therapist at work in the dynamics of clinical situations. Nurse practitioner Lynn Cummings warns of the dangers of exalting ourselves as caregivers and burdening patients with our own needs in "Preventing Harm in the Name of Help."

With her AIDS quilt, physician Wilma Bulkin Siegel depicts how emotionally complex yet meaningful it can be for professional caregivers to make personal connections to patients and their plights. Physician David Hatem and nurse Carol Picard both use the strategy of writing to come to terms with their clinical experiences and indirectly explore their involvement with patients. A trained musician, the Reverend Sally Bailey uses music as a "companion" for herself and others to temper grief.

In a poignant and revelatory graduation address to medical students, Aaron Lazare, psychiatrist and Chancellor of the University of Massachusetts Medical Center, speaks about the death of his young daughter, his personal suffering, and his "transformation" into a more compassionate person.

When we are doing our work effectively, relationships—real connections—occur. We love our patients, we lose them, and we grieve. What should we make of

Cortney Davis's poem "What the Nurse Likes"? What do we think of a healer who likes "giving bad news," "watching patients die," or admits to "forgetting them"? As only the arts can bring to light, the ambivalences, ambiguities, and seemingly contradictory feelings are teased out and scrutinized. For she is the very same nurse who sits with her patients all night, who stays with them while they are dying, and who lovingly closes their eyes and gently bathes their bodies before accompanying them to the morgue, "incorporating [them] into memory":

> I like taking care of patients
> and I like forgetting them,
> going home and sitting on my porch
> while they stand away from me
> talking among themselves.
>
> I like how they look back
> when I turn their way.

Poems, patients, and their caregivers bear close reading.

The most provocative reading in this section is the short story "Comfort Care" by physician Laurence Schneiderman. Are professional ethics violated when the experienced priest-therapist, who recognizes all the "tricks of the trade," becomes the patient and, in weakened condition, is seduced by a novice volunteer? Were the would-be healer Kiki to consult with one of us for either supervision or grief counseling for herself, how would we respond? What would be our treatment plan?[5] While the readings in this section do not and cannot provide ultimate answers, they do challenge our accepted notions of professionalism and stimulate knotty and ethical reflection. They may show us our dark sides, our all-too-human sides, and in so doing, are intended to jar our consciences as well as our consciousness.

SOME WAYS CAREGIVERS USE THE ARTS FOR THEMSELVES AND FOR THOSE THEY COMPANION

Many skilled practitioners have shown the efficacy of the expressive therapies, including music, puppetry, film, and the visual and dramatic arts. The readings in this section discuss a variety of such techniques and interventions used creatively with children—in schools as well as in clinical settings. These same techniques can be just as liberating and enabling for adults. After all, when it comes to grief, is there not a child and an adolescent as well as the mature adult and wise old self in all of us?

When we work with children, who may appear to be limited in their storytelling abilities and their use of words, drawings and puppets allow them to reveal and release their feelings spontaneously. The structured art therapy techniques Barbara Sourkes has developed for use with seriously ill young patients and their siblings are classic. In her essay "Art Techniques for Children with Cancer," a child's drawing of his illness, titled "Family: From Sun to Rain," encapsulates the drastic change in the child's and family's life. Art therapists Linda Nicholas and Suzanne Lester also examine how these children are assaulted by the demands illness makes upon them and further hampered by the severe limits on their choices. Even though they may deliberately leave their pictures unfinished, their art work allows them to gradually "catch up" with the realities of their illness by creating an organization and permanence to inner experience. Their pictures often become cherished heirlooms for their families; one family explains how their deceased child's art, framed and rotated seasonally, continues to be a small extension of the child's self in their ongoing lives.

With Brenda Eng's techniques of puppet play, we see how readily adaptable these expressive modalities are for all ages, in either individual or group settings, and, equally important, how they tune us into our own system of symbols, our own multiple inner voices. Forum theater is an adult version of creative puppetry where the audience participates directly with the actors. In *A Wake for Dying,* Kate Wilkinson and Judith McDowell provide a working script offering grown-ups the opportunity to act the role of others, to play out alternative approaches to situations, and to express thoughts and behaviors they might otherwise avoid or repress. Regina Kelley's application of participatory visual arts to hospice care allows us "to document the priceless moments of heart-to-heart communication in which the patient becomes teacher" and to honor these special people who pass through our lives. We practitioners too need to be ignited by the process—to be able to express surprise, delight at new insights, and feelings of appreciation and kinship.

For those adults who may have difficulty accessing or articulating their own stories—and who are reluctant to use expressive art therapies—what safer medium than film? Films permit viewers to reflect on the more distanced lives of others and, by offering a contained time and place, legitimize "appointments with grief," thereby gaining reprieves that enable grieving persons to go about their difficult business of day-to-day living. Lynne Martins in "Movies as Movement" suggests a number of choice films readily available on video that model the gamut of grief behaviors and traumatic situations.

In "What Does Death Sound Like to You?" Kevin Kirkland suggests that sound for the living is meant to engage us, whereas music for the dying can free patients from literal, mundane time by moving them to a different—one hopes calmer or more spiritual—realm. In "Keeping Emotional Time," Lesleigh Forsyth, arguing that grief must be "acknowledged rather than hidden" and that music, in particular, acts to free grief, offers a selection of classics for the express purpose of releasing emotions.

In situations of sudden or traumatic death, Maria Trozzi—in the case of a crisis in a high school cafeteria—clarifies how therapists can husband all the community resources, put in place supports and coping strategies, and thereby diffuse the intensity of adolescents and adults mourning in isolation. Artist Christina Schlesinger and thanatologist Roberta Halporn demonstrate how a group mural and a gravestone rubbing became meaning-making rituals and creative commemorations of the tragic murder of young Yusuf Hawkins, victim of a racially motivated crime. In another form of commemoration, using the old practice of posthumous photography, social worker Mindy Gough demonstrates how remembrance photographs can be a cherished gift for families of infants who die at birth.

*　　*　　*

We, as clinicians, are always on the lookout for evocative materials to offer to those we serve. The various stories and templates, suggested in so many of these readings, are not for our eyes only but are meant to be shared with clients and colleagues at an opportune moment. The mark of a good therapist is the ability to sense just when to offer the gift of a metaphor, an idea, a revelation, or an experience. In Barry Lopez's children's book *Crow and Weasel,* we are reminded that stories have a way of taking care of us:

> If stories come to you care for them. And learn to give them away where they are needed. Sometimes a person needs a story more than food to stay alive. That is why we put these stories in each other's memory. This is how people care for themselves.

In addition to a professional audience, I hope this book will be a resource and even late-night compendium for patients and clients to find—even in one passage or one suggestion—a way to quiet their own suffering. Not everyone wants to express grief by engaging actively in therapy, expressive or otherwise; some find more solace and strength retreating into worlds of others—preferring memoirs, biographies, nonfiction, film. Still others find comfort by sharing their personal stories, as members of a group, supporting and supported by those who are in the midst of a similar situation. As so many researchers concur, it is not so much the content of the stories that heals as the sense of community derived from sharing them. Groups are a valuable resource, both person-to-person meetings and the very recent electronic groups. Dialogue and support groups are the most effective therapy for some; others find safety in the anonymity of the Internet, and only in the privacy and intimacy of that setting are they comfortable enough to acknowledge their suffering.

As an artist, Picasso defined art as the lie that enables us to see the truth. As a therapist, Freud wrote of the basic human need to make sense of one's thoughts and to create stories—even at the expense of fabrication. Somewhere between the two perspectives is the key to what it's all about: finding congruence with the meanings of our lives. Is this not the hoped-for miracle of any "therapy"? To relieve, to re-live, to relevé (from the French, in ballet, to rise above, to stand on one's toes) . . . to transcend.

LESSONS FROM CULTURES OLD AND NEW

Why and how the sacred texts, the classics—and their creators—transcend time is the essence of J. Havelka's "Culture, Creativity and Death." The time-honored measures used in traditional Protestant, Catholic, and Jewish rituals continue to bring relief to mourners because they are effective, offering consolation, hope, and forgiveness to those who believe. Let the Psalms continue to soothe our souls—the Lord is still our shepherd. Every tradition grapples with four basic spiritual questions: Who am I? How shall I live knowing I am to die? How shall I die appropriately? What legacy can I leave to the earth and the human family? And every tradition acknowledges the questions of meaning and grief that each of us must experience when confronted with mortality. Stasiak's "Visible Words" affirms the power of prayer and reenactments and the ancient sacramental acts of anointing the sick. Examining Jewish law and tradition, Hannah Sherebrin focuses on the value of long-standing traditions in the psychodynamics of grief resolution.

In the essays on Edvard Munch (by Judith Stillion) and Kaethe Kollwitz (by Louis Gamino), we learn how two major artists confronted their suffering through the creative act. In their painting and printmaking both repeatedly made visual images of the deaths in their immediate family circles. Part autobiography, part metaphor, these wrenching works vividly depict their inner landscapes, haunted by fear, sadness, horror, and at times even terror (Figure 2). Were Munch or Kollwitz or even Shakespeare's Hamlet or Beethoven or Brahms to seek us out in their time of grief, how would we counsel them? Are they not expressing their angst exceedingly well through their craft? What is psychotherapy all about, anyway?

We all know loss and grief are not restricted to bereavement, but also accompany the loss of bodily function or of a limb by amputation, as analyzed in "To Know of

Figure 2. Edvard Munch, "The Scream," woodcut, 1885.

Suffering and the Teaching of Empathy." Like Munch and Kollwitz, contemporary sculptor Nancy Fried demonstrates how fortunate artists are, for they can purge some of their grief by wrestling with it on canvas or in clay. In "Cradling Her Sorrow" (Figure 3), a woman's headless torso tenderly rocks a pained face in the crook of her arm, directly below the deep mastectomy scar, the site of a recently amputated breast. Fried tells how she came to accept her changed body through the making and remaking of the pieces: "Over and over again, I made that scar and lovingly smoothed it out. Looking at the sculptures—they look beautiful and complete."[6]

But one would be misled to assume the serenity in "Cradling Her Sorrow" epitomizes Fried's grief process. Other works in this series show anger, horror, preoccupation, her dallying with the idea of a prosthesis, and ultimately accommodation with her changed body and self. As with Kollwitz and Munch, the act of expressing pain is a means of healing for the artist, as well as a documentation of the healing process for us.

The head in "The Nightmare" (Figure 4) viewed from the back exposes a tumble of detached breasts. Contrast this with "Breast Flap," "Hanging Out," and "The Flirt" (Figures 5, 6, and 7), which display not only survival and comfort, but wellness, pride, even a bit of humor. Yet, lest there be any doubt about the circular staircase metaphor for grief, or that new losses can unstitch mercilessly the scars of old wounds, we note how unconscious knowledge plays itself out in Nancy Fried's recent

Figure 3. Nancy Fried, "Cradling Her Sorrow," terra cotta, 1989.

Figure 4. Nancy Fried, "The Nightmare," front and back views, 1987.

Figure 5. Nancy Fried, "Breast Flap," 1987.

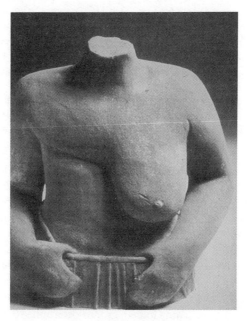

Figure 6. Nancy Fried, "Hanging Out," 1987.

Figure 7. Nancy Fried, "The Flirt," 1988.

work, "Sculpting Through Grief" (see pp. 313-316), where the catalyst of the anguish is the end of a fifteen-year relationship rather than the mastectomy.

Just as clay harnessed the grief and rage of Nancy Fried, young writer Martha Davis in "Against Daily Insignificance" tells us how she mourned for her irreplace-able brother by repeatedly using the written word:

> There was something satisfying about writing these poems. I managed to distill some part of what I was going through into a shape, a color, a single feeling. The sorrow itself eased only a little after writing a poem, but working with language again, trying to craft it, was healing; it began to give me another self.

Works of art help us to grieve not only for our individual losses but also for communal ones. Large-scale architectural monuments commemorating Hiroshima, the Holocaust, and Vietnam fortify the living memory of survivors while they provide space for their mourning—a place to walk, share, recall, honor. In James Miller's "AIDS Time: A Passage Through Cawthra Park," we visit—and probe the meaning of—a memorial honoring men and women who have died from AIDS. Whether communities choose the ancient Hebrew rite of rending their clothes, create multi-paneled murals in their classrooms, visit public parks designed to honor those who have died of AIDS, or log onto the global World Wide Web and Internet sites described by Carla Sofka and Tom Golden, groups determine for themselves appro-priate ways of both memorializing the dead and comforting the living.

BASIC NEEDS OF GRIEVING PEOPLE

An essay on "Therapeutic Touch" by Mary Simpson opens the final section. You don't have to be an ordained member of the clergy to understand and apply the laying-on-of-hands, the techniques of gentle massaging, centering, breathing along in the same rhythm—and the art of simply being and promoting the comfort of those "in transition." In the poem "Hello, David," the anonymous night nurse who stays with, touches, and is touched by the dying soldier David, embodies the heightened responsibilities borne by the caregiver. In "My Mother's Hands" the adult daughter Elaine Freed Lindenblatt looks . . . remembers . . . and makes the gift of a parable-like story for us and for herself, and as explicitly as any theory, validates the self-discovery latent in the process of reminiscence and life review. The baking ritual in Lesleigh Forsyth's "The Sourdough Father" invites us to reenact the sacred measures of touching, kneading, looking, musing, simply being.

We see—and rejoice at—the innate abilities of adults and children to invent their own creative rituals, without needing professionals to prescribe them. In Jessie Kesson's "Dear Edith"[7] we meet an old lonely woman confined to a nursing home who keeps in touch with a dead friend by writing her letters, for the most part in her imagination. In "Silent Conversations" by Leigh Westerfield, we witness one-sided conversations with a much-missed therapist (an example of another disenfranchised loss) at her gravesite. As chronicled by distinguished photographer Elsa Dorfman in "The M(ortality) Word and the L(ove) Word . . . ," we see the inventiveness of families and friends who commission handsome colored photographs, often before and after a loved one's death (see Figure 8). Her photographs are, I would guess, the newest variation of posthumous and Victorian remembrance photographs.

THE CHEMISTRY OF PARTNERSHIP AND THE HEALING ART OF GRIEF

In Kurt Stasiak's words, "The subtle temptation in health care (or in any form of ministry) is to consider patients or parishioners as the receivers, while deeming those who care for or minister to them as the givers and providers. To the extent we acquiesce to this mutually exclusive relationship, we disregard what the patient can give us—what the patient, in fact, *must* give us." After all, what but time and vanity separates "us" from "them"?

When the chemistry of partnership meshes well, therapist and "client" enter into a magical pas de deux. What the experienced physician tells young doctors about disease applies as well to grief, that it magnifies both sufferers and those who tend them.[8]

For me, the African sculpture (Figure 9) symbolizes the client/therapist relationship; it epitomizes rapt attention, sincerity, openness to spontaneity and vulnerability, and mutual respect. Together the figures are partners in the healing process, neither one donning a mask or focused on power disparity, or pretending to be what he or she is not. Neither person engulfs the other. At different times in the encounter, as energy flows between them, both are nurturer and nurtured.

Figure 8. Elsa Dorfman, "Jamon, Dad, Elise, November 23, 1996."
Photograph taken on first anniversary of mother's death.

In my interpretation, this work of art suggests that a good therapist is not fearful of emotional bankruptcy, of being used up, of not knowing. Comfortable, indeed inspired by models of shared power,[9] the therapist too is on her knees, in a posture of humility, perhaps responding to a bodily cue to honor distance . . . to "push" no further. Even more, this sculpture shows how significant a part of the interaction *concern* and *attention* are, and how communication depends on more than words.

The competent therapist understands that anxiety, emptiness, and meaninglessness can be allayed, even retroactively, by enabling those in pain to

- connect with their wholeness
- make peace with, discover, and respect the coherence of their life's story
- seek reconciliation with alienated family, friends
- give and receive love, forgiveness, appreciation, and expressions of affection
- say good-byes (or, if you prefer, au revoir)
- complete relationships with others
- assure continuity, relationship, and meaning beyond death.

To whatever degree these are accomplished, loss ultimately can animate our lives.

Figure 9. African Sculpture. Ward St. Studio Archives, date unknown.

Human grief exists both in time and timelessness. I, like so many of my colleagues, believe there is a healing trajectory. And like them, I believe that periodic revisits of grief—planned and unexpected—are part of the process. Grief, therefore, is not "resolved" in the medical sense of the word; rather it becomes a repositioning and re-vival of the loved one in an inner space and time, accessible forever, whenever one needs, wants, or is forced to feel the connection. This is the paradox—the healing power of grief. At that moment of connection, the emptiness and void are gone, or at least temporarily held at bay.

Since grief is not a cerebral problem but a subjective experience, we understand grief only and entirely as we filter and interpret it through our own experience. Initially it captures us, but we can capture it back and reshape it; and the expressive arts and therapies function beautifully as vehicles to help us reshape grief. Ultimately, the potential for healing in the midst of suffering exists because grief is about creating and transforming bonds of attachment, not severing them irrevocably.[10]

ENDNOTES

[1] Although I use the terms "patient" and "client" here for practical purposes, I do so with much hesitancy. I am much more comfortable with the idea of patients as people with whom we make bonds and connection. I am also using "helping" advisedly, for implicit in this Introduction is the belief that each of us has within us the seeds of our own healing, and for

those of us in the palliative arts, which is how I see grief "therapy," the means of our own creative "treatments."

[2]There is a plethora of fine research on bereavement—handbooks that focus on the anatomy of bereavement (Rapheal, Stroebe, Kastenbaum), complicated mourning (Rando, Lazare, Saunders), disenfranchised grief (Doka), traumatic death (Stillion, Redmond, Williams, Figley), tasks of grieving (Worden), continuing bonds (Klass, Silverman, Nickman), childhood, sibling, and family grief (Martinson, Bluebond-Langner, Davies, Koocher), counseling skills and the coping capacity (Weisman, Parkes, Worden, Neimeyer)—to mention but a few.

[3]Cassell, E. J., The Nature of Suffering and the Goals of Medicine, *New England Journal of Medicine, 306*:11, pp. 639-645, 1982.

[4]*Intoxicated by My Illness,* Fawcett Columbine, New York, p. 40, 1992.

[5]I asked Laurence Schneiderman, the physician author of this story to complete the same assignment I use in my training: "Kiki, the protagonist, seeks you out for grief counseling." His answer follows: "Usually, as an ethics consultant, my work engages me before the fact and requires that I deal with treatment disputes, including helping survivors prepare for the imminent or inevitable death of a loved one. This involves a complex interweaving of emotional and rational threads. Many times, the grieving has already begun, expressing itself in difficult ways, for example denial, distrust, anger, threats, storming off in the midst of discussions, and so forth. My task is to absorb and redirect the emotional energy of those who love the patient, make clear my compassion for their suffering, and gently help them find rational understanding that nature allows us only so much life, that death is part of the human condition, that we all die. Much like Father Julian I try to transform destructive acts of love into constructive acts of love—helping everyone including the patient to seek not a tormented final act but one that is peaceful and dignified. This often involves dealing with private agendas—guilt, unreconciled estrangement, family feuds, and so forth. I try to help people identify with the patient (Would he want to be kept alive now by all these machines only to suffer? Would you want that if you were he?) I reassure them (and the physicians, too) that "doing everything" doesn't just mean adding more tubes and needles and machines, but at some point "doing everything" means doing everything possible to alleviate suffering and enhancing comfort, dignity, privacy, intimacy, for the sake of what we all want in the end for ourselves—a good death.

After death, grief counseling for me involves many of the same complex interactions of emotion and reason. Kiki is unusual in that for a layperson she is very experienced in the ways of death. Hence, she will be particularly alert to insincere uses of "technique"— as was Father Julian, her teacher. Going over memories of the one who died from beginning to end is a well-known technique to help survivors bring closure to their mourning. This is what Father Julian taught her. If a grief counselor attempted to do this, it would have to be spontaneous and uncontrived. Because Father Julian was such an unusual man, Kiki may find herself responding to genuine interest and not feel manipulated. This, of course, requires genuine interest. The grief counselor must genuinely love life in its varieties and feel comfortable about death. Kiki's grief may well be intensified by feelings of guilt. (He was a sick man. Did I have to challenge and further weaken his faith? Then cause him to commit a sin of the flesh? What about the morphine? Did he deliberately kill himself with it? In short, was I the cause not only of his death but his spiritual annihilation?) These are deep questions and one is grateful when survivors can find comfort in their religion. In the case of Kiki, I would not expect *her* to find such comfort directly since she is not particularly religious but would try to have her gain comfort by seeing Father Julian's death in his own context, which *is* religious whether or not he believes. It is almost the reverse of Pascal's wager. If there is no God, then Father Julian will have ended his existence in the way most suited to him. He was very much a man of this world of flesh and blood. He received from you just what he taught: loving comfort, the very kind of physical comfort he made sure he provided. He received it from someone close to him. And, best of all, he passed away in his sleep. If there is a God, then Father Julian died knowing he will be judged by all his works—his years of devotion to his many patients over the course of his life along with the momentary lapse at the extremity of his illness. In our conversations I would encourage Kiki to express her fears along with her grief, gradually leading her to expand the pain of uncertainty into the larger, still painful but ultimately restoring wonder of mystery.

[6]Quoted in New York newspaper *The Village Voice*, "Body Beauty," by Arlene Raven, January 26, 1988.

[7]An assignment that I use following the reading of "Dear Edith," particularly for nurses in a geriatric subspecialty—and one that stimulates the development of specific procedures, practical guidelines, and usable protocols—is "Were you the clinician called to the nursing home, Anson House, what would be your problem assessment and treatment plan for staff and residents?"

[8]Selzer, R., Rounds, *Letters to a Young Doctor,* Simon and Schuster, New York, 1982.

[9]Quill, T., and Brody, H., Physician Recommendations and Patient Autonomy: Finding a Balance between Physician Power and Patient Choice, *Annals of Internal Medicine, 125*:9, pp. 763-769, 1996.

[10]I am grateful to Patricia Marshall for this insight.

Sandra L. Bertman
University of Massachusetts Medical Center
Worcester, Massachusetts

THE ARTS, PERSONAL GRIEFS, PROFESSIONAL ROLES

On the Psychology of Loss

William M. Lamers, Jr.

INTRODUCTION

Before my training as a physician I had little interest in the way people reacted to loss. This changed one night during medical school when an ambulance brought two young men to the emergency room where I was working. Both had been killed instantly when their car slammed into a concrete bridge abutment. When I realized their identities, I was unable to work for the rest of that night. Both of them were friends of mine. I had been with one of them only the night before. I sat in my room in the on-call quarters, overwhelmed by strong feelings that I could not understand. I had previously experienced the deaths of friends and family members. This was different. These two deaths of men my own age were unexpected, and I was not prepared to deal with them. I withdrew into myself and wondered why I could not go back to work in the emergency room.

As my medical training progressed, I developed an interest in the way people reacted to loss. There was little information available in the medical or psychiatric literature. I read Freud's *Mourning and Melancholia* [1] and Lindemann's *The Symptomatology and Management of Acute Grief* [2]. Lindemann offered a simple analysis of reactions to death based on his work with survivors of the Coconut Grove nightclub fire in Boston. I came upon an early copy of Feifel's *The Meaning of Death* [3], and also Bowlby's papers on separation and loss experiences of children [4, 5].

I began to perceive that loss experiences could provoke a wide variety of physical changes and psychological responses. I saw that some persons sensed the connection between loss and the appearance of symptoms while others were totally unaware of the relationship. I observed how individuals in a family reacting to the same loss often had very different responses. Further, I saw that loss did not necessarily produce negative changes.

During the late 1960s I observed that over half the patients in my practice of adult and child psychiatry sought assistance for problems ultimately derived from some sort of loss, whether recent or remote. Most of these patients had been referred from health-care professionals in the community, very few of whom knew of my interest in the study of loss. My personal experiences and interest in loss led me to see relationships between loss and subsequent behavior that would otherwise not have been obvious.

During my training in psychiatry I worked with several patients who provided me with unusual reactions to loss. Each taught me something new about the way we respond to loss. I began to see that early childhood experiences of separation and loss set a pattern for the way adults respond to loss. I saw that some persons have more difficulty dealing with loss than others, and that some conditions can aggravate and extend the period of reaction to loss. After experiencing the death of two friends in the emergency room, I could identify with those who experienced difficulty in dealing with loss. I wanted to see if I could somehow help them resolve the problems created by loss. I found that working with persons who displayed unusual reactions to loss provided new insights into the psychology of loss.

Prior to his experience with survivors of the Coconut Grove fire, Lindemann conducted research on patients with ulcerative colitis. Lindemann suddenly realized that many of his patients experienced the onset of their symptoms shortly after the death of a loved one [2]. I began to wonder about the possible psychological and physical mechanisms involved in converting feelings about loss into a life-threatening illness.

The early work of Bowlby and his coworkers on separation and loss fascinated me. It was clear that we begin to respond to losses in childhood, that we develop set patterns of reaction to loss, and that we can expend considerable energy trying to protect ourselves against loss.

My years of training in child psychiatry provided broad experience in the ways in which children react to loss. In my own life, the unexpected death of my sister forced me to put some of my experience into practice in helping her six young children adjust to the death of their mother.

POETRY AND GRIEF

The loss experiences of my own children were also instructive. One of my sons emptied a jar of tadpoles into a small pool behind our house into which I had just poured some kind of liquid to kill mosquito larvae. My son's anguished crying and insightful questions about death ("Does this mean that I'll die, too?" "Will you die too, Daddy?") immediately brought to mind a poem that I had enjoyed but not fully understood from a high school literature course:

> SPRING AND FALL: TO A YOUNG CHILD
> Margaret, are you grieving
> Over Goldengrove unleaving?
> Leaves, like the things of man, you
> With your fresh thoughts care for, can you?
> Ah! as the heart grows older
> It will come to such sights colder
> By and by, nor spare a sigh
> Though worlds of wanwood leafmeal lie;
> And yet you will weep and know why.
> Now no matter, child, the name:
> Sorrow's springs are the same.
> Nor mouth had, no nor mind, expressed

What heart heard of, ghost guessed:
It is the blight man was born for,
It is Margaret you mourn for.

Gerard Manley Hopkins

Certain poems, I began to realize, offered insight into the ways people deal with loss. Some descriptions of loss found in poetry are not only more detailed but clearer and more memorable than descriptions in textbooks. The power of a few well-chosen words to describe, perhaps in a symbolic way, emotions difficult to verbalize, makes poetry a valuable tool in grief therapy. Poetry, and literature as well, can provide bereaved persons with a description of their feelings and fears. After identifying their fears and feelings in poetry, they no longer see themselves as unique. Someone else has not only experienced what they are going through but, more important, has lived to write about it. I recall one agitated young woman who attended one of my inpatient hospital poetry therapy sessions. She reacted to the word *death* in a poem I had brought to the session and suddenly this woman, who had been mute, began to talk with great urgency about the death of her sister ten years earlier. Then she shared the story of her sister's accidental death and confessed that she had never been able to talk about it with anyone, including her parents or a succession of therapists.

In time, I learned that there is a unique constellation of earlier experiences associated with each current loss, and each new loss can awaken memories of past losses and stir anxieties about losses yet to come. As a hospice physician, I occasionally came to know a particular family quite well, and while visiting their home during a final illness, I observed the changes in family members as they reacted to the impending death of a loved one.

GRIEF REACTIONS

Shoor and Speed described the relation of loss to delinquent behavior [6]. I saw in my work the relationship of loss reactions to unplanned adolescent pregnancy, which led to my co-authoring a book titled *Teenage Pregnancy* [7]. Working with young drug addicts I came across a surprising number of persons who began using drugs as a way to extinguish feelings arising from the death of a loved one. One young addict eventually revealed that she began to use drugs to try to escape from feelings of responsibility for her father's accidental death. She had persuaded him over her mother's objections to drive her to be with friends. He was killed on the return trip. As this young woman attempted to subdue her feelings, she relied on alcohol, amphetamines, barbiturates, and eventually heroin. Following one of her accidental overdoses, I visited her in an intensive care unit where she suddenly revealed to me the basis for her dependency on mind- and mood-altering drugs. After that turning point, we could speak directly about her grief and could seek alternative ways to deal with her beliefs and feelings.

When provided with support and guidance, grieving persons can experience rapid change in attitudes, emotions, and lifestyle. Without adequate expression of some sort, grieving can be arrested, and appropriate response denied, giving rise to a host of maladies: physical, psychological, and social. Unresolved grief is like a ticking time bomb.

NEEDLESS GUILT: "I KILLED MY SISTER"

A woman in her late twenties presented herself at my office for her first appointment. When I asked her what I might do for her, she said, "I'll give you one month, and if things aren't better by then, I am going to kill myself." This was an unusual opening statement, especially for a woman so young with seemingly her whole life before her. I learned she was in excellent health, had a fine education, and held a good job, but she had trouble with relationships. She saw no future in marriage, no hope for following what should have been a productive, if conventional, life. Seeing her friends falling in love, marrying, and beginning to raise families added to her depression. She felt very strongly that she could never achieve happiness in her lifetime. But she had no awareness of what was causing this distress. Preoccupied with a gloom of foreboding, she predicted a future so bleak that she saw no alternative to suicide. She asked if I could help her.

I decided to gather some basic history so that I could get a better understanding of this person who seemed so desperate. She was the oldest of six children born to a successful professional couple. While telling me about her siblings, she began to cry out loud, and then to shout with distress and tears, "I killed my sister! I killed my sister!" When asked to explain, she told of being competitive with her sister, who was about fifteen months younger. Her parents must have noted something wrong with this sister because they took her to doctors and began to treat her differently. My patient became increasingly resentful at the way her parents favored the younger sister; out of control one evening, she yelled at her sister, "I wish you were dead!" That very evening her sister died. Her parents, she learned later, had been told by specialists that the younger sister had an inoperable brain tumor and that nothing could be done. And so they indulged her while frustrating her older sister, who did not know the grim prognosis.

As my patient told the story of feeling responsible for her sister's death, her tears increased. As we talked, I was surprised to learn that she had not thought about it for many years. The memory, while suppressed, had continued to influence her life. She saw herself as unworthy, as undeserving of any happiness. It was as if she were still punishing herself for the fatal anger she felt toward her sister. At the time of her sister's death, she did not recall anyone taking the time to explain that she did not actually kill her sister. The life of this young woman was strongly influenced by needless guilt over the unfounded belief that her anger had "magically" killed her sister.

THE DYNAMICS OF LOSS

On experiencing loss, people begin passing through an irregular continuum that encompasses thoughts, feelings, physiological responses, and observable behavioral changes. There are several clinically distinguishable phases of reaction to loss. I found that Bowlby's terminology of the phases, *protest, despair,* and *detachment* [4], fit with my observations. The phases tend to succeed one another.

Protest, or remnants of the phase of protest, persists as long as denial is a viable mechanism. Elements of protest can recur as attention wanders, during sleep, or during periods of increased stress. When denial can no longer hold back the reality of the loss, despair supervenes. Detachment similarly follows despair when active grieving begins to resolve, whether through completion of post-death activities, through the need to return to occupational activities, or through a need to refocus attention on other priorities. Return to an earlier phase of active grieving can occur during periods of increased stress, during sleep, and during periods of altered states of consciousness.

People can benefit from being told that the sequence of reactions they experience is normal and that successful completion of grief work takes time. There is no way to avoid the necessary grieving process without paying an emotional price, nor is there a "geographic cure" for grief. One widow who left on an around-the-world cruise the day after her husband's funeral returned to discover that she was a year behind in her grieving and had lost the support of friends who saw her as non-caring.

When I work with people who have difficulty facing the tasks of grieving, I tell them that it will take time to do the necessary work and that I know of no short cuts. I have seen children as well as adults of all ages gain a new dimension to their lives because they have somehow managed to transcend a major loss. How does this occur? Those who experience loss often feel forced to re-assess their lives, to re-prioritize their activities, to decide which things are important and which are not, and to develop new objectives. They learn to let go of fantasies about people "living happily ever after" and take a more pragmatic stance toward life. Some turn away from organized religion, saying, "If there is a God, how could this have happened?" Others find strength and support in religious beliefs and practices. Many go through a period of extended, undirected searching, marked by phases of recurrent longing, feelings of remorse, and mild to moderate depression.

To facilitate the course of bereavement, I encourage patients to keep a simple journal in which they record their physical and psychological reactions and adjustments over a period of time. I stress the normalcy of a host of emotional reactions that may be foreign to them and reassure them that some persons feel, if they let their feelings take over during grief, that they may lose control. I let men as well as women know that crying and anger are normal reactions to loss. I tell them the reaction to this loss may also trigger remembrances of earlier events, other losses from the past. And then I present them with a copy of the diagram (Figure 1) on p. 6, together with a brief explanation of the phases, in the next four sections. This enables them to have a sort of "road map" of territory that may be new to them.

Protest

During the initial response to loss, shock and confusion predominate. As realization of the loss accumulates, a sense of denial develops. Anger is a common feature during this early response to the loss. This includes anger at oneself

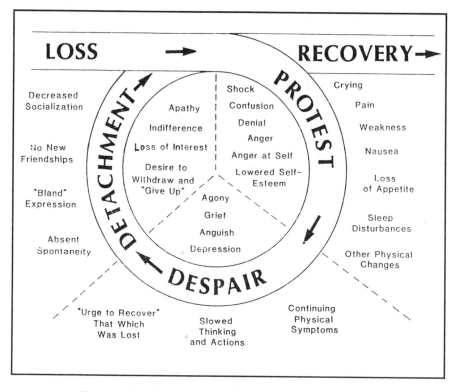

Figure 1. The Grief Cycle. © 1978, Wm. Lamers, Jr., M.D.

(self-recrimination for things said, unsaid, done, or not done) as well as anger at the deceased ("How could you do this to me?") plus anger projected at anyone deemed responsible for (or contributing to) the death, including family members, physicians, and anyone else. Crying, weeping, disorganization, difficult breathing, and weakness are commonly observed. When denial is no longer effective, helplessness and lowered self-esteem begin to dominate, and the bereaved person progresses into despair, the next phase of grief.

Despair

The predominant feelings in the despair phase are characterized by grief, anguish, and depression. From a psychological and behavioral point of view, the inability to effectively deny the death prompts the survivor to vacillate between dejection and the hope of reuniting with the deceased. Searching and an urge for reunion are commonly observed. Survivors may imagine seeing or hearing the deceased person. Agitation, hyperactivity, restlessness, and a variety of physical symptoms dominate the physical and social aspects of behavior. Crying is a common feature of this phase.

Detachment

During the phase of detachment, people describe their feeling states using terms like apathy and loss of interest. They tend to avoid social situations: "I'm no fun to be around. I feel like a fifth wheel." People in this phase have said to me "food tastes like sand." Life seems to have lost its meaning; formerly enjoyable activities now seem empty of meaning and pleasure. A Greek term, *anhedonia,* has been taken to describe this absence of feeling, this absence of "hedonism." Persons in this phase of loss have modulated emotional and physical responses. Their level of energy is low. They can work, but derive little satisfaction in the process and are usually characterized as "depressed" by coworkers.

Persons progressing through the last phase of the "grief cycle" rarely cry as heavily as those newly experiencing loss, although laughter is usually inhibited. They are generally reluctant to develop new relationships and have a sense of detachment from the future as well as from the past. They may speak of "taking one day at a time" to illustrate their dissociation from the usual integrated continuum of life.

Recovery

In time the bereaved person generally adapts to the loss and enters into a period of readjustment during which it is possible to look objectively at the loss or death without the disturbing and distorting effect of profound emotions. Recovery does not mean the same as "total cure" or "amazing turnaround"; it is not a dramatic change. The loss remains in mind, though not always in the foreground. Not everyone recovers from every loss. There is nothing "automatic" or spontaneous about what we call "recovery."

Many persons require assistance to recover from loss. Some need a great deal of assistance; others require less. Some find within themselves the seeds of their own recovery; others look outward to find solace and support in religion, spiritual search, new relationships, old friends, or new endeavors.

Some persons develop a "flight into health" that serves to deny the reality of their loss. This may be manifested in the development of a new relationship that merely substitutes a new love object (or new baby) for the person (or child) that died. Men appear to be more likely to deny the pain of the loss by seeking involvement in new relationships, new love, or new activities.

It is imperative to recognize that there is no set time for recovery from loss, no recipe or timetable for all the work that must be accomplished to react to major loss. For the loss may be greater than it first seemed. The loss of a spouse imparts a loss not only of the person, of companionship, of security, but loss of love, loss of the future, loss of support in the years ahead. Each aspect of the loss must somehow be addressed. And this takes time, effort, and passing again and again through uncertainty, anxiety, indecision, and perhaps healthy self-doubt. Recovery implies a reworking of the ways in which one looks at life, at oneself, and at the future. Recovery is not an event; it is an ongoing process. We never fully recover, but must deal with a succession of losses. As long as we are alive, we are never exempt from loss. The complexity of our existence suggests that we never fully recover from major loss; we only make repeated efforts at better levels of adjustment to loss.

VARIABLES IN PROGNOSIS RE: LOSS

Some age groups are particularly vulnerable to loss. Infants and children under the age of five are prone to develop serious emotional and behavioral sequelae as a result of the loss of one or both parents unless a satisfactory surrogate parent is available. Those over sixty who lose a mate experience an increased morbidity in the year following the loss compared to persons the same age who had no such loss. Parents who experience the death of a child from cancer have an increased incidence of separation and divorce. Middle-aged persons generally have sufficient social and physical support to assist them through the emotional distress of the death of a loved one [8].

Individual Variables in Loss

The above descriptions of behavior and feelings commonly associated with loss serve only as a general guide. Individual reactions differ widely depending on a number of variables. Children, for example, do not react as adults do, nor does an adult react the same way to the death of an individual as they do to multiple, concurrent significant losses. I have found it valuable for several reasons to ask a series of questions that probe the depth of a survivor's grief. Bereaved persons sometimes lack understanding of their response to loss. They may consciously suppress or unconsciously repress their intellectual awareness of the reality of the loss. They may find themselves involved in behavior foreign to their usual routine. They may experience feelings that superficially appear to be inconsistent with the loss. They may develop apparently exaggerated depression, anxiety, fearfulness, agitation, or physical symptoms. Further, they may be unable to describe their feelings because they do not know the descriptive terminology. They may also be unable to associate the onset of their physical changes with the loss.

The following are useful questions to ask when working with grieving persons. The answers often indicate the significance of the loss and often suggest approaches to help in the satisfactory resolution of the loss.

The Basic Questions

- Who died?
- How did the death occur?
- When did the death occur?
- Where did the death occur?
- Under what circumstances did the death occur?
- Were there any unusual circumstances surrounding the death?
- What is the impact of this loss on the survivor?
- What was the quality of the survivor's relationship with the deceased?

- What "unfinished business" remains from the relationship?
- Was the survivor involved in caring for the deceased?
- What prior losses has this survivor experienced?
- What is the age of the survivor?
- What are the strengths of the survivor?
- What was the impact of the funeral?
- Are there any "survivor symptoms"?
- Was this a "sanctioned" loss?
- What financial and legal matters remain?

Each of these basic questions opens an area for further consideration and discussion. Each of the questions on the following "expanded" list provides opportunity to reflect on what happened and to begin to resolve any unfinished business.

THE EXPANDED LIST OF QUESTIONS

Who Died?

- What was the relationship of the deceased person to the survivor?
- How does the survivor describe the person who died?
- Is the description primarily subjective? Or primarily objective?
- Is the deceased described in terms of a person or merely as the source of the survivor's woe?
- What roles, if any, did the deceased and the survivor play for each other?
- Were the roles clear or confused?
- Did the death occur with certainty, or is denial of the death still a reasonable possibility?
- Has the body been found? It is very difficult to proceed with timely grieving when the death cannot be finally determined, for example when the body is lost at sea or when the deceased is "missing in action."

Example: Geoffrey Gorer, the English sociologist, learned many years later that his father had died with the sinking of the *Lusitania.* As a boy he had been told that his father was "on a long journey" from which the child mistakenly presumed he would one day return. As a response to this and other cultural denials of death in England, Gorer wrote the important book *Death, Grief and Mourning* [9]. Knowledge of the reality of loss and death may be quite painful but can also, as in Gorer's case, initiate creativity, productivity, and a search for meaning.

How Did the Death Occur?

- What was the cause of death?
- Is the cause of death known?
- Was it an easy or peaceful death?

- Was it a painful death accompanied by distress or other physical problems?
- Was it a sudden or accidental death?
- Were any resuscitative measures employed?
- Was suicide suspected?
- Was there openness prior to the death, or was there collusion among family and/or caregivers to withhold information from the dying person?
- Did the survivors experience distress in trying to obtain help for the dying person?
- To what extent was there physician involvement? Was it beneficial? Did the physician say, "There's nothing more I can do."
- Was the dying person able to transcend the rigors of the moment and leave the survivor with a positive farewell?

Example: On the morning of his death one young hospice patient was asked by his mother what he wanted for breakfast. He replied simply, "A kiss." Their last communication characterized their relationship.

Where Did the Death Occur?

- Did death occur in a health-care institution? At home? Elsewhere?
- Were any health-care personnel present at the death?

When Did the Death Occur?

- What time of the day was the death?
- Was the survivor present?
- Was there any premonition of the death?
- Had the survivor been present before the death?
- Was the death sudden and unanticipated (accident, cerebrovascular accident), or was it anticipated, as in old age or after a long illness?
- When did the survivors learn of the impending death?
- When did they first arrive on the scene?
- Was there time for survivors to say good-bye?
- Did the death occur on any anniversary or significant date?
- Was the dying person conscious, able to communicate?

Example: A physician and his wife were reluctant to have hospice involved in the care of their only child who was dying. The day before his death the father called, said the child had been unconscious for a week, and asked how he should say "good-bye." The parents hoped until the very end that their son's cancer would be cured. I suggested that the father speak gently to his son as if the son could understand, that he and his wife should tell their son all the things they wanted to say, and that they should stay with their son until the time of death.

Are There Symptoms of "Survivor Identification"

- Has the survivor developed any physical, social, or psychological behavior characteristic of the deceased? (The dynamics of this may be as simple as identification with the deceased or as psychologically complex as the reactivation of latent self-images, as described by Horowitz [10]. The survivor may be clinging to a symptom in order to hold onto at least a part of the deceased; the adopted symptom may be a metaphor for mortification. Or the symptom may serve as a symbol, an equivalent for or residual of the prolonged, elaborate, intense mourning rituals of our ancestors. Whatever the particular dynamic, symptom, or symptom complex, discussion may facilitate the direct expression of feelings, the verbalization of unrecognized ambivalence, and the dissolution of impasses in the extended grieving process.)

Example: I accompanied a friend of mine to the hospital where his father had just died of a sudden heart attack. As we were leaving the hospital he remarked to me that in the last half hour he noticed the onset of pain radiating down his left arm—the same symptoms his mother had described as presaging the father's fatal illness.

What Was the Quality of the Relationship?

- What is the history of the survivor's relationship with the deceased?
- Was there a history of dependence on the deceased?
- Was there an element of abuse in the relationship?
- Was the deceased a mentor, a friend, a support?
- Was the relationship fulfilling or inhibiting?
- To what degree did (does) the survivor identify with the deceased?
- If the death was unanticipated, was it apparent to both parties that it was a fulfilling relationship?
- Had the deceased and the survivor talked about death?
- If so, had they come to some understanding of how the survivor would deal with the death of the other person?
- Was there any unresolved anger between the survivor and the deceased?
- Is there a sense of relief at the death?
- Is there a sense of guilt regarding things done or not done, things said or unsaid, feelings expressed or unexpressed in the relationship?
- Was the deceased idolized by the survivor?
- Does the survivor feel that life is now over for him/her as well?
- To what extent does the survivor acknowledge ambivalence toward the deceased person?
- What was the nature of the relationship of the survivor to the deceased person?

Example: Several middle-aged siblings asked me to help persuade their mother, who lived in an adjoining state, to let them visit her during the final days of her illness from cancer. She said she did not want to let them visit but offered no good reason. I talked with the siblings and learned that the mother had remarried many years previously. She had abused and abandoned them as small children. She had even tried to sell the youngest child. Despite the abuse they had suffered over a number of years, their desire to be with their dying mother was stronger than I had seen, at times, in adult children who had been treated with love and respect by their mother. They wanted one more opportunity before she died to hear that she loved them. For her to die without telling them she loved them would confirm the ultimate rejection, namely that they were unlovable. It was possible to discuss the fallacies in this line of thinking objectively and to help these adult children separate their sense of worthfulness from the actions of a biologic parent who continued to be unable to meet their basic need to be loved.

Was This a "Sanctioned" Loss?

• Can the survivor let others know of the loss and anticipate some social support?
• Or was the relationship a covert one with others not knowing about the loss? (The most common unsanctioned grief situations in our society are the death of a (married) lover, the death of a stillborn child, death from HIV disease, death by suicide of a family member, and incarceration of a family member. Persons unable to make their loss known to others cannot benefit from the social support of friends, family, or the larger community. Those who cannot announce their loss are also denied the psychological benefits of a funeral.)

Example: A widow sought to prevent her husband's lover from attending the funeral. The lover obtained a court order allowing her to be alone in the funeral home parlor during her visitation. After the lover left, the widow and other mourners returned to find scratched on the inner surface of the open casket, "I'll always love you."

What Unfinished Business Remains?

• Was there "unfinished business" in the relationship?
• Promises unfulfilled?
• Does the death for the survivor cast doubt on anticipated projects, plans of raising a family, a common business, travel, or other activities?
• Did the untimely death of a spouse or partner provide a focus for exaggerated anger as a way to avoid feelings of loss and grief?

What Is the Financial and Legal Picture?

• Had the dying person and the survivor discussed financial matters in view of the impending death?
• Had they executed a will, a trust, or any other legal instrument to help the survivor?

Example: A bride-to-be refused to sign a generous premarital agreement on the grounds that she did not want the stepdaughters to feel that she married their father simply for his money. He died on the return from their honeymoon, and her grief at his death was compounded by her self-recrimination for not signing a document that would have made her a wealthy woman.

Did the Survivor Provide Care for the Dying Person?

• Was the survivor involved in care of the deceased?

Example: A young woman diagnosed with cancer of the ovary said she did not want to have her six-year-old daughter in the room where she was dying. We explained the benefits to the daughter of being able to help in some small way with mother's care. The mother allowed the daughter to help feed her. This opened communication between the mother and daughter, and both began to offer expressions of love mixed with tears.

If all else is equal, involvement in caring may enhance communication, help resolve unfinished business, serve as a symbol of love, and contribute to the facilitation of grieving. For some, involvement in caring may seem a needless burden. Each situation must be considered on its own merits.

What Is the Impact of This Loss?

• What is the impact of this loss on the survivor?
• How vulnerable is the survivor? Is the survivor's assessment of his or her vulnerability accurate?
• Is the grief response appropriate or apparently inappropriate in terms of locally accepted notions of grief?

Example: Several couples went boating. The young child of one couple was missing and soon was found to have drowned. When the dead child was brought to her, the mother smiled and said, "Now we have an angel in Heaven." Her husband came to me after the funeral and said he was frustrated by his wife's positive response to the accidental death. He said he felt like crying much of the time but that he did not want to "rain on her parade." She came from a different ethnic and religious background in which her reaction was typical and appropriate. He needed time to react in a typical and appropriate way for his background.

What Is the Short-Term Impact of This Loss?

• What will probably happen as a result of this loss over the next six to twelve months?
• What changes will this death bring to the survivor?
• Physical loss—loss of cohabitation and protection, increased susceptibility to illness, sleep disturbances?
• Social loss—loss of identity as a couple or as a family, change in level and frequency of social interaction?
• Economic loss—loss of financial security, income from insurance?
• Emotional loss—ongoing grief, anxiety, depression?

The Long-Term Impact of This Loss?

• How has the loss affected the survivor over the course of many years?
• Has the reaction to the death been a positive one?

Example: Four children under ten years of age were devastated by the accidental death of their mother. Their father soon remarried a woman who tyrannized them. The new stepmother wanted to be married, but she did not want to care for someone else's children. This brought the surviving children closer to one another. The gained strength from surviving their ordeal.

Has the Survivor Experienced Prior Losses?

• Is this the first significant or major loss of the survivor?
• Have prior losses been resolved to some degree?

Example: A psychiatrist asked me to see a woman in her seventies who he said was "very depressed." She was the widow of a psychiatrist. During the first visit she cried so profusely that she could tell me only part of her story. It seems she had become enamored recently with a gentleman and finally persuaded him to visit her on the West Coast. In anticipation of his arrival, she planned a welcoming party. All went well until the "boyfriend" left with one of her best friends. My new patient expressed anger at the suitor as well as at her woman friend, and grieved the loss of two friendships as well as a cherished future. The next day she was crying less. I asked what else might be troubling her, and she told me it was silly to even talk about it but that her trusted dog of many years had recently died, and she had not realized how much the dog meant to her. She now expressed fears of walking in the hills without the dog, for there had been a murder in the area earlier that year. She also acknowledged that she was too old to ever get another puppy and train it, and she had to admit to herself that she was getting older and that her days were numbered.

The next day, she focused on her husband's death ten years earlier. She was saddened to think that she had survived him all these years. Among the things that remained as supports to her, she listed her religious beliefs, her remaining friends, and her love of art and beauty. She then became very subdued and shared with me the loss of a lifetime when in the late 1940s she realized that almost all of her relatives had been killed in the German concentration camps.

I asked her to return the following week and to my surprise she entered my office carrying a puppy in her arms. She had done a lot of thinking over the weekend, she said, and she was determined to continue to do things that made her feel better. We also talked about her "spirit" and about the internal and external resources she used to provide direction for her life and focus for her energies and interests.

Needless to say, this woman made another successful adjustment to loss. Those who have learned to adjust successfully to significant loss seem to have learned something that enables them to adjust to subsequent losses. At minimum, they may learn not to expect too much of the world. They may learn that life is not "fair," and they therefore do not expect too much of life or of other persons. They may still be available to love and therefore still vulnerable to further losses. This woman was willing to try to love again, even if at first it was with another young puppy. Those who have successfully survived a prior loss have the feeling that somehow they made it through grief once before and they can do it again.

What Are the Strengths of the Survivor?

- What internal resources are available to the survivor?
- What is the strength of personality?
- What are the survivor's religious belief systems and practices?
- What are the survivor's philosophical belief systems?
- Are these beliefs helpful in resolving the loss?

Example: An identical twin experienced the loss of her sister in an automobile accident. Being a twin was a major part of her identity. In the years that followed the death, the survivor often expressed bewilderment in situations in which others expected her to have clarity of thought. She could not fully grasp the impact of the death of the sister who was part of her identity. She was puzzled that she, too, had not been killed and experienced a certain amount of confused guilt that she was alive and her sister was dead. When her parents tried to comfort her, she responded with what they sensed as inappropriate anger.

How Did the Dying Person Approach Death?

- Did the dying person make a satisfactory adjustment to the impending death?
- Was there time to do this? Or did death come too soon for any resolution to occur?
- What memories does the survivor have of the way the deceased person faced impending death?

Example: As he neared death from intestinal obstruction secondary to cancer of the bowel, I mentioned to the ninety-year-old patient lying comfortably in bed without benefit of any analgesics that he seemed to have things in "pretty good control." He shook his head in contradiction, pointed upward with his hand and said, "No; He does."

What External Supports Are Present?

- What is the family structure? Is it supportive?
- Is the atmosphere in the family positive in the face of loss?
- What support is available from friends?
- What social support is available?
- Will social contacts be maintained during bereavement?
- What economic liabilities and assets are implicated?

Example: A father of three young children died at home during the middle of the night. The mother initially wanted to have the funeral home remove the body before the children woke up, but we agreed it would be important for the children to have a chance to say "good-bye" to their father while he was still at home. We awakened the three children, all under ten years, and brought them to the bedside where the mother explained their father had just died. They could see with their own eyes that he was no longer breathing. They said their good-byes. In the respectful silence that followed, the oldest child looked up to his mother and said, "Mommy, are you all right?" When she answered in the affirmative, he said, "Then I'm all right, too."

What Was the Impact of the Funeral?

- Was there a funeral? If so, what sort?
- What was the impact of the funeral and related ceremonies?
- Was the body present for viewing? How did the survivor respond to the viewing of the remains?
- Was the survivor involved in the planning? In the ceremony?
- Was the service satisfying to the survivor? If so, why? If not, why not?
- Did the funeral help the survivors realize the finality of death?

A properly planned funeral can be beneficial to the immediate survivors as well as to their friends and families. In hospice we encourage families to talk about funeral plans before the last stages of life. This exchange allows for the open expression of feelings about dying and death, helps develop a mutually agreed upon course of action, and lays the groundwork for communication with funeral personnel. We encourage families to involve children in funeral ceremonies and to learn to answer children's questions about death and funerals. We support the inclusion of religious, spiritual, ethnic, and family traditions in funeral services. Personalizing funeral services assists in the development of feelings of closure, resolution, and satisfaction.

RECOVERY FROM LOSS

Some people have sufficient internal and external strengths and sources of support that they resolve their grief in a minimal time without formal assistance or counseling. Others require temporary professional assistance or a supportive group experience to assist them during their recovery. A small number, because of their pre-existing personality or because of the circumstances surrounding their loss, will require extensive psychological support before they can resolve their grief and resume normal, productive functioning. Ethnicity affects the resolution of loss. In some cultures, bereaved persons are treated with respect. In others, they are spurned and seen as a source of bad luck [11]. Bereaved children, more vulnerable than bereaved adults, cannot begin to make a positive adjustment to a death until they are reassured they will be cared for. In time they will require answers to questions that may be difficult for them to ask. Did I cause the death? Will I die the same way? Will I die when I reach the same age? With proper support, children can survive loss and in some ways be more sensitive about personal relationships than would otherwise have been the case. If they are not encouraged to grieve, the effects of inhibited grieving may adversely influence subsequent emotional and social development.

SUMMARY

My nearly forty years of clinical experiences have taught me about the resiliency and resourcefulness of the human spirit. A small amount of the right kind of support, guidance, and encouragement at the right time can help grieving persons make successful adjustments where they previously thought none was possible. No single answer or formula serves everyone, but the guidelines collected here can be a starting point for productive work with grieving children and adults. Throughout my experiences, I have been guided by Erikson's benevolent dictum, "Grief, successfully handled, can serve as the focus for new social and psychological growth" [12]. This knowledge can help in the development of creative interventions to relieve the discomfort that usually accompanies major loss.

REFERENCES

1. S. Freud, *Mourning and Melancholia,* in Collected Papers, Hogarth Press, London, 1956.
2. E. Lindemann, The Symptomatology and Management of Acute Grief, *American Journal of Psychiatry, 101,* pp. 144-146, 1944.
3. H. Feifel, *The Meaning of Death,* McGraw-Hill, New York, 1964.
4. J. Bowlby, Grief and Mourning in Infancy and Early Childhood, *Psychoanalytic Study of the Child, 15,* pp. 9-52, 1960.
5. J. Bowlby, Childhood Mourning and Its Implications for Psychiatry, *American Journal of Psychiatry, 118*:6, pp. 317-340, 1961.
6. M. Shoor and M. H. Speed, Delinquency as a Manifestation of the Mourning Process, *Psychiatric Quarterly, 37*:3, pp. 540-558, July 1963.
7. J. Semmens and W. M. Lamers, *Teenage Pregnancy,* Charles C. Thomas Co., Springfield, Illinois, 1968.
8. P. Clayton, L. Desmerais, and G. Winokur, A Study of Normal Bereavement, *American Journal of Psychiatry, 125*:2, pp. 168-178, 1968.
9. J. Gorer, *Death, Grief and Mourning,* Doubleday, New York, 1965.
10. M. Horowitz, Pathological Grief and the Reactivation of Latent Self-Images, *American Journal of Psychiatry, 42,* pp. 341-361, 1980.
11. P. Elsass and J. Schneider, Application of Western Approaches to Grief Counselling of Non-Western Clients, in *Chinese Americans in Loss and Separation: Social, Medical and Psychiatric Perspectives,* C. L. Chen (ed.), Foundation for Thanatology, New York, 1992.
12. E. Erikson, personal communication, 1978.

BIBLIOGRAPHY

Carey, R. I., Weathering Widowhood: Problems and Adjustment of the Widowed During the First Year, *Omega, 10,* pp. 163-172, 1979.
Doka, K., Expectation of Death, Participation in Funeral Arrangements, and Grief Adjustment, *Omega, 15,* pp. 119-129, 1984.
Edwards, D., *Grieving: The Pain and the Promise,* Covenant, Salt Lake City, 1989.

Engel, G., Is Grief a Disease? *Psychosomatic Medicine, 23,* pp. 18-22, 1961.

Feifel, H., *New Meanings of Death,* McGraw-Hill, New York, 1977.

Fulton, R., and Fulton, J., A Psychosocial Aspect of Terminal Care: Anticipatory Grief, *Omega, 2,* pp. 91-99, 1971.

Fulton, R., *Death and Dying: Challenge and Change,* Addison-Wesley, Reading, Massachusetts, 1971.

Gerber, I. et al., Anticipatory Grief and Aged Widows and Widowers, *Journal of Gerontology, 30,* pp. 225-229, 1975.

Glick, I., and Parkes, C. M., *The First Year of Bereavement,* Wylie, New York, 1974.

Grollman, E., *What Helped Me When My Loved One Died,* Beacon Press, Boston, 1981.

Grollman, E., *Living When a Loved One Has Died,* Beacon Press, Boston, 1987.

Hardt, D. V., An Investigation of the Stages of Bereavement, *Omega, 9,* pp. 279-285, 1978.

Hinton, J., *Dying,* Penguin Books, Baltimore, 1967.

Jackson, E., *You and Your Grief,* Channel Press, New York, 1961.

Kalish, R., and Reynolds, D. K., Widows View Death, *Omega, 5,* pp. 187-192, 1974.

Lamers, W., *Death, Grief, Mourning, the Funeral and the Child,* Bulfin Press, Milwaukee, 1965.

Lamers, W., Funerals Are Good for People, M.D.s Included, *Medical Economics,* pp. 46-49, June 1969.

Marris, P., *Widows and Their Families,* Routledge, London, 1958.

Owens, G., Fulton, R., and Markusen, E., Death at a Distance: A Study of Family Survivors, *Omega, 13,* pp. 91-225, 1982.

Parkes, C., Effects of Bereavement on Physical and Mental Health, *British Journal of Medicine, 2,* pp. 274-279, 1964.

Parkes, C., *Bereavement: Studies of Grief in Adult Life,* International University Press, New York, 1972.

Parkes, C., Determinants of Grief Following Bereavement, *Omega, 6,* pp. 303-323, 1975.

Pollock, G., Mourning and Adaptation, *International Journal of Psychoanalysis, 42,* pp. 341-360, 1961.

Rando, T., An Investigation of Grief and Adaptation in Parents Whose Children Have Died from Cancer, *Journal of Pediatric Psychology, 8,* pp. 3-20, 1983.

Rees, W., Mortality of Bereavement, *British Journal of Medicine, 4,* pp. 13-16, 1967.

Sanders, C., A Comparison of Adult Bereavement in the Death of a Spouse, *Omega, 10,* pp. 302-322, 1980.

Silverman, P., *Helping Each Other in Widowhood,* Health Sciences Publishing, New York, 1975.

Volkan, V., The Linking Objects of Pathological Mourners, *Archives of General Psychiatry, 27,* pp. 302-322, 1972.

Winnicott, D., Transitional Object and Transitional Phenomena, *International Journal of Psychoanalysis, 34,* pp. 87-89, 1953.

Worden, J., *Grief Counseling and Grief Therapy,* Springer, New York, 1982.

Yalom, I., Group Therapy with the Terminally Ill, *American Journal of Psychiatry, 134*:4, pp. 396-400, 1977.

What the Nurse Likes

CORTNEY DAVIS

I like looking into patients' ears
and seeing what they can never see.

It's like owning them.

I like patients' honesty—
they trust me with simple things:
They wake at night and count heartbeats.
They search for lumps.

I am also afraid.
. . .

I like the way women look at me
and feel safe.
Then I lean across them
and they smell my perfume.

I like the way men become shy.
Even angry men bow their heads
when they are naked.
. . .

I like lifting a woman's hair
to place stethoscope to skin,
the way everyone breathes differently—

the way men make suggestive groans
when I listen to their hearts.

I like eccentric patients:
Old women who wear purple knit hats
and black eyeliner. Men
who put makeup over their age spots.
. . .

I like talking about patients
as if they aren't real, calling them
"the fracture" or "the hysterectomy."
It makes illness seem trivial.

I like saying
You shouldn't smoke!
You must have this test!
I like that patients don't always
do what I say.

. . .

I like the way we stop the blood,
pump the lungs,
turn hearts off and on with electricity.

I don't like when it's over
and I realize

I know nothing.

. . .

I like being the one to give bad news;
I am not embarrassed by grief.

I like the way patients gather their hearts,
their bones, their arms and legs
that have spun away momentarily.

At the end of the gathering they sigh
and look up.

. . .

I like how dying patients become beautiful.

Their eyes concentrate light. Their skin
becomes thin and delicate as fog.
Nothing matters anymore
but sheets, pain, a radio, the time of day.

. . .

I like watching patients die.

First they are living,
then something comes up from within
and moves from them.

They become vacant and yet
their bodies are heavy
and sink into the sheets.

I like how emptiness is seen first
in the eyes, then in the hands.
. . .

I like taking care of patients
and I like forgetting them,

going home and sitting on my porch
while they stand away from me
talking among themselves.

I like how they look back
when I turn their way.

Preventing Harm in the Name of Help: Ensuring Ethical Care Through the Concept of "Preserving Own Integrity"

Lynn Cummings

INTRODUCTION

Here we will explore one dimension of "Preserving Own Integrity" as developed by Davies and O'Berle in their research into a Supportive Care Model for the role of the nurse in palliative care [1]. Referring to "Preserving Own Integrity" as a core concept, these authors maintain that nurses must attend to their own self-care needs if they are to provide support for others.

Although true in all aspects of nursing, "Preserving Own Integrity" becomes an ethical imperative when caring for dying patients. As this term implies, we as nurses have a moral obligation to our patients to attend to the full spectrum of what the preservation of our integrity entails [1]. Not only is self-care necessary to prevent stress and burnout, it is essential to ensure that we, as caregivers, do not further burden the dying with our own needs. By attending to our emotional and psychological integrity, we maintain our boundaries and avoid imposing on others who are vulnerable. This process ensures that we are accountable to our patients in providing care that does not exalt us as caregivers but, instead, respects and honors the dignity and individuality of those facing a life-threatening illness.

Over the course of a progressive illness, a person moves from a state of having a potentially treatable disease to having one that is incurable, with death as the inevitable outcome. Palliative care focuses on comfort and support at a time when traditional treatments claim that "nothing more can be done." Nurses have a pivotal role in providing supportive care to dying patients and their families. Only recently has research been undertaken to explicate what this supportive role is [1-6].

One of the potential consequences to the patient and family if the nurse disregards Preserving Own Integrity is that the caregiver might burden the patient in the process of caring for him as he dies. To prevent this, the concept of Preserving Own Integrity insures that nurses are accountable for providing care that is patient-centered and not caregiver-centered, and for respecting the person's dignity and personhood through the transition from life to death. Preserving one's own integrity should be an unalterable condition of nursing that assures practices are in keeping with the ethical principle of nonmaleficence, or care that will not harm the patient [7].

THE SUPPORTIVE CARE MODEL

Davies and O'Berle developed their model to describe the specific components of the supportive nursing role in palliative care [1]. The authors found that although the literature on the subject describes the supportive concept as central to palliative care nursing, little research has been done to identify the specific knowledge and skills required of the nurse to provide supportive care. To articulate these specific care components, Davies and O'Berle, using a qualitative descriptive approach, examined in-depth interviews with an expert practicing nurse as she described the care she gave to ten patients and families. The model that emerged from the data identifies six separate but interconnected dimensions in the supportive role: Valuing, Connecting, Empowering, Doing For, Finding Meaning, and Preserving Own Integrity. For our purposes, we will limit the discussion here to the dimension of Preserving Own Integrity (POI).

Preserving Own Integrity describes the nurse's ability to maintain his or her own feeling of self-worth and to maintain an energy level sufficient for effective functioning. By looking inward, valuing personal worth, and acknowledging and questioning behaviors, reactions, and needs, the nurse maintains self-worth and esteem. Energy levels are sustained by various psychological strategies, such as distancing, using humor, hiding personal feelings, learning from mistakes, and sharing frustrations. Self-reflection on the nurse's part regarding his or her own behavior and motivations becomes the focal activity of this dimension.

Aimed at strengthening the inner resources of nurses and maintaining their wholeness, the above strategies assist them in acknowledging work-related grief and in finding meaning in the work of caring for dying patients. The goal is to prevent the nurse from experiencing burnout from emotional and physical exhaustion brought on by the demands of caring for dying patients and their families. The dimension of Preserving Own Integrity confirms that the nurse as a professional cannot be separated from the nurse as a person.

According to Davies and O'Berle, recognition of the interaction between human characteristics and "nursing behaviors" has been missing in the research on supportive care and has led to an incomplete conceptualization of this role. This chapter will therefore focus on the interaction of our human characteristics and our nursing behaviors in the context of preserving our own integrity. We ask the question: At what risk is the patient if the nurse is not aware of the need to preserve his or her own integrity as an essential part of the preparation and commitment to care for palliative patients? We will address the question after a brief review of the literature on Preserving Own Integrity.

LITERATURE REVIEW

Recent literature has attempted to describe the domains of nursing behaviors involved in the care of dying patients, including issues analogous to Preserving Own Integrity. Degner et al. identified enhancing personal growth as one of seven critical nursing behaviors in caring for dying patients [2]. The authors highlighted the need for nurses to define a role for themselves so that they could "receive emotional rewards and experience personal growth as a result of their involvement in the care" [2, p. 249]. Some nurses, particularly students, they noted, had difficulty confronting their feelings about caring for dying patients, lacked confidence in their ability to care for palliative patients, and inadequately managed their feelings as well as other aspects of nursing care. Negative nursing behaviors communicated lack of respect for the patient and family, conveyed in actions that ignored patients' specific requests for information, blocked discussions about death and dying when the patient clearly wanted to discuss them, and communicated an attitude of blaming patients for their circumstances. Other negative nursing behaviors were compulsively taking control at death scenes, taking action based on their own needs and agenda rather than the patient's, and responding to patient's anger in a harsh and defensive manner. The investigators associated these problems with the nurse's failure to adequately define a personal role in caring for dying patients.

After reviewing the literature on hospice nursing, Dobratz culled a description of nursing functions specific to care of the dying [3]. The author described four categories: 1) intensive caring, 2) collaborative sharing, 3) continuous knowing, and 4) continuous giving. The last category describes what nurses must do to balance their own self-care needs with the demands of repeated death encounters. Dobratz acknowledges the occupational stress of day-to-day encounters with death; however, she refers to Vachon's work wherein stressors in the work environment are identified as more detrimental than stressors associated with death and dying [3]. These stresses can be relieved, she suggests, by the nurse verbalizing the frustrations through effective team communication, and by team building to ensure a supportive work environment.

McWilliam et al. researched palliative nursing as part of a multidisciplinary support team [5]. The authors found that the challenges associated with caring for dying patients, such as unpredictable time frames, psychosocial care skills, and family-centered care, threatened the nurses' commitment to provide quality care, creating both internal and external conflict. The management of these conflicts required considerable energy on the part of the nurse in role adaptation and intra-personal and interprofessional conflict management. The authors referred to these efforts as secondary work aimed at reducing the impediments to the primary work of caring for patients. The nurses managed by a continuous process of reflecting on their own professional practice and on the everyday work experiences of palliative team nursing. Their findings, they concluded, were consistent with Davies and O'Berle's concept of Preserving Own Integrity in explaining nurses' secondary work to preserve their professional integrity [1]. McWilliam et al. corroborated that Preserving Own Integrity was a core component of palliative-care nursing, and was essential for maintaining job satisfaction by dealing with the stress associated with the care of dying patients.

Literature examining caring behaviors, as identified by the patient and family, offers different emphases on what constitutes a supportive relationship. Kristjanson's research demonstrates that patients and families rank clinical competence, sharing of information, and attention to physical care as indicative of caring [4]. Results varied somewhat according to the locale of care; for example, home-care families valued the patient being treated as a whole person.

Other researchers identified more interpersonal aspects of care to be important to patients and families. Hull conducted in-depth interviews with ten families who identified four areas of hospice nurses' caring, including effective communication and nonjudgmental attitude [8]. Actions that conveyed these caring qualities were the hospice nurses' willingness to talk, listen attentively, answer questions honestly, have a calm and unhurried demeanor, and have an accepting and tolerant manner. In an illuminating comment, one family described nurses who wore street clothes as "real people rather than starched professionals" [8].

Raudonis conducted a similar study with fourteen terminally ill adults to determine the patient's perspective on the nature, meaning, and impact of an empathic relationship [6]. The author found that patients experienced an empathic relationship when the nurse entered into a reciprocal sharing and revealing of personhood with the patient, within the context of a caring and accepting relationship. This sharing had the effect of making the patient feel acknowledged as an individual and a person of value. The participants in the study went so far as to describe the development of an empathic relationship with their nurse as a "friendship" with reciprocal sharing of deep and meaningful feelings.

What are the implications of these findings for ensuring that the care provided to the terminally ill is perceived as caring by patients? What role does Preserving Own Integrity play in the quality of the relationship the nurse forges with the patient? And what are the consequences for the patient if the nurse does not recognize the critical nature of the POI dimension?

DISCUSSION

Much in the nursing literature documents the stresses of caring for dying patients and their families and the needs of caregivers [9-13]. Also well documented is how these stressors can lead to intrapersonal stress, which threatens the nurse's sense of worth. Davies and O'Berle contend that these stresses threaten the nurse's integrity [1, 12].

Latimer speaks of ethics as the moral grounding that guides our way of treating patients [7]. Ethical principles clearly articulate philosophy, and valued beliefs and attitudes from which care practices flow. From this ethical perspective, Preserving Own Integrity becomes a way of ensuring accountability to those in our care. One must first understand the impact of a life-threatening illness before comprehending how care may enhance or detract from the patient's sense of integrity.

Renowned palliative-care physician Dr. Balfour Mount quotes ethicist David Roy in describing five consequences of a terminal illness experienced by a patient [14]:

- the fracturing of a sense of control and mastery,
- the giving of power to others,

- the breaking up of one's vision of the world,
- the fragmentation of how others perceive the expression of the individual's self, and
- the fracturing of relationships that are based on how one relates through one's body as one sees, touches, smiles, and gestures with others.

Some processes of disintegration of the self are brought on by the physical disintegration of the body. As caregivers, we must be vigilant that we do not add further to this disintegration by burdening the patient with care that is caregiver-centered and not patient-centered.

An important question to ask ourselves is whether we as helpers look honestly at our motivations for helping. Is our involvement to demonstrate some superior skill or knowledge, to meet our need for control over others, to bring about change in another person, to meet a job requirement, or truly to offer ourselves as an instrument of competence and compassion to the terminally ill?

Self-knowledge and self-appraisal must accompany our humanitarian inclinations. Many are motivated to help the dying based on a genuine desire to bring about a "good death" or to ensure that some bedside "horror story" that we have witnessed does not recur. In our zeal, we may forget who should define a "good death" and who should make the care choices. If we lose sight of this vital consideration, we risk forcing patients into situations which meet our need to be "good helpers," but cause our patients harm in the name of helping. I speak of the "I know what's best" syndrome, whether it be a ward nurse who dismisses the patient's request to die at home, after unilaterally determining that the family cannot cope, or the home-care nurse that badgers the family into accepting aid in the home before they really want it. True patient-centered care trusts that patient and family, given adequate information, will make choices that are best for them and their situation. This approach recognizes and honors the individual's autonomy and accepts that decisions may not always meet with the health-care team's approval.

In a debate with Dr. Roy in the *Journal of Palliative Care* over what constitutes a "good" death, Dr. Henteleff talked of taking the "low road" in caring for the dying [15]. He spoke of serving the dying at the frontlines and being accountable for their dignity by not further burdening them with what he termed "hateful actions" by caregivers [15, p. 52], such as:

- deceiving the patient,
- mistreating the patient through over-treatment or inaction,
- abandoning the patient by ignoring, avoiding, or not treating the person as a whole,
- taking advantage of the person's vulnerability to exert our own need for control, demonstrate our zeal as caregivers, or impose our beliefs and solutions,
- to exalt the person by treating the patient on a level above the human experience and thereby caricaturing their dying.

As nurses, we are not immune to these "hateful actions" in our practice. Nor do we suggest that these infractions are deliberate. These errors may occur through care which, though grounded in a genuine desire to help, lacks reflective appraisal of its true motives and consequences for the patient.

O'Berle and Davies write about the disillusionment of nurses, arising from their frustration at not being able to give care in the manner they value [12]. Their personal integrity is eroded when a dissonance occurs between the technical competence that the health-care system rewards and the caring competence that nurses value. McWilliams et al. identified the effort nurses must make to ensure that their needs, goals, and expectations of service to others were not jeopardized [5]. To fulfill their own performance expectations, nurses may unconsciously shape the patient and family situation to meet their image of good nursing practices.

Sourkes identifies some of the traps into which caregivers may fall in the process of helping [16]. She describes the caregiver as being plagued with the "rescuer fantasy," wanting to protect the vulnerable patient and make everything better. Working with dying patients means we must put aside our own agendas and accept one that is defined by the patient with an uncertain future. Caring for the terminally ill calls for, Sourkes says, someone who can flow with the experience and neither become entrapped by it nor try to superimpose a rigid structure on it [16]. The caregiver must be committed to the patient's and family's quality of life as defined by the patient and the family.

In their zeal to help, caregivers are in danger of over-involvement and of becoming a surrogate family member, inserting themselves into the lives of the patient and family more as intruder than as invited guest. Burucoa cautions palliative-care providers to guard against exclusiveness in care, which risks creating a suffocating enclosure around patient and family, invading their space and privacy [17]. Sourkes reminds us that we must know how to enter a family's circle while at the same time maintaining our own boundaries and preserving our sense of integrity [16].

From over-involvement to under-involvement, the reluctance of a nurse to engage fully in a balanced relationship with the patient can have a detrimental effect. The emotional toll of death anxiety and caregiver grief in working with dying patients, and the coping strategies employed by nurses for these feelings, has been recognized in the literature [9, 11, 13, 18]. Warren found that nurses may deliberately prevent themselves from caring too much because of the high personal cost, actualized by distancing and objectifying the patient, a process that buffers the nurse from a deep interaction with the person [19]. This technique, in effect, contributes to a depersonalization of the patient by attending to only a part of the patient's whole. Nurses need to engage in an ongoing, honest appraisal of their limitations in taking emotional risks [16]. We need to learn about the context of our own psychic reality from knowing ourselves and confronting our own loss history. It is within the context of knowing ourselves that the ability to risk emotionally, and to experience and witness deep feelings, has meaning.

If we fail to recognize the impact of grief on us as individuals, we may not recognize when we need to deal with these feelings as professionals. We may seek support from those we are caring for and inappropriately burden them. Although there is a reciprocal nature to caring relationships, the dying person is experiencing his or her own grieving, and it is unethical to expect that the patient has the capacity to support the caregiver. Each person in the relationship has needs that must be met, but the inviolate boundary is crossed when the nurse's needs are met at the expense of the patient's. Looking inward and assessing our reactions will safeguard the patient and ensure self-control.

CONCLUSION

As nurses, we bring many things to dying patients and their families—a soothing touch, a cool drink, a kind word, medication to ease the pain. However, the most precious gift we offer is ourselves. This gift must be recognized as a powerful tool with the potential for great healing and, equally, for great harm. What enables a caregiver to sustain quality involvement with the dying in a manner that ensures that care is ethical and beneficent?

The concept of *Preserving Own Integrity,* as described by Davies and O'Berle, leads to an active process of exploring the concepts of life, illness, death, and grief, and the meaning of these concepts for ourselves and for others. Understanding what we bring to the care of the dying in the form of our beliefs, attitudes, motivations, and reactions is a fundamental part of palliative care and a moral obligation that honors the rights of dying patients. Thus, introspection must be the caregiver's constant companion, with the attendant willingness to acknowledge his or her own vulnerability [16]. The process of preserving our integrity is embraced as a covenant between two human beings, one offering professional skills and personal integrity and the other facing the universal journey from life to death.

> Do not walk in front, I may not follow.
> Do not walk behind, I may not lead.
> Walk beside me and be my friend.
> *Unknown*

REFERENCES

1. B. Davies and K. O'Berle, Dimensions of the Supportive Role of the Nurse in Palliative Care, *Oncology Nursing Forum, 17*:1, pp. 87-94, 1990.
2. L. F. Degner, C. M. Gow, and L. A. Thompson, Critical Nursing Behaviours in the Care for the Dying, *Cancer Nursing, 14*:5, pp. 246-253, 1991.
3. M. C. Dobratz, Hospice Nursing: Present Perspectives and Future Directives, *Cancer Nursing, 13*:2, pp. 116-122, 1990.
4. L. J. Kristjanson, Quality of Terminal Care: Salient Indicators Identified by Families, *Journal of Palliative Care, 5*:1, pp. 21-30, 1989.
5. C. L. McWilliam, J. Burdock, and J. Wamsley, The Challenging Experience of Palliative Care Support-Team Nursing, *Oncology Nursing Forum, 20*:5, pp. 779-785, 1993.
6. B. M. Raudonis, The Meaning and Impact of Empathic Relationships in Hospice Nursing, *Cancer Nursing, 16*:4, pp. 304-309, 1993.

7. E. Latimer, Ethical Challenges in Cancer Care, *Journal of Palliative Care, 8*:1, pp. 65-70, 1992.
8. M. M. Hull, Hospice Nurses: Caring Support for Caregiving Families, *Cancer Nursing, 14*:2, pp. 63-70, 1991.
9. J. P. Adams, M. J. Hershatter, and D. A. Moritz, Accumulated Loss Phenomenon among Hospice Caregivers, *The American Journal of Hospice and Palliative Care*, pp. 29-37, May/June 1991.
10. G. A. Hartrick and M. D. Hills, Staff Nurse Perceptions of Stressors and Support Needs in their Workplace, *The Canadian Journal of Nursing Research, 25*:1, pp. 23-31, 1993.
11. C. M. Parkes, The Caregivers' Griefs, *Journal of Palliative Care, 1*:2, pp. 5-7, 1986.
12. K. O'Berle and B. Davies, An Exploration of Nursing Disillusionment, *The Canadian Journal of Nursing Research, 25*:1, pp. 67-76, 1993.
13. M. L. S. Vachon, *Occupational Stress in the Care of the Terminally Ill, the Dying, and the Bereaved*, Hemisphere, Washington, 1987.
14. B. Mount, Whole Person Care: Beyond Psychosocial and Physical Needs, *The American Journal of Hospice and Palliative Care*, pp. 28-37, January/February 1993.
15. P. Henteleff, To Die with Dignity: You Take the High Road and I'll Take the Low Road (Letter to the Editor), *Journal of Palliative Care, 2*:2, pp. 52-53, 1987.
16. B. Sourkes, Views of the Deepening Shade: Psychological Aspects of Life-Threatening Illness, *The American Journal of Hospice Care, 4*:3, pp. 22-29, 1987.
17. B. Burucoa, The Pitfalls of Palliative Care, *Journal of Palliative Care, 9*:2, pp. 29-32, 1993.
18. K. O'Berle and B. Davies, Support and Caring: Exploring the Concepts, *Oncology Nursing Forum, 19*:5, pp. 763-767, 1992.
19. L. Warren, cited in reference No. 18, 1988.

Becoming the Patient

1.
For years the same dream:

a pit beside the road, walls
made of dirt, women with matted hair
who called to me, their wails

sounding like lullabies.
I'm tired of being the nurse. I bend
close to the edge.

Will I be drawn into the patient
like thin wires of pain?

2.
First, the white gauze.

I probe the patient's wound;
its steep walls retract—
muscle and veins, their red glow

a lantern.
Voices come and go.
The hall lights dim. Then,

skin pressed to bone,
I enter the patient. My heart
becomes soft; its blood

echoes back unfamiliar places:
toes, temple, belly.

Who else knows what this is like?

3.
All day, my fever rages.
I see the nurses are crying,
eyes full of waiting, eyes
shiny as ice.

Beyond my window,
a field. The nurses sing to me.
They hold me
in the tall meadow grass.

I cannot turn from their bodies.

4.
My nurse smells cold as January.
Birds dart at her hair,
plucking for seeds in this long winter.
The birds see the window near my bed
and think it is air. One by one,
their soft bodies against it;
they have tried to go home for the night.
What is the point of being here?

5.
I open my eyes.
There is a moon in the hallway;
under it, nurses talk, their voices
like water traveling long viaducts.

When pirates with knives in their teeth
bend over me, I call my nurse.
She says *They don't want to kill you—
only to look.*

I close my eyes.

6.
The wound's edge has sucked shut.

My nurse tells me I am so good
I am free to go. After this,
nothing else is important.

I tell her my dream.
We have something in common, she says,
but she will forget me.

She says *It's time,*

7.
and everything is aflame.

Standing beside my patient,
I point out the thin scar.

Music—A Companion for the Journey from Mourning to Morning

Sally S. Bailey

As a young child being raised in a small rural midwestern town, there were few opportunities for hearing classical music. I looked forward each day to the music broadcast from the state college's radio station just before it went off the air at sundown. I was particularly drawn to the program's theme song. I never discovered its title nor composer until some years later when, as a teenager, my piano teacher assigned the piece which I recognized from my youth. It was Maurice Ravel's *Pavane pour une Infante defunte* (pavane — a slow stately sixteenth-century dance— for a dead infant).

I began with this story because I am a musician and my earliest childhood memories include music—first playing the piano by ear and singing, followed by years of lessons and a lifetime of joy from making and listening to music. However, only in my later years have I become conscious of the very special place music has always had in facilitating my own mourning and grief work, while simultaneously preparing me for my life's work—integrating music and other art forms in ministering to the dying and bereaved to enable persons to mourn, grieve, and celebrate life. Now I more fully understand the truth in Goethe's words: "The future enters into us to prepare us, long before it happens."

There is growing research on using sound to assist healing for body and soul. Among the pioneers in these fields are Helen Bonny [1] in using music therapeutically, and Don Campbell [2] in studying the effects of sound. I have chosen here to share reflections on the role music has had in enabling me and those to whom I've ministered to move from "mourning to morning."

Albert Schweitzer's words also hold much truth for me: "There are two means of refuge from the miseries of life: music and cats." As an introspective child, I found (and continue to find) comfort from music and cats. I remember how sad I was when my beloved "Tom" died. I insisted on creating a funeral for him, digging his grave outside the sunroom window through which the sounds flowed as I played Handel's *Largo* and simultaneously wept. On other days when I felt bereft or sad from life's realities, I would play a contemplative Chopin etude or nocturne or Tchaikovsky's *None but the Lonely Heart,* or the theme *Goin' Home* from Dvorak's *New World Symphony.*

I grew up during World War II and remember the many nostalgic songs played to comfort those separated during wartime. After I went to bed I would hear my mother play on the piano such songs as *My Buddy* and *Now Is the Hour*. They became a part of my repertoire of songs for mourning too.

Then there are the memories of funerals. I was frequently asked to sing—old hymns such as *The Old Rugged Cross, Lead Kindly Light, Rock of Ages, Shall We Gather at the River, Nearer My God to Thee*—to remind the mourners that their departed had gone to a better place. I observed how the music often drew forth tears and weeping among the bereaved. It was not an easy task to sing songs for mourning.

As I matured, I learned that throughout history music has been integral to the grief work of people of all religious faiths—lamenting not only those who have died but also the loss of a community or country. One of the earliest accounts of loss is found in the Book of Psalms, which includes many laments. In Psalm 137, the Children of Israel are exiled into Babylon and cry out:

> By the rivers of Babylon we sat down and wept
> when we remembered Zion.
> There on the willow trees
> we hung up our harps,
> for there those who carried us off
> demanded music and singing,
> and our captors called on us to be merry:
> 'Sing us one of the songs of Zion.'
> How could we sing the Lord's song
> in a foreign land?
>
> PS 137:1-4 (NEB) [3]

However, we know they did "keep singing."

A more recent example of oppressed people who have continued to sing in a foreign land are the African Americans. They have produced a tremendous wealth of music in their spirituals, many of which have texts related to life and death. One of the most hauntingly beautiful is *Sometimes I Feel Like a Motherless Child*—a universal lament that can gather people together. I learned to sing this spiritual when I was a teenager, and it has become one of the songs of my soul since my mother's death.

In my musical development, along with the requiems and passions by master composers, I was exposed to the literature of great art songs, song cycles, and operatic arias, many with themes of separation or loss through the death of a beloved. I poured out my soul singing "When I Am Laid in Earth" from *Dido and Aeneas* by Purcell and "The Empty-Handed Traveler" from *The Consul* by Menotti.

However, the ultimate occasion that gathered the height, depth, and breadth of my experiences and feelings related to death and mourning was my opportunity to sing Gustav Mahler's *Kindertotenlieder* with orchestra. The cycle of five songs with poems on the death of children by Friedrich Rueckert takes one through the reflection of the father (poet) whose children die in a storm. In the final song, through expressing anger and remorse that the children were permitted to go outside, the father finally regains a sense of peace:

In such a tempest, they rest
As in their mother's house;
By no storm frightened,
By God's hand protected,
They rest, they rest, as in their mother's house.

For me, the experience of the father's emotions of sadness, anger, remorse, and grief did not come solely through the poetry. Rather, I felt these through the power of the music with its tonal color, harmony, tempo, and rhythm. After singing about the raging storm in which the singer must project intense, raging sound, the song concludes with the words above, with the singer projecting the quality of a croon, a lullaby. Through the union of poetry, the timbre of the voice, and selected instrumentation, Mahler creates a mystical spirit of transcendence and conveys a sense of peace to the listener.

On one occasion, I was accompanying a cellist and playing Max Bruch's *Kol Nidrei* (a Hebrew melody for Yom Kippur). In the midst of our playing, a young woman who had been listening to our music suddenly rose from her seat, burst into tears, and fled the room crying: "I can't listen to this . . . you know what happened to my brother!" Thirteen years previously her brother had been murdered in another country, and when his body and possessions were returned home, inside the suitcase was the music of Bruch's *Kol Nidrei*. She never wanted to listen to it again, for it brought back the horror of her brother's death as well as the pain of her being left behind. She, it would appear, had not tended her own grief work.

When my father died, I wanted to participate in his funeral service. My father was a man of faith, and I was thankful he had been liberated from physical suffering. I thought Bach's *Jesu, Joy of Man's Desiring* would celebrate his life. However, with its vibrant, joyful sound and tempo, my mother thought it would be inappropriate for the occasion. I realized that we in fact were at two different places in our mourning at that time, and I must not project my experience of my father's death onto my mother and other members of the family. My mother requested Bach's contemplative *Arioso in G*, which I had frequently played for my father. I will associate this composition forever with my father. I continue to play it from time to time and remember—giving thanks for what was and what is.

We need to stay "in tune" with our own grief work throughout our life—for we shall always be encountering losses. Some years ago, a hospice nurse said that she was feeling the need to go to a sad movie. When I asked her why, she replied: "So I may cry a while." She was feeling blocked and unable to release her tears. As a musician when I know I need to mourn, I will sit at the piano and play "my repertoire" of nostalgic pieces—both classical and popular. But the time comes when one must get beyond the melancholy. I find much wisdom in these words from Ecclesiasticus:

My son, shed tears for the dead;
raise a lament for your grievous loss.
Shroud his body with proper ceremony,

and do not neglect his burial.
With bitter weeping and passionate lament
make your mourning worthy of him.
Mourn for a few days as propriety demands,
and then take comfort for your grief.
For grief may lead to death,
and a sorrowful heart saps the strength.

Eccls. 38:16-18 (NEB) [3]

At a time when I was "stuck" in my sadness from a loss, I was playing several preludes and etudes of Chopin that made me even more morose and fatigued. I happened to turn to a Beethoven sonata, commonly known as *The Appassionata*. One cannot touch the keys lightly when playing this sonata. It requires much vigor and strength and plunges one to the depths of one's soul as well as lifts one to the heights. As I played the first movement, I realized I had also struck a vein of anger and rage that I felt surrounding my loss. Discovering this new emotion, another facet of my grief, helped lift me out of my "pit of sadness." I was able to face the reality of my loss with greater equipoise and make the appropriate decisions I needed to make.

A reader may say, "I will not be able to tend my grief in the ways you describe because I neither sing nor play an instrument." However, the reality is that everyone can be a listener. Only a minority compose or actively make music. The rest of us listen to music—and we join with the composers and musicians in responding to sounds. There is only silence until the music is given sound.

From my experience, music more than any other art form holds lifelong associations for most people in relation to the significant people and events in their lives. On hearing a piece of music one never knows when the tears will flow, either from longing for something that no longer is present, or from remembering wonderful and poignant times. Once a patient broke into tears after hearing two of her favorite Irish songs, which her husband had previously sung. Since his death several years earlier, the first time she had been able to cry was at the sound of those Irish songs. Music clearly can facilitate grief work if one will engage with the pain of the loss.

One of the most dramatic occasions I have witnessed of a patient's being moved by music occurred in the hospice on the morning of Good Friday. Along with other patients, a patient came to the hospice commons to listen to music and watch the creation of a visual piece of art by a gifted Japanese artist.

The artist used a bed sheet for the canvas and stretched it across one end of the commons. Unseen by the people present, he stood behind the canvas and began to paint while I accompanied a flutist who played several contemplative pieces by J. S. Bach. First there emerged what appeared to be a circle of dancers, but soon the figures were filled in and the image of the crown of thorns formed on the canvas. Simultaneously the music was taking the patient to the depths of her soul, and she began yelling loudly: "Get me out of here. I am sick of this death and dying." And then she burst into tears and wept.

A nurse gently wheeled her back to her room where she wept much of the day. Heretofore the patient had not dealt with the reality of her dying nor made decisions about her possessions. The artist, nurses, and pastoral staff visited the patient throughout the day allowing her to grieve her own dying. These events enabled her to begin to make the decisions she needed to make and to move through her dying with gentleness and peace. I feel it was the combination of the visual creation, the music, the other people gathered to share a common experience, and the compassionate staff that helped evoke a freeing response in the patient. She was not alone.

Music also brings much comfort on "the journey from mourning to morning." Many times surviving family members have commented that listening to music helped them as they kept the vigil with their loved one. The wife of a patient said she was happy that her last memory with her husband was of their hearing music together on the night he died. They enjoyed going to concerts, and shortly before he died in the hospice, a string quartet was playing in the patient/family living room. The sound of the music floated down to all the patient units.

Another example of music facilitating grieving involved an eight-year-old girl whose mother died in the hospice. The child began to withdraw when she learned of her mother's death and refused to be touched by staff who tried to comfort her. She fled from the viewing room, where her mother's body was laid, down the stairs to the commons from which she heard music playing. The movement/dance therapist had just concluded her afternoon session. The music being played was a recording of Paul Winter, which captures the sounds of the sea and whales. The child accepted the therapist's invitation to create a dance together with movements like the rolling surf. In the midst of it, the child wept, was cradled and held—as she began a new dance of life: "from mourning to morning." Perhaps all of us could more easily enter into our mourning if we allowed ourselves to respond and move to music with our entire body, like the child who danced.

As I reflect on all the examples given here of the role of music in grief, the common thread is that the music "touched" the listener or got inside one's body and soul—literally as well as figuratively. And when this happens, we might say that music has brought us "home"—to a place of comfort and repose—even if we can only arrive there by way of tears. There is much truth in Willis Elliott's words:

> Great music plays the entire pianoforte of human feelings
> which are the memory carriers of the soul
> as it sings and
> suffers and
> shapes its destiny.

Mourning is part of the journey of life—and when entering the journey with music assisting our steps, morning will come, and we will be "home."

REFERENCES

1. H. Bonny, *Music and Your Mind,* Station Hill Press, Barrytown, New York, 1990.
2. D. Campbell (ed.), *Music: Physician for Times to Come,* Quest Books, Wheaton, Illinois, 1991.
3. *The New English Bible with the Apocrypha,* Oxford University Press, New York, 1971.

ENDNOTES

Some of the stories of music facilitating persons' grief are included in S. Bailey et al., *Creativity and the Close of Life,* The Connecticut Hospice, pp. 78-80, 1990.

The quote at the conclusion of this chapter is from the unpublished writings of the Rev. Dr. Willis E. Elliott, Biblical Scholar in Residence at Craigville Conference Center–Cape Cod, and my mentor.

Night Nurse

CORTNEY DAVIS

> behold, the angels of God
> Genesis 28:12

Angel,

hold their hands while I hurry
from patient to nameless patient,

feeling their skin beneath my hands
like tattered dresses stinking

of urine. Now they are sobbing.
Touch me! an old man says, *Touch me.*

The women want to steal my flesh.
They cry out, *Take my place!*

Angel, you go. Go into the corridors
where their bodies wither before me.

They die rolling in their beds,
they die sitting on their toilets.

When I try to give them breath
their vomit comes into my mouth.

Angel,

when a patient's skin is moist with pain,
and pain wakes him and sings him to sleep,

when a patient's family turns away
and his hands fall empty to the sheets,

then everything is multiplied.
A sip of cold water could be a thousand lakes;

a nurse appearing uncalled in the doorway
could be someone who loves him.

Angel, when their lungs stop and their eyes
slick over and stare, when their skin

purples from toe to thumb to hollow cheek,
you be the one who gentles the world;

you be the one who stays,
all these lives flying from us.

Comfort Care

L. J. Schneiderman

Father Julian Chiochio's Comfort Care Group. *An oasis of old-fashioned humanity in the high-tech desert of the modern hospital,* the article called it. And a picture showed Father Julian with protruding jaw, in what could have been compassionate exhortation or the effort to dislodge something stuck in his teeth. It struck her as a much better way to mark time while waiting to make babies than subbing for burnt-out teachers in South-Central Los Angeles. Whatever makes you happy, her husband Jonathan said.

The operator paged Father Julian and put him through; she heard his gravelly voice on the other end of the line: Sure, what the hell, join the crowd, the more the merrier. Followed by a weird almost barking kind of laugh.

The next morning while they passed around sticky buns and coffee he asked: What's your name? Kiki, she told him. Kiki Fishberg. No kidding. Again that strange laugh, a cough mostly. Call me Woppy. We'll be the Seven Dwarfs. To her dazzlement the others picked up on it right away; they started working on Dwarf names. Sarah, one of the nurses, became Lumpy. Maynard the psychologist became Bitchy. Deenie, another nurse, Mammoplasty. Ruth, the social worker, Emesis. Sam, the psych resident, Fuckup. Embarrassed, she felt her face erupt in a tingling heat, but by the time they had gone around she had tucked her stocking feet under her, joined the laughter, and was bouncing up and down in her chair. You see, he said. The way we rev ourselves up.

He mocked everything you would expect of priests. Instead of a clerical collar he wore rumpled shirts and loose clashing ties picked up years ago at Goodwill outlets, when you still could get bargains, he said. And pushed behind his ears what was left of his gray hair, securing it with thick black-rimmed glasses and a scruffy ponytail. Sloping nose, tangled brows, moist lips, a tongue always in motion, shaping some raunchy joke, usually, as though it were his idea of a fine cigar. Not at all attractive. And not exactly mainstream thanatology. He made a feast of foul words as though they were one of the last great pleasures of life. People don't give a fuck about heaven or hell. They just want to die in their sleep.

But everything the article said was true—he brought people comfort. At the bedside he would deposit his thick hand, this huge clod wormy with veins, unerringly

This short story is reprinted with permission of *Black Warrior Review, 18*:2, Spring/Summer 1992.

on the part of the body that hurt the most. And it never failed—eyes squinting like a cowboy's against hot gritty wind would instantly soften and a gaunt face would fill up and smile.

Her first solo assignment was a Mrs. Bogatescu with breast cancer. One after another, silent explosions of masses in her armpits, under her ribcage, circling her neck, had exhausted her husband and two children to the point that they could no longer bear to be with her; nor was she in her denuded almost embryonic shapelessness able to summon up the stoicism necessary to keep them brave. The woman spent most of her waking hours weeping.

Which is what Kiki found herself doing at morning report. She shook her head with embarrassment. For Chrissake! She had been on the case less than a week! But Father Julian looked at her. I'll come with you today.

As usual they just sat there at first, the only sound the muted racket from the hallway outside. Then with one hand in Mrs. Bogatescu's, the other settled on a mound of flesh, Father Julian began his routine. He was curious. How had she met her husband—what was his name? Chuck. How had she met Chuck, tell me about it—Where? When?—waiting patiently in the long silences. The woman's lips nibbled against gluey saliva. Funny story. They met. At this gas station. Chevron— they took Mastercard. While trying to figure out how to use the pump. This guy came over. Soon Father Julian and Mrs. Bogatescu—Carla—were laughing over the crap- game called love. What if their gas tanks hadn't been in synch? What if Chuck had come a few minutes earlier, or she a few minutes later? They had achieved simul- taneous gasups, so to speak. What if, what if—the possibilities and *double entendres* were limitless. By early afternoon they were revelling in the unforgettable adventures of Carla and Chuck. And Mona and Thelma—by the time night came around she was gasping out her daughters' favorite scatological jokes, a faint blush on her yellowish face, joining Father Julian with her croaky laughter until exhausted she fell into a deep sleep and died.

Kiki found herself being awakened by Father Julian gently stroking her hair. Outside the black windows traffic slid by, clicking like tumblers behind a safe. Want some coffee, he said. She looked at her watch. Jonathan would already have taken his dinner into the bedroom to pore over loose-leaf binders. He was in the management training program of a large detergent company. She had learned to fall asleep in the glow of his desk lamp. Coffee sounded nice, she said.

They drove in his unconvertible convertible, an old Karmann Ghia whose shredded top wouldn't go up—in the dash lights it looked like something made of dried mushrooms. What about when it rains, she asked. He jutted his thumb toward the back: a poncho.

They shared a peach tart, picked at it listlessly in one of the leatherette booths, their eyes half-closed and swollen. She found herself showing him pictures from her wallet. What is this, she wondered, his routine again? But he looked at each one methodically, tilting it under the fluorescent lights. Mother, father, sister, Jonathan. He liked Jonathan. Good-looking. No, better than that. Corporate looking, know what I mean? Graduation portrait, wedding shots. It annoyed her now, that same chipmunk smile stamped on her face. Her childhood, she thought for the first time. What's this, he said. It was a honeymoon shot, both of them crouched in parkas, her left hand bulbously swathed in bandages—this huge Q-tip. Jonathan's idea, to camp across the country. Naturally, the first night out while trying to cook dinner in the dark she practically cut her thumb off. Almost in reflex Father Julian's hand plopped down and covered hers. Then quickly he smiled, patted it ironically. They both laughed. The routine. Anyway, no problem. She has a Cuisinart now and a clean well-lighted kitchen. What about you, she said. Any pictures? No, sorry. No pictures, no family. He'd grown up in foster homes, mostly. Could he go for another peach tart? Why not, he said.

So, she said when he came back with the tart. That it? Deprived childhood? The coffee, she realized, was beginning to kick in. That how come you're so weird? She flicked her fork toward his purplish plaid shirt and yellow and black tie.

He shrugged. Not all that weird. You end up wearing what you wore in college. In the sixties everyone dressed like this. The only rebellious thing he did those crazy days was become a priest. It appealed for some reason. Discipline.

She said it sounded like something out of a porno mag.

He gave his barking laugh and looked at her, startled obviously, but not without admiration. Well, I suppose. Celibacy. Just another form of pornography.

The weirdest of them all, too, seems to me.

He rubbed his face. It helps me keep the faith. He rubbed again. You keep the faith hoping someday to believe. What about you?

She told him God was not one of her hangups. Far as she was concerned, far as what she believed—and she thanked her Cognitive Science major for this—religion was wired into the brain just like hunger, thirst, lust, what have you. Survival of the species, that's all. Otherwise Homo sapiens would've looked around eons ago at all the shit going down and said, What's the use, why go on? You remember the Stockholm Syndrome? These women held hostage by a gunman who threatened to kill them. What'd they do? They fell in *love* with the bastard. They began to *worship* him. Even though he didn't give a *shit* about them. That's religion, far as I'm concerned—a humongous Stockholm Syndrome. She was Jewish, of course, if anyone asked. But all that meant was she was brought up to celebrate Hanukkah along with Christmas (lighting a menorah and topping the tree with the Star of David) and knew the way to make her parents happy was by marrying Someone Nice Like the Jonathan Feldman Boy.

Through the whole thing Father Julian sat hunched over his coffee, amused not so much by what she said, she knew, but by the way she said it, his brow furrowed with that kind of ironic skepticism you see in French movies. She liked that. When she was in the mood to be cynical—and coffee unfailingly stirred it up—she would perch up on her stocking feet and flop her hair about, very much aware that her petiteness took on a particular archness that men found stimulating. In fact the only thing lacking to make this cafe scene French-perfect, she thought, was the sensual wreathing of cigarette smoke. But she didn't smoke and was just as glad Father J. didn't either.

In the room, while you were sleeping, he said. I was watching you.

She blinked. Oh yeah?

The way you were sitting. The way you were . . . draped. Bathsheba. By Rembrandt. You know that one? She shook her head. She must have died while I was looking at you. And I thought: It's true. Life *is* short. Art *is* long. He laughed and ended up coughing and punching his chest comically. They agreed—time to be getting home.

The next time she needed help it was Mrs. Kettleman, an old black woman with white hair and bowel cancer. In an effort to stifle her pain the medical resident had given her larger and larger doses of intravenous morphine and ended up shutting down her intestines. For the last two days the old woman had been vomiting so wretchedly the doctor avoided her room. This time they not only sat with her, but Father Julian showed her how to give a bed bath. Twice—when they didn't get the kidney basin up in time—they rolled her from side to side and changed the rank, swampy sheets. As Father Julian ran the washcloth over the prunish body, lifting the flaps of her breasts to clean under them, Kiki felt a wave of heat flood her face. For Chrissake—what was going on? She shook her head, felt her hair sting her ears.

This time the coffee only made her feel more agitated. Her ankles banged against each other on the chair.

What I want to know is what would've happened if we weren't there?

Well for one thing it would've been a lot worse, wouldn't it.

That's what I mean, that's just what I *mean.* I mean does it *have* to be so fucking ugly?

Why we were there, right? So it wouldn't be.

Oh, nice. Some people get to throw up so that other people can feel good about wiping it off.

What can I say? The ways of the Lord are mysterious.

She felt her hand tighten around her coffee cup, actually saw it turn white, saw it bulge at the base of her thumb, like an adder puffing.

You, he said quickly—he launched a mocking finger which made an aborted bulky dive like something shot from a circus cannon—*you* got the answers, not me. And in the midst of his protracted laughing and coughing she jumped up, knocking the table, spilling the coffee.

Then the fantasies began. At first they were the kind of harmless pleasures some of her old college professors had inspired: soaring in a balloon, rolling in waves, seatmates on a hijacked jet, sweaty rock singers joined over a spotlit mike, that sort of thing. She let herself enjoy them, why not. Time and again the Anne Tyler book she was reading in bed would drop on her chest. Startled, she realized she was imagining his thick hands washing *her* body, lifting *her* breasts. It terrified her—this idea, this *image* of her emaciated body; she actually sneaked her hand under the sheet and rolled her plump breasts for reassurance; and lay awake waiting for Jonathan to come to bed. But when he moved in and entangled her legs she couldn't help imagining that it was Father Julian. Still that was okay. Nice, actually. Only when Father J.'s massive face began to haunt her dreams, when things started getting out of hand, did she get uneasy.

It was amazing in retrospect that no one in the group said anything about that barking laugh, his cough—which kept getting worse and worse—until a patient on rounds pointed out what was obvious: You really ought to go see a doctor about that. The group all laughed, but really it was true. They had just gone along with it as one of their beloved leader's peculiarities.

Sure enough, the chest X-ray showed trouble. And one of his testicles was more like a rock, which on biopsy proved to be cancer. The group was stunned. You of all people, they said. Why not me of all people? And he cursed abundantly to keep the group's spirits up. If I had been using the fucking things—fucking things, right?—if I'd been using them I would have been checking on them. Gathered around his bed they laughed, albeit with some constraint. Soon everyone in the hospital was repeating his latest quip. They could just as well have lopped off my appendix for all the difference it makes.

Now her fantasies took on a vividness, a microscopic glow and particularity she found breathtaking. As though she and the cancer—like terrorists from opposite sides—had met and formed a conspiracy of expediency. They would seep into his flesh, divide the territory, occupy, possess. Borders and rules were for others, not for them. Picture this: what if, what *if* one night while he was lying there she entered his room and before he said a word climbed on top of him, engulfed him, pressed him down, invading his mouth with her tongue, digging into his anus with her finger the way she did in the heat of making love? What would he do, what would he *do?* The scene's sheer implausibility made her feel free to let it loose, let it fly unchecked. His mouth, her tongue; his anus, her finger. It became an obsession—it would never happen—what harm then? Except that now when Jonathan turned off the light and came to bed she pulled him onto her, and even though with the utmost sweetness he complied with all her requests she was left sleepless and thrashing.

Tenacious spots remained on the X-ray. Specialists conferred. Another biopsy. Chemotherapy had failed. Law and order had given way. Like a fanatic mob, cells were rioting through the alleys of the lung. The fiery drugs left him wide-eyed and ashen, like someone pulled from a car wreck. He would feel better in a few days, they said. But now when the group assembled around his bed there was an audible heave of dismay. Fucking Jesuitical cancer, Father Julian whispered. What did you expect? But the laughter churned and died.

She figured out ways to be alone with him—after the others in the group had gone home, after visiting hours, between nursing shifts, best of all in the evening right after medications. She too would ignore restraints. She had bonded with her enemy, the way generals do who keep a picture of their adversary before them. At first she sat, just as she had been taught, held his hand as he fell asleep, nothing more. But one night she lay her head down and felt—a gasp escaped her—his other hand come down. She seized it, pressed down on it with all her might, felt it deep in her hair, holding, holding fast.

At last he was deemed strong enough to go home. It was Kiki's suggestion that the group look in on him now and then to help him with his laundry, the cleaning, garbage, shopping and such. All agreed—she had the most free time.

That morning she pranced back and forth in front of the mirror and flung what must have been a dozen outfits on the bed. What does a priest's housekeeper *wear?*

The spearmint dress looked too minty, the denim wraparound too suggestive, shorts—now that the weather had turned chilly—too blatant. Tweeds? Jeans? Forget leather. Flinging, flinging. Her one cashmere sweater was flattering but too Symphony-Boardish, her baggy turtleneck too artsy fartsy, worse it made her boobs look like day-old bread. For Chris*sake!* She blindly stabbed into her closet and hauled out white cotton pants. Okay. Next. What she always wore around the house with them: a t-shirt. She threw it on. Done. Finished. Decided. She slammed the door and hurled herself down the steps as though leaving the scene of a crime.

He lived toward the back of a pinkish two-story singles complex which featured stenciled parking spaces and an oval swimming pool. The crucifix was there, just as she expected, stark and assertive as she opened the door. Yet it was as though he had made one brutal sweep of his arm across the wall to clear it, then could do no more. The rest was a dizzying mess, as though the whole place had been tipped on its side. Newspapers, magazines, books, shoes, towels, cereal boxes, Kleenex, tuna fish cans, abandoned dishes—she had to pick her way. Wrinkled venetian blinds scattered pale pink light into a dank smell of immobility. The man himself was off in a corner, gloomily watching acrobatic ski jumpers on television. Gray sweat shirt and milky blue pajama bottoms. His terry cloth bathrobe lay open revealing puckered folds of flesh.

Then for the first time it occurred to her: This will not be easy. And she stood there wondering how to begin.

I've come to cheer you up, she said. Cheerily. Don't make my trip a total waste of time.

He grimaced, lurched a bit—a laugh? a cough? I know the routine, he said. All the tricks.

She sighed. Her shoulders fell. I know you know. She started going around, picking things up, pushing other things into more-or-less piles.

Look at that, he said. Ski jumpers used to be happy if they could just come down on their skis. Now they do all these fucking loops. The bursts of cheers from the TV caused him to cringe.

Like bagels and croissants, she said. You don't get the plain old-fashioned kind any more. She started slapping books into the bookcase. *Greek Bronze Statuary, Russian Art Nouveau, Paintings of the Lotus Sutra.* She saw he had an Escher print on the wall. In college she had studied Escher four different times—in Art History and again in Cognitive Psychology and again in Modern Philosophical Theories and again in a course entitled Man and Machine: Is There a Difference?

Must you make all that noise?

That's why I'm here. To ruin your day.

He still didn't take his eyes off the TV. He was armed, prepared. He would not be provoked. He would not be comforted. She started stacking the dishes. On the way to the kitchen she was brought to a halt by his surly voice.

Lucky you, they said. Cancer of the testicle we can cure. Completely. Permanently. Ninety percent of the time.

She turned and looked at him.

I'm one of the ten percent. Don't look at me like that. I'll throw you out. He lurched again, a low-pitched rumble, it hardly made a sound. One of the Chosen People. Like you.

She put down the dishes and came back to him, was about to take his hand, but caught herself. Careful. One of the tricks. Instead she knelt down next to him, pushed her face between him and the TV. Look at me when you talk, she said.

You want to know how I feel?

She nodded.

Like the punchline in a bad joke.

That's better, she said. He scowled. Not a trick, she said hastily. Sarcasm. Honest. It just slipped out. When was the last time you ate?

He lifted his elbow in the direction of a bowl yellowed with grit. She picked it up. I'm not hungry, he said. Remember, I know them all. His hand toyed with a plastic container of pills. Then dropped it on the table next to him. Then picked it up again. She took the container out of his hand. Morphine for pain. Come on, she said. You need a shower. She heaved him up by the lapels of his robe. He looked at her startled. Come on. Which way? Glowering. This he was not prepared for. She gave him a push and started working off his bathrobe, pushing, raising his arms and hauling his sweat shirt over his head, getting a pungent whiff of each item as she flung it behind her.

The hallway was crowded on both sides with scrambled books, and boxes filled with record albums—mostly operas, it seemed. On the walls were a few unframed oil paintings, sheepishly crude and scratchy. Yours? she asked as they came to the first one. He grunted. A murky cafe scene showing old men playing odd instruments including one with a broom handle sticking out of a can. He waved his hand giving his undershirt a flip as they went by. Florence. The next, an old woman and man scraping the hull of a boat—mostly muddy blue and green. Bellagio. She reached around and started working on the knotted drawstring. Then the largest picture of all, full of agitated colors, a young woman slouched by a stone fountain. Another wave of the hand. Bathsheba. Me, you mean? They paused to look at it. The face was so crudely done it could have been anyone. You, he said. And me. Aha, she said. He turned and looked at her and started to sway and for a moment she thought she was going to have to grab him, but he caught himself on the wall and turned and she got back to work, bumping him forward with her body. The last thing she pulled off was his pajama bottoms, stepping on them to keep them anchored while he shuffled out of them. By the time they reached the bathroom he was naked.

To keep from embarrassing him she occupied herself with the shower. Let's see. How do these things work? It's been so long.

The stall was one of those single-piece units made of a white plastic, the door was frosted sliding glass, the showerhead the kind popular in motels, that could be adjusted to give pulsating jets of water. Only after she got it going did she turn and let herself look at him. She had to, of course. Really look at him.

It was what she had always heard—the eyes of an animal before slaughter. Not for food though, nothing so rewarding as that, but because he was no longer any use.

His torso, slack, his arms, which he held in front of him, thin and furry burs of hair. And his buttocks—truly negligible. Negligible, that's all she could say. She was used to Jonathan's bulk.

Come on, she said. In you go. But he didn't move. And she realized it would never work, unless . . . unless. . . . And with sweep of her hand threw back her hair. And took off her clothes.

For a while they just stood there, the two of them, he with his hands gripping his elbows, eyes squeezed shut while water bounced heedlessly about, oblivious to how she had to duck and bob to keep the spray out of her face. Damn, had no one taught this priest the rules, the simple *courtesies* of shared showering? She started to laugh, but caught herself when she saw how miserable he looked. Back, she ordered, and pushed him against the wall. The soap was Irish Spring, hinting mischievously of men's colognes and skin bracers—a secret life? Whipping up a lather she first did his neck, then his back (Turn), his chest—carefully along the raw-looking scar—then under his arms—he flinched, he was ticklish—all in workmanlike fashion. Turn again. And all the time he continued to cringe, his outsized hands hanging in midair, eyelids buried shut. Both arms, the hands, squeezing their girth as she rubbed, squeezing the webs too between his fingers. Then his buttocks, his thighs, making him raise each leg over hers so she could do his calves and feet, again rubbing carefully in the webs between his toes. Then, only then, did she acknowledge with her soapy hands his rather hangdog erection, carefully—the skin around his scrotum was still yellow-green from the surgery.

And then rose up on her toes and embraced him and enclosed him between her thighs. And in that one swift move under the silky flesh of the water put flesh to her dream, invading his mouth with her tongue and probing, probing until she felt the heat of his anus around her finger. And so they remained. And sometime in the midst of the warm orchestral thudding she heard him sigh.

It was by far the longest shower she had ever experienced. Later she realized one can hope for such endless supply of hot water only in major league apartments and hotels, settings far beyond her present budget, but well within her dreams, for someday, she was certain, Jonathan and she would routinely shower in such luxury, and secretly she would always think back to this, the first time— rebellious, irreverent thoughts—the kind she had long since discovered would buzz through her head as she sat in the hushed and sacred presence of the dying, holding the patient's hand—as she sat now holding Father Julian's hand until he fell asleep—or so she thought. The moment she withdrew to leave he opened his eyes.

What, she said.

He waved his hand, almost negligently, the way he had dismissed an article of clothing or one of his paintings, then turned his head away.

She closed the door softly behind her.

The next morning he was found dead by the visiting nurse and everyone agreed it was just what he would have wanted—to die in his sleep. And that night she drew Jonathan under the water with her, letting him comfort her and kiss her tears. He understood. Such a good man, such a good man, so very sad. Whispering they soaped each other the way they had always done. Jonathan was first rate in the shower. Only a few more years, he promised. Then he would feel ready to start a family. A few more years of subbing, that's all. And she agreed, she had to agree, that was not too much to ask. Under the comforting water they continued to soap each other, planning their future. And as the water started to turn cold she realized that Father Julian would never know—perhaps it was just as well—and now it was too late to tell him. Art is short. It is life, *life* that is long.

To Know of Suffering and the Teaching of Empathy

Sandra Bertman and Melvin J. Krant

Medical education is geared primarily to the mastering of an enormous amount of information on the nature of the body, on diseases or injuries afflicting the body, and on techniques for elimination or at least dissipating the impact of illness. How to promote a humanistic or an empathetic grasp of the hurt and pain that often accompanies these illnesses, particularly those that cannot be eased by standard treatment, is another matter.

A valuable source of teaching material can be found in creative literature. Creative artists have long struggled to explicate their personal visions of pain and to communicate these visions to their readers. In this essay we would like to focus on some literary descriptions associated with a specific area of human pain, namely amputation of a body part, and offer some concepts of empathy. Our hope is to encourage greater use of fiction and poetry for helping both patients and physicians cope with the impact of serious illness.

A person can lose a part of his body by accident. In Robert Frost's "Out, Out—," a poem set in rural Vermont, a boy is at work on a woodpile in the family farm [1]. Responding to his sister's call for supper, he meets with sudden violence:

> . . . the saw,
> As if to prove saws knew what supper meant,
> Leaped out at the boy's hand, or seemed to leap—
> Neither refused the meeting.

The physical reality of the amputation is clear to the boy: his body is no longer whole. The thought of living without his hand seems unbearable:

> . . . the boy saw all—
> Since he was old enough to know, big boy
> Doing a man's work, though a child at heart—
> He saw all spoiled.

Yet the reality is too overwhelming to fully acknowledge. The boy turns to his sister to deny that he has actually lost the hand, and to plead for restoration:

Reprinted from *Social Science & Medicine*, © 1977, pp. 639-644, with kind permission from Elsevier Science Ltd, The Boulevard, Langford Lane, Kidlington OX5 1GB, UK.

> ... "Don't let him cut my hand off—
> The doctor, when he comes.
> Don't let him, sister!"

The medical response seems typical of an emergency—orderly and technical. The boy is operated upon. But the meaning of the devastation to his body is more than the boy's heart can bear. To the astonishment of the medical staff, he dies on the operating table:

> ... The watcher at his pulse took fright.
> No one believed. They listened at his heart.
> Little—less—nothing! and that ended it.

The staff is surprised; but nothing more is made of it. There are no questions asked. All go about their business:

> No more to build on there. And they, since they
> Were not the one dead, turned to their affairs.

To the image of the violent trauma and the boy's rejection of a diminished future life, Frost adds the bleak absence of caring. The poet knows the efficient, technical response, by itself, is insufficient. The boy's wound is deeper than his hand. A comforting word from the sister or from the medical staff is glaringly absent. No one moves toward relieving the hurt within. The staff becomes concerned momentarily— only when the boy's pulse is failing during surgery.

The need to be understood, to let out hurt, to be touched and cared for, becomes more pronounced with illness. In Tolstoy's *The Death of Ivan Ilych,* the protagonist, a mature lawyer, falls ill. As his health perceptibly fades, Ilych reflects:

> (though he would have been ashamed to confess it) . . . He longed to be petted
> and comforted. He knew he was an important functionary, that he had a beard
> turning grey, and that therefore what he longed for was impossible, but still he
> longed for it . . . Ivan Ilych wanted to weep, wanted to be petted and cried over. . .
> [2, p. 138].

Age and important accomplishments do not pare away the need to find solace and to be cared about. Yet no one seems to respond to the unvoiced urgency in Tolstoy's mature Ivan Ilych any more than anyone responds to the young boy in Frost's poem.

The absence of caring, and the loneliness of suffering as far as the rest of the world is concerned, is again the theme in W. H. Auden's *Musée des Beaux Arts:*

> About suffering they were never wrong,
> The Old Masters: how well they understood
> Its human position; how it takes place
> While someone else is eating or opening a window or
> just walking dully along . . . [3, p. 3].

Auden describes the fatal calamity in the Brueghel painting *Landscape with the Fall of Icarus.* Icarus, who dares to fly too near the sun, falls in his hubris, and plunges into the sea while the day-by-day world goes about its business, barely looking up to notice (Figure 1).

Figure 1. P. Brueghel, *"Landscape with the Fall of Icarus"* ("La Chute d'Icare") 1558. Courtesy of Museés royaux des Beaux Arts, Brussels.

> . . . everything turns away
> Quite leisurely from the disaster; the ploughman may
> Have heard the splash, the forsaken cry,
> But for him it was not an important failure . . .

Perhaps it is understandable, this unconcern of the world at large; many events in it seem too distant. One must draw limits to what one can devote attention and care. But when is suffering close enough? What relationship should exist before someone must show concern? In Frost's poem and Tolstoy's story, even when a family member is in pain, neither a sister nor a wife seems able to respond or help. How then should a physician respond?

Even maimed war heroes are avoided by many people. Losing a leg or an arm for one's country might seem a fitting sacrifice to support a person's self-definition. However, both Siegfried Sassoon and Wilfred Owen, young British poets of the World War I era, tell us otherwise. Sassoon's poem *Does It Matter* is filled with the irony of alienation, the feeling that no one in a civil society ever cares to see, or really understand, the bitterness that exists when one has been maimed. The feeling of being out of touch in a world that superficially seems civilized enough, helping out through decent actions and good intentions, yet never quite touching the bitter feelings within, is conveyed in the imagery and tone of each stanza:

Does it matter? losing your leg? . . .
For People will always be kind,
And you need not show that you mind
When the others come in after hunting
To gobble their muffins and eggs.

Does it matter?—losing your sight . . .
There's such splendid work for the blind;
And people will always be kind . . . [4, p. 75].

The cynical stab of the poet almost pushes us away. Is he trying to make us feel guilty? Isn't it ungenerous to question and nag at us when we are not responsible for his grief? Perhaps it is only in a poem that such self-pity can be expressed, for in life, people will avoid those who allow such bitterness to surface.

In *Disabled,* Owen causes the intact reader even greater anguish, giving a picture of a bleak limbless man:

He sat in a wheeled chair, waiting for the dark,
and shivered in his ghastly suit of grey,
Legless, sewn short at elbow. . . . [5, p. 67].

The amputee reflects on his past, and regrets how unlovable and unattractive he has become:

And girls glanced lovelier as the air grew dim.—
In the old times before he threw away his knee.
Now he will never feel again how slim
Girls' waists are, or how warm their subtle hands:
All of them touch him like some queer disease [5, p. 68].

Dredging up events from memory, he mourns the past. He questions resentfully why he joined the army, blaming his own vanity and his girlfriend. And as he reflects, he sees his present and his future:

Now, he will spend a few sick years in Institutes,
And do what things the rules consider wise,
And take whatever pity they may dole.

Women not only will see him as "some queer disease" but will discount him when they look for real men. Like Frost's boy, all is spoiled:

To-night he noticed how the women's eyes
Passed from him to the strong men that were whole.

And for solace he "waits the dark." All he wishes for is to sleep:

How cold and late it is! Why don't they come
And put him into bed? Why don't they come?

Owen's amputee is even more despairing than Frost's. Frost's boy dies; Owen's soldier must live in this state of hell where only sleep can obliterate the pain.

If one were near him, how could one communicate with a man like this, whose pain is so pressing and immediate? He must mourn the image of self-past, and identify reasons to live with far more restrictions. Yet he might make us feel so helpless, speechless, and guilty that, out of embarrassment, we avoid him, adding to his isolation and torment.

Amputation is frequently the result of medical intervention, in which case the removal of a leg, an arm, a breast is invariably couched in the language of sacrifice— a person gives up a part of the body's integrity in order to avoid the ravages of disease. However, diabetes may worsen, cancer may spread, and the patient may have to sacrifice even more:

First they took off one breast
then the other
then her ovaries came out
then her pituitary gland.

Slowly they dismembered her
to keep her alive.
They started with the things they understood
cutting her womanhood away,

the most obviously infected part,
and then the module whose function they weren't sure of.
It is a matter of taking out the fuse
so the lights won't go on [6, p. 5].

So begins Karen Swenson's poem *Virginia*. A cynical hue is cast on the sacrifice, painting the surgeons almost as savages pulling a person apart, analogous to killing the woman so the cancer will die. But these feelings of futility and rage at the uncertain surgeons, hacking away pieces of the body in procedures that may not work, appear to be those of a friend, not of Virginia, who keeps going back as a patient even if in vain:

She leaves me to go to the hospital,
moving from biopsy to biopsy
as they cut her back to the bone,
but the more they minus
the more multiples there are [6, p. 5].

Not infrequently friends and family take their anger out against the doctors for the incurable illness—even when not enough is known about the disease—although physicians are doing whatever they believe might help. A young man, whose mother had undergone six years of multiple surgeries for metastatic breast cancer, was furious at the doctor who asked permission to perform an autopsy on her body following death. He screamed, "She was autopsied in life!"

Timing is often critical in decisions to consent to the body-part sacrifice. Even when urgency exists in the doctor's opinion, a person may need to think through the diagnosis and discount other options before allowing the surgeon to proceed with the amputation. In Norma Klein's novel *Sunshine,* a twenty-two-year-old woman with osteogenic sarcoma cannot make the sacrifice despite the medical urgency. Kate lashes out at the surgeon trying to persuade her that amputation of her leg will save her life. "My leg?" cries Kate, "you take my leg off? . . . No! you can't" [7, p. 47]. Rushed too fast and too hard to make a decision for which she is unprepared, she refuses, and eventually dies of the illness.

Solzhenitsyn, in *The Cancer Ward,* introduces two adolescents to each other in a regional cancer hospital in Siberia. Both are patients awaiting medical decisions about their conditions. Demka, the boy, reveals to Asya, the girl, that he is in the hospital because of a sarcoma of the leg:

> He spoke of his leg almost as he did of his wages, with embarrassment . . . "Well, you see . . . They're not saying, but they want to cut it off." His darkened face sought Asya's bright one as he said this. "You can't be serious!" Asya clapped him on the shoulder like an old friend. "What do you mean cut your leg off? Are they crazy? Or don't they want to bother curing you? Don't let them do it! Better die than live without a leg. What sort of life is the life of a cripple? Life has to be enjoyed" [8, pp. 148-150].

Demka thought of what Asya had to say:

> Yes, of course, she was right again. What was life with a crutch? Suppose he were sitting here next to her, what would he do with his crutches? And what would it be like with a stump? He would never have been able to bring that chair over himself. She would have had to fetch it for him. No. Life without a leg was no life at all [8, pp. 149-150].

Like Frost's boy and like Klein's Kate, Solzhenitsyn's adolescents see life without an intact body as not worth having. Better die.

Demka's leg gets worse. But with time, and as the pain becomes more intense, he comes to see the limb as a curse, a burden that is interfering with recovery, and accepts the operation as a necessity. After the surgery Demka foresees his life going on and tells himself that now he won't be distracted from his studies by such frivolous diversions as dancing or racing. He is, in fact, better off without the leg. His thinking is quite different from Sassoon's and Owen's soldiers; the absence of rancor and bitterness makes us feel less pained and less guilty. But is Demka's attitude rationalization? Will his argument break down as time goes along? Should we be prepared for depression and resentment when Demka leaves the hospital and goes home?

Solzhenitsyn describes a most poignant moment when Asya, in a state of terror, enters Demka's recovery room shortly after his operation. She has learned that she is to have her breast amputated because of cancer. Asya cries, moans, and throws herself on Demka's bed:

> "Who w-w-wants m-me n-n-now?" She stammered inconsolably . . . She buried her cheek in the pillow . . . "Who wants a woman with one breast? Who? At seventeen," she screamed at him as though it were all his fault. He didn't know what to say to comfort her [8, p. 456].

Thoughts of the beach and of bathing suits that would never be worn flood the girl's head. Silly, we might say, of all the superficial vain thoughts—bathing suits! Yet Asya is overwhelmed. Asya pushes her breast into Demka's face, demanding that he fondle it and kiss it. She pleads with him never to forget it. Demka, fascinated and absorbed, kisses and kisses her lovely breast, as Solzhenitsyn concludes, "Today a marvel, tomorrow into the basket" [8, p. 458].

Accompanying hoped-for rescue from cancer is a disfigurement far worse than cosmetic. The woman may be made to feel ugly and sexless. Asya's breast amputation touches on definitions of her womanhood: sexuality, attractiveness, marriage, maternity. "Cutting away her womanhood" was the image Swenson used to describe Virginia's breast amputation. The breast, says Anne Sexton in her poem *The Breast,* "This is the key to it" [9, p. 4].

In *Semi-Private,* Helen Yglesias describes the plight of a twenty-eight-year-old woman waking up in the hospital after a breast amputation. Jealousy rages as she thinks of herself dying and leaving a husband "who will run right out and get himself a beautiful two-breasted wife." The young woman tries to convince herself that Matt, her husband "will love [her] with only one breast." This preoccupation extends even to the nurse who comes to help her:

> The nurse washed my face again with a warm, soapy cloth . . . She smelled delicious. Everything about her was very nice. Matt will be crazy about her. Two breasts, too . . . [10, p. 36].

Images of husbands abandoning their wives, of lovers leaving, concerns of being deformed and freak-like, and intensely jealous feelings of intact women are thoughts commonly present after mastectomy. Still another concern—that of past losses being dredged into present time—is introduced by Alice Davis as she looks at her body in *After Surgery:*

> I am lopsided
> Flatter than a boy;
> S-shaped stitchery
> Frames wash-board ribs;
> Why should I remember
> After seven years
> The way a hand
> Curved my breast?
> Old griefs sift through this excavation [11].

A loss of a precious body part not only throws her off-balance, but kindles up remembrances of a long-gone lover and a lost husband, thoughts of whom still bring back old pain. Today's hurts make yesterday's anguishes again vivid.

The world of the maimed with its hurt, embarrassment, shame, and uncertainty is caught with special poignancy by Marjorie Kellogg in her novel *Tell Me That You Love Me, Junie Moon.* The heroine, Junie Moon, a patient on a hospital ward unit, has been doused with acid by an assailant. Scarred in face and body, she has lost the fingers on one hand. Another young man on the ward, John Goren, has lost his leg but "could no more tolerate deformity in himself than in those around him."

Solzhenitsyn's adolescents, Asya and Demka, demonstrated that the maimed can understand and help one another, but Kellogg focuses on another perspective: the difficulty of accepting oneself and others as deformed, even among other maimed people. At one point, Junie Moon offers John a part of her Hershey bar, but Goren "did not want to take it because there were fingers missing from the hand that held it to him . . . he did despite himself, feeling pale and shaky" [12, p. 57]. Why does a deformity in someone else arouse such repugnant feelings, especially in one who has lost a limb himself? Avoiding contact with other disabled persons seems like a denial, an attempt to escape reminders that now one is like them.

Similarly, facing herself is Junie Moon's great problem, and she persistently delays both looking at her burned, scarred face and allowing anyone from outside the "safety" of the hospital ward to see her. A dying woman, who by the nature of her own pain feels authorized to deal with the unmentionable, helps Junie Moon to make the long-delayed confrontation with her "new" face:

> "He got you real bad, Junie Moon," says Minnie [referring to the man who poured the acid] . . . "have you seen yourself?" "Why should I go around looking at myself, can you tell me that?" She wanted to tell Minnie to mind her own damn business . . . Minnie's voice was almost like a whisper, "Of course. I didn't know you before, Junie Moon. You probably was a good-looking woman, that would be my guess." "But now. Minnie?" "Now, it's like you say: pretty bad." There. The words fell like stones. She did not think she could tolerate the sound [12, p. 25].

That night Junie Moon looks at herself in the mirror and is horrified. She returns to Minnie, who says:

> "You went to look? . . . It won't ever be so bad as it were there . . . Let Minnie see your hand. Come on now. I heard you smash the mirror" [12, p. 26].

But living among fellow-sufferers is not enough; the maimed need their contacts with the outside world. They need to know that they are still acceptable and needed— though they may dread the first meeting with lover or spouse. So it is with John Goren who waits for his girlfriend to visit, excusing her prolonged absence to his teasing roommates. One day he catches sight of her in the corridor:

> He turned to run. He would have to see her another day—another time when he felt up to it. She would have to understand that. But his leg was missing and he was not about to run anywhere. Instead he sat down and crossed his good leg over his stump and looked wildly for a blanket with which to hide himself [12, p. 59].

Goren's hopes and shames are revealed. He needs to be in touch with people he loves, but, simultaneously, he fears being found unacceptable. He echoes the worries of the young woman in *Semi-Private* who tries to convince herself that her husband will love her even with only one breast. Kellogg and Yglesias emphasize these conflicting feelings of rejection coupled with great need for reassurance, acceptance, and love.

Kellogg's novel focuses attention on interactions between the medical staff and the sufferers:

The doctors who treated Junie Moon were friendly and candid because there were no mysteries about her troubles. They had a few regrets, such as they could not supply her with new fingers. "Just can't give you a new hand Junie Moon," they said, wagging their heads and winking at her. One day she said to them: "Why not!" and they looked at her in genuine surprise. "Why not, little resident? Why not call up the hand store and have them send one over?" One of the residents scratched his nose and gave her a long look, "because," he said "the hand store was sold to a tire factory, and that's the truth."

Junie Moon loved to be taken down by young boys like this one with the hard eyes and silly smiles, and she poked him in the ribs: "You got a bedside manner that will end you up in jail," she said, and they laughed together [12, p. 62].

There appears to be an easy enjoining between Junie Moon and this resident physician, accomplished through bantering and playful ridicule. They seem to intuitively understand each other. The young resident accepts the banter on its own terms, and becomes the one doctor granted a unique trust:

He was to have the questionable privilege of being the first and last physician to whom she said anything that mattered to her, and he was so touched by it that he had not mentioned it to anyone, for fear he might be asked to discuss it at a staff meeting.

We are not told why he fears discussing Junie Moon's revelations at a staff meeting. Does he fear "exposing" her real self, kept hidden from the medical staff? Will he be violating her trust? Or does he fear that in talking about Junie Moon as a person he will be ridiculed for bringing such irrelevant concerns into a medical meeting? Whatever the reasons, caring for Junie and sharing in her story become a lonely privilege and responsibility for this young doctor. The alliance, however, does afford Junie a place to share her hurts:

"It's like being sentenced," she said to the resident. "You're right," he said putting his hand gently on her face. "You're a cheery cuss," she said to him and loped away [12, p. 66].

Sick people are dependent on their doctors, but often feel that the physician does not understand their pain. An older woman patient in *Semi-Private* comments:

"You and I know how it is with doctors, with them everything is fine because does it hurt them? No, it hurts you and me and it puts money in their pocket, but God bless them they do their best" [10, p. 36].

Tolstoy describes with singular clarity the gap between the essential concerns of a sick man and the analytical gyrations of the physician. Growing sicker, Ilych revisits his doctor:

There was the usual waiting and the important air assumed by the doctor . . . [The physician asked] . . . questions which called for answers that were foregone conclusions . . . and [Ilych noticed] the look of importance which implied that "if you only put yourself in our hands we will arrange everything—we know indubitably how it has to be done" [2, p. 121].

Ilych understands the techniques employed by the physician when addressing a sick man, for Ilych himself, as a lawyer, frequently acted similarly when prosecuting "an accused person." Being sick is like being accused, and the lawyer and the doctor, stressing their righteousness and self-importance, are really no different. Ilych feels not only condemned and helpless but disregarded:

> To Ivan Ilych only one question was important: was his case serious or not? But the doctor ignored that question as inappropriate. From his point of view it was not the one under consideration, the real question was to decide between a floating kidney and appendicitis.

Ilych feels the barrier between his need to be understood and the physician's mechanical deliberations. Yet he is helpless to express his disappointment and his frustration. He has to grasp what is happening to him by indirection:

> From the doctor's summing up Ivan Ilych concluded that things were bad, but that for the doctor, and perhaps for everyone else, it was a matter of indifference. . . . And this conclusion struck him painfully, arousing in him a great deal of pity for himself and of bitterness towards the doctor's indifference to a matter of such importance [2, p. 122].

It is not that the physician does not attempt to do good; it is more a matter of style and manner. If the physician makes his objectives only technical, if he does not recognize the fear and loneliness invoked by suffering, and if he avoids the patient's emotional concerns in order to protect himself, he communicates feelings of indifference or, worse, a sense of hostility.

Another technique that physicians sometimes employ to avoid genuine contact is to be paternalistic and inappropriately garrulous. In *Semi-Private,* the young mastectomy patient is treated by her surgeon in such an irritating manner:

> "That's the girl. Best way to sleep, elevated. How are you? Feeling good? Fine." My surgeon's loud, fast voice infuriated me. "Your chart is great. Keep up the good work. Don't use your left arm—we don't want these sutures to tear. Do anything else you want. Been out of bed yet? We need you out of bed—it's twenty-four hours since your operation. The nurse will help you to the bathroom, you'll smear a little make-up on, you'll feel better for it. What do you say there, Dr. Guerrero?" He drew Bob into his frenetic activity. "Doesn't she look great?" [10, p. 39].

The surgeon's simplistic advice and vigorous encouragement seem organized to exclude the patient's voice from entering into dialogue. Not a moment is given to the fact this his patient has lost a breast and must live with the threat that cancer may recur. Such behaviors can be classified as anything but empathic.

Kellogg helps us grasp another essential characteristic of a true therapeutic alliance between the caregiver and the patient. Empathy requires that one penetrates into the inner world of another in order to identify the wound (or the wounding possibility) in oneself. At one point, Junie Moon reveals to her physician-confidant how the maiming occurred. The physician feels himself identifying with the assailant and begins to wonder whether, if properly provoked, he could disfigure a woman with acid. The thought disturbs him, and he tries to discuss the issue with his wife one night, but "the look of horror which crept over her face prompted him to put a stop to the entire discussion." The young doctor is not allowed to share his doubts about himself. Just as the wife cannot bear it, one might ask how often physicians signal that they cannot endure their patient's pain, putting a stop to sharing even before it gets started.

Sacrificing a body part is a horrendous ordeal, even if it is to save a life. People are worried that they'll be treated without real compassion, and the absence of genuine caring simply adds to their painful lot in life. Empathy is not denial, avoidance, false optimism, obfuscation of the issues by clever professional jargon, or inappropriate cheering. An empathic therapeutic bond, on the contrary, requires contact, an accurate exchange and sharing of knowledge, a daring to touch, and the creation of a safe environment to share inner doubts.

Yet another insight is found in literature—the insight that life may be enhanced through suffering. When a person endures the trauma of an unbearable loss, life can become truly intense. Transformed through suffering, a person can be virtually reborn, as the speaker in *Virginia* describes the woman with breast cancer:

> She stands on the corner and talks to me,
> wearing her scars behind the soft sculpture of foam,
> tells me that living with death is not too bad.
> It gives life salt, not depending
> on any other time to make up your present tense,
> and days become what they always should have
> been pungent with the present [6, p. 5].

Though pieces of my body may be taken away from me, Virginia seems to say, life goes on, not in the ordinary sense, but "pungent with the present." No whining here; rather a sense of great courage, even gratefulness—days become what they should have always been, rich and truly lived in the moment, without postponement for a future. Virginia goes back for more biopsies and more surgery; life is ever worth living because it is life.

Karl Shapiro, in *The Leg,* also offers a transcending message—a person is more than his or her body parts. The subject of the poem wakes fitfully in a hospital room to the realization that his leg is gone. Mourning his loss, he comes to realize that he has not just lost a leg, he has, in fact, gained something:

> . . . [he] now smiles to the wall
> The amputation has become an acquisition [13, p. 38].

Shapiro talks of the duty this man feels for his orphaned leg, still a part of him, though no longer an integral part. The limb continues to have a life that must now slowly die, and the man must honor this passage. Though the leg is now separated from him, he must continue to respect the lost part—it is yet life. There is an essential Hebraic threnody in this concept. In Jewish tradition, a part that is separated from the body is still part of that person, and must be accorded rites of internment, to be rejoined to the body when it is buried at a later date. Not a thing of waste to be discarded in a basket, as Solzhenitsyn's physicians so cynically threw away Asya's breast, the amputated part remains sacred:

> Pray for the part that is missing, pray for peace
> In the image of man, pray for its safety
> and after a little it will die quietly.

With the power of such belief, hurt is transcended. Through the strength of such belief, a person is indomitable. He or she can adapt to the loss, and can go on with living, or if need be, face death with trust.

Molly Holden, in *Hospital*, insists that this strength is not only in traditional religion, but is to be found somewhere within her human center. She rejects the priests, the churches, the holy speakers who come to offer their way of salvation as she lies sick in the hospital. Instead, she searches inside herself to find the human force:

> And all the while I lay, under the words and attempted curing
> seeking inside not out for a human grace
> that would give me a strength and a courage for enduring against great odds
> in a narrow place [14, p. 39].

Here we find the essential ingredients of hope—the strength and courage to endure, with all the medical help that one can get, and to remain a person.

And so with Theodore Roethke's protagonist, rising through his diminished body in *Infirmity*. Despite his body's betrayal, repeated amputations, and multiple side effects, he can still define an inner essence that is his humanness:

> I love myself: that's my one constancy
> Oh, to be something else yet still to be!
> Sweet Christ, rejoice in my infirmity
> There's little left I call my own.
> Today they drained the fluid from a knee
> and pumped a shoulder full of cortisone;
> Thus I conform to my divinity
> By dying inward, like an aging tree [15, p. 244].

REFERENCES

1. R. Frost, *The Poems of Robert Frost*, Random House, New York, 1946.
2. L. Tolstoy, *The Death of Ivan Ilych and Other Stories*, Signet, New York, 1960.
3. W. H. Auden, *The Collected Poetry of W. H. Auden*, Random House, New York, 1954.
4. O. Williams (ed.), *The War Poets*, John Day, New York, 1945.
5. W. Owen, *The Collected Poems of Wilfred Owen*, C. D. Lewis (ed.), New Directions, New York, 1963.
6. K. Swenson, *An Attic of Ideals*, Doubleday, New York, 1975.
7. N. Klein, *Sunshine*, Avon, New York, 1974.
8. A. I. Solzhenitsyn, *The Cancer Ward*, Dell, New York, 1968.
9. A. Sexton, *Love Poems*, Houghton Mifflin, Boston, 1967.
10. H. Yglesias, *The New Yorker*, Feb. 5, 1972.

11. A. Davis, *After Surgery,* unpublished manuscript.
12. M. Kellogg, *Tell Me That You Love Me, Junie Moon,* Popular Library, New York, 1968.
13. K. Shapiro, *V-Letter and Other Poems,* Royal & Hitchcock, New York, 1944.
14. M. Holden, *To Make Me Grieve,* Hogarth, London, 1968.
15. T. Roethke, *Collected Poems of Theodore Roethke,* Doubleday, New York, 1966.

The Body Flute

CORTNEY DAVIS

O my body! I dare not desert the likes of you
in other men and women, nor the likes of the parts of you
Walt Whitman

I go on loving the flesh
after you die.
I close your eyes
bathe your bruised limbs
press down the edges of tape
sealing your dry wounds.

I walk with you to the morgue
and pillow your head
against the metal drawer. To me
this is your final resting place.
Your time with me
is the sum of your life.

I have met your husbands and wives
but I know who loved you most,
who owned the sum
of your visible parts.
The doctor and his theory
never owned you.

Nor did "medicine" or "hospital"
ever own you.
Couldn't you, didn't you
refuse tests, refuse to take your medicine?
But I am the nurse
of childhood's sounds in the night,

nurse of the washrag's sting
nurse of needle and sleep
nurse of lotion and hands on skin
nurse of sheets and nightmares
nurse of the flashlight beam at 3 a.m.

I know the privacy of vagina and rectum
I slip catheters into openings
I clean you like a mother does.
That which you allow no one,
you allow me.

*   *   *

Who sat with you that night?
Your doctor was asleep,

your husband was driving in.
Your wife took a few things

home to wash, poor timing,
but she had been by your side for days.
Your kids? They could be anywhere,
even out with the vending machines

working out just how much
you did or didn't do for them.

*   *   *

You waited
until you were alone
with me. You trusted

that I could wait and not be
frightened away.
That I would not expect

anything of you—
not bravery or anger, not even
a good fight.

At death
you become wholly mine.

*   *   *

Your last glance, your last
sensation of touch,
your breath

I inhale, incorporating you
into memory.
Your body
silvery and still on the bed,
your lips fluttering into blue.
I pull your hand away from mine.

My other hand lingers, traces
your finger from the knucklebone
to the sheets

into which your body sinks,
my lips over yours,
my cheek near the blue

absence of your breath,
my hands closing
the silver stops of your eyelids.

Reflections on Suffering

Graduation Remarks for the
University of Massachusetts Medical Center, June 2, 1996

Aaron Lazare

Welcome to all of you on this extraordinary occasion. Today is a day for celebration, a day for thanksgiving, and a day for deep reflection.

You are now within minutes of becoming physicians, doctoral scientists, and nurses with graduate degrees. You are now amongst the most *fortunate* people on earth. *You* will be amongst a minority in our society who will have the opportunity to *contribute so much,* to be *respected by so many,* and to receive *intellectual and emotional satisfaction* from your work.

This has been a difficult year for you, the class of 1996. You have lost a remarkable classmate and friend, Flicka Rodman. You also lost his wife Jane, another remarkable person known to many of you and also the daughter of one of our faculty members. They died in late November, after being struck by an out-of-control vehicle while on a hiking path twenty feet off the road in the Mojave Desert.

This leads me to my message to you on this day: responses to suffering.

Suffering in one's life is neither an aberration nor a stroke of misfortune. It is part of the human condition. It is to be expected. You cannot be human and not suffer. It is absolutely unavoidable. Most of you have suffered or will suffer loss through illness and death of family and close friends. Some of you who desire children will have trouble conceiving. Some of you will have children who suffer from serious illness. (I recently received an anguished letter from a former graduate of our medical school whose child is suffering from a serious birth defect.) A few of you will lose children to death. Many of you will have children who suffer from learning disabilities. All of you who become parents will suffer disappointments in your children. All of your children during their adolescence will torment you so that you will wonder why you wanted children in the first place. (Ask your parents.) A significant number of you who marry will experience the suffering of marital discord. Many will suffer from dissatisfaction with your jobs. Some of you will suffer the humiliation of malpractice suits. Many of you will suffer the betrayal and estrangement of family and friends. Most of you will ultimately have to come to terms with your own diseases and physical limitations. Some of you will suffer in making the transition from an active medical career to retirement.

I list these events not to depress you but to challenge and prepare you.

We all have choices as to how to respond to suffering. On one hand, we can become confused, isolated, cut off from others, self-protective, bitter, envious, enraged, blaming of others, vengeful, stagnant, guilty, and depressed.

There are alternative responses. We can transform suffering into a new self-awareness, a new sense of purpose, new meaning, renewal, new discovery and development, and a new capacity for compassion.

Our Jewish and Christian heritages speak eloquently to transformation from suffering.

How does one transform one's suffering and that of others? I will share two personal experiences.

The first story is an experience which occurred in 1968 but which I thought of in a new light just one week ago. It is a story of suffering I inflicted on my father. After adopting two Caucasian children, my wife and I decided that we would adopt children who otherwise would not have a home. In 1968, these were African-American children. Adopting a black child would be a serious offense against my father and his conception of loyalty and family—perhaps a betrayal of my relationship to him. He was, after all, an uneducated working man in a blue-collar city similar to Worcester. He was born in a small living room behind his father's store, just two years after his parents arrived from eastern Europe through the gates of Ellis Island. One of his greatest aspirations in life was to provide higher education for his three children. My wife and I, graduates of elite liberal arts colleges, then at Yale and on our way to Harvard, could easily espouse the great egalitarian virtues of transracial adoption. Not so easy for him. In a heated argument at the time, he said: "You can *prove* to me that you are right. But I know you are wrong." (Although I still believe I was right, I can now appreciate that this is a profound statement. "Intellectual" proof is not always superior to intuition.) But I was as stubborn as he; and we went on to adopt not one but ultimately four African-American children and two Vietnamese children, in addition to our first two adopted Caucasian children. My father could have responded to his suffering by rejecting me, my wife, and our children. He could have become bitter, isolated, and withdrawn. He could have harbored grudges, which he was quite capable of doing. (He used to say of someone against whom he harbored a grudge: "He is no good; he never was any good; he will never be any good.") Instead, he presented the newly arrived child with a government bond from the state of Israel (a powerful symbolic gesture of acceptance) and became a wonderful grandfather to all of our children. With the arrival of the new infant, he immediately decided—and told all his friends and neighbors—that his son and daughter-in-law, whom he previously declared "crazy," were wonderful people. He was no longer ashamed. He was now proud.

I will always remember when, years later, one of my children suffered internal bleeding and was hospitalized in Boston, he immediately flew from New Jersey to be with us at the bedside. I will also remember my father's role surrounding the survival of our two Vietnamese sons. These two half-brothers, eight and nine years of age, were scheduled to fly to the United States on the ill-fated C-5 transport that crashed outside of Saigon killing all the children from their orphanage. A Canadian friend of ours, who was flying orphans out of Cambodia, removed our boys before they boarded the plane and flew them to Montreal. When my wife and I arrived in Montreal, my father was there waiting for us to arrive, and was there at our side to welcome his sixth and seventh grandchildren.

I wonder why, just one week ago, I thought of this story in this new light of *his* suffering and *his* transformation. Perhaps it is because I have now reached my father's age at the time this event occurred back in 1968.

The transformation of my father's world view following our adoption of our first black child reminds me of a story someone told me.

A seven-year-old boy was walking home in a field. He was wearing a baseball cap and carrying a baseball and bat. Speaking out loud, he said "I am the greatest hitter in the world." With that, he tossed the baseball two feet in the air and swung at it with his bat. He missed and announced "strike one." He picked up the ball, gazed at it and again declared "I am the greatest hitter in the world." He again tossed the ball in the air and swung at it. He missed and announced "strike two." Now he seemed perplexed. His confidence was waning. He inspected the ball and inspected the bat. With less confidence than before and some tension in his face, he declared again "I am the greatest hitter in the world." With considerable apprehension, he tossed the ball in the air and swung. He missed again. "Strike three" he said. For several seconds, he appeared despondent, ashamed. He was suffering. Then his face lit up with pride and he declared: "If I struck myself out, I must be the greatest pitcher in the world."

How was my father able to overcome his suffering? I can surmise there was his desire and ability to forgive his son, his willingness to reexamine his values and attitudes about the meaning of race and family. His compassion for the suffering of the early deprivations of his new grandchildren, his desire and ability to reach out to form new and unexpected relationships with his grandchildren, and his courage to face friends and neighbors not too happy with his new grandchildren. He was transformed.

The second story is the experience of suffering when my twenty-nine-year-old daughter Jacqueline, our first child, died on May 12, 1995, after a two-year struggle with breast cancer. It is also the story of suffering of her seven siblings, my wife, Jacqueline's birth mother, and myself. There was enormous suffering from losing her. For me there was even greater anguish in helping her bear her own suffering: of losing her hair, losing two inches of height (from collapsed vertebrae), losing ovarian function and with it dreams of being a mother, losing the ability to walk, losing the ability to work, and having to endure the indignities of near total dependence. Her original hopes for cure and a future were soon replaced with hopes for the management of pain and death with dignity.

What was so remarkable to me was the response of others, particularly during her last four months when she lived at home with us. Two of her seven siblings remained at home to be with her instead of moving on. An older brother (with whom she frequently quarreled), a master carpenter, completely redecorated the master bedroom for her. With its beautiful Wedgewood blue walls, white woodwork, and floral arrangements, several people remarked that it looked like their image of heaven. Another son, who had been estranged from Jacqueline since the beginning of her illness, moved home and quit his job in order to provide twenty-four-hour nursing care. Her biologic mother, whom she discovered five years ago, lived with us during weekends to share the nursing care. Friends from work gave up vacation days so Jacqueline could continue to receive paychecks. Parishioners at my wife's church brought hot dinners daily for three months. Both friends and complete strangers at the medical center reached out with friendship, interest, kind words, prayers, and compassion. All of these gifts were unsolicited. Following Jacqueline's death, I wrote a personal message to 6,300 employees of the University of Massachusetts Medical Center. This began a new kind of relationship between me and dozens of employees who came forward in person and in letters to tell me of their losses and their own suffering.

I cannot put into words how I have been transformed. Our entire family is stronger. My wife and I now have a special connection to Jacqueline's birthmother. I feel closer to the employees of this Medical Center. I feel more cared about as a person (not just for the moment but permanently). I feel more connected to the larger community, to the universe. I feel more generous, more sensitive, more compassionate. I know I am a better physician, a better father, a better friend.

In conclusion, I urge all of you (graduates, family, and friends) on this wonderful day of celebration and thanksgiving to rededicate yourselves to offering compassion to those who suffer and to accept compassion from others for the relief of your own suffering. I urge you to renew and strengthen relationships through generosity, by offering and accepting apologies, by forgiving and accepting forgiveness.

This will enable you to grow and be transformed by the inevitable suffering ahead, so that you will be not only intelligent people but wise people.

Hope and Millie

David Hatem

I had thought as I entered medical school that I might become a pediatrician until I realized that, while I liked children, I did not like sick children. Maybe this explained my discomfort when several of my patients who were infected with HIV brought their children with them to their clinic visits. As I spoke with my patients, I would repeatedly notice out of the corner of my eye their daughters playing joyfully in another corner of the room, running, falling, laughing, and sometimes crying. The hardest question seemed to be asking the mother whether the child was infected as well. I was never sure that I wanted to know the answer.

*   *   *

Rosa was always quiet, kept to herself, spoke very softly. It was hard, she said, keeping her sons off the street, teaching them values, and caring for her young daughter. She had to be well, she had to be strong. It was a secret, her infection, a secret that she held inside. She seemed so alone at times, and as she got sicker, her voice got softer. She couldn't sleep, she couldn't remember, she couldn't concentrate. She couldn't stand the weight loss, the loss of appetite, the loss of strength. She had to be strong, she had to lead the family. From a wheelchair she led them to Disneyworld, waning energy, wasting muscles. She finally told them. They already knew.

What energy she had spent holding on to herself, holding such news inside herself. What energy she had spent holding a mirror up to herself, a mirror that reflected back her feeling of emptiness. How could she share this news with anybody? She had already shared her forbidden infection with her daughter, her daughter who was her future, her daughter who was her life, her daughter who was all that she could wish for, her daughter who she had named Hope.

*   *   *

Carmen was always laughing, always amused, always happy in her thoughts. Sometimes she brought her Millie with her who ran around the room, looking up with her big brown eyes, curious, young, beautiful. Millie's strength, her voice, her energy, her curiosity filled the room, sometimes displacing her Mom, sometimes diverting my attention. It was easy to be captivated by someone so young, someone so vibrant, someone who avoided (or escaped) the infection's transmission. She allowed us to forget about sickness and death, she allowed us to look to the future.

And look to the future we did, Carmen working hard to stay clean, stay positive, and stay alive. She began to look forward, to what she did not know, but she looked forward. She pressed on.

The liver failure, the abdominal swelling, the feet that were bursting with fluid. She continued to laugh, now softer and tinged with irony, but she laughed. And she talked. She was getting prepared, she was talking to her family, explaining her wishes, explaining her plans. They would care for Millie, they would watch over her, and Carmen would watch over them. Strength over strength, sight over sight, it was vision over vision. This bond was so strong, this connection so tight. Then the story was told.

Young Millie was Milagros. (Millie was the Miracle.) Named for her aunt who had played a vital role in her existence. Carmen was waiting to get into detox, waiting on a long list of names, destined to wait too long to get any help. She was tired of using, she needed some help.

> And my daughter-in-law, Milagros, saved my life. . . . I couldn't get in, and didn't want to get into trouble, so she "picked me up" while I waited.

Picked her up meant that she bought her drugs so that Carmen could avoid withdrawal before she got into detox. And into detox she went, coming out sober, coming out clean. Carmen, now clean, but pregnant, went through with the pregnancy, and gave birth to her own Milagros.

*   *   *

We should look to their children to see how they feel and we should listen to their names as they are called to see what they wish the future to hold. Millie and Hope, Hope and Millie. Hope and Milagros, Miracles and Hope.

THE FACES OF AIDS:
AN AIDS QUILT

WILMA BULKIN SIEGEL

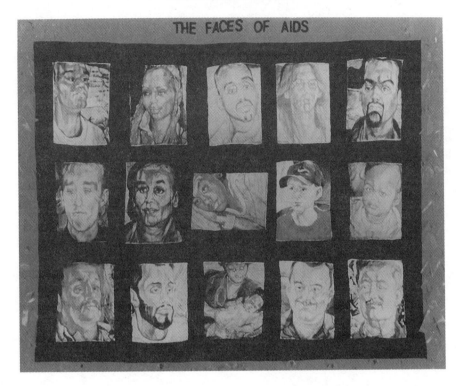

Among those immortalized in Wilma Bulkin Siegel's AIDS Quilt are IV drug users, hemophiliacs, a stockbroker, a hairstylist, a prostitute, a nurse, and an eighteen-month-old baby born with AIDS, whose mother was dying of AIDS and who spent the last five months of her life in hospice care. In the artist's words: "As a physician, I was affiliated with one of the first hospices to care for patients with AIDS at Montefiore Medical Center in the Bronx. Upon my retirement, I felt "burnout" and could not return to medical issues. As my art became professional (I had done art as a hobby during my medical career), I combined my two professions. I felt that painting patients with AIDS could give them comfort and hope as well as dignity and long-lasting identity on paper."

Seeing Fred on a Respirator

CAROL PICARD

Oh God
I will never take breath,
breathing, blowing a kiss, a candle
for granted again.

The breath
Take a breath
The in breath
The out breath
The infinite possibilities of what we can do with
the gift of breath.

What we take in first on our arrival
and the last we give up on returning to
that place without the rhythm of breath.

SOME WAYS CAREGIVERS USE THE ARTS FOR THEMSELVES
AND FOR THOSE THEY COMPANION

Using Art Therapy with Pediatric Oncology Patients

Linda G. Nicholas and Suzanne Lister

> ... I woke to find myself in a dark wood,
> Where the night road was wholly lost and gone.
> ... It is so bitter, it goes nigh to death;
> Yet there I gained such good ...
> Dante, *The Divine Comedy* [1]

Current Canadian statistics from the National Cancer Centre Institute of Canada (1996) [2] show that approximately 800 children under the age of fifteen are diagnosed with some form of cancer each year. Almost 200 of these children will die. Cancer, surprisingly, is the second leading cause of death in children. Since 1960, the survival rate has grown from approximately 25 percent to roughly 70 percent. Unfortunately, the incidence rate has also increased by 4 percent, which translates yearly to about one child per 100,000 being diagnosed with some form of cancer.

INTRODUCTION

Most of this chapter will focus on children who are very seriously ill, though not necessarily terminal. Working with the dying is preceded by working with those who have continued expectation and hope of living on, overcoming illness, and returning to health. Children demonstrate a great capacity to endure, adapt, and continue under adverse and stressful conditions, serious and possibly terminal illness being among them. They will often doggedly survive until their birthday has come, or Christmas, or a special event of some kind. They will seize the day in a way that adults often find hard to do, rarely allowing anything to stop them from continuing with the things that they still can or want to do. Of course, there are difficulties that get in the way of this productive creativity—fear (see Figure 1), withdrawal, pain, and anger being among them. Recognizing these difficult responses to living with cancer, pediatric oncology teams have come to understand the needs of these children, their siblings and parents, and have greatly enhanced the psycho-social support which is offered to them and their families.

The multidisciplinary team at the Children's Hospital of Western Ontario includes a social worker, a psychologist, a nurse clinician, and several art therapists. Patients also utilize the child-life program, which offers support to inpatients and outpatients, a socialized pediatric pain program, and a nutritionist. Team members

Figure 1. *"I'm afraid to go into the woods. It's frightening!"* (Boy, 6, Leukemia)
After the young patient had talked about how much longer his treatment would be,
he painted this picture. Though Dante felt that he entered his dark wood
in his mid-life, these sick children confront fears early in their lives.

present special teaching packages to the schools that the sick child attends,[1] and
provide outreach into the family home and help with financial concerns. Art therapy
has proven to have multiple benefits for the children and families seeking treatment.
As an important link to the child's inner world, art therapy can help make sense of
the medical treatment for these patients. It covers the areas of greatest need for the
child and can provide extra input for the team regarding the patient's strengths and
vulnerabilities.

We will begin this discussion with a brief definition of art therapy, its history and
theory, and then provide a more detailed outline of the evolution of the Art Therapy
program at the Children's Hospital of Western Ontario. In order to elaborate on the
role of art therapy in the context of illness and medicine, it seemed prudent to include
information about the treatment of cancer, focusing on childhood leukemia, how this
illness affects the child, along with the role of art therapy and how it may help.
We conclude with a short section on working with children who are dying and the
effects of this work on the art therapist.

---

[1] School issues have been studied extensively: see Deasy-Spinetta and Spinetta, 1980 [3]; Noll,
Burkowski, Rogosch, LeRoy and Kulkarni, 1990 [4]; Stehbens, 1988 [5].

Figure 2. *"In the art room"* (Girl, 13)
A drawing of the art therapist and volunteer assistant from the rear.
Care and humor are both illustrated in this picture.

ART THERAPY

Art Therapy Defined

Art therapy is a human service profession that utilizes art media, images, the creative process and patient/client responses to the created products as reflections of an individual's development, abilities, personality, interests, concerns, and conflicts (Figure 2). Art therapy practice is based on knowledge of human developmental and psychological theories. These are implemented in the full spectrum of models of assessment and treatment including educational, psychodynamic, cognitive, transpersonal and other therapeutic means of reconciling emotional conflicts, fostering self-awareness, developing social skills, managing behavior, solving problems, reducing anxiety, aiding reality orientation, and increasing self-esteem.

Art therapy is an effective treatment for the developmentally, medically, educationally, socially, or psychologically impaired. It is practiced in mental health, rehabilitation, medical, educational, and forensic institutions. Populations of all ages, races, and ethnic backgrounds are served by art therapists in individual, couples, family, and group therapy formats [6].[2]

[2] Linda Chapman, A. T. R., is presently the Chair of the Committee on Professional Practice of the American Art Therapy Association.

For populations of terminally ill children, art provides a special contribution to their treatment and healing process. By expressing powerful feelings and impulses on paper, the child is able to start to bring order out of chaos. Both the process of doing the art and the final art product are inherently therapeutic, creating an organization and permanence to inner experience that is the crux of child art therapy.

History and Theory of Art Therapy

Very simply put, the emergence of art therapy can be connected to the development of analytical psychology, particularly to Carl Jung [7, 8].[3] For Jung, images both from our dreams and those that we consciously produce ourselves held symbolic significance. He understood symbols as healing agents [9] and believed that in the creation of symbols the creator moved toward psychological health. Through the creation of images the artist reveals and connects with the unconscious self, providing release.

Art therapy, then, can be used in two basic ways, both resting on the assumption that art tells us something about the artist's inner self. The first approach can be termed art as therapy where the focus and the therapeutic value are achieved in the process of creating the work. The second approach, art psychotherapy, takes a closer look at the product, and what that art work might reveal about the artist. These two approaches are often not mutually exclusive, and most art therapists will testify that they employ both during the course of therapy.[4]

The Art Therapy Program at Children's Hospital of Western Ontario

Starting this work in 1978 was a little like pioneering a new land.[5] We were unable to find any substantial literature, other than medical, on therapy with leukemic children, let alone art therapy. Susan Bach, who had been working in Switzerland for some years, had at that time written two papers [11], both in German, which had to be translated. Kübler-Ross had made passing mention of patients' art work but nothing else could be found [12]. What to do? It was clear that there were particular needs for these children and teens, and we would have to think carefully about what these were. Asking "Who are my clients and what are their needs?" helps the art therapist focus on the most beneficial approach for different client populations.

---

[3] For more detail into Jung's work related to art and symbolism see *Man and His Symbols* (1964) [7], and *The Archetypes and the Collective Unconscious* [8].

[4] In her text, *Approaches to Art Therapy*, Judith Rubin [10] provides a broad spectrum of the varied theoretical bases of art therapy.

[5] Selwyn and Irene Dewdney had already pioneered art therapy in Canada through their work with psychiatric populations in southwestern Ontario since 1946. In and around London, art therapy was spreading due to their innovative work in the field. The program at Children's Hospital was one such spin-off from their successful efforts.

In the case of children in our hospital, it is clearly their leukemia or other cancer and the challenges of the hospital and treatment that are the dominating difficulties. The medical environment can be a threatening, disempowering, and intimidating setting for the physically ill youngster and his or her family, and once we recognized this we were able to structure a program that would meet the clients' needs rather than our expectations. Outlining these specifically is helpful in clarifying the difference between working with children who are *physically ill*, especially acutely and dangerously, as these children are, and those who need to be helped for behavioral, developmental, or familial problems. Although these three areas play a part in how a child (and the family) copes with the illness, they are not the main therapeutic focus. The primary concern is to support the child and the family in tolerating the treatment and medical environment that hopefully lead to recovery.

Cancer Treatment

Lifting out the core issue in this way means that one is able to focus on and develop a suitable program. So to start we need to know facts about the illness, then information about child development from birth to age eighteen (the age range of the children attending for treatment). Apart from understanding some basics about the drugs and procedures that the child with leukemia will receive and undergo, there are consequential experiences that are important because of their relevance to therapy. So let us first consider treatment, as this is fundamental, and it is what the child is coming to the hospital to receive. The medical experience usually consists of the following:

1. No choice of place; it has to be the hospital,
2. No choice in undergoing procedures, as they have to be done and sometimes require surgery (i.e., tumors, bone cancer). These procedures generally include:
   Blood work
   Lumbar punctures
   X-rays and/or radiation
   Intravenous treatment (see Figure 3)
   Taking pills
3. No choice in timing: it has to occur once to three times a week,
4. A duration of treatment that has to continue for up to three years (see Figures 4 and 5).

You will notice that one of the common themes is that the child does not have a choice. This is a very important issue that will be returned to later. The physical effects of this treatment are varied, but will include the following:

Loss of hair
Nausea
Mood swings
Weight changes (see Figures 4 and 5)

Figure 3. *"Me getting my IV in"* (Girl, 9)
This young girl with leukemia focuses her attention on the treatment
in this drawing. Notice the contrast in facial expressions between
the drawing of the nurse and the patient/child.

Lassitude
Destruction of natural and immunized immunity

and occasionally,

Mouth cankers
Reduction in intellectual ability
Hospitalization

Obviously such dramatic body changes are dreadful for the child, family and, to some extent, the friends and extended family. There are psychological as well as concrete effects on the functioning of all these groups.[6]

It is not surprising that one of our main therapeutic goals evolved into helping the child and his or her family to survive the time in the outpatient unit: waiting for

---

[6] When children with cancer were interviewed about the things that they did not like about the disease, they listed medical procedures (needles, bone-marrow aspiration and lumbar puncture); feeling nauseous; losing their hair; having restrictions on peer and play activities in case they were hurt; general school problems such as missing school and being unable to keep up; worrying constantly [13].

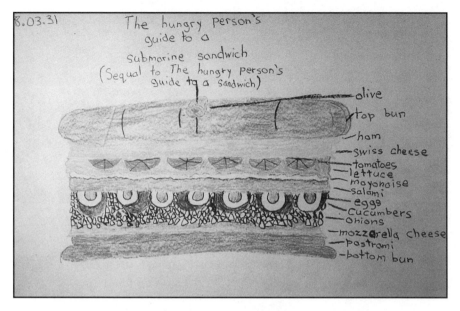

Figure 4. *"The hungry person's guide to a submarine sandwich"* (Girl, 12)
Some of the medication produces fierce hunger, and food
becomes central to these children.

all the procedures, and then enduring the procedures themselves. The key issues here include *waiting* and *tolerating pain* and *discomfort.*

The Waiting Game

The mixture of difficult emotions experienced and the long periods of waiting for children and their families during their treatment days soon became clear. Being with them, while trying to provide some relief with the distraction of art materials, gave an understanding of their terrible frustration with *time.*

It is worth looking at the process of the typical treatment day for families struggling with the serious illness of a family member. There are many experiences that are inevitable for seriously ill people that require understanding on the part of the worker. One such important matter is that the hospital often becomes an ambiguously experienced second home.[7] As such, hospital and treatment experiences often

---

[7] Hospital appointments/stays create conflicting feelings for parents who must care for their children during this traumatic time. Parents have stated *categorically* that they both dread and desire the child's stay in hospital. While it often symbolizes their only hope, it also represents the feared outcome, death. Many parents and children feel that they will always retain some feelings of hope and comfort with respect to the hospital and staff. However, upon terminating treatment their feelings often change to resistance, reluctance and separation, probably a most healthy response.

Figure 5. *"Spotty dog"* (Boy, 6).
After treatment, when medication is finished, there are side effects, as
this drawing demonstrates. Here the skin irritation is so bad that the
itchiness feels as if it is also outside the parameter of the body.
This is very annoying for the child.

become the central point of conversation and interest, alienating friends and others who are not willing to be tolerant of this obsession. Consequently, there is more of a sense of community with others in the same situation, who understand the vocabulary *and* the feelings. Friendships developed in this setting, because of the commonality of experience, often survive past the child's treatments, particularly if the outcome for both families is successful, less so if the child dies.

The waiting, then, is a surprise for both child and parent who, after all, have been told they have an appointment time. The procedure upon arriving at the hospital is commonly as follows:

1. The child's finger is pricked for a drop of blood to ascertain the blood count for that day (see Figure 6). This determines the levels of treatment and how the child's body is coping with the leukemia. The child and parent wait in the waiting room until the results are in, and the doctor is ready. Sometimes the blood was not adequate, or something goes wrong, and the process has to start again, adding additional waiting time. If all goes well, it will take one-half to two hours to see the doctor.
2. The actual treatment takes one-half to one-and-a-half hours more depending on the schedules of hospital staff that day.
3. Instead of treatment, the child may have a lumbar puncture and/or x-rays. The lumbar puncture is a difficult procedure that is nerve-wracking for everyone involved. The children must lie flat on their backs after completion of the procedure for some time in order to prevent severe headaches afterward.

Figure 6. *"True"* (Girl, 11)
Getting the finger pricked for blood takes some time to get used to,
and it hurts, as this picture clearly tells us.

From reading this you can begin to understand how much time a typical appointment may take. What is the result of all this? A variety of powerful and difficult feelings such as frustration, puzzlement, and anger from parents who are still trying to lead their own lives during the child's illness. In most cases somebody has to give up his or her own time to be at the *disposal of the demands of the illness*—the crisis situation requires it. It does not take long to come to see what is necessary in terms of therapeutic support. It was a common sight to see fathers particularly, walking up and down the halls or waiting room, coat on, ready to go, looking at their watches before they had even been to see the doctor. Consequently, one of the goals for art therapy was to help the child pass this stressful time as pleasantly as possible. This took some of the strain off the parent, allowing them to talk to other parents. The art experience also encouraged the child to talk to other children. So the large art therapy table was set up, and children would come and sit at it as they desired.

The art therapy experience provides a fairly large range of choices, within the limitations of the space. One result of this is that children often *opt to return* to us, and even look forward to coming to the hospital in order to do some art.

Over time, the children themselves have taught us what they need. By watching and listening over the years, seeing children come in at diagnosis, begin the period of stringent treatment, settle in to the routine of long visits and waiting, share their excitement and worry as they reached the end of medications, experience their anxiety during their monthly off-treatment check-ins, the terrible sadness of relapse, the exhilaration of those reaching three, four, five years off treatment, the grief with and for parents whose child has died, the long haul for the child that is dying, we have come to know the frustrations of the waiting game and its outcomes.

Offering Choice

As mentioned earlier, the need for having choices comes from the reality of having no choice about what is done to you. Parents, who would normally rush to defend their child from a fall or threatened hurt, suddenly find themselves allowing their children to undergo uncomfortable and difficult procedures. It gives new meaning to the description "being torn." Over time both the child and the parent become familiar with and more tolerant of these inevitable miseries, and with the support of pain therapists, loving nurses, and understanding doctors, the child generally recognizes and accepts the longer-term goal of getting well.

Such resignation is in many ways a highly maturing experience, but it has its price—anger, frustration, outbursts of resistance, depression. In this continuum of no choice, no matter how you feel, or what you do or say, the art therapy can play a role by first giving obvious choice of materials (including various media and art techniques, crafts, games, puzzles, toys, and books) and, second, by allowing children to take as long or short a time as desired, to do or not do, giving them as much freedom with their time as possible. They may also choose to keep or give away their work, or store it forever in the drawer. The feelings associated with the no choice position are also able to be expressed through the art. Anger at doctors (Figure 7), parents, and treatment; fear at receiving treatment and procedures (Figure 8); joy at being released (Figure 9) can be shown and shared as the child wishes. Frustration may be expressed physically by pounding clay or playdough, painting furiously with large brush work. All these things are available to the child.[8]

How the child works at the art also provides evidence of his or her efforts to cope with the situation surrounding the illness, giving an indication of the child's stress, anxiety, and coping strategies. It is not uncommon for children to leave their work unfinished so that they can anticipate a little pleasure in returning to the hospital. There have also been instances of children resisting the completion of art work. This has had several meanings for the child: a desire for continuity, and often an anxiety about ending. After all, if the picture is still unfinished, you have to be there to finish it the next week: a logical way to cheat the fear that you might not be there. This occurred mostly with children who had relapsed and were less likely to live.

Along with our respect for the child's self and suffering, the expectation that the child is encouraged to achieve respect of self and others goes hand-in-hand. As with many other things in life, there is a paradox related to this self-respect. One of the difficulties associated with such a devastating illness is the separation that the child

[8] This does not mean that we do not expect reasonable behavior. Children are given certain limits which include respect of others and self, pertinent to their age, as well as care of the art therapy room. It is interesting to note that we have rarely had difficulty with the children who use our facilities.

Figure 7. *"To: all doctors here in London, From: ___"* (Boy, 12)
Doctors are very understanding, knowing that children often need to
"get back" at them. Here this boy has shown himself ready to
give a "shot" to all the doctors in London.

Figure 8. *"Nervous wreck"* (Drawing by a teenage boy)
This picture shows, in graphic detail, how this boy experiences his treatment week.
By the end of it, as his title proclaims, he is a nervous wreck. Such a negative
view needs to be not only expressed, but also discussed and modified.

Figure 9. *"Untitled"* (Drawing by a teenage girl)
Her treatment is over and the bunny is up the hill and away!

experiences from the normal and routinely accepted things: inclusion in groups of friends that are playing games, having an ordinary cold without worrying, being able to get through a school day without feeling exhausted. The differences inevitably set these children somewhat apart from their peers, consequently making them stand out. In their family they become the center of concern. This shift in their previously experienced space can make children feel awkward and self-conscious. The sense of self becomes distorted, moving them toward a sense of importance that rings hollow for them because it is based on their illness. Children might become angry, demanding, and frustrated not just because of the obvious demands that the illness makes upon them, but because others have changed their response toward them. They are no longer sure of where they stand, what the boundaries are, or what the "self" really is. Their sense of self-esteem sometimes becomes falsely inflated, and they instinctively know that things are not right, the world has skewed. Such feelings and experiences may be displayed in their art work (Figure 10).

Art therapy can help the child return to the more established sense of self. Our observation shows that the art produced at the beginning of illness relates almost exclusively to the *time before* the child was diagnosed. It recalls the normalcy that is lost [5] and often bridges the sense of shock by relating back to a time of higher stability. As treatment continues, the child is likely to gain in maturity as he or she

Figure 10. *"Billy"* (Boy, 7)
Here the young patient expresses the sense of being off-balance.
In this picture everything is that way, including his house.

endures things that must be. Gradually the child's art work reflects the present, and occasionally the future. It is as though children produce art which is most useful for them in regard to the period of their life that it reflects, allowing them to catch up gradually with the reality of their illness. Consequently, the art work usually connects to the child's most healthy self-esteem position, in a sense discouraging the move toward the falsely inflated self, quieting the panic that goes along with such disruption. The need for demonstration of high control in areas that were, previous to the illness, not really within the child's domain of decision (parental expectations, school attendance, regulation of food, etc.) reflects the other side of the coin: the great loss of control of one's body and what is done to it [14] as well as choices regarding long- and short-term plans for the future. The child becomes a king or queen without a real domain, able to request more of his or her subjects, but unable to leave the castle.

Parents will, quite understandably, join in most readily: old rules are dropped or become flexible, the sick child becomes the center of the family's life; and things are brought, given, or allowed which would normally have been waited for or denied. Several foundations spend their time raising money so that these sick children may have their heart's desire, for it is impossible to give them the thing most wished for: a cancer-free life.

The Dying Child

As Michael Bull[9] points out in his paper "Death in the Family," the word "crisis" in Chinese is represented by two symbols, one meaning danger and the other meaning opportunity [15].

Trying to imagine what the opportunity might be for children with cancer seems almost impossible. What possible good can come out of such a dreadful situation? In fact it would seem that one of the main objectives of the therapist at this time is to help dying children use the time left to them in a way that is rewarding. This does not exclude the recognition of sadness and fear, but rather includes the acceptance of all feelings as pertinent to the self and its situation. The child is encouraged and supported to communicate the widest range of feelings to family and friends. Art therapy increases the possibility of the expression of thoughts and feelings that children may not have the ability to express due to excesses of anxiety, an inability to express themselves adequately, or even a wish to not upset those around them. Art therapy takes advantage of children's natural ability to express themselves through art and play.

The child's art work takes on an extremely valuable position at this time, for the art is recognized by the parents, and often by the child, as potentially extending beyond the life of the child. Its permanency makes it a small extension of the child's self. Consequently, the child's work may be treasured, with the knowledge that the child actually produced the work.[10] As an example of this, one family in the program gathered together all the work their daughter had produced, framed it, and now take a piece out, season by season, putting each on an easel in their hall. It is as though their daughter follows them through the year. This sense of "time extended" is a very important part of art, and has been a valued part of the Art Therapy program at the hospital.

While children are still able, the art therapist has an opportunity to help them express fears, reveal and talk about thoughts of what it will be like after they die (see Figure 11), make concrete (through creating pictures) hopes and feelings for their family. Showing parents their child's art work can help them to literally see what their child sees. Commonly the child understands and knows more than the parent imagines or even wishes (Figure 12), and it is not unusual for the child to protect the adult by keeping quiet about how much he or she knows. The sharing of knowledge is a large part of the opening up that can happen at the time that the child is dying, where the inner self can courageously come in contact with others. These very sick children have expressed not only knowledge of their dying, but a wish to die bravely or to be allowed "to go" by parents who are continuing to "hold on" to them. We are often astonished by the courage and acceptance children show as they get close

---

[9] Michael Bull's paper gives a very helpful overall account of working with families who are trying to cope with the death of a child. When the Art Therapy program first started, Michael was the social worker with the pediatric oncology team.

[10] With financial assistance from Childcan, a parent-run organization, we have been able to frame a chosen piece of art work for the family. Childcan has also supported the Art Therapy program from its inception.

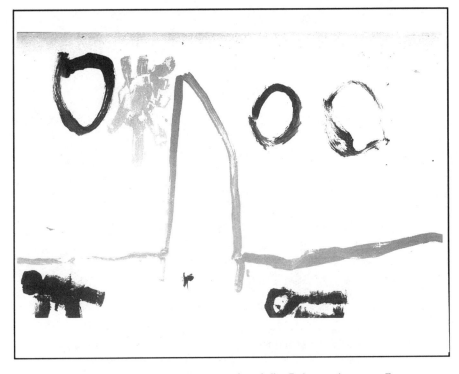

Figure 11. *"What will happen when I die. Being underground"*
(Painted by a boy, 7)
Notice that the child is not alone.

to dying; their ability to enjoy any moments that they are able to, leaving behind them a small legacy of art work, valued because it was touched by them and came exclusively from themselves (Figure 13).

How This Work Affects the Art Therapist

No discussion on working with childhood cancer is complete without some commentary on the multiple stresses of working with the dying child. The hectic quality of the treatment, the cheerfulness that we see as helpful for the child, our own need to protect ourselves from too much of the reality of the work, all lead to an avoidance of what this work may mean for us. Necessarily, it reminds us of our own death, and as such requires an enormous amount of energy to defend against this continual "Momento mori."[11] Nevertheless, although paradoxical, the recognition and acknowledgment that we will die are vital to help free ourselves from the fear

---

[11]See [16] *The Denial of Death,* for a wonderful account of the fears of death that we all struggle with.

Figure 12. *"My friend in the funeral home"* (Girl, 12)
The young artist shows her friend's funeral. She knew that she too was
dying and needed to talk about the funeral and her feelings.

of it. While not intending to enter into a discussion of such philosophical issues, we urge those who work in the field to avail themselves of some of the thinking in this area. The time will never be wasted.

Not only is our own death reflected in the struggles of these children, but also the possible and terrifying indication that this could happen to our children, or children close to us. This puts a tremendous strain on workers who are parents, many of whom have admitted to checking regularly for the first signs of leukemia in their child. When one works on a daily basis with childhood cancer, the possibility of such an event in one's own life becomes distorted toward an inevitability.

Most pediatric oncology teams understand the stress that their team members experience and have regular meetings that allow for discussion of events and feelings. Even so, the sense of guilt that accompanies those who have normal, healthy children competes with their relief.

A small anecdote may help to illustrate the broader recognition that this work is difficult and stressful: while we were raising money at a foundation banquet for the Art Therapy program, a few slides of the children's art work were shown. The audience found this extremely moving, and afterward the master of ceremonies got up and said that he and his colleagues would give us money because they could not face doing this kind of work; it was too sad. He stated that they donated to us in order to help them reduce their own guilt.

Figure 13. *"Two empty swings"* (Girl, 12)
This child was dying of a genetic blood disorder, as was her sister.
Here the empty swings are highly expressive and a single bird flies out
of the picture. Flying away is a common theme in sick children's pictures.

In saying this, we must also state that, like the word "crisis," this work contains both dangers and opportunities. In opening us up to our greatest anxieties, it allows us to touch and know ourselves in a way that is not often available to us in our protective culture. One of the gifts that these children have given us is the possibility of knowing ourselves more deeply, of understanding what other experiences mean for us. For this we offer thanks (Figure 14).

REFERENCES

1. A. Dante, *The Comedy of Dante Alighieri. Cantica 1. The Inferno,* D. L. Sayers (trans.), Penguin Books, New York, 1966.
2. National Cancer Centre Institute of Canada, *Canadian Statistics,* 1996.
3. P. Deasy-Spinetta and J. J. Spinetta, The Child with Cancer in School, *The American Journal of Paediatric Haematology/Oncology, 2,* pp. 89-94, 1980.
4. R. B. Noll, W. M. Bukowski, F. A. Rogosch, S. LeRoy, and R. Kulkarni, Social Interaction between Children with Cancer and their Peers: Teacher Ratings, *Journal of Paediatric Psychology, 15,* pp. 43-56, 1990.

Figure 14. *"Untitled"* (Painted by a girl, 15)
This picture of a boat sailing into the sunset is rendered in beautiful sunset colors
of orange and yellow. It took a long time to complete, and was started just
before the end of treatment. She continued to respond well.

5. J. A. Stehbens, Childhood Cancer, in *Handbook of Paediatric Psychology,* D. K. Routh (ed.), Guilford Press, New York, pp. 135-161, 1988.
6. L. Chapman, Professional Practice, Newsletter from *American Journal of Art Therapy, 16,* Winter 1996.
7. C. G. Jung, *Man and His Symbols,* Dell, New York, 1964.
8. C. G. Jung, *The Archetypes and the Collective Unconscious* (Collected Works, *9,* Part 1), Princeton University Press, Princeton, New Jersey, 1968.
9. G. M. Furth, *The Secret World of Drawings: Healing Through Art,* Sigo Press, Boston, 1988.
10. J. A. Rubin, *Approaches to Art Therapy: Theory and Technique,* Brunner/Mazel, New York, 1987.
11. S. Bach, *Spontaneous Pictures of Leukaemic Children as an Expression of the Total Personality, Mind and Body,* Schwabe, New York, 1975.
12. E. Kübler-Ross, *On Death and Dying,* Macmillan, New York, 1969.
13. B. M. Sourkes, All the Things That I Don't Like About Having Leukaemia: Children's Lists, in *Psychological Aspects of Childhood Cancer,* J. Kellerman (ed.), C. C. Thomas, Illinois, pp. 289-291, 1980.
14. D. B. Golden, Play Therapy for Hospitalized Children, in *Handbook of Play Therapy,* C. E. Schaefer and J. O'Connor (eds.), Wiley, New York, pp. 213-233, 1983.

15. M. Bull, Death in the Family: Structure and Stresses, Crisis and Coping, in *Thanatology: A Liberal Arts Approach,* M. A. Morgan and J. D. Morgan (eds.), King's College, London, Ontario, 1987.
16. E. Becker, *The Denial of Death,* Free Press, New York, 1973.

BIBLIOGRAPHY

Bach, S., *Life Paints Its Own Span,* Daimon, Einsiedeln, Switzerland, 1990.

Cane, F., *The Artist Is Each of Us* (Rev. Edition), Art Therapy Publications, Craftsbury Common, Vermont, 1983.

Kramer, E., *Art as Therapy with Children,* Schoken Books, New York, 1971.

Naumburg, M., *Dynamically-Oriented Art Therapy: Its Principles and Practice,* Grune and Stratton, New York, 1966.

Rode, D. C., Building Bridges within the Culture of Paediatric Medicine: The Interface of Art Therapy and Child Life Programming, *Journal of American Art Therapy Association, 12*:2, pp. 104-110, 1995.

Rubin, J. A., *Child Art Therapy,* Van Nostrand Reinhold, New York, 1984.

Art Techniques for Children with Cancer

Barbara M. Sourkes

I felt much better because I knew that I had somebody to talk to all the time. Every boy needs a psychologist! To see his feelings!

Ricky [1]

Psychotherapy with the child who has a life-threatening illness is profound and poignant, and it powerfully attests to the struggle toward survival. Within its framework, the child seeks to reintegrate the shattered facets of his or her life. Through words, drawings, and play, the child conveys the experience of living with the threat of loss and transforms the essence of his or her reality into expression.

ART TECHNIQUES

Art therapy can be a powerful tool to facilitate the child's expression and integration of complex experiences. Structured art techniques allow the therapist to pose questions earlier in the process and with more specificity than might be done through verbal means alone. Three structured techniques developed by the author are described below.

Mandala

The mandala—a graphic symbolic pattern or design in the form of a circle—originated in Eastern religions. Jung believed that a mandala could mirror the state of the inner self [2]. The mandala is used in art therapy today, when a therapist asks a person to fill in a blank circle to reflect "how you are feeling now." The steps in a more structured version of this projective technique include: definition of topic, guided visualization, set of feelings, color-feeling match, proportion of color-feelings, and discussion of the completed mandala.

The therapist *defines a topic* around which the mandala will be focused. An example would be: "How I felt when I heard that I had cancer." The therapist begins by providing the child with a brief *guided visualization:*

This chapter has been adapted from B. M. Sourkes, *Armfuls of Time: The Psychological Experience of the Child with a Life-Threatening Illness,* University of Pittsburgh Press, Pittsburgh, 1995.

> Close your eyes and think about the day you were diagnosed with cancer. Remember where you were (hospital, doctor's office, clinic), who was with you, who told you the diagnosis, what words were used. Remember how you felt. You may open your eyes.

The visualization sets the stage for the concrete task that follows:

> Now I am going to give you the names of feelings which other children have told me they felt when they heard the diagnosis. I want you to think about each feeling and see if it fits for you.

The therapist then presents a *set of feelings* that are commonly attributed to the experience. Each feeling should be written on a separate file card and arranged randomly on the table to avoid the order bias of a vertical list. The feelings might include: shocked, scared, sad, angry, lonely, hopeful. A category called "other feelings" should also be included. It is best to limit the number of feelings to a maximum of eight. The therapist then gives the child a set of markers or crayons and a sheet of paper with the outline of a circle on it:

> Now, *choose a color to match each feeling.* I want you to color in a part of the circle for each feeling. If the feeling was big, then make it a big part of the circle; if it was small, color in a small area [*proportion*]. You may use the same color for more than one feeling as long as you label it clearly. If you had other feelings that I have not mentioned, put them in. When you are all finished, we can *talk about the feelings and the colors* you have chosen.

Because the mandala requires little time and minimal exertion or coordination, it can be used even with a child who is very ill. Most children find the technique nonthreatening and enjoyable, and they often express relief at having an array of feelings already articulated for them. Interpretation of the mandala is based on the child's choice of feelings, colors, proportions, order, overall design, and verbal associations. At its simplest, the mandala is a tool for facilitating expression; at its most complex, it is powerful in its symbolism and depth.

Figure 1 is a mandala drawn by an eight-year-old boy diagnosed with leukemia two months earlier. (The reader can color in both mandalas below to obtain the finished effect.) He explained his drawing: "Shock is yellow because I turned pale when I heard that I had leukemia. Scared is red—for blood. I was scared of needles, thinking what was going to happen, seeing all the doctors. I was MAD [black] about a lot of things: staying in the hospital, taking medicines, bone marrows, spinal taps, IVs, when they wake you up in the middle of the night. I was sad [purple] that I didn't have my toys and that I was missing out on everything. I chose blue for lonely because I was crying about not being at home and not being able to go outside. Green is for hope: getting better, going home, eating food from home, and seeing my friends."

Figure 2 is a sophisticated mandala drawn by an eighteen-year-old girl who was diagnosed with osteogenic sarcoma at age ten. Art therapists think that her mandala looks like a cross-section of a bone or a roulette wheel. The girl comments: "When you first hear the diagnosis you feel shock to the very core of your being. The shock

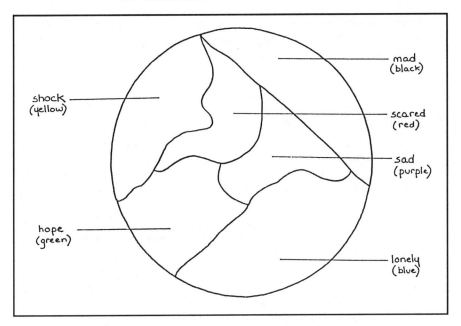

Figure 1. *How I felt when I heard that I had leukemia.*

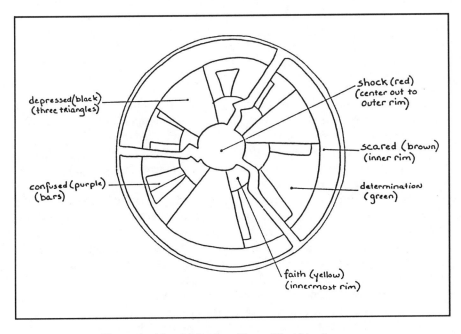

Figure 2. *How I felt when I heard that I had cancer.*

waves reverberate outward and totally envelop you. Being scared surrounds you. Depression presses down on you—but you can't let it get the better of you or you won't make it through. So you must have faith that things will turn out all right and the determination to fight. Confused—you're always confused—about how this could have happened to you."

Change-in-Family Drawing

The Kinetic Family Drawing is a widely used art therapy technique. The child is asked to draw a picture of the entire family and to show each member engaged in an activity. The drawing is then analyzed for the child's perception of his or her position within the family and the nature of the family relationships. If the child is hesitant to engage in this task, he or she can be encouraged simply to draw stick figures. Although the richness of individual representation is lost, the dynamics of the family system nonetheless emerge. The author has added another step to this technique. After the child has completed the basic family portrait, the therapist asks: "What changed in your family after you got sick? Show the change in your drawing, either in picture or in words." The responses to this simple question are often dramatic and can be used for any "before and after" situation.

A ten-year-old boy, who had been diagnosed at the age of six, drew an active and engaging family portrait. When asked what had changed after he got sick, he added slashes of rain to the sky. He then crossed out his littler brother with the commentary: "My little brother wasn't alive then." His choice of words—"wasn't alive then"— rather than "wasn't born yet" attests to the valence of the life-death dichotomy of the diagnosis. He added tears to his mother and showed his father thinking, "poor kid." He erased himself playing ball and reportrayed himself as he was then— in a wheelchair (Figure 3).

Scariest Image

The therapist asks: "Think of the *scariest* experience, thought, feeling, or dream that you have had since you became ill. Draw it." Through this technique, the therapist invites the child to bring out the extreme fear, often the very image that he or she is most afraid to express. The drawings tend to focus on medical procedures, being alone, and death. They often represent a blend of actual and imagined experiences (Figures 4, 5, 6, 7, and 8).

Figures 4 and 5 illustrate the invasiveness of needles. These drawings, done in a group setting, sparked a lively debate on whether needles in the "butt" are worse than needles in the arm. Both pictures demonstrate a partial dissociation: the child's full body is omitted; only parts are suggested. The ten-year-old boy who drew the needle "in the butt" had actually had a leg amputated. Although the leg is not severed, he depicts it as "less present" by showing it as smaller. In the eleven-year-old girl's drawing of the needle, the precise markings on the syringe attest to the extreme vigilance that many children maintain over their treatment.

In Figure 6, drawn by a ten-year-old girl, the child lies in her bed in stark isolation, accompanied only by an ominous-looking television set.

Figure 3. Family: Sun to rain.

In Figure 7, a ten-year-old boy depicts a skull and crossbones leering above a bone-marrow aspiration needle.

In Figure 8, an eleven-year-old boy portrays himself lying in a hospital bed, the finality of death symbolized in his thoughts of a tombstone.

*   *   *

Drawings enable profound disclosures to emerge. Although these art techniques are simple to administer, they evoke complex and powerful responses. The therapist must be prepared for the conscious and unconscious material that the pictures reveal.

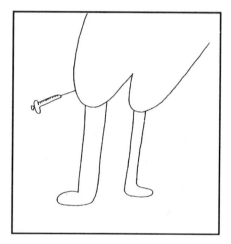

Figure 4. Needle in the butt.

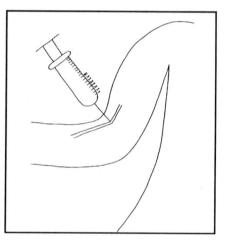

Figure 5. Needle in the arm.

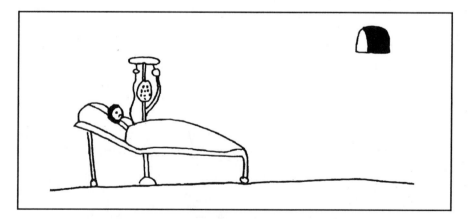

Figure 6. Alone in the hospital.

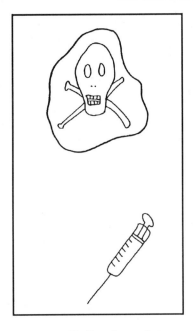

Figure 7. Skull and crossbones.

Figure 8. Tombstone.

REFERENCES

1. B. M. Sourkes, *Armfuls of Time: The Psychological Experience of the Child with a Life-Threatening Illness,* University of Pittsburgh, Pittsburgh, p. 3, 1995.
2. S. Fincher, *Creating Mandalas,* Shambhala Press, Boston, 1991.
3. R. C. Burns and S. H. Kaufman, *Kinetic Family Drawings,* Brunner/Mazel, New York, 1970.

Puppets: Bridging the Communication Gap Between Caregivers and Children About Death and Dying

Brenda Eng

Figure 1. Young boy with camel puppet.

Communication is the key to providing care for children and their families. Talking with children is a unique art and comprehending what children are saying requires special knowledge and understanding of children's language and cognitive processes. According to Pontius, communication is a process in which two or more individuals share their thoughts, feelings, ideas, and experiences [1]. Specifically, communication is the generation and transmission of symbols (verbal and nonverbal behaviors) by a sender and the perception and interpretation of a message by a receiver. Art, music, crafts, poetry, play, and other modalities have increasingly been appreciated as vehicles for communication and for constructive interventions.

Understanding and knowledge of the therapeutic value of play are essential. Caregivers can then incorporate play into their plan of care to provide children a means to communicate their feelings, concerns, and thoughts about death and dying. This chapter discusses puppet play as a creative and therapeutic intervention, explaining its premises and its application to children coping with issues of death and dying. Developmental considerations, basic strategies, and principles of intervention are discussed. These considerations are equally applicable to children whether they are experiencing the death of a significant other or whether they are facing their own death through illness.

BACKGROUND RATIONALE

In Bluebond-Langner's study of children with cancer, she proposed that, whether told or not, children learn very quickly that they have cancer and learn eventually that the disease is potentially fatal [2, 3]. The observed passivity, the lack of direct expression of the awareness of their prognosis, and the lack of questioning about death in terminally ill children do not necessarily mean they are unaware of the prognosis and what is happening; "(the child) knows and observes the restrictions against speaking about death. If he tries to break taboos, he rarely does so directly, and then, perhaps only in a highly symbolic manner" [2, p. 180]. As children lack adult intellectual ability and maturity, they may indicate their feelings, thoughts, and concerns in other than straightforward, verbal ways. Kübler-Ross proposed that dying children use three "languages" to communicate their knowledge of their impending death [4]. The first of these is the language in which the children verbally articulate their knowledge. The second, symbolic nonverbal language, refers to those behaviors through which the children indicate their feelings and thoughts. The third is symbolic verbal language. The children may use one, two, or all three of these languages to communicate their concerns, feelings, and thoughts about death and dying. In caring for children, one must be observant of and responsive to all modes of communication.

Providing children with an outlet to express, directly or indirectly, the thoughts, feelings, questions, and needs aroused by illness, hospitalization, and impending death is essential. Play is the most basic way children symbolically express their feelings. According to Erikson, children tend "to play it out" [5]. Play offers an illusionary world for the child to control; it provides the child with some sense of power over the environment. In play, the child becomes the decision maker and master. There are no directions to follow and no adult rules and regulations to observe. In a socially acceptable way, play provides the child with supportive experiences for dealing with specific issues aroused by the illness. Observation of play can also caregivers some insight into the child's thoughts, feelings, and needs. According to Piaget, play assists the child with self-understanding, with exploring and comprehending the environment, and with accomplishing successive stages of development [6]. Piaget stated a particular need for dramatic play in children up to age twelve. A form of dramatic play, puppet play helps reduce tension caused by drawing parallels between a child's feelings and the actual events of the external world. Puppet play frees the child to take on the imaginary emotions of inanimate objects or other people. Puppet play is an unstructured, nondirective form of therapeutic play which allows the caregiver to help the child communicate in a nonthreatening way. To avoid misinterpretation, it is important to make a clear distinction between play therapy and therapeutic play, with puppet play considered a form of therapeutic play (see Table 1).

A MATTER OF DEFINITION

Puppetry has been used as a valuable education tool on a worldwide basis for centuries. Often it was combined with magic and mystery to evoke feelings of fear

Table 1. Comparison of Play Therapy and Therapeutic Play [7]

	Play Therapy	Therapeutic Play
Primary Goal	To provide an opportunity to the child for self-expression.	To provide an opportunity to the child for self-expression.
Secondary Goal	To assist the child to gain insight into his or her behaviors, expressions, feelings.	To assist the caregiver to gain insight into the child's behaviors, expressions, and feelings.
Therapist	Psychiatrist, psychologist, or psychiatric nurse clinician.	Primary caregiver, nurse.
Client	Emotionally disturbed, neurotic, or psychotic child.	Any child (chronically or terminally ill).
Environment	Specially prepared playroom.	Hospital playroom, bedside, or any convenient safe physical space.
Length	Usually one hour.	Usually fifteen to forty-five minutes.
Duration	Usually several months duration.	Varies from one time only to daily during period of care.
Reflective Technique	Reflection of verbal expressions and nonverbal feelings.	Reflection of verbal expressions only.
Interpretation	Significant behaviors, expressions, and/or feelings interpreted to the child to promote insight.	No interpretation made to the child.
Main Proponents	Axline, Moustakas	Petrillo and Sanger, Green-Epner.

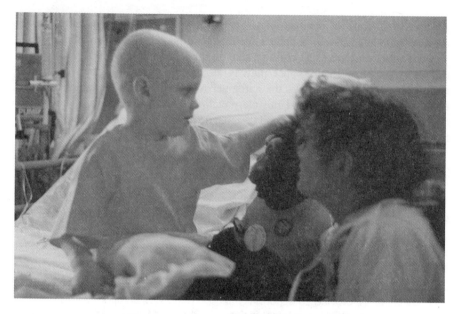

Figure 2. Therapist joins the dialogue.

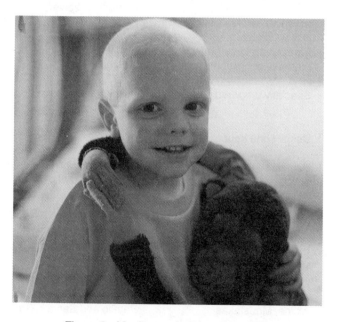

Figure 3. Monkey puppet hugging child.

and awe. It is accepted in other parts of the world as a serious art form, but the United States and Canada have been reluctant to accept puppetry as more than child's play.

Puppetry is a form of dramatic communication. Whether it is used by hobbyists or professionals, by educators or therapists, in a classroom or a hospital, for adults or children, communication is its function [8]. While puppets often resemble dolls and are sometimes made from the same materials, they are usually more detailed and are meant to be brought to life in front of an audience. A child will react to a doll and that doll may come alive for that one child, whereas a child can become the puppet and can project a part of his or her own self through the figure. The child will talk *to* the doll but will talk *through* the puppet. The puppet offers a degree of anonymity to the child, allowing children to "speak" more freely, express thoughts and feelings more readily, and act in ways that might not be acceptable as themselves, but perfectly acceptable through the gentle disguise of the puppet.

Creative puppetry may: 1) improve self-concept [9], 2) increase creativity and self-expression, 3) expand acceptable avenues for emotional release, 4) enhance social skills [10], and 5) provide the child an opportunity to experience life vicariously. It is important to note, however, that existing knowledge of puppet play is based on anecdotal description and clinical impressions. Therefore, caution is warranted regarding the therapeutic value of puppets.

A puppet is the caregiver's ticket into a child's world because it speaks the child's language. A puppet, whether it is a realistic image or an abstract form, is an instrument through which ideas, thoughts, and feelings are conveyed.

CAUTION AGAINST INTERPRETATION

It is natural and tempting for the caregiver to want to interpret the child's style and content of play. However, puppet play is not intended for the purpose of in-depth clinical analysis and/or interpretation. In therapeutic play, the caregiver should reflect only the child's verbal expressions and carefully determine if and when it is appropriate to go beyond these to the underlying feelings. There should be no attempt to interpret or explain the expressions or the possible feelings behind the nature or content of the child's play. To do so would be inappropriate and is entering the domain of play therapy. In addressing children's art as another potential mode of expression, Williams proposed that it may be useful to regard the observations made during puppet play as a kind of weather report—one can make a forecast based on some evidence and then be on the lookout for the signs indicated [11].

WHAT IS A PUPPET?

Essentially, a puppet is an inanimate object made to come alive. In addressing puppetry as a form of dramatic communication, Vincent-Davis emphasized that a puppet is not a work of art [8]. It is only a tool, an instrument like a violin through which feelings, concepts, and ideas may be conveyed, and like a violin, it helps to have a good one, but it is not the violin that makes the music, it is the violinist. A puppet, be it hand puppet, rod, shadow, or marionette, requires as much skill and dexterity to manipulate well as does a musical instrument.

TYPES OF PUPPETS

Basically, puppet types are determined by the way the puppet is manipulated, e.g., with the fingers; hand or body; by rod or with strings. Champlin and Renfro suggested that choosing the right puppet should be more than a guess or a feeling [13]. It is important to consider the intent of its use, the physical space available, the age of the child and who will be primarily using the puppets. Consider the context in which the puppets will be used, and determine which character to acquire. Invest in a few sturdy, washable puppets of good quality, then supplement this collection with home-made puppets, and purchase more as resources become available. Key concepts to remember are flexibility and creativity. A well-chosen basic collection can offer many imaginative and creative opportunities.

Stick Rod Puppets

- simplest puppet
- basis of puppet is a cut-out picture or a three-dimensional form
- made from small toys, stuffed bags, paper plates with features added
- form is attached to a stick or rod control

Limitation: limited in ability to express action and emotion

Figure 4. Some puppets.

Finger Puppets

- draw features on finger
- use small pictures cut from books, greeting cards, magazines attached to finger tip or glove
- introduce nursery rhymes, simple poetry, uncomplicated stories
- more elaborate puppets may be constructed from felt, etc.

Hand Puppets

- best known type of puppet
- flexible-body hand puppet can interpret a wide range of emotions and actions
- talking-mouth hand puppet is capable of sounds and talking
- should fit comfortably over hand and be easy to manipulate
- make sure head is not too cumbersome or weighty as will be awkward to manipulate
- acceptable to use both types for variety and interest

Plush Toys Converted into Puppets

- stuffed toys can make excellent puppets
- make hole in back of head for finger, create a pocket on the back for hand, add a stick in the bottom, or attach strings to the limbs

String Puppets or Marionettes

- perhaps the most difficult style of puppet for the beginner to use when portraying emotions

BEGINNING WHERE YOU ARE

When puppets are mentioned, people usually imagine a formal stage with window opening, drapery, and scenery props. However, this formal approach is only one option. With the many alternatives available, we recommend that caregivers begin where their abilities or interests already lie. Other considerations include: 1) maintaining consistency of the personality of the puppet, 2) puppetry can become tedious if overdone, replacing motivation with boredom, 3) puppets that moralize and preach are not as effective as ones that children can identify with as having faults like theirs, and 4) puppets bound by puppeteer techniques may lose their potential value.

ENLISTING YOUR SKILLS

One's own skills and interests will determine the general selection of puppets and related materials used. Individuals with dramatic voices should experiment with projecting diverse personalities through voice. Those less comfortable with voice expression should adapt puppets to pantomime activities, which can be just as

Table 2. Puppet Play—General Trends during Childhood [13]

	Early Childhood	Middle Childhood (early)	Middle Childhood (late)
Age	3 to 6	6 to 8	9 to 12
Cognitive Sphere	Preoperational	Concrete operations (inductive reasoning and beginning logic)	
Purpose of Dramatic Play	Initiating social life	Learning of social roles	Learning of social roles
Play and Story-Telling Content	Everyday world • animal stories • fairy stories	Expanding world • adventure	World of fantasy, historical events, and science fiction • myths, folktales • adventure
Attention Span	Short: concentration can be enhanced through active participation	Able to concentrate for long uninterrupted periods	
Developmental Considerations	• Magical thinkers • Generally accept puppets as real characters (believing what they say and putting great trust in their inherent natures) • Puppet characters should retain a truthful nature at all times (use within a consistent framework so as not to confuse the child)	• Are fully aware that the actions of puppets are controlled by somebody else • Shared sense of pretending • Rich, fertile imagination helps them to fill in voids whenever necessary (puppets do not have to be as realistic as those for younger children)	
Type of Puppet	• Finger • Hand (maximizing gross motor movement)	• Hand (requiring simple manipulation), e.g., talking mouth puppet	• Generally require more sophisticated material in both content and selection of puppets • Capable of manipulating puppets using fine and gross motor skills
Key Criteria for Selection of Puppets for All Ages	• Lightweight, durable, washable, well-sewn seams, scaled to size of children's hands if intended for their use. • Puppets resembling stuffed toys of soft materials and furs are particularly appealing to younger children.		

Figure 5. Child engaging with monkey puppet.

compelling. Others may engage in spontaneous puppet play or use pre-existing stories, which can be great springboards for children and caregivers to begin using puppets.

Puppets can be used in almost any physical location, with activities adapted to the physical dimensions of the space available. When caring for a child confined to bed, presentation is usually most effective on a one-to-one basis. Story aprons and story totes make excellent vehicles for transporting puppet materials. Finger puppets and small stick puppets are easy to use in the limited space of the bed.

Visually impaired children usually respond best to puppets that provide strong tactile experiences; hearing impaired children may prefer sign language around the puppet's face. Developmental considerations are presented in Table 2.

SUMMARY

Communicating with children and comprehending what children are saying require special knowledge and understanding of children's languages. Puppets provide a gentle way of hiding oneself, so they are well suited to act as go-between in communication between caregiver and child. Using puppets frees children to deal symbolically with concerns and problems, helping them to see things in simpler, purer form. Puppet play, combined with the sensitive, careful guidance of the caregiver, can help children and their families gain greater undersatnding of themselves and one another as they deal with the difficult task of talking about death and dying.

REFERENCES

1. S. L. Pontius, Communication with Children, in *Nursing Management of Children,* J. Servansky and S. R. Opas (eds.), Jones & Bartlett, Boston, pp. 3-65, 1987.
2. M. Bluebond-Langner, I Know, Do You? A Study of Awareness and Communication, and Coping in Terminally Ill Children, in *Anticipatory Grief,* B. Schoenberg, A. C. Carr, A. H. Kutscher, D. Perez, and I. K. Goldberg (eds.), Columbia University Press, New York, pp. 171-181, 1974.
3. B. Bluebond-Langner, *The Private Worlds of Dying Children,* Princeton University Press, Princeton, New Jersey, 1978.
4. E. Kübler-Ross, The Language of Dying, *Journal of Clinical Child Psychology, 3,* pp. 22-24, 1974.
5. E. Erickson, *Childhood and Society,* Norton, New York, 1963.
6. P. Piaget, The Stages of the Intellectual Development of the Child, *Bulletin Menninger Clinic, 26:3,* pp. 120-145, 1962.
7. C. S. Green-Epner, The Dying Child, in *The Dying Child: A Supportive Approach,* R. E. Caughill (ed.), Little, Brown, Boston, pp. 125-157, 1976.
8. P. Vincent-Davis, Puppetry: A Form of Dramatic Communication, *Puppetry Journal, 26:4,* pp. 3-5, 1975.
9. T. Hunt and N. Renfro, Puppetry and Early Childhood Education, *Puppetry Journal, 33:3,* 1981.
10. R. Vogelsang, E. Saubiolent, and D. Sullivan, The Development of Positive Attitudes and Social Values in Children Through Puppetry or Listen to Floyd, *Puppetry Journal, 3:2,* pp. 3-10, 1979.
11. Y. B. Williams, Spontaneous Expression of Body and Soul in Children's Art, *1985 Pediatric Hospice Conference Report: Encircling the Circle of Care,* Children's Hospice International Alexandria, Virginia, pp. 69-70, 1985.
12. M. Adams-Greenly, Helping Children Communicate About Serious Illness and Death, *Journal of Psychosocial Oncology, 2:2,* pp. 61-77, 1984.
13. C. Champlin and N. Renfro, *Storytelling with Puppets,* American Library Association, Chicago, 1985.

BIBLIOGRAPHY

The Child and Life-Threatening Illness

Gibbons, M. B., When the Dying Patient Is A Child: A Challenge for the Living, in *Pediatric Oncology and Hematology: Perspectives on Care,* M. J. Hockenberry and D. K. Coody (eds.), C. V. Mosby, St. Louis, pp. 493-508, 1986.

Grollman, E. A., *Talking About Death: A Dialogue Between Parent and Child,* Beacon Press, Boston, 1976.

Grollman, E. A. (ed.), *Explaining Death to Children,* Beacon Press, Boston, 1984.

Jampolsky, J. and P. Taylor, *There Is A Rainbow Behind Every Dark Cloud,* Celestial Arts, Tiburon, California, 1982.

Katz, E. R., Talking with Dying Children, *1985 Pediatric Hospice Conference Report,* Children's Hospice International, Alexandria, Virginia, pp. 57-58, 1985.

Klutik, T., B. Haladay, and I. M. Martinson (eds.), *The Child and the Family Facing Life-Threatening Illness,* J. B. Lippincott, Philadelphia, 1987.

Lonetto, R., *Children's Conceptions of Death,* Springer, New York, 1980.

McIntyre, B. B. and M. Raymer, Expressive Therapies in Pediatric Hospice Care, in *Pediatric Hospice Care: What Helps?* B. B. Martin (ed.)., Children's Hospital of Los Angeles, Los Angeles, 1989.

Rando, T. A., *Grief, Dying and Death: Clinical Interventions for Caregivers,* Research Press, Champaign, Illinois, 1984.

Schmitt, B. B. and M. H. Guzzina, Expressive Therapy with Children in Crisis: A New Avenue of Communication, in *Hospice Approaches to Pediatric Care,* C. A. Corr and D. M. Corr (eds.), Springer, New York, pp. 155-177, 1985.

Share, L., Family Communication in the Crisis of a Child's Fatal Illness: A Literature Review and Analysis, *Omega, 3*:3, pp. 187-201, 1972.

Spinetta, J. J. and P. Deasy-Spinetta, Coping with Childhood Cancer: Professional and Family Communication Patterns, in *Communication in a Health Care Setting,* M. G. Eisenberg, J. Falconer, and L. C. Sutkin (eds.), Charles C. Thomas, Springfield, Illinois, pp. 173-205, 1980.

van Eys, J., Caring for the Child Who Might Die, in *Dying and Death: A Clinical Guide for Caregivers,* P. Barton (ed.), Williams & Wilkins, Baltimore, pp. 222-236, 1977.

Waechter, E., Children's Awareness of Fatal Illness, *American Journal of Nursing, 7*:6, pp. 1168-1172, 1971.

Play

Axline, V., *Play Therapy,* Baltimore Books, New York, 1969.

Bennet, L., The Play Interview, in *Psychological Assessment of Handicapped and Young Children,* G. Ulrey and S. Rogers (eds.), Thieme-Stratton, New York, pp. 230-235, 1982.

Children's Health Care, 16:3, pp. 133-237, 1988. Entire volume dedicated to theme of play in health care settings.

Garot, P. A., Therapeutic Play: Work of Both Child and Nurse, *Journal of Pediatric Nursing, 1*:2, pp. 111-116, 1986.

Lee, J. and M. D. Fowler, Merely Child's Play? Developmental Work and Play Things, *Journal of Pediatric Nursing, 1*:4, pp. 260-270, 1986.

Moustakas, C., *Children in Play Therapy,* Harper and Row, New York, 1969.

Pontius, S., Practical Piaget: Helping Children Understand, *American Journal of Nursing 82*:1, pp. 114-117, 1982.

Rogers, S., Developmental Characteristics of Young Children's Play, in *Psychological Assessment of Handicapped Infants and Young Children,* G. Ulrey and S. Rogers (eds.), Thieme-Strottan, New York, pp. 65-83, 1982.

Shaefer, C. E., *Therapeutic Use of Child's Play,* Jason Aaranson, New York, 1979.

Walker, C., Use of Art and Play Therapy in Pediatric Oncology, *Journal of Pediatric Oncology, 6*:4, pp. 121-126, 1989.

Puppetry

Linn, S., Puppet Therapy in Hospitals: Helping Children Cope, *Journal of the American Medical Women's Association, 33*:2, pp. 61-65, 1978.

Linn, S., W. Beardslee, and A. F. Patenoude, Puppet Therapy with Pediatric Bone Marrow Transplant Patients, *Journal of Pediatric Psychology, 11*:1, pp. 37-46, 1986.

Transformations:
Visual Arts and Hospice Care

C. Regina Kelley

When confronting death, a person often responds with a profound search for wholeness, healing life's wounds and making peace with the world. The arts are a vehicle for self-expression and, therefore, a significant tool for transformation during the dying process. The arts assist patients, families, and staff to understand the whole of their own lives, as well as the profound journey toward death that they share. In this way, the arts uniquely fit the mission of hospice care, which is to assist terminally ill patients and their families to maintain the highest quality of life as long as life lasts.

Hospice generally enters a person's life when a doctor assesses the patient as terminally ill with six months to live. Thereafter, medical care is palliative, and medical personnel are joined by hospice professionals and volunteers who offer a range of services for emotional, physical, and spiritual needs. The arts address all of these areas functioning as an animator, that which endows life or spirit. The arts reawaken the senses often ignored during long illnesses. They address what is possible rather than what is lost. They bring beauty, joy, and every form of expression into a time that we often assume to be unbearably painful.

The arts are an agent of self-expression and therefore are transforming in nature. The artist begins with an ephemeral idea, a vision or possibility. Then the artist faces the blank page and, in doing so, his or her fears as well. As the vision meets concrete reality of materials, the artist sheds preconceptions and steps into the unknown. The reality of the evolving art work is a product of growth and discovery. The artist is empowered not only by self-expression but by tangible nonverbal knowledge. This seed of transformation is present in every art-making process and can help to prepare patients for their final transformation, death. The lessons of letting go and experiencing the present moment are an invaluable component of hospice care.

One patient, Maria, exemplifies the potential of art to transform. Maria, age thirty-nine, came to the hospice homeless and dying of AIDS. In the arts program she began drawing butterflies, a universal symbol of transformation. For the first time in her life, she began to feel fully alive and responded to kindness by making gifts of drawings and painted T-shirts for everyone who had befriended or helped her. In her former life as a drug addict, she had stolen from friends and family. Her true spirit of generosity healed many relationships. As her artistic knowledge developed, she began a "master work," an autobiographical journal/sketchbook that included drawings of her daily feelings and experiences, photographs, mementos, letters to her family, and journal entries. Through her art she found a new way to express both her joy and the pain that once drove her to drugs. It was her hope eventually to publish her book so that "people can understand people with AIDS and be less fearful." Maria was a high school dropout with a twenty-year drug history; during her last year she became an artist, craftsperson, and author.

Maria exemplifies the two motivations to make art that commonly arise: the desire to summarize one's life experiences, and to make gifts for loved ones. Participatory arts offer the opportunity for patients to resume their role as a participating member of the family. They are a significant means of nonverbal communication— offering love and, often, forgiveness. Most important, they are a way for the patient to reclaim his or her power, to say, "I am."

The arts function at three levels in hospice care. Many patients and families believe that lifelong hobbies and craft work are no longer possible with the patients' diminished physical strength. Without these outlets, patients may feel a loss of identity as our culture often associates self-worth with work. Yet many familiar activities can be adapted to new physical circumstances by using lighter-weight tools and materials. Simpler crafts can be substituted for complex projects. Often two extra hands, with a volunteer or family member assisting, can make a special project possible. For instance, a young man in his thirties with AIDS was well known for his oriental rug avocation. As he neared death, he began a "cross stitch" embroidery project for his mother, which he was able to plan and execute with assistance during his last days, even though he was feverish and nearly blind. So first, patients should be encouraged to continue working with activities they cherish, albeit in a new way.

Mrs. O., an artist and homemaker in her late sixties, wanted to continue in her profession as well as make gifts for her family, since much of her work focused on her family. She was able to complete two crosses for a daughter who was to be ordained to the ministry. The process became one that united friends and family. When hospice care began, Mrs. O. was receiving chemotherapy and was extremely weak. She began drawing and designing the crosses. A neighbor and friend cut the wood in his shop, I did some of the machine sanding, and Mrs. O. completed the silver work on the first cross as some of her strength returned. She began the second cross incorporating a design that her other daughter has found on her travels in Europe. A close jeweler friend completed the cross by setting a sapphire in the center. Mrs. O. was able to see the finished work and present it to her daughter the week before she died (Figure 1). Hospice provided encouragement and coordinated the efforts of the participants.

Second, patients should be encouraged to learn a new art form. It is easy to forget during illness that we all love to learn and grow. Suitable techniques and art experiences can be designed for virtually every level of physical capability. Simply by handling unfamiliar materials, the senses may be stimulated. Concentration can divert or relieve pain and anxiety as the patient focuses on the new experience. Patients develop a new sense of confidence as their creativity becomes apparent. A young AIDS patient, who had collected paintings and prints of clowns, was delighted to create his own painting. An elderly woman enjoyed creating abstract water color paintings as thank you notes.

Figure 1. A silver cross made by Mrs. O (photo © Paule French).

Finally, art can lead to a profound expression—a summarizing of one's life. This can take many forms, such as a book, a painting, or a video, each of which fulfills the patients' desire to collect their experiences, their wisdom in a concrete form. Annie was a thirty-one-year-old ALS patient living in an intensive care unit. Her only form of communication was to blink her eyes to indicate yes or no, and she was receiving various medications that affected her concentration. She was an anthropologist/ archaeologist and wished to make a significant artwork to challenge her keen intelligence, now locked in a nonfunctioning body. As a hospice artist I invited her to make a traditional Native American shield that united her goals of contemplating the important things in her life and continuing to learn about Native American customs and artifacts. I served as her hands. I described the process and framed as many choices as possible in questions that could be answered with a yes or no. Annie also painstakingly spelled out important information letter by letter. The resulting shield contains significant animals in her life, the mountains she loved to hike, and an important dream image of an owl (Figure 2). She dreamed that at night her heart burst open and she became an owl that could fly around the hospital. Like many of us, she was very frightened of death and did not wish to speak about it or make decisions, while she could still communicate, about resuscitation or other details surrounding death. One day, however, her breathing machine malfunctioned and she had a near-death experience in which she felt herself to be floating in a night sky. The shield was changed to depict the night sky and was then hung at the foot of her bed reminding her that death could be peaceful. She died two weeks later.

The arts offer families a way to create special memories and conversations during the dying process and a way to remember and grieve during bereavement. So often our imperfect communication patterns become painfully inadequate during times of crisis. Families in the midst of anticipatory grief find it a relief to be offered

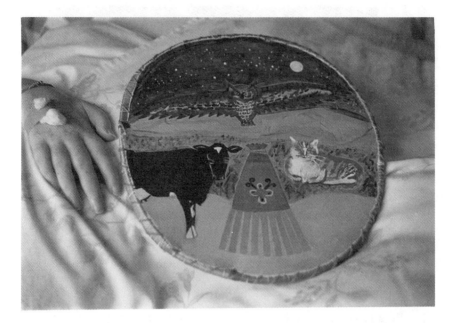

Figure 2. Annie and her medicine shield (photo © C. R. Kelley).

an activity to do together. It creates an emotionally neutral situation, and family members are gratified to find that making art can be fun, can initiate new conversations, and allow participants to assist one another in loving ways. One family gathered in their grandfather's sickroom with three generations present. Each member made a paper collage of a favorite memory of grandfather. The collages were united into a paper "quilt." This day became a special memory for each one, and the quilt will be a treasured heirloom. Artworks like this can also be part of the bereavement process, uniting a family, sparking remembrances of activities and qualities of the loved one.

Hospice ministers to medical personnel and to its own staff and volunteers as well. Everyone who works with the dying needs to come to terms with his or her own beliefs and understanding of death. The arts are a means to explore this issue and to restore harmony during times of intense grief. Caregivers need multiple ways to remember their experiences with patients. The intensity of caring and resulting feelings of loss when death occurs can become a burden unless we realize all that we receive from the people we assist. The arts allow caregivers to honor the special people who pass through their lives, to document the moments of heart-to-heart communication in which patient becomes teacher. In the sculpture *Annie and the Owl*, I was able to explore the transformation of death, and honor the remarkable young woman I had worked with so intensely, telling both of our stories in the sculpture (Figure 3).

Figure 3. Annie and the owl (photo © C. R. Kelley).

Art can also be a significant means to build community among people. At the Connecticut Hospice, an in-residence facility, the entire staff, along with patients and their families, helped to create a bronze sculpture. All members of the staff, from the janitor to the president, were asked to create a small wax sculpture that symbolized how they renewed themselves after a difficult day in the hospice. The responses were both varied and beautifully similar. A nurse discovered that she, a volunteer, a patient, and a doctor all turned to music for solace, yet each pictured it differently. With jeweler Melinda Bridgeman, I then integrated the wax images into a column that supports a bell (Figure 4). The entire sculpture was placed in an outdoor garden designed by the staff. The soothing sounds of the bell and the rich imagery serves to remind the staff of the many ways they can care for themselves and one another. With the arts helping to create a supportive environment, staff members are able to provide ongoing compassionate care for patients without feeling depleted.

The courage of the human spirit is never more evident as when patients choose to take creative risks, to transcend physical limitations, to examine their lives through the arts in order to meet death with equanimity. The artwork, or gift, becomes a visible symbol of their love and will, a triumph of their spirit. The whole process of making art is healing, as patients, families, and staff experience well-being and heightened awareness, approaching the great mystery of death.

Figure 4. Column with bell (photo © C. R. Kelley).

Sound and Silence:
Music Therapy in Palliative Care

Kevin Kirkland

THE RHYTHM OF LIFE AND DEATH

In many religious and creation myths, the world began with sound, the primal sound, the Word, Nada Brama, the Big Bang. Sound, vibration, resonance, music permeate the universe. Every molecule vibrates, producing sound. From our first moments in the womb, life is sound and rhythm: your mother's heartbeat, her speaking voice, the music she listens to. This ocean of sound and rhythm stays with us throughout life internally: heartbeat, pulses, circadian rhythm, breathing. Rhythm engages the body to respond, an event called *entrainment*. You hear lively rhythmic music and your body can't resist tapping a toe, swaying, or jumping up to dance. We are rhythmic beings.

Music for the living is meant to engage us. Music for the dying is meant to free us, as the so-called "New Age" music (music without a set pulse, that balances sound and silence, that is repetitive in nature without shifting keys or tempi) or the plainchant or Gregorian chant free us.

The burden of time, as Therese Shroeder-Sheker says, is replaced with eternity. In one approach to palliative care described by her, the prescriptive music is done with the patient almost anonymously, with little verbal communication. The music, in this case plainchant or Gregorian chant, is provided by a singer/harpist, sometimes in pairs, and only by the previous consent of the patient whenever possible. There is no dialogue, no emphasis on interaction or engagement. Though the text is Latin and religious, there is no agenda to convert. The music is used because of its structure, its ancient appeal, and its sacred nature. The patient does nothing but receive. Repetition is often an important element, with the same chant sometimes sung over and over. Her belief is

> the qualities of music can unbind or loosen a patient from what it is that binds one so deeply to the physical body. All memories (wounds and joys) are woven consciously or unconsciously in the human biography and attached to qualities of time within the body in the muscles, organs, even the bones, and in physiological rhythms [1].

Originally published as part of *The Art of Dying: The Art of Caring, Victoria Hospice Society Dealing with Death Conference,* and reprinted with permission.

The task is to free the physical body from literal time, burdened time, and replace it with eternity.

WHAT DOES DEATH SOUND LIKE TO YOU?

This may sound like a funny question at first, and your first thought might be of someone choking out their last breath, but think about it musically. When you reflect on people you have known who have died, what do you imagine death sounding like if it were music? Is it dissonant? Painful to hear? Or do stringed instruments play tender melodies? Is it lulling or gentle? Heavenly? Sorrowful or joyful? Does it depend on the situation? How would you imagine your own death sounding? Such questions may help you understand what your belief system is about and what your experiences have been (Table 1).

We often admire the beauty of the leaves in autumn, and yet those leaves are dying. Is death just as beautiful? Perhaps it can be. The beauty inherent in music can facilitate a beautiful death experience. Would you like to die in the presence of music? Is there a certain piece of music or song that speaks to you, music so beautiful, dignified, reverent that it arouses deep inner calm, rest, a sense of what sacred means to you?

> I'm coming out of a dark cave . . . in the jungle . . . there's light over the horizon . . . I'm following the path alone . . . I've come to a clearing . . . I see my mother . . . I'm so glad to see her (Jean weeps softly) [2, p. 50].

Originally developed by Dr. Helen Bonny as a method known as *Guided Imagery and Music,* GIM is an individual form of therapy, healing, or self-actualization that involves imaging to mainly classical music in an alternative state of consciousness while dialoguing with a guide. Rather than a therapist-imposed guided imagery script, the imagery is client-generated in response to the music, and the therapist deepens the process through reflective, supportive, probing responses. When used in psychotherapy, GIM is an uncovering technique that accesses unconscious material, facilitates cathartic releases, and leads to deep insights into the inner psyche. Central to its effectiveness is a client-therapist relationship that provides the safety and trust needed for the client to investigate deep inner regions of the psyche. In addition, the therapist needs in-depth training to use the technique.

In my approach, the music of contemporary composers is used because it is evocative, unfamiliar (which can free the client from humming along or guessing the

Table 1. Recommended Listening

Andrew Lloyd Webber: *Pie Jesu* (from his *Requiem*); Tomaso Albinoni, Oboe Concerto, Op. 9, No. 2; Vivaldi, *Gloria:* Et in Terra Pax; Bach: *Magnificat,* "Suscepit," Fauré, *Requiem:* "In Paradisum."

Jean-Guy Ropartz: *Pie Jesu;* John Ireland: The Forgotten Rite; Tobias Picker: Old and Lost Rivers (for orchestra); Marcello: Oboe Concerto in C minor, Adagio.

name of it), and because of how it is written. Twentieth-century composers write from experiences and from a consciousness similar to our own. The music is also free from the restrictions of form found in classical music. It can be deeply symbolic, engaging, painful, or beautiful. Some of the music-imagery programs include: Transformation, Lamenting, Empowerment, Grieving, Traces of Becoming, Program "R" (Remembering, Resolving, Reflecting).

Each session begins with an exploration of issues, concerns, or objectives pertinent to the client at the time. Using the themes or images that emerge through this preliminary exploration, the therapist guides the client through a relaxation induction, and then focuses the client on a starting image in preparation for an experience with the music. The music may be one of several programs specially designed for this method. Each program has been carefully selected and sequenced for specific therapeutic uses. In the music-imaging process, the client may have body sensations, visions, feelings, memories, fantasies, or any variety of internal experiences, all of which are regarded as "images." A dialogue is maintained throughout the imaging, with clients describing their experiences as they occur, and the therapist probing, supporting, reflecting, and amplifying them. The therapist writes a transcript of the dialogue for later reference. When the imaging and the music come to a close, the therapist helps the client return to a normal state of consciousness. A verbal discussion follows, focusing on the client's reaction to the imagery and aspects of the experience that are therapeutically significant. Nonverbal techniques such as mandalas, musical improvisation, expressive movement, clay work, and journaling may also be used to process the imagery [3].

PAIN MANAGEMENT

Specially chosen music can stimulate a decreased sense of pain. But what kind of music? That's the difficult part. Some say Baroque music (Bach, Handel), with 60 beats per minute, is relaxing. It's similar to a resting heart rate which the body entrains to, or matches, bringing about relaxation. For others, personally meaningful music is best. Studies have shown that a person's favorite music, or music he or she finds relaxing, can be a powerful distraction from pain. The pleasure and stimulation of music can release endorphins, reducing pain. But what one person finds very soothing and relaxing, another may find irritating or boring. A person's "taste" for music can also change when palliative: the adolescent who always liked heavy metal may now find classical music more soothing. Lastly, music can be a stimulus that overrides the experience of pain.

LIFE REVIEW THROUGH MUSIC

Sometimes a music therapist will do life review through music with a patient. Songs of different eras, favorite songs, and songs with lyrics that relate to life experiences are incorporated into a tape, along with the stories and reminiscing shared. Often the patient will sing too, or a segment will be included where friends or family sing together. The process provides an opportunity for reflection and closure for the patient, and the tape can be a wonderful keepsake for loved ones.

MUSIC AS A BRIDGE TO
CONNECTING AND COMPANIONING

Patients frequently choose music, consciously or unconsciously, which symbolically expresses something of their current emotional state or needs. It is not uncommon for a patient to show surprise when the lyrics of a casually requested song reveal a more profound feeling. On one occasion a woman in her sixties dying of cancer requested the song "Time in a Bottle." It immediately made her cry, opening up feelings and fears of dying, of being cheated out of living, about precious memories. On another occasion, I sat down at the piano to play some gentle songs during a quiet time after supper on the palliative care unit. The first song I chose was "As Long as He Needs Me." A woman in her late fifties came running over, hugging me, crying, saying that was her son's song, that he had played Oliver in the high school musical. Now thirty-five, this son, a lawyer, was dying of AIDS. Bringing along my guitar, we went to his room where his father and sister were visiting, and I sat by his bedside to sing this song, which immediately caused everyone to weep. The poignant words seemed to sing about the parents' unconditional love and acceptance of their son, a man with a sometimes unaccepted disease and sexual orientation.

As long as he needs me I know where I must be, I'll cling on steadfastly, as long
as he needs me. As long as life is long, I'll love him right or wrong, and somehow
I'll be strong, as long as he needs me.

He died that night, and to this day I'm sure we all share the precious memory of that experience.

REFERENCES

1. T. Schroeder-Sheker, Music for the Dying: A Personal Account of the New Field of Thanatology—History, Theories, and Clinical Narratives, *Advances: The Journal of Mind-Body Health, 9*:1, pp. 36-48, 1993.
2. V. Weeks and G. Hewitt, Music Therapy: Variations on a Theme, *Journal of Palliative Care, 9*:4, pp. 37-55, 1993.
3. K. E. Bruscia, Embracing Life with AIDS: Psychotherapy, Guided Imagery and Music (GIM), in *Case Studies in Music Therapy*, K. E. Bruscia (ed.), Barcelona Publishers, Phoenixville, Pennsylvania, 1991.

BIBLIOGRAPHY

White, M. E. and R. C. Blom, Guided Imagery and Music with Hospice Patients, *Music Therapy Perspectives, 3*, pp. 24-28, 1986.

Songlines

CAROL PICARD

In the fresh grief of early mourning,
this dancer, deer-like, stunned before the lights of the ICU.
Forgetting her name, body and place.
The majestic power of the leap, gone.
The ability to move delicately and then disappear, gone.
The deep knowledge of both inner and outer landscape, gone.
The space between the eyebrows filled only by this blinding moment.

We clothe the naked sorrow and sing her home with
soothing words, and slow, graceful dances of comfort.
We witness, with small gestures,
so that she may remember
not why, but how
we live.

Movies as Movement: Films as Catharsis in Grief Therapy

Lynne Martins

INTRODUCTION

In 1962 the short French film, *An Occurrence At Owl Creek Bridge,* was introduced to American audiences. Its popularity in the United States came, in part, from its debut on television as episodes of *The Twilight Zone* and *Alfred Hitchcock Presents.* In a brief twenty-eight minutes, we are exposed to a gamut of emotions as our minds enter the escapism of fantasy. Although the first few minutes of the film explain the hero's fate of hanging, we are surprisingly vulnerable to the fantasy of his escape despite the fact that there is not a single clue in the film to suggest this possibility. This adaptation of a short story by the American Ambrose Bierce seems to symbolize, in part, our preoccupation with avoiding death even when it is inescapable and, ultimately, inevitable.

We erroneously believe that we are as progressive in our attitudes toward death and dying as we are in our technological advances. But death is still a taboo topic. Until we pick death up in our hands and touch it, we remain unaccustomed and unprepared for its assault upon our lives.

As we continue our work with the dying and bereaved and seek to incorporate creative strategies, one powerful tool is the use of films. Visual media can be a creative catharsis to unlock those who are held captive by their grief or dying processes. Because films are easily accessible, they can be used by the professional seeking to enhance the therapeutic process. In addition, films are an invaluable teaching asset when we are training others in this field.

THE EVOLUTION OF DEATH EDUCATION IN MEDIA

Although many freedoms were espoused in America in the 1960s and 1970s, we did not completely liberate our thinking about death education. We did, however, begin to approach death more openly through the medium of film. In the 1970s, such films as *Brian's Song* and *Love Story,* dealing with terminal illness, were introduced. While *Brian's Song* taught about the camaraderie and grief of men, *Love Story* unfortunately gave the message that "love means never having to say you're sorry." In anticipatory grief work, the opportunity to finish business is crucial to a healthy adjustment, including the need to say, "I'm sorry, please forgive me," several times.

151

However, these films were our introduction to the issues surrounding catastrophic illness and death. A film about cancer in the 1970s was as taboo as a film about AIDS was in the mid-1980s.

Fortunately, the 1980s saw a multitude of films that explored a variety of previously forbidden topics. The films ranged from the now acceptable theme of terminal illness to the unmentionable theme of attempted suicide in the classic *Ordinary People,* a film with some very interesting insights into family dynamics and individual coping styles when sudden accidental death occurs.

A venture into adolescent grief comes with such films as *My Body Guard* and *Stand By Me,* involving tremendous loss and grief through accidental death, and attempted suicide. *Sophie's Choice* touches on the pain and unfinished grieving of survivors of Auschwitz; *Crimes of the Heart* is an off-beat comedy dealing with some very serious issues in a not-so-serious way.

Near the end of the 1980s several choice films were produced—among them *Fields of Dreams,* a fantasy film that addresses unresolved grief. Although most would see this as a film about baseball and perhaps a premature mid-life crisis, the questions about mid-life ultimately lead the main character to resolve his relationship with his deceased father. *Accidental Tourist,* a humorous dramatic film, looks at the effect a child's death has upon a marriage and how differently men and women grieve. *Dead Poet's Society* looks at youthful suicide and its relation to parental expectations. In late 1989 *Steel Magnolias* shows, with fresh understanding, the grief process, accurately portraying a young woman who dies from diabetic complications. This brilliant film is based on the true experiences of Robert Harling and his sister Susan, portrayed as Shelby in the film. Robert wrote the screen play in a staggering ten days, and described his cathartic experience in *Life Magazine:*

> The events that inspired the play were difficult . . . Six months after my sister's death in the fall of 1985, at age 33, I was still a mess . . .
>
> She was my best friend and I missed her desperately. I was depressed. In the midst of my ranting and raving that my two-year-old nephew would never know how wonderful his mother was, an old friend . . . suggested I write it all down . . . she insisted. I protested. But my spirits couldn't sink any lower, so I decided to try.
>
> The whole experience was a catharsis for me and my family. All of this has been an amazing journey for me. Sometimes I feel very uneasy. I didn't deliberately set out to do any of this. When I started "putting it all down" for my nephew, I wasn't interested in writing a hit play or creating a star-studded motion picture.
>
> All I wanted to do was tell a story, to make sure a little kid would have a better understanding of who his mother was.
>
> I often wonder what my sister would think of all this stuff that happened. I wonder what she'd think of *Steel Magnolias.* I think she'd laugh. She laughed a lot [Harling, *Life Magazine,* 1989, pp. 91-92].

Harling's amazing journey was borne out of his need to grieve the death of his sister and move onward. It is a marvelous example of the creative working out of a grief process and the transformative power of grief.

In the early 1990s, *Men Don't Leave* appeared, a drama about a family's journey through the grief process as the father suddenly dies in a construction accident. Two highlights of this film are the very real and accurate portrayal of a nine-year-old's loss and the portrayal of his older teenage brother's grief, which both interrupts and influences key phases of adolescent development. From a pre-teen point of view, the film *My Girl* shows a child's grief process when her best friend dies suddenly from an allergic reaction to bee stings, and offers some very important themes about unresolved loss and grief. By 1993, the barrier against AIDS in films was shattered by the wildly successful film *Philadelphia*. Portrayals of losses, anticipatory grief, and discrimination are among its greatest strengths.

Admittedly, one glaring omission in this exploration of loss and grief themes in films is a multicultural representation. In my opinion, few films as of yet portray loss and grief from the richness of an African American, Hispanic, Asian, or other ethnic perspective. My intent has been to bypass films with powerful competing themes such as poverty, war, or violence in the inner city, and to focus on types of losses directly related to death, however difficult that distinction.

Recent films offer a glimmer of hope that perhaps the future will continue to enlighten us with scripts that realistically portray and wrestle with difficult issues.

FILMS AS CATHARSIS

The use of films as catharsis can be a powerful relief and release for individuals struggling in their grief processes. To explore possibilities of catharsis in the grief process, we will examine: a) permission-giving, b) clarification, c) containment/ safety, and d) escapism.

Giving Permission to Grieve

One of the foundational issues within grief work is the permission to grieve losses. Often therapists give the much sought-after permission that is absent in the support networks of individuals. The need for permission is most acutely felt when grief has been delayed, gone underground, or become complicated. The use of films to give permission has an extraordinary result as clients identify with their heroes and heroines of the screen. Momentarily, clients forget that the actors and actresses are merely portraying "someone else" as they activate feelings within the bereaved that need to be triggered. The identification with the character on the screen, at the very least, gives them a sense that expression and release of feelings are appropriate and necessary when real-life supports tells them otherwise.

Clarification of Emotions

Grief work naturally creates a type of emotional disorientation and confusion with self. At times, clients need assistance in identifying what it is they are feeling. Individuals cannot heal what they cannot name. Films can provide clues and, therefore, a sense of clarity about the seeming disarray of emotions and expressions in grief. Confusion and chaos are unraveled when clients recognize their unvoiced emotions on the screen. When individuals decipher feelings for themselves rather than accept labels which others seek to dispense, they are emancipated in their grief process.

Containment/Safety

One of the greatest barriers to grief work is the client's fear of the intensity of emotions. Tears are forbidden in the statement, "Once I start crying, I'm afraid I'll never be able to stop." The terror of tearful release plays havoc with the client who has difficulty locating, identifying, and expressing emotions. A film is an excellent catalyst due to the simple fact that the length of film creates a safe boundary in which to express painful tears. The anonymity of a darkened theater where one may openly weep, or the privacy of viewing a film at home, strengthens the element of safety which is much needed in the catharsis of intensely painful emotions. The convenience of video rental also allows clients to view a film repeatedly, if necessary, in a way in which they can practice mastery of their emotions. Again, this is an important aspect of containment in grieving for those who feel they have "lost control" of their lives and feel hopeless to gain back that control.

On one level, clients may be well aware of "why" they are viewing a particular film, but on another level they allow themselves to weep knowing that when two hours has passed, they can resume life without being immobilized by tears. Ironically, this approach also helps clients whose tears severely interrupt their ability to function in daily life. Instead of seeking a "release," they are seeking to "contain" their grief. In other words, they are not seeking an escape from grief but, rather, wishing to reserve a time and place for their grief. Most often they are satisfied in knowing that at a specific time and a specific place they will be able to "let go" of their emotions. This appointment with grief enables them to go about the business of day-to-day life, particularly in the stage of grief in which the client yearns to remember the deceased in a healthy way but desires to return to the routines of work and family life.

This containment empowers clients in several ways: 1) they learn they can manage their grief in palatable portions, 2) they begin to trust their emotions as an accurate gauge in their response to death and grief, and 3) they learn to create safe environments for themselves and eventually transfer their experience in the movie theater to those who are capable of lending support.

Escapism During Grief

Generally, escapism connotes negative images of the resistant client who stays firmly based in denial and frustrates the therapist's best attempts to help. However, the grief process is an incredibly exhausting venture. Escapism is appropriate when a client seeks a slight reprieve from grief work, in a sense, a "night off." Films can provide a healthy choice of escape from the grief process that truly offers no respite to the grieving individual. At times, this is the first instance a client has smiled or laughed aloud since the death occurred.

Along with escapism is the permission to enjoy life even in the midst of grief. Many times clients who are racked with guilt find it unthinkable to allow themselves any sense of pleasure. In other instances, clients are so overwhelmed with the demands of family life that they have forgotten that they too need to take care of self.

As appropriate as films are in the therapy process, caution is required in the exploitation of this tool as with any therapeutic strategy. Films, of course, are never a substitute for therapy. They should be used as a creative measure alongside therapy, much as one would use bibliotherapy. The use of films is especially helpful because it is a visual and audio experience for the client. Grieving individuals often find it "difficult" to read due to their inability to concentrate (a common grief response) and so films are a viable alternative. This tool is not an end in itself. It does not work for every client. We further recognize that films are a product of Hollywood and have many limitations.

The following section is especially designed as an aid for training people to work within this field. A brief overview describes the films and the bereavement themes dealt with in each film.

ACCIDENTAL TOURIST (1988)   120 minutes   **Category:** Drama/Humor
Characters: Macon (father)—William Hurt; Sarah (mother)—Kathleen Turner; Muriel (dog trainer)—Geena Davis; Ethan (deceased son of Macon and Sarah)
Bereavement Themes: parent's loss of a child; sudden death by violence

Discussion Points

1. Death is an incredible strain on a marriage. The coping mechanisms for loss and trauma that exist prior to the death will guide a couple through the grief process regardless of whether these coping strategies are healthy or destructive.
2. Parents stockpile guilt as their feelings of helplessness overwhelm them. The protective nature of parenting creates an assumption that somehow the child's death could have been prevented. Often, this is evidence as one spouse blames the other.
3. The loss of a child is one of the most devastating losses for a family. Couples are at very high risk for divorce after the death of a child.
4. Grief cannot be neatly compartmentalized and filed away. It is a wildly untidy and relentless process.

Overview

In *Accidental Tourist,* Sarah announces to her husband, Macon, that she wants a divorce. The sudden death of their son has been too difficult for her; she must separate if she is to go on with life again. Macon is passively blamed for Sarah's inability to cope with her son's death. We recognize that death has delivered the final blow to an already fractured marriage.

Macon's flat monotone affect hints at clinical depression as this father's grief process is now entering its second year. Macon has lived his entire life in safe tight compartments. We learn much about his character through the bizarre life of his two brothers and sister who live together in their grandparents' house. There is a great deal of hilarity in the compulsive and eccentric behavior of his family.

One of Macon's challenges is learning how to curb the biting dog, Edward, who belonged to his son, Ethan. Family members hound him to rid himself of this beast, but he refuses: he cannot let go of the wonderful memories of Ethan's play with the dog. However, the dog does need discipline. This leads to Macon's affair with Muriel, the dog trainer. She does more for Macon than just train the dog. She opens him to an entire world he has never experienced. Most important, he feels needed and accepted as he is.

Sarah, the distraught wife, makes a fleeting attempt to woo Macon back after the wedding of Macon's sister rekindles their affection. Her attempt is unsuccessful because Macon has changed and grown, but Sarah has remained stuck. After some ambivalence, Macon goes back to Muriel as he realizes that he has changed.

This film brilliantly illustrates the intrusion of grief upon everyday life. In one scene, Macon dreams he is having a phone conversation with his deceased son, only to awaken to the ringing of the alarm clock. In another scene, he is shopping for Muriel's son, and encounters one of Ethan's classmates. In an awkward exchange with the classmate's mother, Macon is reminded that Ethan is not around to enjoy adolescence.

BEACHES (1988)   120 minutes   **Category:** Drama/Humor
Characters: CeCe Bloom (singer)—Bette Midler; Hilary Whitney (lawyer)—Barbara Hershey; John Pierce (lover to Hilary, husband to CeCe)—John Heard
Bereavement Themes: Catastrophic illness—viral cardiomyopsis (virus of the heart); anticipatory grief

Discussion Points

1. To honor the dying person with respect to where he or she wishes to die provides unsurpassed dignity to that person.
2. It is unrealistic to believe that a dying person is always capable of drawing close to those around him or her at the point of death.
3. Death is not romantic but relentlessly cruel and harsh.

Overview

Beaches is about two best friends (CeCe and Whitney) from opposite sides of the tracks. They briefly meet as children and continue to keep in contact with each other as adults, moving in and out of each other's lives at various life transitions: jobs, romances, marriage, divorce, and childbirth. Their "friendship" weathers many emotions that would dissolve a normal friendship. Rivalry, jealousy, anger, betrayal, unforgiveness, and silence are the stressors in their relationship.

That their friendship seems disconnected and unlikely is not the most troublesome point in this film. The trouble results in the illusion that after years of turbulence, distance, and silence, we are led to believe that terminal illness somehow transcends the crack in this fragile friendship. This simply does not happen in real life. Unfortunately, *Beaches* grossly misrepresents death as something that reunites people. Thus we are given a romanticized interpretation of death and the events prior to death.

Nevertheless, the portrayal of the duration of the disease is quite accurate. We observe the agony of being diagnosed with a disease with no known cure. We witness the gradual debilitation of Whitney and her frustration at growing increasingly incapacitated. Mood swings, self-pity, depression, and anger—valid aspects of the dying process—are well acted. The care of Whitney's child after her death is another realistic consideration introduced in this film. It would be a mistake to dismiss this film entirely as a teaching model about death. The last part of the film is excellent.

CRIMES OF THE HEART (1986)   105 minutes   **Category:** Black humor
Characters: Lenny (sister who never married)—Diane Keaton; Meg (sister who failed in Hollywood)—Jessica Lange; Babe (sister who shoots her husband)—Sissy Spacek
Bereavement Themes: suicide, attempted homicide, anticipatory grief, complicated grief due to unresolved grief

Discussion Points

1. Suicide ideation is common among surviving family members.
2. Suicide can have self-duplicating patterns in families when grief is unresolved.
3. Suicide leaves an aftermath of unanswered questions, guilt, and abandonment issues for family members.
4. Remembering the deceased is crucial to grief work and adjustment. A scrapbook of photos and memorabilia is healing.
5. Both healthy and normal, humor helps us digest issues that are incredibly painful or overwhelming. For some, humor excavates tears resulting in a much-needed release.

Overview

Crimes of the Heart, a black comedy, is about the off-beat relationship of the three MacGrath sisters and their unresolved grief about their mother's suicide.

The tongue-in-cheek treatment of suicide is shown in each sister's struggle to understand why their mother committed suicide. She hanged not only herself but also the family cat. Part of the sisters' struggle to understand why their mother committed suicide results in self-destructive patterns each sister unconsciously exhibits. Suicide ideation, a strong theme, is demonstrated in various ways.

Because their mother's death was highly publicized, the sisters are branded by the townspeople and other family members—an illustration of the legacy that suicide inflicts on surviving family.

Crimes of the Heart begins with Babe's recent attempt to kill her husband. This crisis reunites the three sisters. As a battered wife who indulges in an affair, Babe contemplates suicide when her husband discovers the affair and abuses her under-aged lover. She turns the rage away from herself and aims the gun at her husband. The shot does not kill her husband, and her first response is to lackadaisically make a pitcher of lemonade.

Meg is the sister whose failed career in Hollywood paved an already worn road for a mental break. And Meg is the child who discovered the body of the mother. Meg's self-destructive behavior is obvious in her abuse of alcohol. She is a constant source of irritation and jealousy for Lenny, and many confrontations take place between the two sisters.

Lenny is the child who took the role of caretaker for granddaddy, sacrificing her personal life along the way. This sacrifice is perhaps one of the underlying issues between her and Meg. Lenny is also obsessed with the diagnosis of a shrunken ovary, which she blames much of her spinster life on.

As a defense is built for Babe's freedom in the homicide case, a crushing blow comes when she receives a threat from her husband to have her committed for insanity. When her lover is sent out of town on the very same day, these events compound to send her on a suicidal binge. Her various attempts at suicide are perhaps the most desperate, hilarious part of the film. Meg comes home to find Babe—after an afternoon of attempts—with her head in the gas oven. Once Babe is safe, Meg confronts her to find better ways to cope with bad days. In Babe's rash of attempts, she realizes the reason why her mother hung the family cat: she didn't want to die alone. The film ends with the three sisters celebrating Lenny's overdue birthday.

Crimes of the Heart shows well how each sister has her own "baggage" to resolve, while it uses humor to reveal some of the issues underlying suicide.

FIELD OF DREAMS (1989)   2 hours   **Category:** Fantasy/Drama
Characters: Ray Kinsella (husband/father/corn farmer)—Kevin Costner; Anne Kinsella (wife/mother)—Amy Madigan; Terrance Mann (author)—James Earl Jones; John Kinsella (Ray's father)—Ray Liotta
Bereavement Themes: son's grief over death of father; unresolved grief; loss of ambition and dreams (mid-life crisis)

Discussion Points

1. Current losses trigger unresolved losses.
2. Time does not resolve irrevocable losses.
3. "Empty" chair/role playing can be helpful in finishing delayed or denied grief.
4. Grieving about "what cannot be" is a natural, necessary part of the process.

Overview

Field of Dreams is a light-hearted fantasy about unrealized dreams and unresolved grief. With a heavy theme of baseball and a hint of mid-life crisis, it is also the vehicle of exploring one man's unresolved grief about his father.

An Iowa corn farmer in his mid-thirties, Ray Kinsella awakens one morning to realize his fear of duplicating the life of his father and of growing old. As Ray walks through the corn fields he hears a voice and sees a vision that spark a passion-turned-obsession to build a baseball field in the middle of his corn field. Despite being heckled and called insane by the townspeople, he plows under his cash crop to build the baseball field. Then he becomes obsessed with understanding what the voice and continuing messages mean. His wife, Annie, supports his venture even when she wonders about how they will survive without the income from the farm.

In the process of understanding what the vision and voices mean, he relays his guilt over an angry confrontation with his father as an adolescent and his remorse in not making peace before his father's death. His grief is compounded by the fact that his father did not have the opportunity to meet Annie or Karin, his child.

Ray believes that the field is being built to redeem the reputation of Shoeless Joe Jackson, accused of throwing a World Series in an earlier era. In his adventure, he recruits Terrance Mann, a gifted writer from the sixties who has become embittered and soured on life.

While the average person cannot see the players on the field, Ray, his wife, his daughter, and Terrance Mann can plainly see them. Near the end, the real reason for the voices and vision becomes clear. The reunion of the players is to give Ray and his father, John, the opportunity to reconcile their past grievances. John is the catcher of this imaginary team. Reconciliation happens when Ray introduces John to his family and then proceeds with a "lost" game of catch.

Field of Dreams is clearly about aspirations and second chances at reconciliation and good-byes, but integrates the unresolved grief theme in a meaningful way.

MEN DON'T LEAVE (1990)　　115 minutes　　**Category:** Drama/Humor
Characters: Beth Macauley (mother/wife)—Jessica Lange; John Macauley (father/husband who suddenly dies)—Tom Mason; Chris Macauley (17-year-old son)—Chris O'Donnell; Matthew Macauley (9-year-old son)—Charlie Korsmo; Lisa Coleman (mother's boss at catering service)—Kathy Bates
Bereavement Themes: parental loss; spousal loss; children's grief process; teenage grief response; subsequent losses due to sudden death

Discussion Points

1. When a child's parent dies, often the surviving spouse is unable to be present for the child and is preoccupied with his or her own grief as well as subsequent losses. It has nothing to do with parenting skills or lack of concern or love for a child.

2. Subsequent losses can be financial or emotional or both, and can create a history of multiple losses in addition to the actual death. Subsequent losses can be as devastating as the death itself.
3. The central issue for a grieving child is: Who will care for me?
4. Anger and depression are natural, normal responses to the death of a loved one.
5. A child or teen's developmental process is powerfully interrupted by the death of a parent.

Overview

Men Don't Leave is both a dramatic and sometimes humorous portrayal of the struggles of a young mother and her children to cope with the sudden death of their father. Beth Macauley suddenly finds herself widowed, unemployed, and struggling to absorb the news that her husband's construction business left her with enormous debts she cannot pay. Unable to find an adequate job in her own small town, she is forced to move to the suburbs to find employment. In this transition, she is forced to sell the family house and her husband's truck.

She faces the defiance of her oldest son, Chris, who accurately portrays a seventeen-year-old's grief response: anger, anger, and more anger. Chris is caught between his own developmental conflict of individuation from parents and "being the man of the house" to fulfill his father's role. Her nine-year-old son, Matthew, becomes an invisible child, very withdrawn and sad, who spends his time zoning out in front of the television. Later, Matty spends a great deal of time worrying about family finances and acts on a belief that if only he could win the lottery for his mother, then they could move back "home." This belief engages him in a string of thefts to earn money for a lottery ticket.

As Beth works to provide for her family, she faces numerous challenges: a new job, a difficult boss, a romantic interest, and a diminishing influence in her eldest son's life as he embarks on his own romantic interest. She attempts to provide family night for the family, but meets resistance on Chris's part and preoccupation on Matty's. During one poignant scene, we see through the eyes of a nine-year-old, who sees nothing else in the museum outing except other children playing with their fathers. Some of the most humorous parts of the film involve Jody, a very offbeat radiology lab technician, who takes a part romantic, part parental interest in Chris and attempts to analyze Beth and her grief process. Jody's response is not unlike what many grieving people experience: a minimization and dismissal of the grief process.

Over time, Beth slowly begins to develop a friendship with Charles and is conflicted and confused about the romantic overtones present. When she is fired from her job, she slips into a deep depression and refuses to come out of her bedroom. Not even Charles can reach her. For one of the first times in the film, we see Chris's concern for his mother and his guilt about his jealousy over Charles. Sadly, Matty is lost in all the commotion.

When Matty's lottery ticket scheme fails, he is bitterly crushed and displays his sense of injustice, rather like the injustice that a child feels at the unfairness of the death of a parent. In response, he runs away—returning to the family home, to his playhouse. In perhaps the most intense scene of the film, Beth, Chris, and Matty sit in the playhouse as Matty reveals to Beth his reasons for running away to the playhouse, not because he misses the playhouse, but because he misses her. What follows is a very honest, realistic conversation about the raw questions children have about death, the afterlife, and their own pain and behavior. We see Beth's ability to answer her child's questions, fears, and erroneous beliefs in a caring, respectful manner without attempting to extinguish or minimize his pain. Part of this exchange may make adults squirm because of an erroneous belief that children should be shielded from pain, but in essence, it is this raw pain that allows Matty to make a very important reconnection with his mother.

Men Don't Leave is an excellent teaching model of a healthy grief process and the stark challenges parents and families face when death triggers a series of subsequent, unwanted changes and adjustments.

MY BODY GUARD (1980)   96 minutes   **Category:** Drama
Characters: Clifford (new kid in school)—Chris Makepeace; Gramma (Clifford's saucy grandma)—Ruth Gordon; Moody (school bully)—Matt Dillon; Linderman (perceived psychopath)—Adam Baldwin
Bereavement Themes: sibling and adolescent grief; accidental and violent death; attempted suicide

Discussion Points

1. Adolescents are ruthlessly intolerant of those who are "different," for whatever reason.
2. Certain types of death are more prone to outrageous interpretations and misunderstandings.
3. Ignorance breeds fear. Accurate information lessens chances for cruel remarks or erroneous conclusions.
4. Delayed and unresolved grief paves the way for complicated grief.
5. Unauthentic guilt can be the breeding ground for suicide. It is crucial to "check out" suicide ideation with grieving clients as thoughts about suicide are often part of the grief process but normally subside. Thoughts that do not subside require immediate intervention.
6. A loss history, including a detailed account of the most recent death, may help to reveal "secrets" that harbor torment.

Overview

An excellent film about adolescent relationships and grief, *My Body Guard* reveals the relentless cruelty of Moody, the school bully, who preys on his vulnerable peers. As a newcomer to the school, Clifford is an attractive target for Moody, but Clifford determines not to submit to the daily threats and sets out to find his own "protection."

Ricky Linderman, massive for his age, is the mysterious loner who sends even the toughest bully cowering: Linderman is rumored to be a cold-blooded killer who has murdered a teacher and even his own brother. Somehow, Clifford embodies the wisdom to question the rumors and to search out the truth about Ricky Linderman. A sympathetic teacher reveals the truth: the previous year, Ricky had discovered the body of his younger brother after a tragic shooting accident. The relief of this news sends Clifford on a quest to recruit Linderman as his bodyguard but Linderman is not interested. The rejection of a "heroic" role among the students puzzles Cliff, who then sets out to befriend this young loner.

With little in common, Cliff and Ricky find friendship while restoring a motor-cycle that Linderman has built from scratch. Ricky's important therapeutic rebuilding of the motorcycle appears to have begun shortly after his brother's death.

Cliff is completely unaware that, as someone needing "protection," he triggers Linderman's guilt over his inability to save his younger brother. Eventually, Linder-man unravels his gut-wrenching secret: he accidentally shot his brother while they were playing with their father's gun. To complicate matters, he put the gun back in his brother's hand to avoid blame. After surviving a suicide attempt, Linderman now believes he deserves nothing except isolation. After all, he only "lets people down."

Cliff's caring persistence sheds light on Linderman's darkened existence. In time, Clifford confronts Linderman about his brother, and Linderman blurts out the truth about the shooting. Eventually Linderman is able to rejoin Cliff and his other classmates.

One of the many outstanding teaching tools of this film is the incredibly accurate flat affect of Ricky Linderman.

MY GIRL (1991)   102 minutes   **Category:** Drama/Humor
Characters: Vada Sultenfuss (11-year-old)—Anna Chlumsky; Thomas Jay Senett (11-year-old)—Macauley Culkin; Harry Sultenfuss (Vada's father)—Dan Akroyd; Shelly DeVoto (employee, Harry's romantic interest)—Jamie Lee Curtis
Bereavement Themes: unresolved grief of a mother and wife; death of a playmate

Discussion Points

1. Unresolved grief does not dissolve with time.
2. Children naturally have questions about death and life.
3. Children grieve in their own individual way, as adults also grieve in their own ways.
4. Children will fill in the blanks the best they can, regardless of how inaccurate the information, when it is not provided by appropriate adults.

Overview

My Girl is mostly about coming of age, which often means having questions about life and death answered. An only child, Vada is a precocious eleven-year-old tomboy. Her father, Harry, is a mortician and widower. His wife died at Vada's birth. Harry cannot discuss death with his daughter, even though their daily lives are surrounded by it, and dismisses Vada's preoccupation with death and her hypochondriac-like concerns. Vada's best friend, also eleven years old, is Thomas Jay, who develops a crush on Vada. During the summer, Thomas Jay and Vada have many adventures and make friendship pacts.

Shelly, a makeup artist, takes up employment in the funeral home, and helps bridge a gap between Vada and her father, a relationship that has been nearly nonexistent. Predictably, Harry and Shelly embark on their own relationship, which Vada resents. She invests herself in an adult writing course, and her teacher, Mr. Bixler, becomes the object of her affection. During a challenge to students in the class to express their innermost thoughts, fears, and desires, Vada reveals her deepest fear is that she killed her mother. Sadly, this reminds us that when children are not allowed to talk or ask questions about their losses, they may concoct outrageous conclusions about their part in a person's death. Death is understood in a brutal cause-and-effect rationale.

During one adventure in the woods, Vada and Thomas Jay come upon a beehive. While escaping an angry swarm of bees, Vada loses her mood ring. Later Thomas Jay returns to the woods alone, to look for Vada's ring. He again is attacked by a swarm of bees and dies of an allergic reaction. Vada, devastated by the news, responds by isolating herself in her room. During the funeral, she approaches Thomas Jay's casket and begins to talk, yell, and cry. Vada is pulled away and quieted, but overcome by grief, she runs out of the funeral home, straight to her teacher's house. In her pain, she confesses her love for him only to be met with the reality of her teacher's fiancée. Next, she runs to the doctor to report her symptoms: "I can't breathe, the bee stings, I can't breathe." This is a brief testimony to the real symptomatology of acute grief.

When Vada finally returns home, she is met by Shelly frantic with worry. Shelly's concern allows Vada to relinquish her jealousies, share her grief and remorse with her: "I should have told Thomas Jay he was my best friend." When she next sees her father, Vada blurts out the burning question: "Did I kill my mother? The bees killed Thomas Jay, so I killed my mother," and this begins the first healthy discussion between Vada and her father.

Overall, *My Girl*, focusing on Vada's responses, is an adequate portrayal of preadolescent grief.

ORDINARY PEOPLE (1980)   124 minutes   **Category:** Drama
Characters: Conrad (17-year-old surviving sibling)—Timothy Hutton; Beth (mother)—Mary Tyler Moore; Calvin (father)—Donald Sutherland; Berger (psychiatrist)—Judd Hirsch; Jeannine (girlfriend)—Elizabeth McGovern; Karen (friend from hospital)—Dinah Manoff
Bereavement Themes: suicide; accidental and sudden death; survivor guilt; sibling, parental, and adolescent grief

Discussion Points

1. Death is an incredible strain on a family system. Coping mechanisms for loss that existed prior to the death, whether healthy or destructive, will guide a family through the grief process.
2. The grief process is very individual. Since every person responds differently to death, we must respect the unique expression of each person.
3. While respecting individuality, families must find some commonality in their grief to preserve the family system during a traumatic loss.
4. Death cuts across all socioeconomic barriers.
5. The release and process of grief allows for reinvestment in previous and/or new relationships.
6. The passing of time, in itself, does not heal.

Overview

In *Ordinary People,* Conrad has been hospitalized for his recent attempt at suicide. His suicide attempt, we quickly realize, is rooted in the unresolved grief over the sudden death of his brother, Buck. A year earlier, Conrad and Buck had a boating accident in which Buck drowned and Conrad survived. Conrad's grief is complicated by the inability of his family to even speak about the incident.

His mother's inability to resolve the death of her favorite son results in her sometimes aggressive hostility toward Conrad, as seen in her refusal to visit him during his hospitalization. The father is equally unable to connect with either his grieving wife, Beth, or Conrad, demonstrating the dysfunction within this family. A further problem for the father is the mounting tension he feels between Conrad and Beth. His dilemma peaks over his love and concern for his son and the increasingly unstable relationship with his wife.

Coming to terms with the death of his athletic brother, Conrad seeks the aid of a psychiatrist. In the middle of therapy, the sudden suicide of his friend Karen (from hospital days) reawakens his deep sense of responsibility for the boating accident and the punitive guilt he has suppressed for not preventing the accident and for surviving it. This guilt, which ultimately pushed Conrad into his suicide attempt, is compounded by his mother's hostility. Though Beth grieves too, she is completely unable to find a commonality with either her husband or her son.

As Conrad progresses, he is able to invite new relationships into his life and accept limitations in the relationship with his mother. Unfortunately, his progress toward wholeness cannot preserve the crumbling relationship between his parents.

Ordinary People, an excellent illustration of family systems, succinctly portrays many difficult issues of sibling and adolescent grief.

PHILADELPHIA (1993)   125 minutes   **Category:** Drama
Characters: Andrew Beckett (attorney wrongfully dismissed)—Tom Hanks; Joe Miller (defense attorney)—Denzel Washington; Miguel Alvarez (Andrew Beckett's life partner)—Antonio Banderas; Charles Wheeler (law firm's

homophobic senior)—Jason Robards; Belinda Conine (Beckett's assistant at law firm)—Mary Steenburgen; Sarah Beckett (Andrew Beckett's mother)—Joanne Woodward

Bereavement Themes: major catastrophic illness; anticipatory grief; parental, partner, sibling loss; coworker loss; disenfranchised grief

Discussion Points

1. AIDS is a type of death highly stigmatized by a homophobic society and results in very blatant discrimination.
2. AIDS deaths evoke highly charged emotions and conflicting points of view. AIDS is still a disease where the victim gets blamed.
3. There are many secondary and subsequent losses associated with AIDS.
4. In many cases, the partner's rights are stripped away; it sets in motion a type of grief that heterosexual relationships do not endure.
5. There is nothing romantic or "quiet" about an AIDS death.

Overview

Philadelphia delves into the AIDS dilemma and speaks boldly about the discrimination that countless people endure. The film shows both very blatant and more subtle instances of homophobia, prejudice, and ignorance. *Philadelphia* was one of the first films to dare broach the subject of AIDS in the 1990s.

Andrew Beckett, a bright attorney in a very influential law firm, has been made senior partner and has been given the most prestigious client of the firm. Andrew Beckett also has AIDS. He chooses not to reveal his lifestyle or his illness to the law firm because of previous discriminatory remarks made about gays. As the illness progresses, we watch the discrimination that Andy and his partner, Miguel, endure from the medical community, the legal community, and the media. His work at the firm is sabotaged and, subsequently, Andy is fired from his job. He knows that he has been discriminated against because of his illness, and he decides to take action, but he is turned down by nine attorneys. The only attorney willing to touch the case turns out to be clearly homophobic. The relationship between Andy and his attorney, Joe Miller, is particularly interesting. Whether Joe ever fully accepts Andy is not satisfactorily resolved in the film, but we see Joe's attempt to educate himself about AIDS, to confront his own prejudices, homophobia, and grief as well as cope with the unexpected prejudice he encounters as Andy's attorney.

The film accurately portrays the all-consuming nature of AIDS in Andy's treatment, symptoms, physical decline and his ability to cope with the unpredictability of AIDS. The film also does a good job of portraying the complications, constant decisions made about treatment and care, and the emotional roller coaster of grief one endures when afflicted with AIDS. We see the tension in the scenes between Andy and Miguel and the awkwardness in Andy's family coping with his rapid physical decline. The support and acceptance of Andrew's family pull at our heart, and we desperately want to believe this type of support exists, but such support is a product of Hollywood, and, in the end, is not very realistic.

The accurate portrayal of the disease and its ravaging effects, the appearance of KS (Kaposi's sarcoma) lesions, the weight loss, and weakness prevent us from romanticizing the illness or minimizing Andy's immense suffering.

Philadelphia is to be commended for its attempt to show the many layers of loss and grief imposed by a catastrophic illness.

SOPHIE'S CHOICE (1982)   138 minutes   **Category:** Drama
Characters: Sophie (Holocaust survivor of Auschwitz)—Meryl Streep; Nathan (Sophie's lover, schizophrenic)—Kevin Kline; Stingo (Southern writer)—Peter MacNicol
Bereavement Themes: survivor's guilt; multiple losses (family, country, national identity); complicated grief; suicide

Discussion Points

1. Survivor's guilt is a very complex issue, and those afflicted with survivor's guilt are vulnerable to complicated grief responses and behaviors.
2. Unresolved subsequent losses do not disappear with time or new circumstances.
3. Therapists should be aware of possible substance abuse with grieving clients. Addictive substances may be common "escape" mechanisms during the grief process.
4. Therapists should recognize what constitutes complicated grief and how persons who have had multiple losses are at risk for this pathology.
5. Suicide ideation is common among surviving family members.
6. Suicide can have self-duplicating patterns in families when death is unresolved.

Overview

Sophie's Choice is a complex film about the atrocities of the Holocaust and issues of survival. The potent theme of survivor's guilt is prominent in the main character, Sophie, a Polish Catholic. Sophie's family is caught in the Nazi conflict even though her father is a professor of law at Cracow University and influential in establishing anti-Semitic policy. Ironically, Sophie's father and husband were the first to be arrested and executed. Sophie's anguish over her father results from her love/hate relationship with him: she loved her father but hated the policy that he stood for. Concurrently, Sophie's mother developed tuberculosis. In Sophie's attempt to care for her mother, she unsuccessfully smuggles a forbidden ham. She is caught by the police. She and her two children are arrested and taken to Auschwitz. At this point, an awful choice is presented to her. During a heartless exchange with a guard, she is made to choose between her two children. When he threatens to exterminate both children she screams out for him to take her daughter. Her daughter is killed and her son is sent to the Children's Camp. She never sees her son again. Sophie is spared at Auschwitz, partly due to her perfect German language and secretarial skills. When released, she finds herself trying to make a new life in America. Malnourished and ill, she is befriended by Nathan who becomes her lover.

Sophie's complicated, heavy-laden grief alone is enough to destroy her, but Nathan's cruelty accelerates the process. As a child, Nathan was diagnosed with paranoid schizophrenia. In addition, he is a benzedrine and cocaine addict. His illness and addiction are hidden from Sophie by Nathan's brother but is later disclosed to Stingo, a mutual friend. With this information withheld from Sophie, she has little ability to understand Nathan's bizarre and violent behavior. In her own self-destructive process, she is addicted to Nathan. Her enmeshment with Nathan is her ultimate statement of guilt over surviving Auschwitz. Ironically, Sophie's first suicide attempt was *after* she was released from Auschwitz, not while imprisoned.

Stingo is a young Southern writer who comes to Brooklyn to pursue his career. A neighbor of Sophie and Nathan, he is mesmerized by Nathan's charisma and Sophie's beauty. The threesome become best friends. Stingo begins to draw the awful truth to the surface for Sophie. His love for her drives him to find out the real story of her life. In their exchanges we see the incredible guilt that Sophie has taken on. She feels guilt for not standing up to her father, for not being able to save her mother or her children, and most of all, for surviving.

Stingo's concern for Sophie erupts when Nathan threatens them with a gun during an extreme psychotic episode. During this flight from Nathan, Stingo confesses his love for Sophie and his desire to marry her. At the mere hint of real trust, Sophie confesses her darkest secret to Stingo: her awful choice between her two children. Perhaps it is the idea of love (and confession) that drives Sophie back into the lethal arms of Nathan. Upon returning, Sophie makes her fatal choice to join Nathan in a double suicide—accomplished through cyanide poisoning.

STAND BY ME (1986)   86 minutes   **Category:** Drama
Characters: Gordie (aspiring writer, sibling of deceased)—Wil Wheaton; Chris (Gordie's best friend)—River Phoenix; Teddie (abused child, nearest to the edge)—Corey Feldman; Vern (plump, insecure member of group)—Jerry O'Connell
Bereavement Themes: sibling grief; accidental death; suicidal tendencies; adolescent grief

Discussion Points

1. Adolescents are frequently misunderstood and ignored in their grief process.
2. For children, participation in the grief process with the family is crucial to their adjustment.
3. While adolescents may not express their grief in the way adults expect them to, they do indeed grieve. While a child of twelve may understand the finality of death, he or she is not necessarily able to verbalize or express grief in "adult" terms.
4. Adolescents are especially vulnerable to the internalization and personification of events and feelings at their stage of development.
5. Suicidal tendencies acted out as flirtations with death are warning signals and require immediate attention.

Overview

Stand By Me, one of the finest portrayals of adolescent grief available, gives an accurate, humorous account of the relationships between four twelve-year-old boys.

Gordie is struggling with the sudden death of his older superstar brother, Denny, who died in a car accident the previous year. Battling for self-esteem during adolescence, Gordie receives an additional burden: at the graveside of his brother, his father says accusingly, "It should have been you, Gordie."

Chris Chambers, Gordie's best friend, believes in Gordie's abilities as a writer. Gordie, in return, believes that Chris can rise above the legacy of a juvenile delinquent brother and alcoholic father.

Teddie, a third friend, suffers from the cruelty of an abusive father. Because of his tendency to flirt with death and the rage that simmers in him, Teddie is a disturbing reminder of the effects of child abuse.

Vern, the youngest and least mature of the group, is vulnerable to the berating and pranks of the other boys.

The accidental death of a local boy draws the four kids together. The boy was killed by a train and his body is missing. Their camaraderie and curiosity send them on an overnight adventure to "find" the body and become town heroes. The search for the body is the rarest and rawest form of "death education." For Gordie, the search becomes an obsession to resolve the death of his brother. In one heart-rending scene, Chris comforts Gordie during a nightmare about his brother that awakens him and leaves him terrified and guilt-ridden.

Upon finding the missing body, Gordie's grief reaches a point of release. It becomes clear that the safety in the friendship of this foursome allows for Gordie's expression of grief.

Stand By Me is based on the novella *The Body* by Stephen King. When King was four years old, he experienced a very traumatic event: he ventured near a train track when a man was struck by the train and killed. It is not known if Stephen King actually witnessed the fatal accident or not, but Dr. Lenore Terr makes a very interesting case about post-traumatic play and reenactment of trauma related to King's preoccupation with death (see Dr. Terr's book, *Too Scared to Cry*).

STEEL MAGNOLIAS (1989)   2 hours   **Category:** Drama
Characters: Shelby (young woman with diabetes)—Julia Roberts; M'Lynn (mother)—Sally Fields; Truvy (local beautician)—Dolly Parton; Ouisa (family's neighbor)—Shirley MacLaine; Clarice (local friend)—Olympia Dukakis; Annelle (beautician's assistant)—Darryl Hannah
Bereavement Themes: anticipatory grief related to diabetes; kidney transplant, donation and rejection; ethical dilemmas of comatose state; maternal/paternal grief

Discussion Points

1. Differences of expression in individual grief work within a family system can be a common bond that strengthens rather than divides a family.
2. There are unique issues for both the father and the mother when a female adult child dies.
3. It is important to create and accept support systems outside the family system.
4. Anticipatory grief allows time for family members and loved ones to put things in order and to resolve issues.
5. Anger is a healthy and normal part of the anticipatory grief process.

Overview

Steel Magnolias, a film about the complications of diabetes, is based on a true story about the death of Susan Harling written by her brother, Robert Harling. It portrays a young woman choosing to follow her desire for children at the risk of her own life. Since the film is also about nurturing female relationships, it has been strongly interpreted as a "woman's film" and has not gained the male audience it deserves.

The main character, Shelby, looks at life less cautiously than her mother, M'Lynn, who instinctively wants to protect her child from the debilitating effects of diabetes. M'Lynn's anxiety rises at Shelby's marriage since she suspects that her son-in-law truly does not understand the complications inherent in diabetes. In M'Lynn's mind, the question of bearing children is not an option for Shelby since it is clearly a life-threatening choice.

It is difficult to know if Shelby lives in denial about her illness or if she makes the most of what opportunities are available, despite the consequences. When Shelby announces her pregnancy, M'Lynn temporarily withdraws out of anger. Shelby's response to her mother gives a clue to her thinking: "I'd rather have thirty minutes of somethin' wonderful than a lifetime of nothin' special."

Shelby's father and her husband are overjoyed at the news of the pregnancy. M'Lynn's four close friends make a commitment to see her through all the consequences of Shelby's choice. After the birth of the child, Shelby experiences kidney failure and undergoes a transplant. M'Lynn is her donor. Within a year, Shelby's kidney fails resulting in a coma and, finally, death. (These scenes touch usually forbidden ethical dilemmas including the decision to withdraw life support systems.)

At the graveside, the rawness of grief is embodied in M'Lynn's confusion, rage, and irrationality. Her friends desperately want to help but have no idea what to say. We feel the tension as the women rage and sob one moment and laugh hysterically the next. Although there is a rich camaraderie between them, they are awkward with M'Lynn's intense emotions and use humor to distract from that intensity.

Steel Magnolias is an excellent model of grief work, showing the different ways men and women process loss.

TERMS OF ENDEARMENT (1983)   2 hours   **Category:** Drama
Characters: Emma (daughter)—Debra Winger; Aurora (mother)—Shirley MacLaine; Garrett (Aurora's neighbor and boyfriend)—Jack Nicholson; Flap (Emma's husband)—Jeff Daniels
Bereavement Themes: anticipatory grief (cancer); unresolved losses

Discussion Points

1. Dysfunctional families do not automatically change when a tragedy occurs. Death does not magically bring families or people together.
2. It is important to include children, often forgotten, in the grief process.
3. Helping professionals need to process their own grief so as not to ask the client to take care of them.
4. At the time of a parent's death, children need to be assured that someone will take care of them. It is highly inappropriate to suggest that they are to care for the surviving parent.

Overview

The opening scene of *Terms of Endearment* shows an overprotective mother (Aurora) pinching her sleeping daughter (Emma) to assure she is breathing and not dead. In a flashback Emma (at about age eight) is admonished to "take care" of her mother after her father dies. In one scene, the mother, unable to sleep, seeks comfort from her grief by climbing into bed with her daughter, beginning the dysfunction that besets their relationship for life. We quickly see that Emma's primary role is to comfort mom at the expense of her own individuality.

It is easy to identify the manipulative Aurora as the villain in this film. Aurora's contempt for Flap (Emma's husband) creates a conflict of loyalty for Emma. Flap and Emma endure many difficulties together: relocation of job, unplanned pregnancies, financial strains, extramarital affairs, and ultimately cancer.

While Aurora achieves some personal growth from her involvement with a neighbor, Garrett, it is not enough to overcome her narcissism and incessant need for control over her daughter's life. Emma's role of caretaker continues to the end of her life. In one poignant scene, Aurora is at Emma's bedside lamenting about a recent date with her boyfriend. Emma responds in anger, reminding her mother that she is dying.

Emma continues her caretaking as she confronts Flap about her impending death and the decisions surrounding the situation. During this exchange, Flap's agenda is about guilt and forgiveness for his affair while Emma's is about care of the children after her death.

Emma's good-bye talk with her children is heart-wrenching, but unrealistic. Where is her husband during this time? Why does she do this alone? Who comforts Emma? Who comforts her children?

The common thread between *Terms of Endearment* and *Beaches* is the fallacy that tragedy will overcome dysfunctional relationships and that an impending death will draw people closer together. While there are moments of care in both films, neither are accurate teaching models for grief work.

BIBLIOGRAPHY

Barnes, D., *Previous Losses—Forgotten but Not Resolved,* paper presented at King's College Bereavement Conference, London, Ontario, Canada, May 1987.

Corr, C., and J. McNeil, *Adolescence and Death,* Springer, New York, 1986.

Fitzgerald, H., *The Grieving Child—A Parent's Guide,* Fireside, Simon & Schuster, New York, 1986.

Harling, R., Local Boy Makes Good, *Life Magazine,* pp. 91-92, October 1989.

Jackson, E., *The Many Faces of Grief,* Abingdon Press, Nashville, 1977.

Jewett, C., *Helping Children Cope with Separation and Loss,* Harvard Common Press, Boston 1982.

Kübler-Ross, E., *On Death & Dying,* Macmillan, New York, 1979.

Kübler-Ross, E., *Questions & Answers on Death & Dying,* Macmillan, New York, 1974.

Lindermann, E., Symptomatology and Management of Acute Grief, *American Journal of Psychiatry, CI, 101,* pp. 141-144, 1944.

Lindermann, E., *Mobilizing Against AIDS: The Unfinished Story of a Virus,* National Academy of Sciences, Harvard University Press, Cambridge, Massachusetts, 1986.

Rando, T., *Treating Complicated Grief,* Research Press, Champaign, Illinois, 1993.

Simos, B., *A Time to Grieve,* Family Science Association of America, New York, 1979 (a good understanding of the complicated issues of survivor's guilt as portrayed in *Sophie's Choice* and *Ordinary People*).

Terr, L., *Too Scared to Cry: Psychic Trauma in Childhood,* Harper & Row, New York, 1990.

Wolfelt, A., *Helping Children Cope with Grief,* Accelerated Development, Inc., Muncie, Indiana, 1983.

Worden, J. W., *Grief Counseling and Grief Therapy: A Handbook for the Mental Health Practitioner,* Springer, New York, 1982.

RESOURCE GUIDE

Accidental Tourist

Johnson, B., Intimate Stories, *Maclean's, 102*:2, pp. 44-45, 1989.

Schickel, R., Dog Eared Doings, *Time Magazine, 232*:26, p. 83, 1988.

Simon, J., The Frenzied and the Frozen, *National Review, 41*:4, pp. 55-56, 1989.

An Occurrence at Owl Creek Bridge

1962—France. Based on the short story by Ambrose Bierce. Available on video cassette from Video Yesteryear, Box C-137, Sandy Hook, Connecticut 06482. Call toll free at (800) 243-0987. $19.95 plus $3 shipping.

Beaches

Johnson, B. D., Intimate Stories, *Maclean's, 102*:2, pp. 44-45, 1989.

Crimes of the Heart

Ozer, J. S., et al., Crimes of the Heart [review], *Film Review Annual,* Film Review Publishers, pp. 250-260, 1988.
Skow, J., Kitchen Comedy on Location, *Time Magazine, 128*:1, pp. 66-67, 1986.

Dead Poets Society

Seidenberg, R., Dead Poets Society, *America Film, 114*:1, p. 57, 1989.
Will. G. F., O Robin, My Captain! [review], *Newsweek, 114*:1, p. 74, 1989.

Field of Dreams

Anker, R. M., The Magical Kingdom's Box Office [review], *Christianity Today, 33*:12, p. 70, September 1989.
Knight, A., Baseball Like It Oughta Be [review], *American Film, 14*:7, p. 76, 1989.
Sanders, J., Illuminations—Can of Corn [review], *American Film, 14*:10, pp. 14-15, 1989.
Wall, J. M., A Playing Field for the Boys of Eternity [review], *Christian Century, 106*:17, pp. 515-516, May 1989.

My Body Guard

Ozer, J. S., et al., My Body Guard [review], *Film Review Annual,* Film Review Publishers, pp. 717-730, 1981.

Sophie's Choice

Ozer, J. S., et al., Sophie's Choice [review], *Film Review Annual,* Film Review Publishers, pp. 1074-1090, 1983.

Stand By Me

Ozer, J. S., et al., Stand By Me [review], *Film Review Annual,* Film Review Publishers, pp. 1339-1347, 1987.

Steel Magnolias

Ansen, D., Three Hankies and No Heart [review], *Newsweek, 114*:22, p. 90, November 1989.
Harling, R., Local Boy Makes Good, *Life Magazine, 12*:11, pp. 91-93, October 1989.
Hart, L., Star Bright, *Life Magazine, 12*:11, pp. 82-88, October 1989.
Schickel, R., Steel Magnolias, *Time Magazine, 134*:21, p. 92, November 1989.

Terms of Endearment

Ozer, J. S., et al., Terms of Endearment [review], *Film Review Annual,* Film Review Publishers, pp. 1202-1223, 1984.

A Wake for Dying
Forum Theatre

Kate Wilkinson and Judith McDowell

Target Theatre is a company of older actors based in Victoria, British Columbia, who frequently use forum theatre techniques to develop plays on issues of concern to seniors. Forum Theatre is a technique of the Theatre of the Oppressed developed over twenty-five ago years by the South American theatre guru, Augusto Boal. It is a form of transformational theatre now being used widely to address social issues in a practical way.

Forum Theatre dramatizes common problems in people's lives, but does not impose solutions or a specific point of view. Instead, the audience members work with the actors in "playing out" alternative approaches to an issue. The power inherent in this form of theatre is that the spectators become "participants" sharing their points of view and taking from one another ideas that are personally meaningful.

A Wake for Dying tackles the theme of personal responsibility for the manner in which we deal with dying. It concerns a family in which the mother is facing a major health crisis. The first two scenes depict specific family dysfunctions in the struggle to deal with the situation. They are designed for forum theatre and stimulate audience participation on the issues of oppression and poor communication. The third and final scene represents a more "enlightened" stage in which the mother is more in control of her experience, and family members who have acquired more information are better able to ease her dying process.

With a play such as *A Wake for Dying,* the director acts as the mediator or "Joker," as Boal calls the role. As the "Joker," I introduce the forum theatre concept to the audience or workshop participants. I prepare them to watch for problems as they view the first two scenes and to think of possible solutions. When the scenes are finished, I ask them to turn to a neighbor, preferably someone they don't know, and chat about what they have just experienced.

After a few minutes, I explained that the actors will replay the second scene, in which the family members are feeling oppressed by their inability to deal with the reality of their mother Diane's imminent death. I ask anyone in the audience to call out "I can help" at any time in the action when the family needs information to help resolve its problems.

| Harriet: | "I wish we knew more about programs for people with mother's concerns." |
| Russell: | "I was thinking maybe we ought to look into this business of a Living Will." |

The person who stops the action comes up on stage and talks about a relevant topic such as representation agreements, the local hospice program, or another community resource that would be useful in advancing the family's discussion. (I like to give him or her a "magic" wand to hold, which transports them into the Hart's kitchen.)

This first exercise warms everybody up so that we can approach the family dysfunctions with more typical forum theatre work. Next I explain that the actors are going to replay a problematic part of the family's discussion. If anyone recognizes that someone is being diminished or that there is anything about the way the characters are relating to each other that is disturbing, that person should call out "Stop!" The actors stop the action until the spectator comes up in the role of one of the characters and demonstrates an approach that will enable the family to make hard decisions and be more sensitive to Diane's needs. The actors respond in character. I encourage as many people to come up as are willing, and I give them the opportunity to work on any specific sequence or line that they feel needs attention.

Exploring the characters' dilemmas leads to a discussion of the meaning of oppression. It begins the process by acknowledging that oppression is not acceptable, and by identifying factors in the situation that people can change. Harriet, for example, is oppressed because she is unable to take time off from work during a family crisis. Similarly, the play contains several instances where self-oppression is a key issue. The family members get in their own way: Russell, the father, is unable to take more of a leadership role; Ruth's religious beliefs translate into dogmatism; Larry's joking but ambitious nature makes him insensitive.

In the doctor's scene we have a dominating character and two who are in a more vulnerable position. Russell and Diane are frustrated because the professional in whom they have confided is not meeting their needs. Here the intervening person can only take over the roles of Diane or Russell, who are the only ones able to change their relationship with the doctor. One premise of the Theatre of the Oppressed is that only the diminished person can bring about change. The dominating person has no motivation to alter the status quo.

Ideally all audience interventions will improve the situation and yield effective suggestions on how "victims" can empower themselves. The Joker supports the process by encouraging people to come on stage, by illuminating the meanings of different interventions, and by drawing attention to "magic solutions," such as endowing a character with a complete personality change. If people are slow to volunteer or have a physical disability that makes coming on stage problematic, I give them a telephone, mimed or real, so they can offer advice to a given character. Similarly, the Joker can freeze the action of a scene and ask someone to speak the inner voice of the character. Ultimately the forum theater is about doing and experiencing rather than passively discussing.

Clearly there are many possible solutions for complex issues, and different discoveries are appropriate for different families. The Joker needs to encourage a broad range of options within the given time and without exhausting the momentum. *A Wake for Dying,* by examining the importance of self-determination in the face of death, gives every individual in the audience the opportunity to examine his or her own response to the situation presented and to make choices accordingly. It encourages them to identify where they may need to acknowledge oppression in their own lives and within themselves.

A Wake for Dying
A Script for Forum Theatre

by Judith McDowell

Developed and Directed by Kate Wilkinson
Copyright 1996: Target Theatre, Victoria, B.C., Canada

CAST

Diane Hart, Russell Hart, Dr. Grieve, Harriet Howard, Larry Hart, Ruth James

FREEZE ACTION SCENE I

*[DIANE and RUSSELL HART are seated stage right in the office
of DR. GRIEVE, holding hands.]*

FREEZE ACTION SCENE II

*[LARRY HART is standing in his parents' kitchen stage left talking to his
wife on a cordless phone. His sisters HARRIET HOWARD and
RUTH JAMES are sitting at the table.]*

SCENE 1

[Lights up on scene in Doctor's office.]

DIANE: I'm glad you came with me.
RUSSELL: I'd rather we didn't have to be here.

DIANE: I need you for moral support. I've got a few things on my mind I'd like to get straight, but I don't know if it's the right time to bring them up.

RUSSELL: I think you need some better answers than you've been getting.

[Dr. Grieve enters.]

DR. GRIEVE: Hello, Dr. Grieve. You remember my husband, Russell.

DR. GRIEVE: [Shakes Russell's hand.] Good to see you again. So, Diane, how are you feeling today?

DIANE: A little better, thank you.

DR. GRIEVE: Not so much pain?

DIANE: No, the pain's better, but I'm wondering about what . . . Well, you know . . . about the next stage.

DR. GRIEVE: Well, it's a bit early to be concerned about that. Though the cancer is metastasizing, nothing's going to happen right away. You should be comfortable for quite a while.

DIANE: But I can't help thinking . . .

DR. GRIEVE: Trust me. You don't need to worry. Are you okay with the medication I've given you? You must tell me if it isn't working, but I don't want to give you too much if it isn't necessary. And how's the digestion?

[Diane and Russell exchange a look.]

DIANE: It could be better.

DR. GRIEVE: This medication might be better for the nausea or stomach upset. Take one pill before meals, until you adjust to the dosage. Then increase as needed. Of course, we can always cut back if you're having problems, or try something else. But the pain . . . Well, it can be a bit of a trade-off.

DIANE: Trade-off? . . .

DR. GRIEVE: That's right.

RUSSELL: The lesser of two evils, you could say.

[The doctor reaches in her desk drawer and pulls out a couple of brochures.]

DR. GRIEVE: Why don't you take these? There's some information here about how to deal with pain management.

DIANE: Thanks. *[Studies them somewhat absently. Russell reaches over and takes them from her.]* I'm wondering how long it's going to go on . . . You know, how long it will take before I'm . . . well, unable to function.

DR. GRIEVE: That's hard to say. I don't like to give a prognosis because I could be wrong. Anyway, why don't we just take things one day at a time?

DIANE: But am I going to be very ill? While I worry about the pain, I know there are other things I just couldn't handle.

DR. GRIEVE: I wouldn't think about that now. If the pain gets worse, we have many ways of keeping you comfortable.

RUSSELL: To tell you the truth, I'm concerned about Diane losing control of the process if she ends up in the hospital. What about a Living Will? Is that something she should look into?

DR. GRIEVE: That's a possibility. If you're really worried about that kind of thing, talk to your lawyer. Make sure everything is in order. That can do a lot to ease your mind.

RUSSELL: But there are a few other things . . .

DIANE: That's all right, Russell. I'm sure we can manage. Thank you, Doctor. I suppose we shouldn't take up any more of your time.

DR. GRIEVE: You're welcome. But are you sure you're okay?

DIANE: Yes, I'm fine, at the moment.

DR. GRIEVE: Good. Now if you'll just speak to the nurse on your way out, she'll set up another appointment in a couple of weeks. In the meantime, give me a call if you have any problems. Okay?

DIANE: Yes, thanks.

[Doctor leaves. Russell and Diane look at each other and shrug their shoulders. Russell takes Diane's hand as they get up to go.]

Figure 1. Diane and Russell Hart in Dr. Grieve's office.

SCENE 2

[Lights up on freeze action in Russell and Diane's kitchen.
Live action starts.]

LARRY: *[On phone]* I'm just waiting for Mom and Dad to get back from the doctor's office. We're having a kind of a conference . . . I hope it doesn't take too long, but Harriet's in charge, and you know what that means. Right! *[Looking at Harriet and laughing, but she is not amused.]* I'll get back as soon as I can. Bye.
[Hangs up.]

HARRIET:	Not funny, Larry. But I understand. Jokes are your way of hiding out.
LARRY:	Oh, for God's sake, Harriet. Don't you ever laugh at yourself?
RUTH:	I wish you wouldn't swear in front of me, Larry.
LARRY:	But, Jesus, I only said . . . Oh, sorry!
HARRIET:	Oh, Ruth, please! Mother has pancreatic cancer, and it's inoperable. The best thing we can do is face the facts.
LARRY:	But do we have to do it now? I've got a lot of deadlines at work.
HARRIET:	Yes, we do. Mother's doing okay now, but she won't always feel so well. And we don't want to leave things until she's really ill.
LARRY:	Be prepared, eh Harriet? You always were a good Boy Scout. *[Grins at his own joke. Looks at his watch.]* Hmm. I wonder what's keeping them.
HARRIET:	You can remain in denial if you want to, Larry, but . . .
LARRY:	Oh, "de Nile!" Isn't that a river in Egypt?
HARRIET:	Very funny! Anyway, it's not helping her if we pretend nothing's happening. A lot of people believe that if you acknowledge death early on, you'll have more time to prepare and that way have an easier passage. . . . Oh, hello, Mother. Dad.
	[All three look at the door as Diane and Russell enter.]
RUTH:	You look tired, Mother. Sit down here.
DIANE:	I am a bit tired.
RUTH:	Let me get you a cup of coffee. *[Brings coffee.]*
DIANE:	But what are you all doing here? I haven't forgotten someone's birthday, have I?
LARRY:	Yeah, mine! No, just kidding!
HARRIET:	I asked them to come, Mother. I guess I should have told you, but I didn't want you to worry. You see, I think we ought to talk as a family—start making some decisions.
DIANE:	You're right, Harriet. We need to talk. I've been putting it off because I didn't want to upset you. And you all have such busy lives, it's hard to get you all together.
HARRIET:	So how did it go? What did the doctor say?
DIANE:	Not much really. Just talked about the medication.
RUSSELL:	She gave us some brochures about pain management. That was about it.
HARRIET:	What about the progress of the cancer? Did she tell you what to expect?
DIANE:	Not really.
HARRIET:	Are you going to have to go into the hospital?
DIANE:	I'm not sure.
HARRIET:	What about home care? Did she mention that?
RUSSELL:	I wanted to get into some of that, but your Mother didn't think . . .
DIANE:	As far as I can tell, she's doing her job. The rest of it is not her responsibility, is it?

LARRY: But, Mom, you don't want to waste too much time with this doctor. If she isn't telling you what you need to know, maybe you'd better find someone who will.

DIANE: I don't think so, Larry. She knows my case. It might not be a good idea to change now. I'm sure we'll manage. *[Looks at Russell.]*

LARRY: Okay, I give up.

RUTH: I'm sure Mother's doctor has her best interests at heart.

HARRIET: But, Mother, it's your life. You have to take charge. Ask more questions. And keep asking until you get some answers. Otherwise, you could be overtaken by events.

DIANE: Taking charge isn't as easy for me as it is for you, Harriet. Anyway, the things I worry about most aren't things the doctor can do anything about.

LARRY: Like what?

DIANE: Like being afraid of becoming a burden. I don't want to get to the point where I'm so drugged or helpless that I can't do things for myself—I don't want to put my family through that.

RUTH: You wouldn't be a burden on us. The Bible says, "Honor thy father and mother." We wouldn't mind looking after you.

DIANE: But I *do* mind. I can't stand the thought of being dependent on other people. It's not the way I've lived, and it's not the way I want to end my life.

RUSSELL: I hate to hear you talk like that. I can't stand the thought of you in pain *[trying not to cry]*.

DIANE: I don't want any of you to have to watch me suffer. That's why I want to be sure that when and if the time comes, you'll respect my wishes.

RUTH: What wishes?

DIANE: For one thing, my wish not to be kept alive after I'm a burden.

RUTH: I hope you're not thinking about doing anything foolish. You're not thinking about taking your own life, are you?

DIANE: I'm just thinking about how to get through this with as much dignity as possible. I don't want to be kept hanging on after there's no quality of life left.

RUTH: *[Puts arm around her mother.]* Don't say that. It sounds like you're giving up. You know we're all praying for you. And miracles do happen.

HARRIET: Well, I don't think it's foolish to want to end your own suffering. That's what I would do if I had to. Personally, I'd rather not be hooked up to a bunch of machines. When it comes to dying, our society really knows how to torture people.

RUTH: But you can't just get rid of people because they're sick—or old. Nobody has the right to make that decision. God made us, and when it's our time to go, He'll call us.

HARRIET:	But if someone would rather choose death than suffering, they should be able to make that decision.
LARRY:	Maybe, but there are too many problems with that solution.
HARRIET:	Well, it can't be right to make people suffer through a painful end.
LARRY:	Listen, time's flying here. This is a fascinating subject, but maybe we could debate it another time.
RUTH:	I don't think we need to debate anything. I think we need to do more praying together. There's a lot of comfort in sharing our fears with God.
DIANE:	I agree, Ruth.
HARRIET:	Prayer's fine, but it's not a substitute for information.
LARRY:	Then let's get some information!
HARRIET:	That's what I'm suggesting, but all I get from you is a lame joke.
LARRY:	Don't sulk, Harriet. It shows your wrinkles. Listen, . . .
HARRIET:	Listen? That would be a novelty around here.
LARRY:	I'm sure there must be humane alternatives to suffering and indignity. We just have to find out what they are.
HARRIET:	Let me check my hearing, Larry. Did you actually say something constructive for a change?
LARRY:	Your hearing's okay—if you ever stopped talking long enough to hear anyone else. What about arranging for some home help, Mother? I could help pay for it.
DIANE:	Thanks, Larry, but I'm not sure I'd like someone from outside coming in and taking over.
HARRIET:	Well, I won't be able to do everything. I have a full-time job.
LARRY:	Yeah, well, with this new shop I'm opening, I barely have time to breathe. Which reminds me, I've got to make a call. *[Goes to phone.]*
RUTH:	I'll pitch in as much as I can. I would have to give up some of my volunteer work, but after all, charity begins at home.
HARRIET:	But I'm sure that's not the whole answer. We're all going to need some extra support. Don't you think so, Dad?
RUSSELL:	I suppose so, but not if it's going to upset your mother.
LARRY:	*[Returns from making phone call.]* Damn. The line's busy. Well, did you get everything settled, Harriet? Can we go now?
HARRIET:	Sometimes you really get on my nerves, Larry.
LARRY:	Hell, sometimes I get on my own nerves!
HARRIET:	Maybe we should look at some other options. I wish we knew more about programs for people with mother's concerns.
RUTH:	I've heard something about the hospice at our church. Someone said that it's not for everyone, and often the family doctor isn't too involved.
DIANE:	I don't think I'd like that.
LARRY:	The people are supposed to be very nice, very caring, but it must be a pretty depressing place—everybody there knowing their time's up.

HARRIET:	That's right, Larry. Think positively. Personally, I like the idea of a place that recognizes that dying is part of the cycle of life. Don't you think it would be good, Mother, to have the support of people who are specialists in this area?
DIANE:	I suppose so, but I don't want to be in an institution, surrounded by a bunch of strangers. I don't care how nice they are. It's not the same as being in your own home. Ruth, could I have more coffee, please?
RUTH:	Of course.
RUSSELL:	Look, I'm sure we can take care of mother ourselves. We don't need to involve a lot of other people.
RUTH:	You know, we're not getting anywhere with this.
HARRIET:	Wait a minute, Ruth. We're not finished yet.
LARRY:	On, no! Here we go again.
HARRIET:	We still haven't made any decisions.
LARRY:	Then I'll make one. You take over, Harriet. Just let us know what you want us to do.
HARRIET:	I know you don't mean that, Larry, but there's germ of sense in it. Maybe we should pick one of us to take charge when we're dealing with the hospital.
RUTH:	As long as you're not the one who decides, Harriet. Your ideas are just too different from mine. I wouldn't feel comfortable. Anyway, I still don't think it's going to come to that.
LARRY:	And if it does, Dad can decide anything important. He's the one who's most likely to be in touch with Mother's wishes. So that's settled.
DIANE:	Yes, but what if I'm completely out of it? What if I can't say what I want.
LARRY:	Then Dad can make the decision. The spouse has the final authority anyway.
HARRIET:	Not always. It depends.
LARRY:	Depends on what?
HARRIET:	Well, for example, what if Dad weren't able to take over? What if he were ill or incapacitated in some way? Then what would we do? Sorry, Dad, I don't like to raise that kind of possibility, but we need to plan for all contingencies.
RUSSELL:	That's okay. I understand. And you're right. In fact, I was thinking maybe we ought to look into this business of a Living Will.
RUTH:	I thought a Living Will was something like insurance, to make sure your family is looked after when you're gone.
HARRIET:	No, it's more like a declaration of intent. You give instructions about what kinds of treatment you're willing to undergo and when it's okay for them to give up and let you go.
RUTH:	Oh, I couldn't do that.
LARRY:	I've heard Living Wills aren't foolproof, because they can't cover everything and they aren't always respected.

RUSSELL: Then it seems like a lot of trouble for nothing.

HARRIET: But at least we ought to find out.

DIANE: I know you're trying to help, Harriet. You all are, and I'm grateful. But all this is suddenly very tiring. I didn't realize how much this morning took out of me. Maybe I ought to rest for awhile.

RUSSELL: Could we leave this until another time?

RUTH: Sure, Dad. We'll go and let you two take it easy.

HARRIET: But nothing's resolved. What have we accomplished?

RUSSELL: I think we've made some progress, but we still have a way to go. Maybe next week we can meet again, if you can find the time.

HARRIET: Good idea, Dad. Is that okay with you, Larry?

LARRY: Sure. I'm up for that. Just let me know when. See you later, Mom. *[Gives her a goodbye kiss. Hugs his father. Exit Larry.]*

RUTH: Me, too. I'll give you a call in the morning, Mom. *[Hugs Diane.]* God bless.

DIANE: Bye, dear.

RUSSELL: Bye, Love. Thanks.

RUTH: You coming, Harriet?

HARRIET: I'm just going to wash these things up for Mother. *[Exit Ruth.]*

RUSSELL: You go ahead, Harriet. I'll do that.

HARRIET: You sure? Okay, then. See you later. Bye, Mother.

[Exit Harriet. Freeze on scene of Diane and Russell holding hands, leaning against each other. Lights down.]

Figure 2. The Hart family in Russell and Diane's kitchen.

SCENE 3
Three months later

*[The scene opens with Diane resting on the living room couch.
Ruth, Harriet, Larry, and Russell are with her.
Larry is serving coffee.]*

HARRIET:	So when is your next appointment with the doctor, Mother?
DIANE:	Next week. Ever since our first get-together, I've been determined to get the information I need at each visit.
RUSSELL:	We realized we had to take responsibility for finding what we needed to know, so we started going with a list of questions.
DIANE:	And if the doctor didn't have the answers, we were prepared to ask her to refer us to someone who did.
RUSSELL:	We took some good books out of the library—*Love Medicine and Miracles* and *Final Gifts*. And several others that helped us understand the process.
HARRIET:	That's wonderful, Dad. I've been reading, too, and I really liked *The Last Dance*. Is there anything else in the way of information I can get for you—maybe on the Internet?
DIANE:	Your father's done some research on palliative care, and we decided to register for the hospice program. It's not at all what we thought it was. Maybe you'd like to read the handbook.
HARRIET:	Of course!
RUSSELL:	One of the best things about the program is having people who listen and help you deal with your feelings and worries.
DIANE:	The people at hospice know a lot about how to control pain and other symptoms.
HARRIET:	And what about your doctor? Is she supportive?
DIANE:	Fortunately, yes. Because I really wanted her to be part of the process.
HARRIET:	What have you found out about Living Wills, Larry?
LARRY:	I talked to a friend who's a lawyer, and actually, in British Columbia, we're talking about something new in guardianship legislation, called a Representation Agreement. You appoint a representative who has authority to look after your affairs if you're incapacitated.
RUSSELL:	That would be good. Mother could be sure her wishes are respected.
LARRY:	You should be Mother's representative, Dad, since you two are so much in tune with each other.
RUTH:	It's probably a good idea to have something in writing. Otherwise, it could be a problem for the rest of us. We don't always agree, and without your wishes to guide us, Mother, we would get into a terrible tangle.

DIANE: I'm glad you feel that way, Ruth.

RUTH: Mother, I talked to my minister, and he was very helpful. He talked about death as doorway, a passage from one kind of life into another, a beginning rather than an ending. Afterward I felt a lot better.

DIANE: That is comforting, Ruth. I might like to talk to him myself, if you think he would come to see me.

RUTH: I'm sure he would.

DIANE: I'm going to need a lot of help with this. It's not going to be easy, but I can make it better by accepting responsibility—just as you said, Harriet. I know now I have to take charge and try to find some peace of mind by being prepared. I can't be sure what's going to happen at the end, and I hate that. But I also can't dwell on the unknown, the negative.

HARRIET: Do you have any ideas, Mother, about the way you see things from here on?

DIANE: A few. I want to be with my family. I want to be surrounded by your love and your strength. I don't want some nineteenth-century scene with everyone standing around looking funereal. I'd like to have some time with each of you to look back at the past, and maybe we could get the family photo albums out and look at them together, maybe help you fill in your memories. I want to have my wake before I'm gone. And, Russell, I'd like you to dig out our old Glenn Miller records, the ones we used to dance to when we were in college. I want to hear them all again and share those memories with you.

LARRY: Well, you'll need some champagne to toast all those memories. I'll see that you have plenty!

HARRIET: And I'll supply the chocolates! I know your secret vice.

DIANE: And I won't feel any guilt about indulging myself. Wonderful! *[pause]* And I want to involve my close friends, too. I've been thinking of inviting each one to lunch and giving them a gift, something of mine that they would appreciate. Do you think that would be all right?

RUSSELL: I think that would be fine—wonderful, in fact.

DIANE: I want to make every second count. And I'd like all of you to help me do that.

RUTH: We're happy to, Mother.

RUSSELL: You kids are great. I can't tell you how much this means to us.

HARRIET: It's a relief to have something positive to do.

LARRY: So, you got your way after all, Harriet!

HARRIET: No, Larry, we're all just struggling to find a way.

LARRY: Well, how's this for a start? *[Brings out a box of chocolates.]*

EVERYONE: *[improvising]* This is great! Oh, good! Lovely! I want the one with the cherry center. Leave me the caramel!
[Freeze action with everyone gathered around the box of chocolates. Lights down.]

END

Editor's Note: For those interested in the books discussed in the script: M. Callahan and P. Helley, *Final Gifts,* Poseidon Press, New York, 1992; L. DeSpelder and A. Strickland, *The Last Dance,* Mayfield, Mountain View, California, 1983; and B. Siegel, *Love, Medicine & Miracles,* Harper & Row, New York, 1986.

Crisis in the Cafeteria

Maria Trozzi

I pulled into my garage late one Friday afternoon, feeling weary but satisfied with the workday just ending. As I came into the house my junior-high-age daughter greeted me with exasperation. "Mom, where have you been? We couldn't reach you. Your secretary has been calling all afternoon. There was a terrible death in Derby. A kid killed himself in school!"

With adrenalin pumping throughout my body, I returned the telephone call from the principal of a mid-sized urban high school. I learned that four hours earlier, a sophomore boy had, without warning, stood up in the center of the cafeteria, pulled a 22-caliber gun from his knapsack, and shot himself in his right temple in front of three hundred peers. His parents, both health-care workers at the local hospital, were alerted and were waiting for his arrival by ambulance at the emergency entrance. It was quickly determined that his critical condition required the services of the major tertiary care hospital fifty minutes away. Sam was airlifted by helicopter to a Trauma Center. He would die several hours later.

That afternoon, as Sam fought a battle he would lose, the principal was meeting in what was to be renamed the "crisis room" with nearly thirty mental health professionals who had heard about the shooting, called Derby High School, and offered their help. Dr. Jack Reardon, Derby's principal, requested my help. What should we do to help the students, the parents, the teachers? How should we use the volunteer helpers? As we spoke the four major television channels' reporters were on the front steps of the school, interviewing hysterical students and anyone who would talk. What should be told to the media? The questions were flying. I asked Dr. Reardon to tell me what had happened in the aftermath of the shooting.

I learned that immediately following the shooting, the cafeteria was voluntarily cleared of the students who had witnessed the event. Cafeteria workers and teachers eating in the adjacent faculty dining room raced to the scene. One used the phone in the cafeteria to call 911. The school nurse held Sam's bloody head in her skirt and quietly pleaded with him to hold on. One of the male teachers found Dr. Reardon, who went to the P.A. system immediately and alerted the entire student body that there had been an accident; a student was hurt; students would hear ambulance sirens. He requested those students who were roaming the corridors to come to the auditorium and the other students to stay in their classrooms. The moment that the injured student was safely in the ambulance, all students and faculty would be called to the auditorium to be informed.

By using the P.A. to gather students together, Jack had ignored the cardinal rule for sharing information in a crisis but in this case it was a brilliant management move. When the safety of students and faculty is a consideration, the leader must do whatever is necessary to contain the situation. Had he not moved swiftly and offered his students information directly, I expect that many distraught students who had witnessed this violent act would have jumped into cars to follow the ambulance or simply have fled the building altogether. To make the situation more difficult, a light snow was falling this Friday in mid-February, and more snow was forecasted.

Jack met with all students and faculty in the auditorium moments after the ambulance pulled away and gave them as many details as he knew. He told them the identity of the student, as well as Sam's apparent condition. Students were then told to return to classes for the last period, and after school if they wished, they could remain in the building. The school would remain open until 11 P.M. that evening; many teachers and counselors would be available. Every forty-five minutes Jack updated those in the library on Sam's condition. Several students had remained in the building. Others came and went. Jack told me that the school was to be open throughout the weekend for students to gather together. Regarding the media, I suggested that he should emphatically request the media not to intrude upon the school community during this time, but to return on Saturday for an interview with the principal and crisis team. By then we would have had an opportunity to talk to the crisis committee about the way the media could actually help in the wake of this traumatic event. I told Dr. Reardon that I was available for telephone consultation throughout the evening, and I planned to arrive at the high school early Saturday morning.

I arrived shortly before 9 A.M. at the high school. The quiet of the snow falling on my windshield contrasted to the chaos that awaited me. The vintage pre-World War II high school building reminded me of my old high school, complete with red brick exterior and hospital-green interior corridors. A few students were scattered throughout the halls in quiet conversation. In the main office, there was a quietness although several people were milling about. Sam had died during the night.

Several people introduced themselves to me: the city counselor, the assistant superintendent, and Jack, the principal. I had many unanswered questions; however, Jack had been at the school all night and looked exhausted and nervous. He provided details of Sam's death. Sam had been brain dead since early the evening before; life support was shut off much later, after the viable organs had been harvested from his fifteen-year-old body. We went down the corridor to a planning meeting. There I met a cadre of twenty-five to thirty psychologists, counselors, trauma specialists, teachers, and the school nurse. I was introduced as the trainer-consultant, whose role would be to provide leadership to the planning committee and direct the school response to this crisis in the days ahead. The Good Grief Protocol,[1] or plan of action, aims to help create a healthy, safe environment in which the school community can understand, grieve, commemorate, and eventually go on. There are four

---

[1] Of the Good Grief Program of Boston Medical Center and Judge Baker Children's Center, Boston [1].

psychological tasks that youngsters must accomplish at the time of death if they are to have "good grief"; that is, a grief that allows children and adolescents to master or strengthen coping skills. Rather than provide a chronology of the next four days of consultation, I will discuss the principal issues that faced us and the responses.

GOALS

Our first goal in the planning sessions was to create an environment of *inclusiveness*. Simply stated, "we're all in this together." This was not simply a school issue; it demanded a community response. Although we would look immediately at which people were at greater risk and assist them, information and support groups would be aimed at all school personnel, including cafeteria workers and custodial staff, all parents, teachers at the middle school and elementary school, and the community at large.

I needed to quickly learn the "culture" of the school and the community so that I could gain their confidence to take what seemed to be an "overwhelming" event and turn it into one that was "manageable." I also needed to build consensus to implement each decision we made. And I needed to build a solid working relationship with the principal, whose leadership would be most important in the days ahead.

THE FIRST TASK: UNDERSTANDING

While firmly believing that youngsters must understand *what happened and why* in order to recover from any loss, I knew how complicated understanding becomes when the death is a suicide, not only a suicide, but a planned, witnessed act of violence. We would focus considerable time and energy making meaning out of this event. The question: why?

It is human nature to distance ourselves from horrific events. Find a reason. Any reason that would make Sam's "situation" different so that we as parents and teachers would not feel as much "at risk." Sam's peers expressed the same need for explanation, since if Sam could do it, then any one of them could.

The gun. An act of violence no one could imagine. Not in this school. Not in this community. Over and over, I heard people say, "Violence happens other places! Not here!" But it had.

Sam had carried the gun in his knapsack throughout the morning schedule. He had attended only his English class. In retrospect, his teacher was appalled at the thought that he actually had the gun in her class. He could have killed other students. He could have shot her. The students reiterated similar concerns about the cafeteria. What if he had fired at them first, or had inadvertently shot one of them in his suicide?

We planned support sessions for both Saturday and Sunday. My work was to help each group validate their fears and challenge the "magical thinking." What might they have been able to do the prevent his death? Why didn't they recognize he was at risk? Will other parents miss the "signs" in their children? Could this happen again?

As for "explaining" the suicide, I encouraged the groups not to point a finger of blame at those possibly responsible: a difficult relationship with a parent was one rumor; a girl friend who broke up with him a few days before was another. Although we can look at the adolescent suicide literature and list risk factors, such as a familial history of suicide or mental illness, sexual identification issues, history of drugs and alcohol, I don't believe that listing these factors to his surviving peers or bewildered parents serves them. Rather, I tell them we know that adolescents often deny the physical consequences of suicide. They see the act as a "permanent solution to a temporary problem." They are unable to see beyond the act itself. When I asked Sam's peers what he "gave up by killing himself" (I didn't euphemize the act when speaking to his peers), there were only three responses: his license, the prom, and graduation.

I reframed the death around the issue of problem solving. Sam was not a good problem solver. In fact, he apparently *isolated* himself from those who could have helped. Perhaps his problems felt so overwhelming he felt they were unmentionable. Perhaps he didn't let anyone know he was deeply troubled. He found the "magical" solution to his problems by killing himself.

Developmental Issues of Understanding

I met with Sam's fifth-grade brother's teacher for a consultation. She needed to know how Sam's brother might respond, and how she could assist him and his classmates. I urged her to acknowledge Sam's death when talking to his brother and then focus the conversation on how his classmates could help him. Most preadolescent youngsters want anonymity when faced with a sibling's death. I told her to expect that but to check in with him from time to time as the weeks turn into months. He will need her quiet, consistent, non-intrusive support.

In addition, I met with all teachers, administrators, and counselors from the town's elementary and middle schools for a two-hour training session. This anxious, concerned group fired questions at me trying to understand how to integrate their personal grief with their professional concern for their students. "What should my posture be? If they don't ask, should I not mention it? You don't think first graders should be told it was a suicide, do you? How do you explain suicide to young children?" Given the nature of this tragedy, even trained staff probably would request some on-site consultation.

I provided a developmental perspective of a child's understanding of death from preschool through adolescence. What are the predictable issues embedded in each developmental stage? What will be required of the adult assessing the child? Most important, I told them to let the students be their teachers. Listen to them. Respond authentically. And, as Earl Grollman states, if it's "unmentionable, it's unmanageable" [2], alluding to the fact that children need details, particularly the grubby ones that adults find difficult to offer. The child will offer the adult hints as to how much to say. Ask children if they understand what are they troubled about, what don't they understand yet, and how can we understand together. There are times when details are not available when we first talk. I ask the children how it feels not to know.

Children need a safe environment in which to mourn; adults must help to provide that safe environment.

THE SECOND TASK: GRIEVING

I asked adults to avoid what I call "competitive grief": Who is hurting the most? Why is he or she carrying on, anyway? How long will she be like this? Such value judgments are understandable at a difficult time like this; yet they isolate people when they need the most understanding. Adolescents, in particular, engage in this competitive grieving. I encouraged their responses of sadness, anger, guilt, terror, and numbness, and validated as normal their somatic responses to their grief. They talked about feeling faint, terrible headaches, and stomach problems, not being able to breathe, or to sleep. I described differences they might observe between boys and girls as well as delayed grief responses. I addressed children's and adolescents' mourning differences and what adults could predict in the ensuing days and weeks.

In the midst of crisis, it is easy for a group to polarize. Yet this is a time for increased *understanding* of one another's vulnerability. Many teachers may already be grieving other losses, such as a chronic illness in the family, a death, or divorce. The trauma of Sam's death could restimulate other griefs from their past, deaths that they may have not resolved.

Modeling

I met with teaching staff Saturday and Sunday (both sessions were voluntary) and Monday morning (mandatory). We began each session by "checking in" with each other. I encouraged teachers not to worry because they were not grief therapists; instead, what was required was their authenticity and openness with one another and with their students. Anxiety about facing their students on Monday was "paralyzing" for some. I suggested rehearsing a classroom dialogue in which they, posing as students, asked the "unmentionable" questions that they feared and I answered with simple directness, giving as much detail as was asked for, and with real feelings: I appreciated their fearfulness of entering the cafeteria, returning to the place where the violence had taken place. I validated their anger at Sam doing this "to them." We talked about suicide as an *interactive* death. They needed to express their anger at the person who had done this, making some of them witness this act of violence, their fear that it could have even been more tragic had he turned the gun on them. Once again, I cautioned teachers about their need to find a reason for the suicide and the danger of doing so. I particularly encouraged the men teachers to know how empowering it would be for their students to see them grieve. My constant message was, "Don't be strong, be authentic."

The Format

Throughout the weekend, more and more students appeared at the high school, joined by several counselors, therapists, ministers, youth workers, and parents. They could engage in activities such as volleyball and basketball or join informal group support sessions. Mostly, they perceived the school, a very threatening place on Friday, as a haven for their confused, frightened feelings. The townspeople responded by providing anything they could imagine to lighten the burden for the kids, the school, and their neighbors. They provided an abundance of food, free taxi rides for any student who needed one; the local cable TV provided the times of parent-teacher sessions, and so forth. The mayor, city counselors, and superintendents were highly visible in the school throughout the weekend. They helped to affirm the nature of the crisis: one of their own had died; a school community was in crisis; this was a community response.

Of the other individuals who had requested time, I met with Sam's next door neighbors (whose gun Sam took the morning of the suicide), the cafeteria workers, the nurse, and Sam's English teacher, who was bewildered about why Sam attended only her class that morning.

The Principal

It was important to form a quick working relationship with the principal, who provides the leadership; gaining trust of the leaders is fundamental to executing any plan. In this situation, the principal's intuitive style and responsiveness to students' needs were correct. The "knee-jerk" response more often found in administrators is to manage the crisis, control the chaos and normalize as quickly as possible. Particularly with a suicide, administrators hide behind the fear of "glorifying" the death. The consequences are unhealthy as grieving goes underground. Jack's response was to create an inclusive environment in which healing could take place in the near future and the months ahead. He was grateful for my managerial role, I was equally grateful for his humanity and spirit of openness and cooperation.

The Parents

In two meetings with parents, and in a televised interview repeated several times, I emphasized what to expect from their adolescents in the wake of their friend's death. Adolescents want to grieve with their peers; they are often not able to share their intense feelings with their parents. However, they do want their parents to be available; and parents often feel frustrated since they want to be more pro-active. It is simply not what is needed. They may find their youngster more clingy, not wanting to engage in anything that could be construed as high-risk; for example, even walking down the street at night to visit a friend, an activity they may have engaged in countless times, might make them feel scared. Acknowledge that the fear is normal and in time will pass. Sadness and anger are the principal feelings in normal grief. Anger may present itself in non-direct ways like moodiness and aggression that challenge the adults who live with them. Also, their mourning is sometimes masked by their normal tasks of adolescence.[2]

---

[2] Separation from parents, sexual identification, moral development, vocational choices.

Parents were desperate to receive information on warning signs of suicide and symptoms of adolescent depression. I did provide them with some written information; however, it has been my experience that when parents are making sense of a teen suicide they feel helpless and scared. If Sam, who apparently showed no particular warning signs, could do this terrible thing, then how can they protect their own teen from this apparent act of impulsiveness? Reframed, their anxiety about suicide is an instance of their ability to help their children deal with stressful life events, to help them develop problem-solving strategies, to learn how to share their feelings before they feel overwhelmed by them. That is where the action is for parents. I shared with them my own anxieties as a parent of two teenagers. I suggested that in the weeks ahead the community might respond by helping parents to address these issues in a workshop format.

The Mental Health Community Linkage

We felt it imperative to involve the community professionals, value their participation, and assure the community that they would continue to respond to needs in the days and weeks that followed, long after my role as trainer/consultant was over. One professional provided linkage to the local mental health community and, as we assessed our needs for the week that was to unfold, placed different people in different positions according to their availability and particular expertise.

Monday

We decided to delay school opening until 10:00 A.M. to allow all staff to feel more prepared for the day by providing them with two hours of training and support. For about one-third of the staff this was the first time they had been to school since Friday. Feeling that sense of unity was mandatory, we spent a few minutes "checking in with each other." I suspected correctly that those who had not participated in the weekend's activities at school would feel left out and judged. For that reason, I asked the group that had been here to "check in" with someone who had not. This helped to bring the entire faculty of nearly one hundred up to speed.

The faculty had stated emphatically that they needed a recipe to get through their classes; how would they talk about it, what would happen, how could they hide their own fears and vulnerability? Knowing the importance of putting ideas on paper, I provided the staff with a paper entitled "Do's and Don'ts" [Appendix A], which reminds us to be real and authentic. They found it helpful.

Another issue they needed to address was the fear of being in the cafeteria. We needed to acknowledge the fear directly. It was also important to provide an expectation that we would eat lunch there. The staff wasn't sure about my strategy. Some teachers felt the need to assure students of an alternate setting for those who were too frightened to go in. I assured them that we would react with sensitivity but if we suggested an alternate place to eat for those students having trouble being in the cafeteria, this would necessarily divide the group. There was the additional problem of weaning them back to the cafeteria later on. Instead, my suggestion was to face the issue together as a group with an abundance of adult support. This theory proved to be correct. Most of the students ate their lunch in the cafeteria. Some students had difficulty the first day and didn't stay. However, by the second day the cafeteria appeared to have the normal level of noise and activity. I assured the teachers that I expected most of the students to walk into school wanting it to feel "normal" in spite of the traumatic death on Friday. We could provide them with that structure.

My final words to the teachers were, again, to let the students be *their* teachers and to be *authentic*. Several volunteer helpers and I were available to assist them at any time during the day.

At 10:00 A.M. the doors opened and I could hear the sounds of metal lockers opening and students' voices. The sounds of nine hundred students filling the corridors encouraged me; I met with the entire student body although I generally don't encourage meeting in such a large group for sharing information or support. However, the weekend had diffused the emotion of the crisis quite a bit, and I felt there was value in the group coming together. I wanted to share a few key themes with the entire group, specifically:

1. the explaining of Sam's death in the context of problem-solving,
2. the need to take care of one another and make room for individual grief reactions,
3. the acknowledged fear of the cafeteria,
4. strategies and support provisions throughout the day and the remainder of the week,
5. information update regarding the wake and memorial service, and
6. the opportunity to search for meaning in Sam's death.

As the entire student body streamed in, I saw a challenge presenting itself. Sitting on the floor in front of the first row was a group of about fifteen students. Some were carrying two-liter bottles of Sprite or Coke. They were locked arm in arm and swaying to a song that they were singing very softly. As Jack attempted to gain the whole group's attention from the stage, these students provided a real distraction. It was clear to me that this small group needed to be noticed. The significance of their pain needed to be recognized. When I was introduced, rather than going to the microphone, I crouched down at the edge of the stage and spoke to the young woman whom I presumed to be the leader, "I can't quite hear the lyrics. Will you share them with me?" She got up and approached me and sang a few bars quietly between her tears. I told her the lyrics were lovely and wondered if she would write them down for me. She nodded and returned to her place. The swaying and the singing stopped. I had the students' attention. In the auditorium—students in their seats, flanked by dozens of teachers, counselors, and others who were on hand to help—we sensed we were all in this together, and the students could feel the support.

After this meeting, students resumed an abbreviated class schedule with the understanding that there was ongoing support in different places throughout the building. The mental health "helpers" had created triage for dealing with student self-referrals. This included informal groups, individual sessions with counselors and psychologists, and psychiatric referrals, if necessary, to the local hospital. Three referrals were made that first day.

I met with two other large groups that morning: the sophomore class and any students who felt they needed more assistance. The self-selected group numbered approximately 150; several were present in the cafeteria when Sam shot himself, some were his best friends, soccer teammates, neighbors. These smaller groups took on a more intimate quality; we were able to dialogue about feelings, somatic responses to pain, and questions still unanswered.

The entire faculty met at the close of school to debrief. They looked like a very different group from the one I met at 7:30 A.M. They were both proud of themselves and emotionally spent.

Next Steps

On Tuesday, the regular schedule was resumed. If students needed further support during the day, they needed a pass; three additional counseling people were on hand. The day went without incident. Two church halls adjacent to the funeral home were open for the kids to "hang out" if they desired. They did. Especially in the evening. The evening of the wake was bitterly cold and students, parents, and teachers lined up for blocks outside the funeral home. They were predictably emotional, and once again there was an acknowledgment of their feelings and the need for being with one another and with caring adults. I also spent some time with a group of cafeteria workers; several of them had been "first on the scene" at the sound of the gunshot.

That afternoon, we invited the print, TV, and radio media to an interview. Although we were not at the end of this crisis, there was much to be learned from the way in which the community had responded, and we felt the timing was appropriate to talk about some themes thus far. If we were to find some hidden "opportunity," it could only be in the modeling of a protocol used to help a community create an environment where mourning and resolution are possible.

THE THIRD TASK: COMMEMORATION

Commemoration, the third task as described by Sandra S. Fox, is simply remembering the person who died [3]. It is a way we affirm life and confirm the death of a friend, as embodied in wakes, memorial services, funerals, poetry, special music, journals, memory walls. The importance of commemoration cannot be overstated. It is empowering and allows us to "do something" in a positive way with our intense emotions of grief.

In general, schools commemorate too quickly; they want to "move on" and normalize. But commemoration should not be rushed; there is time for dealing with an empty student desk or a nursery school cubby. Also, commemoration should not be a whole school activity; rather, only those who wish to commemorate a death should participate.

Many schools particularly object to commemorating a suicidal death, fearing glorification and contagion. Years ago, schools often did not even acknowledge a death if it were presumed to be a suicide. However, school administrators are in a particularly vulnerable position when family members and classmates suggest the typical commemorative responses, such as scholarships, trophies, plaques, believing we give a dangerous message to the surviving students when we commemorate a suicidal death that way.

The difficult issue of commemoration for a suicidal death comes up frequently. Often there is intense pressure from the family to remember their child in a way that may add glorification. However, there is a difference between a family's commemoration of their child and a school's commemorative response. Unlike Sam's family, Dr. Reardon is responsible for nine hundred students and must consider the psycho-educational implications of commemoration.

In the days ahead, I suggested to the planning committee an alternative to the typical commemoration. A more positive approach might be to do a fund raiser in Sam's name with the purposes of helping students learn better problem-solving strategies and of giving meaning to Sam's death; he was unable to deal with whatever problems he had; they became insurmountable and his only solution was a permanent one—death. Perhaps his peers can learn from his death other alternatives that involve reaching out and asking for help.

THE FOURTH TASK: GOING ON

Going on—that is, returning comfortably to familiar activities—is easiest and healthiest after accomplishing the tasks of understanding, grieving, and commemorating. With this said, it is well known that these tasks are not linear. In fact, children and adolescents often talk about these tasks as part of a "wave." One returns to the tasks of understanding, of finding more meaning, of understanding more fully as the need for self-protection diminishes. "Going on" is not about forgetting. Rather, it is about integrating this experience appropriately within one's normal way of living. Anniversaries of the death and holidays are special times when grieving feels intense and renewed. A certain song, a certain smell, any number of things can create what is often called a "memory embrace," and those feelings must be honored.

For a community, the death of a friend creates in its crisis a sense of danger that is obvious. But there lies a hidden opportunity for reconnecting people through the power of the community's grief and pain. This reconnection can be observed when a nation grieves after a presidential assassination, the shuttle disaster, or the bombing in Oklahoma City.

After the formal commemorative rituals are over, the consequences of Sam's death will remain in this community's consciousness for some time. The challenges facing this community are complicated. The Good Grief protocol response to this crisis—as embraced here by the students and teachers, the mental health community, the parents, and even the media—can model a way of facing crises and can promote healing.

APPENDIX A

The Good Grief Program
of Boston Medical Center and Judge Baker Children's Center

Following a Crisis—A Checklist for Adults Helping Kids

DO: Express your authentic or real feelings; they serve as a model.

DO: Listen to each student and encourage the class to listen and talk, one at a time.

DO: Reflect or mirror students' feelings; it's validating.

DO: Encourage students to look after one another.

DO: Challenge their "magical feelings," such as "If only I had . . ."

DO: Make sure that everyone who wishes to contribute does; be inclusive.

DO: *Take Extra Care of Yourself,* especially at the end of each long day.

DON'T: Worry about not having answers. This is one time that the teacher doesn't necessarily know.

DON'T: Try to be strong for the kids (it's a cop-out).

DON'T: Forget to ask for support at any time. You will be regarded as enlightened, not needy.

DON'T: Fall into the easy trap of being judgmental about whose grief is worst, who is the more needy. It separates people.

REFERENCES

1. Good Grief Protocol, *Good Grief Program,* Boston Medical Center, Boston, 1997.
2. E. A. Grollman, *Explaining Death to Children,* Beacon Press, Boston, 1974.
3. S. S. Fox, *Good Grief: Helping Groups of Children When a Friend Dies,* NEAYC, Boston, 1988.

The Life and Death of
Yusuf Hawkins

Christina Schlesinger

Yusuf Hawkins was a young kid who wanted to buy a car. Finding an ad for a used car that sounded good, he made an appointment to go look at it. So it was that on one August evening, Yusuf, a young black male, set out with a couple of buddies to check out the car. They crossed town to Bensonhurst, a working class neighborhood.

A couple of white guys checked out Yusuf and his pals arriving. They didn't like what they saw: black dudes invading their turf. They didn't take the time to see what they were up to: not mayhem or mischief, but ordinary business, which could even boost the economy of Bensonhurst a bit. Instead, the white boys grabbed the African-American boys and began beating them with chains and baseball bats. While Yusuf's friends broke free, the white guys held fast to Yusuf and cracked his head open with their bats. Yusuf fell to his death, a Snickers bar clutched in his hand.

In 1991, I was invited to P.S. 75 in Manhattan to create a mural on the life and death of Yusuf Hawkins. The two 6-foot × 20-foot murals would illustrate poems about Yusuf written by eighth graders working with a poet in the schools; eventually they would find a permanent home on the auditorium walls.

Through the poetry workshop, the kids had immersed themselves in Yusuf's life and senseless death. A mix of African Americans and Latinos, the kids were not far in age and cultural background from Yusuf. They too might want to buy a used car some day and wander into the wrong neighborhood. They told me Yusuf's story from their point of view, focusing on the randomness of the killing: why Yusuf? What he would not have: a future, a family, a life. The awfulness of the event itself. The particular poignancy of the Snickers bar: candy, a symbol of childhood and simple pleasures. The terrible grief of Yusuf's mother, family, and friends. There must be some resolution, some hope, something to hold onto after all this. And that was envisioning a world without violence.

One panel would concentrate on his murder; the other, the aftermath of his death (see Figures 1 and 2). The long, narrow, vertical panel starts with a moonlit sky shining down on the red brick projects of Bensonhurst. Three young toughs hang out menacingly in front of the buildings, carrying chains and bats. Over their heads hovers a chain-encircled vision of fear: a clenched fist, a gun, a knife. As the eye travels down the panel, we find a car, second-hand but clean and shiny. Close to the

Figure 1. Students question violence and racism in a mural commemorating
Yusuf Hawkins (left-hand panel).

car, in a pool of blood, lies Yusuf: blank eyes stare out at the viewer while a lifeless
hand holds a Snickers bar. Over Yusuf's head a cloud of smoke floats: written on the
cloud are these words of the eighth-grade poets: "Why? Why do we have to live in
such a racist world? Why so much violence? And why you, Yusuf?"

The second panel shows Yusuf's funeral. Starting at the bottom of the canvas,
we see Yusuf in an open casket. On the side of the casket, we read: "August 23, 1989,

Figure 2. Coffin, mourners, and escalator to heaven shown in mural
by Yusuf Hawkins' classmates (right-hand panel).

on this day, a poor boy loses his life. He could have had a home, children, a wife."
Huge, oversized flowers and the tear-stained faces of family and friends surround the
casket. Above the funeral scene, an escalator marked "Up" leads to a pink fluffy
cloud. Emerging from the cloud, the brown-skinned, yellow-sleeved hand of God
welcomes Yusuf. On the cloud we read: "How does it feel to be with God in a world
with no violence?"

For the eighth graders of P.S. 75, the poetry workshop and the mural provided them with the opportunity to contemplate and process random violence and death. Writing and painting helped them to organize their emotional responses to Yusuf's killing and empower themselves against their fears. The killers in the mural are small, angry, and white; they are much smaller in scale than Yusuf who, in his death, dominates the mural. The used car is edged in gold paint as if to suggest something larger than a car, possibly a dream, a dream of all the possibilities dashed with Yusuf's death.

In the second mural, the outscale flowers and huge crying faces demand as much attention as Yusuf's casket. The flowers rivet the viewer: they are enormous, bigger even than the faces. The kids intuited something here: amidst grief and loss, we can find beauty. In fact, we *need* beauty at such times: we need to be reminded that life can be beautiful and is worth living. The "Up" escalator is a wonderful touch and a pure invention by the kids. It reassures us that the innocent Yusuf will go straight to heaven. What will he find in this pink-clouded heaven? A world without violence. That is their idea of heaven: a peaceful place. That is the resolution of Yusuf's life and death: the need, the *demand* for the end of strife.

Artists, poets, and painters are a natural resource for developing strategies of mourning. Visual and poetic metaphor shape inarticulate feeling and bridge the gap between inner confusion and outer resolution. Complex and painful emotions can be approached obliquely and in the creative acts of writing and painting, resolution, a way out, can be found. Killers can be reduced in size to little punks and flowers can assume the radiance of a healing sun which dries the tears of the mourners and sends the beloved into the safety of the heavens. Refusing to be brought down to the vengeful level of the killers, the eighth graders of P.S. 75 made something positive and passionate out of Yusuf's senseless and brutal murder. They turned the event around, creating order and beauty where there was once only rage.

Gravestone Rubbing:
Epitaph for Yusuf Hawkins

Roberta Halporn

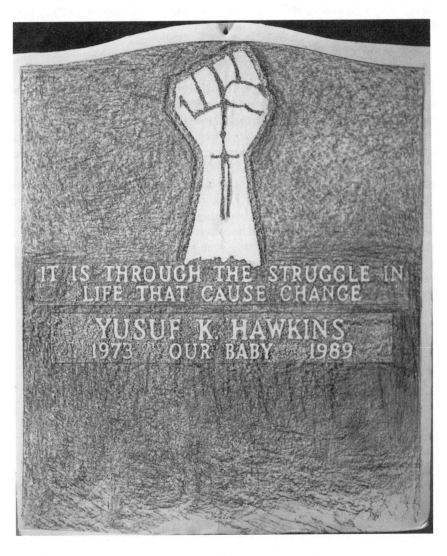

WHY DO GRAVESTONE RUBBINGS?

I cannot think of a more tranquilizing activity than examining the art and ideas of the past in the peaceful, verdant silence of a graveyard. Rubbing itself is an ancient Chinese craft and, through transmission from Great Britain, reached America. It requires no great skill to copy a piece of memorial sculpture—just some paper, tape, and crayons. (So simple a grown-up can do it.) But when you are done, you have tactilely learned something of the lives of three individuals from the past—the deceased whose story is recounted in the memorial, the mourner who commissioned it, and an artisan who designed and created the stone. The attitudes they held, we sense, teach us something about ourselves. And best of all, since no rubbing is the same, we have an original art work to take home.

EPITAPH

In this powerful work, marking the burial site of a young martyr to racism, we see the presence of the three persons who have led to its existence—Robert Pugh, the sensitive artist creating in stone, the person who died whom it commemorates, and the family who commissioned it. Yusuf Hawkins died because he went to the wrong neighborhood to seek out a second-hand car. In an indelible moment of the race hatred that still shadows our country, a group of roughnecks beat him to death because he had the "foolishness" to visit their area. His parents have expressed their grief for a beloved son who had barely begun to live in the moving epitaph, "our baby." By showing us the dark fist representing the "black power" movement, Pugh has carved an image of the only force he feels might defeat this ugliness. But he has gone a further step by comparing this youngster's death to historical incidents that preceded it. Though the fist seems to be holding a rosary, a closer look reveals that the hanging figure is an abstract representation of a lynching, and, at the same time, refers to the memory of a far earlier victim of intolerance—the crucified Christ.

Remembrance Photographs:
A Caregiver's Gift for Families of
Infants Who Die

Mindy L. K. Gough

I'm never sure just how to introduce the work I do when I am asked about it by an unsuspecting acquaintance. Usually when I explain that I am teaching professional caregivers how to photograph infants who have died, the response of my listener is shock. A quick recovery often follows, during which the dismayed listener attempts to respond with polite interest. However, it is evident that many people are taken aback, if not absolutely horrified, by the idea of photographing deceased infants. Our cultural avoidance of death as a painful and unpleasant topic of conversation contributes to this reaction, as does our sense of tragedy and injustice associated with the death of an infant.

Often I am asked questions: "Who takes these pictures? Why do they take them?" "Are they used for medical purposes?" These photographs, known as remembrance portraits, bereavement photographs, or memorial photographs, are taken shortly after the infant's death. Though usually taken by a hospital staff member (a nurse, social worker, member of the clergy), the photographs can also be taken by the families themselves. Remembrance portraits are meant to provide a lasting, tangible memento of the child for the bereaved parents, and are not used by the hospital staff for any other purpose. This article addresses the creation of these photographs from the professional caregiver's point of view.

There is very little literature that directly addresses photographing infants who have died. Many books and articles discussing perinatal loss make at least some positive mention of photographing the infant who has died, although very few provide details about how to make such photographs. However, most authors who have written about this subject do agree that this special kind of photography is beneficial and needed.

A HISTORICAL PERSPECTIVE

Photographing deceased people is not a new custom. Because photography in its infancy was an expensive and difficult hobby, many people did not have portraits taken while they were alive. The death of a loved person, whether infant, child, or adult, prompted families to have portraits made while they still had a chance to do so.

A recent television program on the history of photography noted, "In an age when half the children might die in childhood, remembrance portraits were often taken before the funeral. Deathbed photographs brought no embarrassment—death was too familiar." The practice of photographing deceased children is as old as photography itself. In my personal collection of Victorian photograph albums, I have many images of children and infants who were dead when their photographs were made (see Figures 1 to 4). The inclusion of these photographs in the family albums suggests that remembrance photographs were important and valuable.

CURRENT PRACTICE

The practice of photographing the dead declined in post-Victorian Western society, probably because photography had become inexpensive and accessible to almost everyone. Since people were able to make snapshots and to have studio

Figure 1. Victorian photograph of dead child aged 5 months and 9 days.

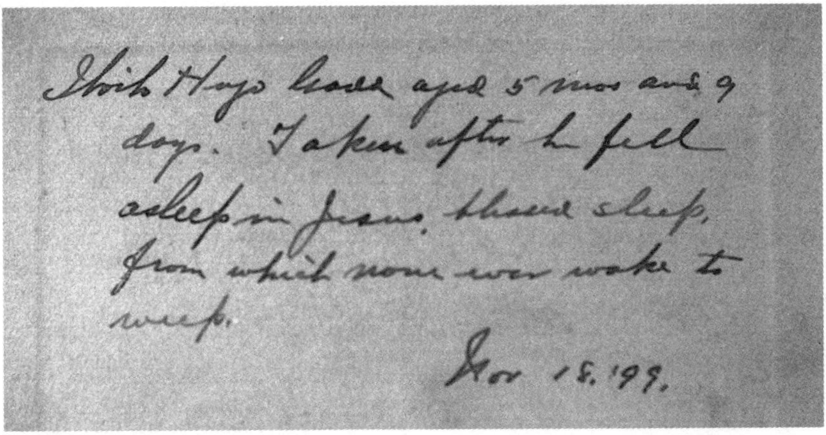

Figure 2. Inscription on the back of photograph in Figure 1.

portraits taken with ease, they did not feel the need to photograph loved ones after death. Most families possessed many photographs taken of their loved ones while alive, and these were preferred to remembrance portraits. This attitude prevails today in Western culture in most cases; however, for families of infants who die prior to birth, who die at birth, or who live only a short time, remembrance photographs provide the only opportunity to make a lasting image of the child. Reddin comments:

> There is no fund of memories or mementos for parents to call upon to ease the burden of their bereavement, and a common result of this enigmatic loss is a psychological disturbance which causes them to wonder if the pregnancy had been real at all, or to think that their baby was only imaginary [1, p. 49].

The remembrance photograph allows bereaved parents to achieve a realistic understanding of their infant's death. Counteracting the effects of emotional trauma on the parents, remembrance photographs "provide parents with a genuine artifact of their lost child, to act as a buffer against a fallible human memory" [1, p. 49].

Primeau and Recht describe interventions that caregivers can offer to parents who lose a baby: "Mementos of the infant can be provided" and one of the most important is the bereavement photograph [2, p. 22]. Rando agrees: "These mementos and a few fragmented memories may be all they have to show for an experience that profoundly marked their lives" [3, p. 154]. Reddin comments that "this photograph may be the only way a baby's existence is ever permanently recorded" [1, p. 49].

Johnson et al. list four reasons for taking pictures of babies who have died:

- A picture helps the family confirm the reality of their baby's life and death.
- A picture shows them exactly how the baby looked so they do not have to rely on memory or fantasy.
- A picture gives them one way to share their baby with other people.
- A picture may be the only tangible memory of their baby [4, p. 3].

Parents of infants who have died confirm that photographs do help them during their journey through grief.

PERSPECTIVES OF PARENTS AND PROFESSIONALS

A young mother told me that the photograph of her long-awaited but, sadly, stillborn son was her most treasured possession. "Without it," she said, "I would have no proof that my boy was ever born. When I went back to work, people tried to pretend Josiah had never existed. I felt proud to be able to pull out his picture and say I had a baby. This is my son. He was nine pounds, two ounces." Most important, to this mother, the photograph of Josiah taken by his nurse showed that he was a lovely, handsome baby who looked like his father.

Another woman shared an instant picture of her tiny infant surrounded by medical equipment, tubes, and dressings. A nurse had taken the picture and, though the mother at first declined it, she later returned to the hospital to retrieve it. She stated that the picture was her only link to her child, as she had refused to view her baby's body after death, and had been very ill during the few hours the little girl had lived. The photograph helped the woman to maintain a realistic image of her deceased child, and despite her initial reluctance, she came to value it highly.

Molly, a four-year-old girl, made a special memory box to commemorate the life of her baby brother who had lived only a few hours. The box contained mementos, toys, and a framed remembrance portrait. Pointing to the picture, Molly told me,

Figure 3. "Sadly deceased."

Figure 4. Woman at rest.

"That is baby Jordan. He is up in heaven with God. He was really cute." Molly's parents had originally decided to hide the portrait from Molly, but she was tearful and preoccupied with questions about Jordan's death. When she was given the portrait and an adequate explanation of her brother's life and death, she became sad but content. The honesty of her parents' explanation and the tangible portrait helped Molly to understand her loss and thereby feel less anxious about it.

The practice of photographing babies who have died continues to grow. Personal conversations with caregivers at the 1995 King's College Conference on Death, Dying and Bereavement in London, Ontario, indicate that those who work with grieving parents encourage the use of these photographs. Many caregivers stated that they had been making such photographs for several years and found them invaluable for helping bereaved families. Hardcover baby books for mementoes, footprints, and photographs are offered by Centering Corporation, a resource company specializing in materials on grief and bereavement. The existence of these very specialized materials lends credence to the idea that remembrance photography is seen as worthwhile both by caregivers and by bereaved families.

THE PHOTOGRAPHS

What kind of images are memorial photographs? Some might imagine these photographs are stark, ugly, or even repulsive. Though this might be true of photographs taken by untrained people, many remembrance photographs now being created are actually lovely, gentle portraits. When caregivers first realized the value of photographing babies who had died, photographic technology was limited, and caregivers had to make do with equipment that often produced harsh, unattractive snapshots. More recently, the instant camera, while useful logistically (pictures appear immediately without the hassle of development), often provided blurry pictures that could not be easily reproduced. Now, however, 35mm autofocus camera technology enables even the nonphotographer to make gentle, pleasing portraits.

Unfortunately, many inexperienced individuals attempt to make these special portraits with the wrong equipment and materials. While a poor photograph may be more desirable than none at all, it is certainly preferable to create an appealing portrait. For those wishing a very practical manual, Johnson et al. offer *A Most Important Picture: A Very Tender Manual for Taking Pictures of Stillborn Babies and Infants Who Die* [4]. Caregivers who intend to undertake this work are advised to prepare themselves thoroughly. A detailed reading of the literature and consultation with professional photographers and caregivers experienced in remembrance photography are imperative.

While we will not address here the technical, how-to aspects of good remembrance photography, we will discuss the qualities that are desirable in these special portraits. While the debate continues as to whether a remembrance portrait ought to be aesthetically pleasing, it seems that many bereaved parents look not at the quality of the photograph, but at the beauty that they perceive in their child. Caregivers report that parents often respond favorably, indeed lovingly, to photographs thought by the caregiver to be most unpleasant.

A photograph that provokes a negative response from those with whom the parents share it may offer more hurt than healing. Because the remembrance portrait is often used as a means of introducing the deceased child to those who never saw him, it is important to make the photograph appealing. Professional caregivers should keep in mind that the maceration and deformities of deceased infants may become less distressing or even routine to them, but to friends and family of the bereaved parents such a ravaged little body may be unbearable. Therefore, the photographer should make a strong attempt to make the child's appearance as visually acceptable as possible. This does not preclude the photographing of the child with any deformities apparent, but it suggests that the photographer should attempt to create a number of portraits appropriate for sharing with others.

A gentle, warm remembrance photograph should show adequate detail to identify the child, yet not be so detailed as to cause a deformity to distract the viewer (see Figure 5). The portrait should be soft and quiet, pleasantly lit, with no distracting background. Care should be taken to avoid hard shadows, glare, and "mug shot" poses. The most common mistakes made by new photographers are cluttered backgrounds and harsh lighting. Natural window light should be used if possible. A variety of poses is suggested, from close-up photographs of the baby's tiny hands or feet, to full-length portraits. Family members, including siblings and grandparents, should be included in some of the poses. The photographs should be easily reproduced, so that copies can be made in the event that the original is lost or damaged.

Portraits can be softened by using soft focus, a technique that renders a soft, fuzzy photograph, and by using high-speed, grainy film, which also produces a slightly fuzzy appearance. Black-and-white film has been used with great success by professional photographers and trained amateurs alike. Black-and-white portraits

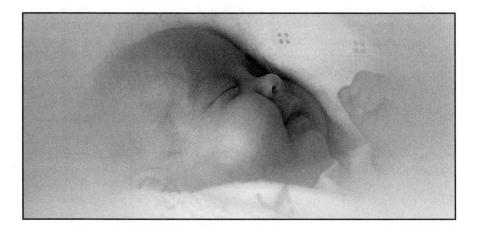

Figure 5. Contemporary photograph using natural light, soft focus, and simple equipment.

are especially helpful when photographing a child whose skin color is very poor. Hand-coloring a black-and-white photograph can also produce a very appealing portrait. Photographing only an undamaged portion of the child's body, such as a hand or foot, can make a meaningful portrait as well. Blankets, special clothing, and items such as soft toys can be used effectively, both to soften the portrait and to mask unpleasant deformities or damage. Creativity and sensitivity are very important. The caregiver who attempts to photograph a baby whose body is badly damaged may wish to consult a professional photographer for ideas and advice.

The baby should not necessarily be made to look alive—the goal is not to hide death, but to acknowledge it gently. However, it should be noted that, historically, many remembrance portraits attempted to create a lifelike appearance in the subject (see Figure 6). For example, several nineteenth-century photographs reproduced in the book *Sleeping Beauty: Memorial Photography in America* depict dead persons sitting up, with their eyes open, and even holding a newspaper [5]. James VanDerZee's beautiful *Harlem Book of the Dead* contains a photograph of a deceased baby holding a bottle and a teddy bear [6]. Many of the remembrance photographs in my personal collection show deceased children dressed in fancy clothing, propped into sitting positions in chairs, with their eyes open (see Figure 3). It seems more natural, though, to photograph the child's body as it is, rather than attempting to create life where there is none.

Family members should be encouraged to take photographs with their own cameras as well. Their input into dressing the child, posing the photographs, and selecting people to include in the photographs should be respected. Because the photography session provides one of the few opportunities for the family to have a positive experience with their child, the photographer should attempt to make the photography session as warm, gentle, and pleasant as possible. Playing music chosen by the family and ensuring the photography location is comfortable can help families maximize the positive aspects of the session.

It does not matter who takes the portraits—nurses, doctors, social workers, members of the clergy, medical photographers, or volunteers are acceptable. What is required is thorough training, sensitivity, and patience. A caregiver-photographer who is not adequately trained may make a serious technical error and spoil the entire batch of portraits, a deeply disappointing event that would cause further pain to already grieving parents. However, if the caregivers have prepared themselves well, through study and in-depth consultation with others, and if they use simple equipment, they should be readily able to make pleasing portraits.

Presentation

Offering a special baby book, folder, or frame with the photographs adds to the special nature of the portraits. Parents should first be asked for permission to make the photographs, and should not be coerced into taking the photographs home with them if they do not wish to do so. Instead, caregivers should carefully store the photographs and negatives for as long as possible, and make the parents aware that

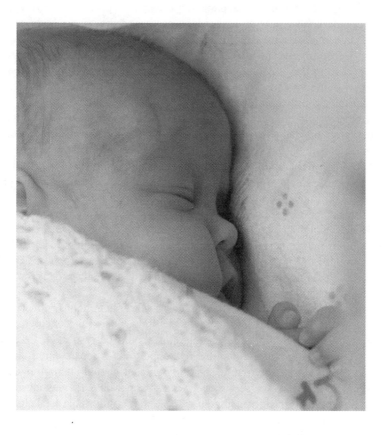

Figure 6. Profile view of child shown in Figure 5.

the portraits will be available to them for a certain length of time. A coordinator appointed to oversee the remembrance portrait program can ensure proper presentation and storage of photographs.

The presentation of the photographs is important. Photographs given too soon, given too late, mailed, lost, unceremoniously handed over in a battered photo-finishing envelope, or damaged in any way may lose some of their special value and even lead to distress for the recipients. To the bereaved parents, careless or insensitive handling or presentation of the remembrance photographs may be construed as a grave offense. Conversely, photographs presented in a respectful manner—appropriate physical presentation at an appropriate time by the appropriate caregiver—give parents the needed message that their baby was important, special, and worth remembering. Sensitive attention paid to these seemingly small details can add warmth and comfort to grieving families and avoid uncomfortable situations for families and caregivers.

Defrain et al. describe the Indian practice of burying babies in the homes of their bereaved parents, and connect this to creating remembrance portraits by remarking that "modern parents keep the spirit of their lost babies from wandering too far by making photographs . . ." [7, p. 62]. This beautiful word image wonderfully encompasses the purpose and significance of today's remembrance portraits. Grieving parents are able to keep an enduring, tangible likeness of the beloved child who existed so ephemerally.

REFERENCES

1. S. K. Reddin, The Photography of Stillborn Children and Neonatal Deaths, *Journal of Audiovisual Media in Medicine, 10*, pp. 49-51, 1987.
2. M. R. Primeau and C. K. Recht, Professional Bereavement Photographs: One Aspect of a Perinatal Bereavement Program, *JOGNN, 23*:1, pp. 22-25, 1994.
3. T. Rando, *Parental Loss of a Child,* Research Press, Champaign, Illinois, 1986.
4. J. Johnson, M. Johnson, J. Cunningham, M. Gough, and I. Weinfeld, *A Most Important Picture: A Very Tender Manual for Taking Pictures of Stillborn Babies and Infants Who Die,* Centering Corporation, Omaha, Nebraska, 1997.
5. S. Burns, *Sleeping Beauty: Memorial Photography in America,* Twelvetrees Press, Altadena, California, 1990.
6. J. VanDerZee, *The Harlem Book of the Dead,* Morgan and Morgan, out of print.
7. J. Defrain et al., *Stillborn: The Invisible Death,* Lexington Books, Lexington, Massachusetts, 1986.

LESSONS FROM CULTURES OLD AND NEW

Culture, Creativity and Death

J. Havelka

Creativity relates to death. Indeed, in its fullest meaning, human culture attempts to create a vision of reality that transcends death of our mortal existence and projects it into the sphere of immortality. Culture is a perennial and massive compensatory activity of humankind. It provides a lofty inspiration and promise of transcendental potentialities of human beings in their encounter with the life-threatening and life-diminishing potency of death. Culture is a noble attempt to escape life's impermanency by promoting the timeless aspects of our existence. Thus, culture will always remain a heroic act of humanity's final victory over death. Creativity, which is the expressive, formal mode of every culture, is a vehicle of human transformation through the trust and contact with the universal "Wholeness" [1, 2].

From time immemorial, human beings have been searching for something which is permanent and imperishable. In a creative act they try to prevent, in a unique way that is both noble and pathetic, the impending threat of mortality and the end. Humankind past, present, and future follows Virgil's celebrated dictum: "Exigi monumentum aere perennius"—'I have created a monument enduring in eternity.' All human cultures create works of art in stone, silk, gold, silver, marble, on paper, leather, in sound, movement, and words that are expected to withstand decay, destruction, and death.

Thus, we all use our creative potentialities to defeat and to mitigate our most pervasive fear, that of passing away, that of impermanence and the loss of personal significance. In endless shapes of artistic forms there emerges the central motive of human existence: to attain both a personal significance beyond the threat of death while still living and a claim to immortality through the memory of others.

In essence, it is a death-denial that forms the driving force behind every genuine creative act. In this context, human creativity is "cosmocentric": it both mitigates our inevitable diminishment and molds our destiny into a continuity that endures in the universal context. There the Promethean spirit of our individuality challenges the mystery of Thanatos. In whatever walk of life, whatever human condition we find ourselves, this cosmocentric, creatively oriented tendency penetrates our living. Through this unique process of liberation from the fear of death, we eventually

Previously published as "Death and Creativity," in *Thanatology: A Liberal Arts Approach*, M. A. Morgan and J. D. Morgan (eds.), King's College, London, Ontario, and reproduced with permission of the publisher.

discover the most basic meaningfulness of our existence. It is meaningfulness through creative intentionality. Such intentionality, as Rollo May correctly notices, is life's organized patterning, which gives meaning to our experience [3, 4]. We intend to be to such an extent that the fear of non-being weakens.

Since death appears to undermine our wish to endure, we can counteract it through a creative act that protects and rescues our endangered existence. To face fully dying and death becomes possible through this intentional creative self-actualization. If, however, this self-actualization fails to materialize, it could lead to what Maslow [5] calls a "Jonah syndrome," which is the fear of our potential greatness. This is essentially a deficiency condition that prevents our inner growth, restricts the range of our capacities, and inevitably leads us to anticipate death with horror.

Those who suffer from this fear syndrome keep retreating more and more from any possible risk and thus fail to challenge their own death. They cannot cope with the threat of disintegration, and progressively lose control of their vital energies that nourish every genuine creative intention. While sinking into a deeper anxiety about death, they run away from life. They mistrust their own unique meaningfulness. The "Jonah syndrome" characterizes a weakened, anti-heroic personality incapable of creative determination, be it in artistic expression or more generally in the process of higher maturation.

Contrasted with the "fear of greatness" is Tillich's "courage to be," the positive aspect of every creative act in its most fundamental encounter with the reality of death [6]. To encounter death courageously is to offer a challenge to our transience through the creatively expressed significance of every existence.

Generally speaking, we choose from two alternatives: we either defensively repress the thought of death or overcome it through a creative act. A non-repressive denial of death occurs in human creativity where our cosmocentric tendency is symbolically expressed as timeless and is oriented toward the universal Wholeness, where death loses importance.

Overcoming the fear of greatness requires a specific courage, a courage to create in spite of the natural biological limits imposed upon us by bodily death. In order to challenge this inevitable reality, we decide to act out something that allows us to reach beyond the boundaries of our physical limits. Through any genuinely creative expression, and its self-actualizing energy flow, we free ourselves, even if only temporarily, from death's universal levelization. In any real, creative act of any culture, we attain a bold denial of death, which is, in a sense, the most essential form of human individuation in its progress toward spiritual maturity.

Creative courage shapes our destiny, unrestricted by the inevitable polarity of our birth and death, and, by symbolically offering a vision of reality that bypasses both of these, aims at cosmic unity. Shakespeare, Michelangelo, Tolstoy, Rodin, Balzac, and Pushkin—all these and many others—forge human destiny into an imaginative edifice that stands as a monument for the denial of death's importance. These outstanding creators courageously formulated symbols, metaphors, myths, and poetical language that crystallize human potentially into its universal significance and thus exempt it from impermanence [7].

Although works of art sometimes deal with human fear, rage, violence, aliena-tion, and hopelessness, they intimate a richer and deeper grasp of existence, thus promoting in us the courage to endure and overcome even the extreme adversities and tragedies that affect our lives and our dying. Without this creative courage to be, no work of art has its central meaning: to dissolve and transform our fears and anxieties that accompany every thought of death. In this context it is significant to note that both modern and contemporary art underplay or ignore the manifestations and meaning of death (entire movements such as Impressionism, Fauvism, Abstract Expressionism, and Cubism are examples). In contemporary art, the emphasis is mostly on the incidental, marginal, and often trivially decorative, an art that lacks a creative intention and courage to face and transcend mortality and mostly favors brutal commentaries on life's violence or inane superficialities. Thematically and formally, most of modern art misses the sense of transcendence central to any genuine culture, and is disappointingly aiming at fashionable avant-gardism through a search for novelties for the sake of novelties, with a complete absence of spirituality.

Furthermore, creativity can be defined as a unique mental process leading to the expansion of experienced reality beyond the already established categorization and classification of it. It is a state of discovery, a new understanding of reality offered to others in an unrepeatable fashion. In it, the creative person formulates an expression based on the subjective, and thus his or her unique inner vision. The created expres-sion becomes a symbolic translation of an internal insight. Only such a creatively shaped vision or insight can be communicated and indirectly shared. At this level the creative individual establishes contact, involvement, and engagement with others in terms of a unique interpersonal sharing. Although artists can never directly render the inner process of their vision of reality, they promote, in viewers and listeners, experiences of expanded reality of their own.

Creativity is at work not only in poetry, music, painting, ballet, sculpture, and the minor arts but also in the new establishment and reorganization of personal relationships. This creative involvement of one person with another person reveals new feelings of inner growth, new ways of confirming the other individual, and a deeper, sharper, and more spontaneous awareness of them. Genuinely creative people want to induce in others change, growth, and a maturation of relationships. They desire an enriched involvement with another and thus hope to prevent in themselves (and in others) personal and even social isolation, alienation, and an unhealthy introverted ego-preoccupation.[1]

---

[1] The criteria for the evaluation of a specific creative act are subjected to changes in social atmosphere and thus sometimes interpreted as detrimental to society. For example, while epochal discoveries of Copernicus, Einstein, Darwin, Pauli, Planck, or Pavlov could open the way to destructive applications, their creative origin was totally unrelated to such a destructive misuse. All of these highly gifted minds offer ideas of creative discovery which in different social and cultural settings can lead to a variety of controversial interpretations, as to whether they are creative or non-creative. Essentially, however, there is no distinction regarding the degree or quality of creativity: creativity has no other basic function than being an act of expanded reality. Once any aspect of reality is enriched and opened beyond the dimension of the predictable, conventional, and morally categorical, it becomes a genuine creative act or expression. And that either in the artwork or in the original process of personal maturing.

The non-creative person, however, seems to be missing the basic precondition for promoting creativity, namely, to be engaged in an activity that invariably relates to the enrichment and expansion of one's own and other people's lives. Non-creative individuals miss that base from which their life is actively directed toward an original discovery and a deeper development of the most significant human values that always point beyond individual death toward life's transcendence. Also, these individuals seem to be unaware of the vital connection with the realities of life that are deeper and richer than the personal achievement required by social conditioning. For non-creative individuals, any work in whatever field of activity is done primarily in order to succeed within the socially approved sphere of behavior. In contrast, the creative person is active and committed as it were "sub specie aeternitatis," that is, from the point of view of cosmic and thus eternal meaningfulness that transcends death [7].

A further aspect of the creative person's involvement is a subjective tendency to actualize the self, to harvest potentialities that can directly or indirectly stimulate other people's growth. Essentially, it is a potent urge to expand in every dimension that of being meaningfully alive. This creative commitment is distinctly different from the ego's desire and security-seeking orientation, which is threatened by the prospect of death. This vital creative involvement is active beyond the fear of life and consequently beyond the fear of death, which characterizes the ego's primary deficiency. This essential creative motivation is engaged in a life-affirming commitment.

In some, this creative tendency may remain hidden under various strata of psychological defense, organized as a protecting wall around the safety- and security-seeking ego. These defensive strategies absorb our mental energies and commit them to the exclusive services of the threatened ego; the result is the rapid weakening and eventually the exhaustion of our basic mental energies. Under these conditions human neurosis sets in.

Should, however, these captive energies become free-flowing again, and differently employed, there could occur a condition of creative "freeing," which strongly facilitates the person's capacities for a healthier transformation of the ego. While preoccupation with the fear of death evokes a variety of psychological defenses, reactivity liberates us to overcome their damaging influences.

We experience ourselves more spontaneously when freed from defensive and eventually neurotic limitations; we open ourselves boldly to the as yet untold experience, and are exempted from oppressive anxieties of death. Thus, creative individuals offer society the fertile and constructive elements of their inner vision, which become potent liberating forces. They also propose new inter-personal encounters not based on the socially established, stereotyped, and often neurotically oriented norms, but on courageous innovation which brings deeper meaning into their lives, even if very often it is of greater personal risk and uncertainty.

Thus, some wider and richer strata of experiences are understood without pervasive anxiety. Such a freed awareness favors life's unpredictability, its constant flow and change, and its ever-emerging novelty; it tolerates a high degree of healthy ambiguity and carries along with it a fearless and serene familiarity with death.

Again, it is rather unimportant whether this creative freeing of awareness results in any work or art. As long as it diminishes our ego-defense and deautomatizes our socially learned responses, it can liberate our creative potential either in art or in enriched interpersonal contact. The courage to create in more open and deeply significant personal encounters minimizes concerns with safety and security devices and wards off the illusory fear of non-being.

One of the more complex aspects of the study of creativity is the understanding of the psychological roots in which the creative act originates. The pertinent neuro-psychological data are not yet fully available beyond the fascinating discovery of the bicameral interaction of our two cerebral hemispheres. Today we are informed about the functions of both the left and right side of the brain—their close cooperation on one level and their radical differences on another level.

Those two levels of functioning display both a massive interaction and, at the same time, a degree of independence in a variety of mental functions. Yet the often attempted interpretation of these two potentialities of the human mind doesn't pro-vide us yet with clear information about the origin of creativity. Further advances in neurosciences may eventually contribute to our deeper understanding of human consciousness in its cooperative left/right brain organization.

Thus, a somewhat different approach follows, one which, although recognizing the existing neuro-psychological data, also examines some other theoretical pos-sibilities. Here the key term used will be *numinosity*, introduced to psychological literature by Freud's early disciple Rudolf Otto [8-13]. Numinosity refers to the most basic mental disposition of experiencing which underlies every response of our mind. This basic mental disposition, or set, is active in two opposing tensions constantly operant within ourselves, through which we react to everything.

Every aspect of our experiencing is permeated by the one or the other opposing mental tensions; we either react positively or negatively to everything. Most of our everyday responses occur within the moderate ranges of these opposing feelings. The extreme ranges of these polar tensions, however, touch the roots of our existence, and numinosity is the experience of these extreme existential feelings.

One of the radical numinous tendencies carries along with it a unique feeling of bliss, of ecstasy, a feeling of the presence of the Holy, or union with the transcen-dental; and the other carries a deeply negative feeling of terror, of non-being, of death. This powerful mental polarity resides in the depth of human existence and keeps manifesting itself in the dual aspect of all our tendencies, strivings, and longings. Through these two different inclinations we long for something on one hand and feel the horror or dislike for something else on the other. In this polarity the most basic dilemma and crisis of the human condition is manifested. Through this polarity we imagine standing either at the gates of heaven or at the abyss of hell. Essentially, the numinosity gravitates toward a contact with the Holy, and recedes in horror from the vacuum of death. Thus, in one of these numinous experiences, there originates our most basic spiritual disposition, our religiosity, our longing for contact with the Holy; and in the other range of numinous tensions there begins the anxiety of ultimate privation, of personal annihilation, and of death. (In Freudian terms, Eros is in a basic conflict with Thanatos.)

In this numinous pool of all the polar ranges of our basic feelings, we may attempt to locate the beginning of the human creative will. Within it is born our creative vision followed by a formalized creative expression that echoes the oscillation between the positive and negative numinous feelings that characterize our desire to exist and our anxiety of non-being. Through a creative act we attempt to capture the dynamic interaction of our deep psyche in its effort to experience reality in the two most significant tendencies: to transcend the fear of death and to seek and merge with the Holy. Any creative act aims at the discovery of a significant and radically meaningful reality; it becomes significant and meaningful because its numinous roots are the deepest and thus the closest to the universal reality.

This "mysterium tremendum" covers in its awesome span the most sublime elements of human happiness, of the profound intimations of love, of the inchoate glimmers of ecstasy, as well as the fear and trembling of those unspecific terrors which threaten to overwhelm us [8]. Numinosity and creativity of every form and content are inextricably linked with this mystery. In their roots they are always in touch with the unfathomable ground of all being. In that sense, the creative urge originating in this ground is universal and thus without any personal character or involvement. Personal involvement occurs later when a conscious patterning takes its shape either in a work of art or in a creative interpersonal engagement. This numinously activated creativity resembles the Jungian collective unconscious, in which begins all our archetypes, myths, fairy tales, sagas, legends, and stories [14]. In this "meta-ground" of all being are pre-formulated humankind's stories and narrations about terrifying demons, as well as about saintly sages, about the horror of death in hell and the bliss of wisdom and of love.

Buddhism refers to this meta-ground of our psychic dispositions as *sunyata,* the objectless cosmic void that is permeated by the bright light [15, pp. 512-526]; and the Aztecs used to call it the "smoking mirror," a reflective aspect of universal reality in which everything originates. In these primitive psychic dispositions is to be found each individual's universal attraction toward merger with the Absolute, but also the horror and anxiety whenever he or she feels a loss of contact with it. In this context, to all ancient cultures, death signifies not only a lamented end of life and tragic separation from the Wholeness, but also a beatific transformation of any suffering originating from our individual impermanency.

Thus, the unarticulated and yet overwhelming notion of death, together with the awesome notion of the Holy, form the preconscious layer of our minds in which the creative process begins. Let us again realize that the numinous tension in its polarity is not rational in its origin. It can eventually become conscious and rational when it is creatively expressed; and that occurs when the internal vision becomes a formally expressed act. Only on the level of this transition does creativity promote the transformation of numinous tensions into a specific expression. Thus, the most significant aspect of creativity is attained: the pre-formal numinous vision is formally shaped.

And how is this transition achieved? The numinous vision can never be directly rendered in its original nature of tension but must be translated through the conscious expression of it into a symbolic act. It should follow that any symbol or poetic expression finds its determining tendencies in unspecific pre-conscious and unconscious processes, which are in turn symbolically translated; thus a symbol is a translation-transformation of numinously pre-cognitive feelings into a conscious formal expression. A symbol has the capacity to "transcribe" the inner intuitive events of the numinous polarities into a form that becomes the vehicle of a deeply significant creative communication.

Thus, by definition, any symbol expands reality by integrating the vision of it with its external expression. In this context the symbol can be known by the formative capacity of our intellect and at the same time understood in its numinous origin by our intelligence. And since creativity is primarily a symbolization of the unfathomable, it depends on the close cooperation of our intellect with our intelligence.

Symbolization is the creative translation of the primarily precognitive elements of reality that are intuitively grasped in its pre-conscious and unconscious roots. The unconscious can be simply defined as a potentiality for awareness that the conscious person cannot fully and directly actualize.

One of the most important aspects of it is the fact that it gives rise to the negative tension of the numinous, namely, to our anxiety. Anxiety can be viewed as the apprehension of an objectless threat to our existence. It originates in that part of our unconsciously determined numinous tensions that apprehend the horror of death through the most archaic aspect of our survival instinct. Through it we notice the world as being full of chaotic terrors which lead to the despair of death.

Under ordinary (non-creative) circumstances, the unconscious roots of anxiety interact with that conscious level, where anxiety becomes molded into specific ego-oriented fears and preoccupations. The creative process, however, forges a unique compromise where the unconscious anxiety of non-being and death is symbolically expressed and is thus exempted from its direct impact upon our fearful and tortured ego. In this process, the creative person achieves a control over this negative unconscious tension, which then frees the individual and allows the individual to minimize the harsh impact of anxiety through the symbolic transformation of it. In this way every creative symbol translates the ego-anxiety of non-being into a detached, non-threatening, imaginative contemplation of death; hereby a unique quality of liberation is obtained.

But for this act of creative freedom from the burden of ego-anxiety, creative persons may pay a social penalty. Sooner or later they may find themselves in conflict with the established conventional responses of society, which are primarily conscious and rational. They will realize that society abhors, fears, and misunderstands the unconscious, while it is vital that they draw from it, control it creatively, and thus use it in a most constructive fashion. They may realize that because they dwell with a consummate interest on their numinous and unconscious functions, society will expose them to suspicion, misunderstanding, and rejection; and these circumstances, in which they feel separated from their own social group, may lead them to the peculiar experience of guilt-feeling toward that group.[2]

---

[2] A somewhat similar argument is developed by L. Kubie [16].

One can assume that such guilt-feelings develop in most cultured and creative personalities. Indeed, such guilt seems to permeate every human culture that is invariably in contact with the mysterious energies of the unconscious and numinous mental universe. And yet beyond this guilt feeling the creative may experience a unique elation and gratification because they have produced a more enriched, universal, and meaningful version of reality; because only in the interaction of the conscious with the unconscious, as they emerge from the numinous through a creative formation, do they celebrate the holiness and significance of life. They fully realize (with greater clarity the more creative genius they possess) that the exclusive emphasis on the conscious process only, so important in any social convention, offers just a fragmentary and superficial reality and leaves behind the other dimensions, so necessary for a complete vision.

This heightened realization is linked with the awareness that a genuine creative act has, momentarily at least, transcended the anxious problem of death, which so viciously threatens our conscious social ego. Thus any creative effort, be it a work of art or the capacity of confirming other persons in their unique meaningfulness, is essentially ego- and death-denying in its nature.

In that sense, creativity is a superbly liberating act that determines the deep significance of our human values and our human freedom. After all, the discovery of the death-minimizing capacity of our mind is the highest expression of existential freedom that no other circumstances, be they social, political, or economic, can give.

REFERENCES

1. K. Wilber, *The Spectrum of Consciousness,* Quest, London, 1977.
2. K. Wilber, *The Atman Project,* Quest, London, 1980.
3. R. May, *The Courage to Create,* Bantam, New York, 1976.
4. R. May, *Love and Will,* Norton, New York, 1969.
5. A. Maslow, *The Further Reaches of Human Nature,* Viking, New York, 1971.
6. P. Tillich, *Courage to Be,* Yale University Press, New Haven, 1952.
7. D. de Rougemont, Religion and the Mission and the Artist, in *Spiritual Problems in Contemporary Literature,* S. R. Hopper (ed.), Harper Torchbook, New York, 1957.
8. R. Otto, *The Idea of the Holy,* Oxford University Press, London, 1928.
9. J. C. Gowan, *Trance, Art and Creativity,* Creative Education Foundation, State University College, Buffalo, 1975.
10. A. Boisen, *The Exploration of the Inner World,* Harper and Row, New York, 1936.
11. E. Cassirer, *Philosophy of Symbolic Form,* Yale University Press, New Haven, 1955.
12. K. Dabrowski, *Positive Disintegration,* Little Brown, Boston, 1964.
13. M. Eliade, *Myth and Reality,* Harper and Row, New York, 1963.
14. C. G. Jung, *Man and His Symbols,* Dell, Laurel Edition, New York, 1972.
15. H. Zimmer, *Philosophies of India,* Meridian, New York, 1956.
16. L. Kubie, *Neurotic Distortion of the Creative Process,* University of Kansas Press, Lawrence, 1958.

Visible Words:
Ritual in the Pastoral Care of the
Sick and Dying

Kurt Stasiak

One of the distinctive characteristics of the Roman Catholic Church is that it is a *sacramental* Church. Catholics maintain that their experience of God is mediated through their experience of, and relationship with, others, and especially through their participation in the symbolic rituals of their worship. Richter summarizes this principle of ritual mediation well:

> Liturgical action depends on symbols because human beings cannot be together and communicate without some kind of encounter in words (verbal symbols) and/or in gestures and actions (nonverbal symbols). All knowledge begins with our senses; this means that an encounter with God is only possible by means of sensible signs [1, p. 9].

Since the twelfth century, the Catholic Church has considered seven liturgical rituals as sacraments—as, to cite the traditional definition, visible signs which confer grace and were instituted by Christ.

The importance of the sacraments in the life of the Church, as well as the richness and complexity of the symbols, words, and gestures which constitute the sacramental ritual, cannot be overemphasized. As Mitchell remarks:

> For many Christians, the sacraments are the primary meeting place of ritual and pastoral care. Many sacraments are symbolic reenactments of some event in the life and ministry of Jesus. Although words accompany, and to some extent give specific meanings to, sacramental acts, sacraments convey meanings "too deep for words." One act may "contain" a very wide variety of meanings simultaneously [2, p. 73].

SACRAMENTAL RITUAL AS THE INCARNATION
OF THE TRUTH

Mitchell's assessment that sacraments express meanings "too deep for words" calls to mind an observation of T. S. Eliot, in which the poet concisely described the

This chapter develops a small-group presentation given at the Death Education Conference at King's College, London, Ontario, May 1990.

goal of his craft. Eliot's definition of poetry speaks equally well to the relationship between symbol and truth:

> Poetry is not the assertion that some-
> thing is true
> but the making of that truth more
> real to us.[1]

Poetry does not make the truth; rather, it assumes the truth as truth and expresses it in a way in which it can be more easily understood and embraced—more easily experienced. In a similar manner, through their symbols and ritual actions, the sacraments express visibly and tangibly the truth the Church teaches verbally. The sacraments are, in the words of Saint Augustine, "visible words": through them the truth Christians profess is made "more real" to them. What the Church acts out in her sacraments is what she teaches as her faith.[2] The sacraments do not simply assert that God is present; they allow the ever-present God to be seen and experienced more readily by all who seek him.

SACRAMENTAL RITUAL AS RESPONSE TO THE TRUTH

The sacraments not only attempt to make the faith we profess "more real" to us, they also suggest and support a response grounded in that faith. An image helpful here is that of light. Upon entering a dark room with the intention of passing through it to another, we face a difficult task. We move hesitantly and, perhaps, fearfully, knowing that wrong turns are inevitable and collisions are likely. But if upon entering a dark room we turn on the light: what a difference is made! It is important to note, however, *what* is different. The room itself has not changed, for the obstacles and boundaries remain in our path. Nor has the light changed our objective situation as we stand at the door: we still need to move through the room and on into the next. What is different is that the light allows us to see more clearly what is there. And because we can see more clearly, a new path—a new direction—for our transit is suggested.

As it is in the above example with light, so is it with the sacraments. Our participation in and experience of the sacramental ritual do not change our objective situation (in the context of this chapter, serious illness or impending death). But, as Glen notes, these symbolic actions do suggest and encourage a response—a religious attitude, a hopeful faith—through which we can confront our situation in life and so more effectively complete our journey:

> Our rituals do not add some superfluous explanation to what we have experienced after the fact. Rather, they provide direction for the living interaction of

---

[1] As quoted by Sally Bailey [3, p. 264]. The exact source of Eliot's verse was unavailable to me.

[2] The classic formulation of this is *legem credendi lex statuat supplicandi:* "the law of prayer establishes the law of belief." That is, as Christian faith is expressed in and through Christian worship, so is that worship a norm for and of faith.

understanding and experience as our lives unfold. . . . In the highly concentrated symbolic language of its rituals, the community both expresses the relational patterns which currently define it and sets out the relational patterns toward which it aspires as its ideal. . . . The symbolic ritual complex of word and action permits the community to own both the present reality and future hope and to negotiate the dangerous passage between the two [4, p. 49].

We approach the sacramental ritual, then, from two perspectives: first, through their words, symbols, and ritual gestures, the sacraments lead us further into the truth we profess by offering us the opportunity to experience that truth more deeply; second, the sacraments suggest to, and encourage in us a Christian response to key moments in our lives.

THE SACRAMENT OF THE ANOINTING OF THE SICK

We will consider now the ritual, the "visible words," of the sacrament of the anointing of the sick. As a detailed commentary on the Catholic rite of anointing is beyond the scope of this chapter,[3] I will limit our consideration to three elements or moments in the sacramental ritual which attempt to offer the sick a guiding light or orientation through their affliction. The first principal symbolic gesture in the rite, an action carried out in silence, is the priest's imposing or laying his hands upon the sick person. A few moments later, a second major symbolic gesture is accompanied by words: as he anoints the forehead and hands of the patient with blessed oil, the priest prayerfully invokes the Lord's love, mercy, and healing power.

These three elements—imposition, anointing, and prayer—express the Church's ministry to her sick in a way that the Christian's hope and trust in the Lord can be more readily seen and experienced. As the prayer expresses verbally what the laying on of hands and the anointing with oil express symbolically, we will consider these "spoken words" of the sacrament.

The Spoken Words of the Sacrament: Redefining the Enemy

According to *Pastoral Care of the Sick and Dying: Rites of Anointing and Viaticum*, as the patient's forehead and hands are anointed with oil, the priest prays:

Through this holy anointing
may the Lord in his love and mercy help you
with the grace of the Holy Spirit.
May the Lord who frees you from sin
save you and raise you up [5, par. 124].

In this prayer the Lord is asked to come to the patient's aid. Specifically, he is called upon to save and raise up the one who is sick. It is important to note that the

---

[3] In addition to the liturgical rites themselves [5], such commentaries include James Empereur's *Prophetic Anointing* [6] and Charles W. Gusmer's *And You Visited Me: Sacramental Ministry to the Sick and the Dying* [7].

prayer neither directly requests a physical cure, nor does it imply (as did a previous version) that the sacrament of anointing offers primarily a spiritual ("sin-forgiving") remedy for life after death.[4] We do not call upon the Lord to deliver the patient *from* his illness; our prayer is that the patient will be saved and raised up *in* his sickness. For it is the patient, and not the tissues, organs, or systems that make up his body, that is the focus of the Church's prayer. As Lawler remarks, "It is the person who is to be raised up, not his infirmity that is to be alleviated" [8, p. 166].

What is the significance of this? What is the religious truth that these words attempt to make "more real" to us? What is the meaning that, even with these prayerful words, is "too deep for words"?

Christians do not hold that Christ abolished sickness or death. The sick whom Jesus healed did not remain forever in good health, and Lazarus eventually returned to the grave from which he had been summoned. To be human is to experience the suffering of sickness; to be human is to die. The recently published *Catechism of the Catholic Church* expresses well the omnipresence of sickness and its inescapable influence upon us:

> Illness and suffering have always been among the gravest problems confronted in human life. In illness, man experiences his powerlessness, his limitations, and his finitude. Every illness can make us glimpse death [9, par. 1500].

Illness and suffering have threatened humanity from the moment our biblical parents ate of the forbidden fruit in the garden. Through that sin, as Paul relates in his Letter to the Romans (5, 12), death was brought into the world. Reflecting upon the biblical account of Adam's sin, however, the late Jesuit theologian Karl Rahner cautions us not to think that if Adam had not sinned he would not have died:

> He would surely have experienced an end to his life, but in another manner; . . . he would have conducted this life immanently to its perfect and full maturity. In other words, Adam could have brought his personal life to its perfect consummation in its bodily form through a "death" which would have been a pure, active self-affirmation. He would have achieved a stage of perfection in which his bodily constitution would not have excluded that openness to the world in its totality which we now expect as the final result of redemption, and as the eschatological miracle of the resurrection of the body [10, pp. 42-43].

Rahner calls this death of the sinless Adam a "death without dying," a dying "free of death in the proper sense, that is, without suffering any violent dissolution of his actual bodily constitution through a power from without" [10, p. 42]. Rahner's reflection upon this "death without dying" allows us to examine with greater precision what it is we mean when we profess that Christ "put an end to death."

Christians do not believe that Christ abolished sickness or death; they believe he defeated their *destructive power*. The distinction is crucial, for in it is found the

---

[4] Prior to the 1972 revision of the sacramental ritual of anointing (which was referred to as "Extreme Unction," the "last anointing"), the priest anointed the senses of the (dying) person, praying that "the Lord might forgive you whatever sins you have committed through the sense of sight, touch . . ."

orientation or *light* of the sacrament of anointing. Death is seldom desired and sickness is never welcomed. Yet, for those who believe that not even death "will be able to separate us from the love of God in Christ Jesus our Lord" (Romans 8, 38-39), sickness and death are not the real enemies. The sacrament of anointing is neither a naive attempt to distract the patient from his or her suffering nor a frantic begging for a miracle cure. Rather, the sacrament attempts to assist the patient in *redefining who the enemy is*. And the real enemy from which the patient must be saved or raised up *in* his sickness or *in* her act of dying is, to use Rahner's phrase, *the darkness of death* [10, p. 46].

The image of darkness is appropriate, for it suggests the many faces with which serious illness or death confront us: the loneliness of the hospital bed, the isolation from family and friends, the despair, anger, and frustration in realizing that our past accomplishments cannot save us now, and the terrifying fear that our present is being raped—and that our future may well be aborted.

The darkness of death is the ground where hope and fear do battle, where religious belief and secular cynicism engage in bitter struggle. As Empereur has eloquently stated:

> The nature of sickness is such that it consumes a person's vital energy to such a degree that it becomes a powerful obstacle to a person's spiritual growth. And in the case of serious illness there is the added possibility of death with all its concomitant fears of the unknown and the loss of meaning. Confrontation with physical dissolution raises questions about the significance of human life. These questions are surrounded with anxiety. Such anxiousness can impede one's further movement toward God. The sacrament of anointing is supposed to make it possible for sick persons not only to manage spiritually during the trials of illness but also to intensify their growth process, their orientation toward God [6, p. 95].[5]

To pray that the sick or dying be saved and raised up is to pray that they be delivered in and through their struggle with sickness or death; delivered through a death or illness in which darkness does not reign, but through and in which the light of Christ shines.

This deliverance from the darkness of death, expressed verbally through prayer, is expressed in ritual or symbolic form (is made more real) through the anointing with oil and the imposition of hands. As I will treat these two gestures together, I must first acknowledge that in so doing I fracture the integrity of the rite. I wish to emphasize, however, that both of these ritual actions of the sacrament act as a light to illumine one's passage through the darkness of serious illness or death. They attempt to "make visible" the words of faith and hope we profess.

As the ritual actions of anointing with oil and the imposition of hands enjoy a rich history in the liturgical tradition of the Roman Catholic Church, it would be

---

[5] The *Catechism of the Catholic Church* expresses a similar assessment quite succinctly: "Illness can lead to anguish, self-absorption, sometimes even despair and revolt against God. It can also make a person more mature, helping him discern in his life what is not essential so that he can turn toward that which is. Very often illness provokes a search for God and a return to him" [9, par. 1501].

inappropriate to consider the following remarks a comprehensive interpretation of their meaning. I have chosen to limit our consideration to two of the several meanings these ritual actions can express. Understanding the sacrament as the "visible words" which sustain the patient's struggle against the darkness of serious illness or death, we will consider the ritual actions of anointing and imposition as expressing, first, the consecration and possession of the patient as a member of the Church and, second, the commissioning of the patient for further service to that Church.[6]

The "Visible Words" of the Sacrament:
The Consecration of a Valued Possession

The "matter" of the seven Catholic sacraments (the elements or gestures used in the ritual celebration) are ordinary human objects and actions which make more real the spiritual effects of the sacraments. For example, one of the effects of baptism is the cleansing of the soul from sin. The pouring of water upon the candidate as the "matter" of the sacrament is a logical choice: the "matter" symbolizes or makes more real the spiritual ablution that the sacrament effects.

The "matter" of the sacrament of anointing is an anointing with oil, and *Pastoral Care of the Sick and Dying* notes that "the Church's use of oil for healing is closely related to its remedial use in soothing and comforting the sick and in restoring the tired and the weak" [5, par. 107]. On a purely practical level, that an anointing with oil is the "matter" of this sacrament is logical and appropriate: oil-based solutions have been among our traditional medicines, and surely part of the "remedial [benefit] in soothing and comforting the sick and in restoring the tired and the weak" derives from the physical contact and action involved in the massaging of flesh.

But, as is the case with all symbols, there is more to an anointing with oil than first meets the eye—or the mind. Symbols may suggest several meanings interrelated to, and supportive of, one another. To recall Mitchell's words, "One act may 'contain' a very wide variety of meanings simultaneously" [2, p. 73].

Another major meaning attributed to the sacrament of baptism, for example, is that through this sacrament the Christian participates in the death and resurrection of Christ. This spiritual meaning is expressed with particular clarity when the person is immersed in, and then raised from, a pool of baptismal water. These very human actions of "drowning" and "rescuing" serve to make more real one aspect of the Church's words of faith concerning baptism: that through baptism Christians die to themselves and are raised up by Christ to a new life in his Church.

As is clear, then, the symbolic actions or the "matter" of baptism expresses more than one meaning. Water cleanses and purifies; water drowns. To bathe in water is to be cleaned; to be rescued from water is to be given back one's life—to have one's life redeemed or restored. In a similar way, the symbolic action of anointing with oil in our sacramental ministry to the sick suggests more than medicine or massage.

---

[6] Other interpretations are referred to briefly in the following remarks. For a more comprehensive exposition, see *Pastoral Care of the Sick and Dying* and the works cited in [3].

In Catholic liturgical tradition, anointings are rare and accompany only the key or defining moments of one's life within the Church. For example, an anointing precedes and follows the baptism of an infant. An anointing of the forehead is the principal ritual action in the sacrament of confirmation, and one part of the rite of ordination to the priesthood involves an anointing of the hands. While the symbolic weight of the anointing varies in the ritual celebration of these three sacraments,[7] the role of anointing indicates the richness and complexity associated with this action.

First, to anoint with oil is to *consecrate*, to make holy, to distinguish and set apart from the ordinary or secular that which is special and sacred.[8] Related to this is a second meaning: that is, as is clear in the biblical accounts of the anointing of kings and prophets, one is anointed for a special *vocation* or mission (we will examine this in greater detail below). Third, and again related to the notion of anointing as consecration, an anointing can symbolize also the act of *taking possession.* What has been made holy and so now has a special mission belongs to those who have administered the anointing. The anointing with oil of a sick member of our Church signifies that it is the Lord and his Church to whom this person belongs, and that we respect this member of our Church as a "valued possession."

This consecration, this "taking possession of" the sick or dying by the Church, is expressed symbolically also by what many patients have described as the most significant and healing experience of the rite, the laying on of hands. *Pastoral Care of the Sick and Dying* notes that this ritual gesture too is rich and complex in meaning:

> With this gesture the priest indicates that this particular person is the object of the Church's prayer of faith. The laying on of hands is clearly a sign of blessing, as we pray that by the power of God's healing grace the sick person may be restored to health or at least strengthened in time of illness. The laying on of hands is also an invocation: the Church prays for the coming of the Holy Spirit upon the sick person. Above all, it is the biblical gesture of healing and indeed Jesus' own usual manner of healing: "They brought the sick with various diseases to him; and he laid hands on every one of them and healed them" (Luke 4:40) [5, par. 106].

Of the four meanings given in the above citation, I wish here to comment only upon the first, and to do so in the context of the individual's relationship to his Church.

The laying on of hands symbolizes the continuing relationship between Church and patient.[9] At a time when the patient may feel isolated and alienated from family and friends—indeed, when the sick or dying person may feel abandoned by

---

[7] For example, while the anointing is essential to the celebration of confirmation, it is considered an explanatory (albeit important) element in the celebrations of baptism and orders. Some readers will know also that different oils (chrism, oil of catechumens, oil of the sick) are used for different occasions. Our point here is to explore the various meanings suggested by the ritual act of anointing.

[8] That an anointing with oil is a consecration, a "making holy," is further reflected in the Catholic tradition by the practice of anointing not only people but *things* which are consecrated—dedicated—for a special and holy purpose, e.g., the cup and plate used during the celebration of the Eucharist, the altar or table of the Lord's supper, or the church itself.

[9] I rely here upon, and highly recommend, Jennifer Glen's excellent article [11].

them—the imposition of hands expresses symbolically the relationship which does in fact continue to exist. As Glen says, the laying on of hands "asserts implicitly that he is fully acceptable to and accepted by the community in his present state. . . . It is a gesture of identification and of aggregation" [11, p. 404]. The sick or dying person is accepted by the community as a member of the community: as one not forgotten, but one who is recognized, desired, and desirable. Rahner notes that, given the sacramental structure of the Church, the actions of imposition and anointing are particularly significant with regard to the patient's continuing identification with and identity within the Body of Christ.

> Baptism, first of all, makes Christian death possible; the Holy Eucharist continuously nourishes the life of the Christian in order that, through assimilation to Christ's death, his own life, in his daily actions and suffering, may grow from within toward that consummation which achieves its full perfection in death; Extreme Unction [or anointing of the sick] is the consecration of the end of this life to the death of Christ. The beginning, the middle, and the end of Christian life, as it is an appropriation of Christ's death, are marked and consecrated through these three sacraments; for they all implant in the mortal life of the Christian soul not only the Lord's death, but his eternal life as well [10, p. 86].

This discussion should indicate clearly that the symbolic actions or "visible words" of an anointing with oil and an imposition of hands have multiple meanings. The meaning "too deep for words" which they attempt to express is actually several meanings—each of which is related to the other, each of which reinforces the other. This is the nature of symbols and rituals: they do not try to convey information so much as they try to capture our imagination.

The "Visible Words" of the Sacrament: The Commissioning of a Vocation

Just as the gestures and symbols of the sacrament of anointing are not restricted to one meaning, these ritual actions are not "visible words" for the benefit of the patient alone. The sacrament of the anointing of the sick is not only the Church ministering to one of her own; it is also a commissioning of that member's new and special ministry to the Church.

The subtle temptation in health care (or in any form of ministry) is to consider patients or parishioners as the receivers, while deeming those who care for or minister to them as the givers and providers. To the extent we acquiesce to this mutually exclusive relationship, we disregard what the patient can give us—what the patient, in fact, *must* give us. One theologian has observed, "For most, death does not come soon enough. Through the sense that death is distant and insignificant, life becomes corrupt and decayed. . . . One leads a better life if one has made a rendezvous with death" [12, p. 445].[10]

---

[10]Comment of W. Kaufman, quoted by Gisbert Greshake [12, p. 445].

We spend a good part of our lives building our careers, reputations, and names, and in that regard we often resemble the tower builders of Babel (Genesis 11, 1-9). Their sin was not the work in which they were engaged (it was, after all, good work), but was, rather, that as they went about the important task of constructing a tower to make a name for themselves, they ironically lost sight of the God whose heavens they were trying to reach.

Making a "rendezvous with death" (and this is done if and when we confront a serious illness, whether in ourselves or in others) reminds us of what the tower builders of Babel forgot: that we live ultimately not for ourselves or what we can accomplish, but to grow in and toward God's grace. Serious sickness reminds us of what we know but want to forget. We nevertheless carry within us always the knowledge that we must and will die, and that the way we will die is determined largely by how we choose to live—a choice we must always make *now*. The sick and dying come face to face with the limitations and weaknesses of human existence we all share, and as we accompany them in their journey we recognize ourselves. For while it may be one patient's body that is diseased, it is the body of Christ and his Church—the many individuals and groups with whom and around whom the patient has built his life—that are disrupted and afflicted.

Seen in this way, serious illness or approaching death invite the healthy to consider and evaluate their lives now, even as the sick or dying must evaluate theirs. This evaluation is guided by "Christian memory," the reminder that our strength is given, not self-created, and that our weakness and sin—far from excusing us—are opportunities for us to do now with our lives what we should be doing always: surrendering to the grace of God.

The vocation of the sick and dying[11] is that of witnessing their hope for and faith in the ultimate victory to which all are called: that victory which shares in Christ's putting an end to the destructive power of death. As the General Introduction to *Pastoral Care of the Sick and Dying* maintains:

> The role of the sick in the Church is to be a reminder to others of the essential or higher things. By their witness the sick show that our mortal life must be redeemed through the mystery of Christ's death and resurrection [5, par. 3].

This witnessing, this vocation, asks more of sick and dying patients than their reaching an acceptance of their impending death, as important as that acceptance may be. The sacrament does not call upon the sick or dying to accept death simply as an inevitable part of human life; it encourages them to witness their belief in the One who begins and continues life. Lawler echoes this notion of the vocation of the sick, observing that the sick "are told that in sickness they are not just people who need to be ministered to, but Christians who can now minister to the Church in a way that was not open to them when they were healthy" [8, p. 167]. The sick and dying who accept this commission to be witnesses are a sacrament, a visible sign, to others that they do

---

[11]I take the phrase from Empereur's *Prophetic Anointing* [6]. Chapter 4 of his work presents an excellent commentary on the notion of the *vocation* of the sick and the dying.

indeed know "Who it is in Whom I have put my trust" (2 Timothy 1, 12). As Power has suggested:

> Through sickness a person is put in crisis, for it makes his relation to the earth and to the human community an ambiguous one. *It is not by coming out of sickness that the crisis is resolved, but by some word that indicates its meaning and reshapes the sick man's relation to the earth and to the human community.* In Christian sacrament, the word is one of eschatological hope. The sick person who receives this word in faith and makes it his own becomes in turn a sacrament of meaning for the community [13, pp. 146-147; emphasis mine].

In the face of the darkness of sickness or death, the power who defeats all darkness is invoked and, through the ritual actions of anointing and imposition, is conveyed. Thus, the sacrament not only reaffirms and strengthens the identification and acceptance of the sick or dying with and by the Church, but also empowers them to continue the ultimate mission of the Church: witness to the ultimate victory, witness to the Ultimate Victor. Glen expounds upon this notion of the commissioning of the vocation of the sick or dying:[12]

> It is a commission which in itself constitutes a symbolic reaffirmation of the future in two respects. First, it offers him the support of the community's faith that he will indeed negotiate the dark passage of sickness successfully, a faith which they confirm in their willingness to stand by him through the struggle. Secondly, it accords to his life even in the midst of sickness a significance which will endure beyond his personal passage in the transformation of consciousness which it effects in the community as symbol expressive and directive of its corporate passage through death to the final realization of the kingdom of God. Thus to lay hands upon the sick person may be in a very real sense to empower him for his own immediate future within and for the sake of the eschatological future of the community itself [11, p. 407].

CONCLUDING REMARKS

Christ did not abolish sickness or death. The freedom and strength offered the Christian are Christ's victory over the devastating power, the destructive darkness, through which death and illness so often present themselves.

The sacrament of the anointing of the sick encourages and calls upon Christians to walk through this darkness. Making visible and tangible the words of faith the Church professes, the sacrament reassures Christians that their community of faith, founded in and grounded by its hope in Christ Jesus, continues to stand with them even when they no longer have the strength to stand by themselves. In the name of Christ and his Church, the priest calls upon the Lord to save and raise up the sick and dying through their darkness into the light of Christ. Through an anointing with

---

[12]Glen acknowledges her dependence upon David Power's fine article [13], particularly for the metaphor of "negotiating the dark passage of sickness."

holy oil and an imposition of hands, ritual gestures rich and complex in meaning, the holiness of our sick and dying is recognized. These ritual gestures also support the sick and dying in their unique ministry in the Church: their witness to the belief that victory ultimately will be theirs because they have placed their hope in the Ultimate Victor.

As a constant image in this study has been the darkness of death, we conclude by recalling that darkest of days in human history—a day which, paradoxically, infused the world with a new and stronger light. Good Friday, with its alternating themes of despair and hope, of hollow darkness and God-filled light, is that day which allows hope in the face of serious illness or death[13] [14].

On that Good Friday, there is one hanging on a cross who does not fight to save himself (although he is the only man who *could* have done that). Rather, hanging between heaven and earth, wavering between calling upon his own strength or summoning that of his Father's, he chooses words of truth: "Father, into your hands I commend my spirit" (Luke 23, 46). This is the death Christ died, the death which makes possible our life through and after death. This is Christ's death, which destroyed forever the destructive power of the darkness of human death.

As the gospels record time, it will be three days before the Father's hands guide Christ through death's darkness and lead him into eternal light. But one need not wait three days to uncover evidence of Christ's victory over this darkness. For the gospel records two others who also hang on that dark hill next to Jesus. The first, who asks that Jesus remember him when coming into his kingdom, "has indeed understood death, understood it rightly and received it as . . . salvation" [14, p. 293]. This first thief looks through the darkness of death, sees the light, and moves toward that light. Christ's response to him is the promise to which we all aspire: "Truly, I say to you, today you will be with me in Paradise" (Luke 23, 43).

But there is another hanging there, and this one chooses to remain in his darkness. He curses Christ and mocks his own act of dying, all the while turning away from the light offered him. Christ turns to him as well, but to him the Lord of all life says . . . *nothing.* As Rahner reminds us, "the darkness and silence which hung over this death serve to warn us that death can also be the onset of a deeper death still, a death that is eternal" [14, p. 293].

We cannot choose not to die. We cannot deny the powerful chains of the darkness of death. Yet we are not without choice, nor are we without freedom: for we can choose in whom, and with whom, we will die. We must fight against illness, and fight well we must. We must attend carefully to our battle against death, although we need not fight for life at any cost. For the Christian believes that life has already been paid for at great cost: the death and resurrection of Jesus Christ.

---

[13]In developing this conclusion I acknkowledge my special debt to Rahner's brief but excellent article, "On Christian Dying" [14].

In all this we must remember what it is and for whom we are fighting. Let us not be deceived that the battle is won by recovery or lost at death. Victory is victory in Christ for He is the Ultimate Victor: Christ who, by dying our death, enabled us to die his.

REFERENCES

1. K. Richter, *The Meaning of the Sacramental Symbols*, L. M. Maloney (trans.), Liturgical Press, Collegeville, 1990.
2. K. R. Mitchell, Ritual in Pastoral Care, *Journal of Pastoral Care, 43*, pp. 68-77, 1989.
3. S. Bailey, The Arts as an Avenue to the Spirit, *New Catholic World, 230*, pp. 264-267, 1987.
4. J. Glen, Rites of Healing: A Reflection in Pastoral Theology, in *Alternative Futures for Worship*, (Vol. 7: Anointing of the Sick), P. J. Fink (ed.), Liturgical Press, Collegeville, pp. 33-63, 1987.
5. *Pastoral Care of the Sick and Dying: Rites of Anointing and Viaticum*, English translation by International Commission on English in the Liturgy, various publishers, 1983.
6. J. Empereur, *Prophetic Anointing: God's Call to the Sick, the Elderly and the Dying*, Glazier, Wilmington, 1982.
7. C. Gusmer, *And You Visited Me: Sacramental Ministry to the Sick and Dying* (Rev. Edition), Pueblo, New York, 1989.
8. M. G. Lawler, *Symbol and Sacrament: A Contemporary Sacramental Theology*, Paulist, New York, 1987.
9. *Catechism of the Catholic Church*, English translation by United States Catholic Conference Inc.*, Libreria Editrice Vaticana, 1994.
10. K. Rahner, *On the Theology of Death*, C. Henkey (trans.), Herder and Herder, New York, 1961.
11. J. Glen, Sickness and Symbol: The Promise of the Future, *Worship, 46*, pp. 397-411, 1980.
12. G. Greshake, Extreme Unction or Anointing of the Sick: A Plea for Discrimination, *Review for Religious, 46*, pp. 435-452, 1986.
13. D. N. Power, Let the Sick Man Call, *Heythrop Journal, 19*, pp. 256-270, 1978.
14. K. Rahner, On Christian Dying, in *Theological Investigations* (Vol. 7: Further Theology of the Spiritual Life I), K. Rahner (ed.), D. Bourke (trans.), Seabury, New York, pp. 285-293, 1979.

The Role of the Visual Image in Psychodynamics of Grief Resolution (Viewed Through Jewish Law and Tradition)

Hannah Sherebrin

SWORD OF THE RIGHTEOUS

And they have torn their garments; and have turned
. The portraits to the wall, and hid the bright
Reflections of a mirror in a white
Cloth; they have stared on Sorrow and discerned
Fatality; they have mourned . . .
    And ceased to mourn. On stools in stolid plight
    Shoeless they sit; suddenly stand upright
And chant the *Kaddish* they have lately learned.
    For why be desolate, and why complain
Seeing that Death has always his last say?
    Let rather piety accept his reign.
Rather let worthy unconcern allay
    The anguish, iterating the refrain:
He who has given, He has snatched away.

A. M. Klein [1]

To find universal principles guiding grief resolution and to test them on the bases of different psychological theories, I selected the Jewish model because, in spite of its ancient origins, it is still practiced largely unchanged. Since a system has survived almost intact for over two thousand years, its principles may be of benefit to the therapist dealing with the bereaved. I undertook, therefore, a survey of literature pertaining to grief, grief within Jewish law and tradition, and the use of Art Therapy in grief resolution. Although literature about death and bereavement existed even in antiquity, psychological investigation of the subject begins with the publication in 1917 of *Mourning and Melancholia* by Sigmund Freud [2]. The importance of the visual image and the use of art in therapy were explored extensively by Carl G. Jung, considered to be the "father" of Art Therapy [3]. The bulk of the literature on the use of visual images in grief resolution has been published in the last twenty years. The study of this topic is still in its infancy.

This chapter reviews basic ideas of grief and loss, and compares normal and pathological grief reactions. My objective is to understand the principles behind the visual images created in Jewish rituals, using a psychoanalytic, individual,

237

behavioral, and humanistic/existential theory base. Therapists involved with the bereaved, the dying, and other clients resolving various losses often play the role extended family and clergy used to perform, comforting the bereaved and facilitating normal grief resolution.

The first definition of *resolution* in Webster's is the act of analyzing a complex notion into simpler forms. This, in a way, is what therapists do in grief work. The second definition, however, fits my model better, describing resolution as the progression of a chord from dissonance to consonance—in other words, as *integration*. It seems we never "get over" our losses. The best we can do is to integrate the loss into our lives so that we can continue in harmony. Understanding why a system or a body of rituals has worked for centuries might suggest more effective modes of grief therapy.

BASIC IDEAS OF GRIEF AND LOSS

The words *bereavement* and *grief* stem etymologically from the old Frisian word *reva,* to rob. Western society regards death and bereavement as a robbery, and an acute deprivation of a significant person in our lives, hence the adversarial attitude toward the subject. Reactions to death vary greatly in different societies.

Volkhart and Michael observe that some conflict is also generated by disparities between subjective, personal reactions and a specific society's expectations [4]. In Western society, according to this study, there are some provisions for healthy grief, but individuals who suffer from accumulated guilt and hostility may become extremely vulnerable to psychic breakdown.

Lindemann, an early pioneer in the study of grief, stated in his 1944 study of the survivors of the Coconut Grove fire in Boston, that grief is a "definite syndrome with psychological and somatic symptomatology" [5]. The symptomatology of the grief syndrome can be defined as an intense emotional suffering, set off by a loss. Beyond loss through death, Peretz identified four categories of loss: loss of a significant person, loss of a part of the self, loss of material objects, and developmental loss [6]. Divorce, separations, geographical moves, surgery, physical disabilities, various assaults, unemployment, enforced retirement, the empty nest syndrome, immigration, and intermarriage are not rare occurrences in our society. Other losses are predictable developmental occurrences such as weaning, toilet training, birth of siblings, starting school, leaving home, and ageing. There are even losses in psychotherapy, as one learns to give up neurotic patterns, a childhood body image, or wishes and unfulfilled hopes.

Bertha Simos warns that the practitioner must know the difference between loss and basic deprivation, which is known as compounded loss [7]: the "practitioner must know the difference in dynamics between never having had at all and having had and then not having" [7, p. 338]. The two experiences demand different therapeutic approaches. Here I will deal exclusively with loss, separation, and fear of loss, which are lifelong experiences, common to all peoples in all cultures. The understanding of loss and grief by clinicians, as stated by Simos, lies in the realization that "the fear of loss, loss, and separation, all related in the unconscious, are important underlying dynamics in much of the pathology seen in their work, hidden under various diagnostic label" [7, p. 337].

NORMAL GRIEF PATTERNS

Solomon tries to present a consensus on grief based on the writings of Lindemann, Engle, Parker, and Green [8]. He concludes that grief is normal, healthy, and appropriate, and that the feelings expressed are complex. The emotional reaction to loss is usually accompanied by a range of contradictory feelings and seemingly aberrant behaviors, yet grief follows a predictable course and is usually of a self-limiting nature.

From a psychiatric orientation, we could classify grief among the Transient Situational Disturbances that appear among the age-related adjustment reactions listed in Diagnostic and Statistical Manual II [9]. However, in the revised edition, DSM-III-R, grief, mourning, and cognate terms are not so listed [10]. Simos claims that childhood and old age are possibly the most precarious times for a loss to be damaging [7], based on the view that the old "have diminished narcissistic supplies with little opportunity for restitution, while the immature ego of the child is too fragile to allow the pain of catastrophic grief to be worked through" [7, p. 340].

In general, grief from bereavement eventually resolves itself completely. But Solomon warns against dismissing the syndrome as insignificant because "pathological grief may, at times, appear deceptively normal because it is a familiar universal experience" [8, p. 55].

Lindemann proposes essentially four stages in the dynamic expression of grief: 1) the early stage of shock, disbelief, and denial; 2) ventilation of affect in the form of anxiety, sadness, and anger; 3) modulation of second-stage emotions by a variety of defense mechanisms; and 4) replacement of early defense mechanisms by more sophisticated behavior, resulting in a process of coping and adapting [5]. By general consensus, the acute phase lasts six to eight weeks, but mementoes and questions can trigger emotional reactions throughout the first year—or even years later. The anniversary date is widely recognized as a trigger for emotional reactions, and different religions and therapy modalities have devised rituals to commemorate anniversaries.

The somatic symptoms of grief cover a wide range: general feeling of malaise, hyperventilation, throat constriction, "lump in the throat," anorexia, dyspepsia, insomnia, or a "hollow feeling in the chest." The physical distress of the mourner frequently includes dull headaches, backache, dry mouth, eye irritation, and nasal congestion.

The stunned reaction of the first stage is normally accompanied by intense confusion and denial, and a feeling of numbness, sometimes called "nature's anesthesia." The numbness is nature's way of allowing us the time to mobilize coping mechanisms. As the anesthesia wears off, the distress symptoms set in with a growing awareness of the reality. Many mourners report, according to Solomon, "an obsessive preoccupation with the image of the deceased," to the point of generating an "insanity panic" [8, p. 58].

Rage and anger at the "robbery" are often expressed vocally and with crying outbursts, mingled with guilt. A self-blaming attitude is accentuated in cases where there was some tension in the relationship. These rage and guilt feelings are related to missed opportunities to express affection, to share feelings, to tell secrets, to say goodbye. The closer the relationship was with the deceased, the more anger seems to occur [11]. This anger stems from the interruption of shared plans, the feeling of being deserted, and the feeling that we deserve to have our plans and hopes continue. Usually the anger is not expressed at the deceased, but rather is misdirected at the self or at others.

Within four to eight weeks, the acute grief normally subsides. As the loss is faced realistically through allowing the flow of feelings, sorrow, and tears, reminiscing about the deceased, sharing mementoes with family and friends, "the mourner gradually draws back into himself in readiness for a future investment in another relationship with a person or an object" [8, p. 60].

Acute grief is a time of crisis. In most crisis-intervention models, the major focus is on helping the bereaved resume task-oriented behavior as quickly as possible. Crisis intervention practitioners, whose belief system reflects the attitudes of today's society, in which problem solving takes precedence over emotional expression, may in fact become a deterrent to the working through of grief. Simos also cautions:

> Because of our cultural emphasis on competence, adequacy, and strength, the bereaved are often prevented by family and friends from experiencing the emotions which should follow loss in order to find a healthy resolution. This lack of social validation often brings the bereaved to the clinician, who socialized into the same value system as everyone else, is in danger of making the same errors [7].

Mourning, which is the process of the expression of grief, involves the psychological task of breaking the emotional tie with what has been lost, and eventually reinvesting in attachments to living individuals and existing objects. Our unique reaction to a loss is governed by our past experiences of a loss or separation. Problems of separation, individuation, factors of age, sex, cultural and social attitudes toward loss all play a role in our individual reactions. The family style in grieving, coupled with current supports or stresses, also has to be considered.

PATHOLOGICAL GRIEF REACTIONS

In spite of the individual patterns for mourning, there is some consensus about pathological grief patterns, as discussed in Solomon [8]. One of the most common and serious obstacles to grief resolution is denial. Although discussed previously, denial as a normal immediate reaction may block the natural pattern of dealing with bereavement. The problem becomes more menacing, in Solomon's view, by the pervasive denial fostered by the entire institutional configuration of American society. Parson and Lidz, however, contend that American society meets with denial only loss that is premature, adventitious, or inappropriate [12]. Pathological denial blinds the individual to the reality of death, no matter whether it stems from within the person's psyche or from external social influences. The illusion that death did not occur prevents the person from exercising any initiative to deal with the loss.

In *The Pornography of Death,* Gorer claims that in the twentieth century, death has replaced sex as a forbidden theme [13]. In contrast, in the Middle Ages, popular manuals like *Ars Moriendi* instructed the reader how to "die well" [14]. We find an early description of a man preparing for his death in the story of Isaac in the Bible. Jacob's deathbed scene shows the development of respect and dignity accorded to the dying person. When Jacob realizes he is going to die, he calls his sons to gather around him so that he can tell them "that which shall befall you in the end of days" (Genesis, 49:1). Jacob charges his children to bury him in the family plot where both his parents and grandparents are buried. This moving account concludes: "When Jacob made an end of charging his sons, he gathered up his feet into the bed, and expired, and was gathered unto his people" (Genesis, 49:33).

The shift from the traditional attitude where the dying person was in charge of his farewells began in the twentieth century with the notion that it would be kinder to conceal the truth and spare the person the anguish of death. The leap from that position to the notion of sparing society the ordeal of death was inevitable. The site of death shifted from the home to the hospital. The hospital staff assumed the role of presiding over death, stripping both the dying person and the family of participation, and leaving them as helpless onlookers. Solomon reports in an article on "the Death Industry" that funeral homes have now taken over the funeral service from the clergy, causing de-ritualization of the rites [8, p. 74].

A common side effect of the grief process is depression in varying degrees. Some physicians use antidepressants to alleviate the symptoms and allow normal grieving to occur. At times the normal mourning process is blocked. When the loss is overwhelming, or the mourner's emotional condition is fragile and unstable, when previous bereavements stay unresolved, or the family and the social surroundings are unsympathetic, the mourner may use psychological defenses to obscure the unresolved grief, thus creating morbid grief reactions. However, Simos states: "what appears as most pathological may, when seen through the grief model rather than the medical model, have a surprisingly quick outcome" [7, p. 342].

Chronic grief can be seen as a result of unresolved and unexpressed hostility toward the deceased. The conflicting feelings of "good riddance," or relief from the dead person, and guilt at the "inappropriateness" of such feelings may bring about intense feelings of self-blame. Other causes of chronic grief may include rage over a brutal murder or a tragic death caused by accident or suicide. The person will usually display endless anger toward God, physicians, and any other number of others, perhaps reflecting an attempt to diminish the pain associated with the loss. Feuchtwanger discusses a case of a teenager who witnessed the tragic death of her mother at the vulnerable age of six [15]. In such cases, we see a reaction of self-blame and chronic grieving, reaching a crisis situation when triggered by another possible loss. Current research by Lindemann and others claim that overreaction to current bereavements may constitute a delayed, distorted response to earlier unresolved grief.

Delayed grief can manifest itself in overactivity, withdrawal, emergence of symptoms related to the terminal illness of the deceased, character changes, and unwarranted hostility toward specific individuals. Events leading to the eruption of delayed grief may be anniversaries of the death or the year the mourner reaches the age of the deceased. Barry warns of internal and external factors that tend to inhibit mourning [16], such as too much personal or family responsibility that does not allow time to mourn or social norms where open displays of grief run counter to the tradition of "stiff upper lip." The prevailing view in the current literature is summarized by Solomon: "Grief is a normal reaction to bereavement; absence of grief is a deviation from the norm; unexpressed grief will tend to find alternative channels of expression" [8].

Loss of parents or siblings in childhood contributes to later problems with subsequent losses and, in the view of some researchers, to depression and mental illness later in life. All schools of psychology agree on the importance of psychic development in childhood, even if the developmental stages and the importance of dealing with loss are viewed differently. Bowlby understands childhood bereavement from the point of view of the Adlerian theory of Individual Psychology [17]. The loss of a primary nurturing figure during the formative years robs the child of the ability to develop a powerful independence, leading to pathological mourning as a reaction to consequent loss.

Juvenile delinquency is seen by some researchers as an alternative expression of mourning, or a substitute for pathological grief. My own observations of juvenile delinquents concur with Solomon's findings, which reveal in case after case, "suppressed grief compounded by guilt eventually surfacing in 'acted out' anti-social behaviour" [8, p. 94]. Professional intervention in cases of childhood bereavement is thus deemed important, no matter what school of psychology the therapist follows.

RITUALS FACILITATING THE MOURNING PROCESS

Gorer believes that the inability of our society to resolve grief is connected to the absence of rituals. A ritual, as defined in Webster's, is "the established form for a ceremony; a ceremonial act or action; any formal and customarily repeated act or series of acts." Rando suggests that the acts in a ritual are behaviors "which give symbolic expression to certain feelings and thoughts of the actor(s) individually or as a group" [18, p. 23]. As aids to mourning, rituals that prescribe a specific grief strategy exist in all cultures, mainly incorporated into religious practices.

With recent global mobility, barriers of cultural isolation have been broken, leading to shifts away from traditional rituals. The changes can be clearly seen in the last decade in the United States, where distinct ethnic cultures have been subjected to outside influences. We see such change in Italian and Jewish communities where, despite differences, rituals were designed to give the mourner a period of bereavement and a traditionally accepted emotional outlet for grief. The present shift toward de-ritualization of the funeral and mourning practices does not allow grief to follow a natural course to resolution.

Colman, in *Abnormal Psychology and Modern Life,* argues that the shift toward an attitude where a mourner is expected to return to normal life immediately may contribute heavily to the recent increase in mental health problems [19]. "If present trends continue, approximately one person in ten now living in this country will at some time require professional treatment" [19, p. 18]. Rando remarks that today's mental health profession frequently has the task of helping create therapeutic rituals to replace traditional ones [18].

If a therapist needs to develop a ritual to assist individuals to complete their grief, an understanding of the components of a ritual may be helpful. Moore and Myerhoff state what a ritual entails: explicit purpose, explicit symbols and messages, implicit statements, social relationships, and culture versus chaos—the same dimensions exist in traditional and religious ritual [20]. As Rando notes, the compelling outcome of translating thought or affect into action was dwelt upon by Boss, Freud, and Langer, who remarked on the ritual's capacity to transform experience, as word-bound thought usually cannot. Symbolic acts that are performed embed themselves into our memory as mental images.

JUDAISM, DEATH, AND MOURNING

In an attempt to understand the role of the visual image in the psychodynamics of grief, a brief study of traditional Jewish mourning rituals may be useful as a model. Judaism offers a comprehensive bereavement code, a mourner's manual, which is the oldest known code for the bereaved. It has served its adherents for thousands of years, offering them a holistic strategy for mourning. It continues to serve: in Gorer's words, "The most complete pattern of time-limited mourning still observed in England is that followed by Orthodox Jews . . . " [14, p. 76].

The *Halakhic* Components of Mourning

Halakha, The Way, or The Jewish Law, originates in the statutory *Torah* of Moses. Details were transmitted through the oral law, and thereafter in the codes, rulings, and decisions recorded in the common law down to the present. The laws of mourning, as prescribed by *Halakha,* reflect the Jewish attitude toward life and death. Death is taken for granted as part of life, and is considered inevitable. In the Bible, death is accepted, not denied or avoided, and Job's words: "The Lord gave, and the Lord hath taken away; blessed be the name of the Lord" (Job, 1:21), are still said by mourners today.

The laws governing mourning are systematic, regulated, standardized, and detailed. In every aspect, they reflect the concept of human dignity, not only the dignity of the living but also of the dead. Solomon remarks, "In this warm and reassuring ambience of mourning, shame and denial were out of place . . . grief and mourning were exercises in healing which concomitantly glorified God, ennobled man and quickened society" [8, pp. 165-166]. Death is also perceived as the great equalizer. Man and woman, rich and poor, are all treated equally. Rabbi Gamliel, almost two thousand years ago, instituted the practice of *tachrichim,* uniform shrouds, to protect the poor from shame, and the rich from exhibitionist competition.

Preparing the body for burial is a unique *mitzvah* (a divine commandment), the performance of which is free of ulterior motive. There is no tangible compensation for time, effort, and cost expended on behalf of the dead. The performance of the *mitzvah* is incumbent upon every Jew, and therefore considered a communal responsibility.

The burial is performed as soon as possible in order to shorten the period of *aninut*, the pre-burial mourning period. The *onan*, or the "one who feels grieved" [21, p. I:85], is exempt from the observances of all the *mitzvot* (positive commandments) in order to allow all energy to be concentrated on preparations for the burial. This practice recognizes the psychological needs of the early stages of shock, disbelief, and denial—and the need to separate oneself from all that is worldly—yet tries to counteract denial by imposing on the *onan* the responsibility of expediting funeral arrangements.

Keriah—The Rending of Garments

The most striking, graphic, and powerful expression of grief is the practice of *keriah* or rending of the garment, performed by the mourner prior to the funeral service or before interment. As the symbolic expression of anger and frustration, the

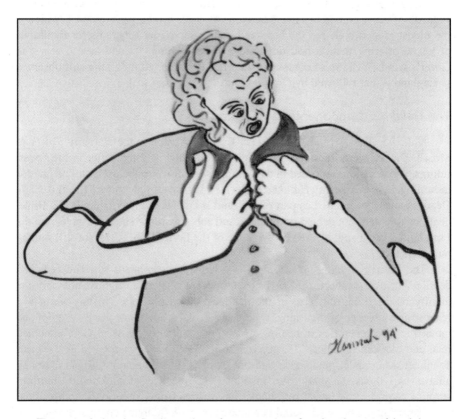

Figure 1. A drawing by the author of a mourner performing the act of *keriah*.

ritual of *keriah* is seen by Solomon as "a model of the interface of psychological theory and normative Judaism" [8, p. 347]. It symbolizes the rending of a relationship, and establishes in the mourner the stabbing finality of the separation. The expression of this rent on the mourner's own clothing is significant, since clothing can be considered an extension of one's own person.

Solomon states: "Narcissism finds eloquent expression in modes of dress . . . as an extension of the ego" [8, p. 35]. Therefore, it appears reasonable that *keriah* performed on a personal garment rather than on an ordinary piece of cloth would maximize the effect. Venting one's rage by tearing a rag may indeed be helpful; however, rending an article of clothing, an object closely related to the ego, an externalized extension of the mourner's inner self, seems to have greater dynamic significance.

Although the rending of garments, like the destruction of any property, would normally be prohibited, the *Halakha* accords a special dispensation to the grief-afflicted individual, recognizing the *keriah* as an acting out of a dangerous, self-destructive internalization of fury. Maimonides, as reported in Solomon, considers *keriah* as an emotional outlet providing some release for the anguished mourner, thus receiving the same dispensation as any constructive act of destruction, such as burning fuel to produce heat [8, p. 344].

Recognizing that complete spontaneity may eventuate in excessive mourning, *Halakha* regulates closely the way *keriah* is performed. Lamm states that the law requires the rending to be performed while standing, explaining: "The posture of accepting grief in Jewish life is always erect, symbolizing both strength in the face of crisis, and respect for the deceased" [22, p. 44]. The minute detailed instructions (about the place and length of the tear) forces mourners who are reluctant to express grief to act their way into feeling.

The obligation to perform *keriah* rests equally on men, women, and even minors. The *Talmud* states: "Children may be made to rend their clothes in order to stir up sadness" (*Moed Katan,* 26b). One is obligated to mourn, and therefore perform the act of *keriah,* for parents, children, spouses, and siblings. It is also performed upon the death of a great teacher or rabbi, and upon the destruction of a scroll or *Torah* or of a great religious site, like the temple. The place of the tear is governed by the relationship of the deceased to the mourner. The tear is on the right side of an outer garment for all but parents, for whom the tear is on the left—above the heart.

The act of *keriah* symbolizes the finality of a relationship, the emotional severing of ties. Gordon notes that the *keriah* is a "visible, dramatic symbol of the internal tearing asunder that the mourner feels in his relationship with the deceased [23].

Pursuing the hypothesis of a sound psychological dimension in the *Halakhic* approach to mourning, we will look at the *keriah* from the perspective of several schools of psychology. From a Freudian point of view (based on *Mourning and Melancholia* [2]), *keriah* can function as the reality testing that leads to "libidinal decathexis" or, simply stated, the severing of emotional ties to the love object. Adler understands grief as an actual shrinkage of the psychic front, a prerequisite to the subsequent expansion in which the sad person achieves his personal elevation through an "anti-social manoeuvre intended to register a hostile gesture against society" [24, p. 232]. The manoeuvre, which Adler sees as manipulating the society for sympathy, can be expressed through the act of *keriah*. The sympathy it generates, it is hoped, will lead to the understanding environment that Adler prescribes for grief resolution.

Bereavement and depression are seen through Behaviorist eyes as a consequence of extinction. The theory explains a large proportion of an individual's behavior as a consequence of the withdrawal of positive reinforcements, which occur with the traumatic severing of channels of communication with a loved person. Behavior-oriented therapy would probably suggest treatment that includes both operant and respondent conditioning. The *keriah* could be seen as an act that helps the individual to establish a new behavior of grieving, one which will be reinforced by the community around him—and the first step toward re-establishing new channels of communication for other positive reinforcements.

Humanists like Carl Rogers and Abraham Maslow, as reported in Solomon [8], stress a person's need to feel safe and accepted for normal development and "self-actualization." Losing a loved object threatens one's sense of safety by exposing one's helplessness and mortality. By dying, the deceased abandoned, and thereby implied rejection of, the living. The act of severing the ties, the *keriah*, is a confrontation of one's inevitable subjective suffering over the loss—and one's own eventual death.

According to Frankel, the ultimate existential objective is to transcend anguish and death [25]. Death forces individuals to use time constructively, by rendering life finite. This finiteness does not negate the individual's responsibility to the community, just as death does not jeopardize life: "Death itself is what makes life meaningful" [25, p. 74]. Existential and Humanistic psychology both prescribe as a modality of therapy the direct confrontation with, and the acceptance of, the reality of death. They also offer respect for human dignity and understanding of a person's social predicament and need for acceptance. The act of *keriah* can therefore be seen as a challenge to grow emotionally and mature spiritually—a challenge, "to surmount the sorrowful vicissitudes of the mortal condition" [25, p. 63].

No matter from what angle the different schools of psychology view death, they all seem to agree about the basic issues. The immediate mourning process should take place so that the "work of mourning" can progress through its various stages. Whereas denial is rejected as inappropriate, an accepting attitude toward bereavement is deemed appropriate and desirable.

The Burial

In the Jewish tradition, the funeral and burial service are based on concern for the honor and dignity of the deceased. Burial, or interment into the earth, is the honorable end accorded anything sacred. A deceased person is compared to a burned scroll of the holy *Torah* and requires similar interment in the "House of Eternity," an expression still used in modern Hebrew for cemetery. Customarily, seven pauses, with reading of lamentations, are observed on the last procession to the grave. The ritual of the seven stops may be a symbolic demonstration of the reluctance to hasten the actual interment. This reluctance is similarly reflected in the custom of filling in the grave, a *mitzvah* in which all able-bodied people participate. This final tribute is part of the "act of loving kindness" in which relatives and friends participate. The three spadefuls of earth dropped into the grave by each participant symbolize a person's soul, spirit, and breath. The spade is not transferred from hand to hand, but planted back into the mound of earth for the next participant to pick up, as though not to make haste.

The bereaved, now joined by the congregants, chant the time-honored mourner's *Kaddish* Lamm writes:

> The *Kaddish* is a vigorous declaration of faith. It is one of the most beautiful, deeply significant and spiritually moving prayers in the Jewish liturgy. . . . It is a call to God from the depths of catastrophe, exalting His name and praising Him, despite the realization that He has just wrenched a human being from life [22, p. 150].

With the conclusion of the service, the congregants part to form two rows, as if a guard of honor, and the mourners pass between them into the mourning period, with its emphasis on the honor and needs of the living. "May the Omnipotent comfort you among the other mourners of Zion and Jerusalem," the congregants chant. They offer the mourners the support of family, friends, community, and tradition as they begin the journey back to the world of the living. Explaining the tradition of washing the hands as one leaves the cemetery, Solomon quotes Rabinowicz's view that it may demonstrate symbolically that we are not responsible, that we "wash our hands of the death" [8, p. 230].

The Seriated Mourning Process

At the conclusion of the interment, the bereaved enters a series of mourning stages, consisting of three distinct periods. The most intense stage of grief occurs during *shivah* (Hebrew for "seven"), the first seven days of mourning. The next more moderate mourning stage is the *shloshim*, literally "thirty," a month-long period, which includes the seven days of *shivah*. The full year, including *shloshim*, can be described as shallow or emblematic mourning, and is observed only following the death of parents.

At the house of the mourner, the stage is set for the first phase of grief work. Many of the customs still seen today stem from the book of Job. Low stools await the return of the mourners; some people sit on pillows on the floor. Mirrors are covered or turned to the wall. The origin of this custom is not clear. Some explain the mirror as a symbol of vanity, and therefore their use is forbidden during mourning. A tall *shivah* candle is lit, and burns for the entire seven days. This candle is also called *ner neshama*, a candle of the soul. A smaller version, which burns for twenty-four hours, is lit on every anniversary of the death.

Upon returning home from the harsh reality of the burial, the mourner, in slippers or socks, is seated on a low stool, and fed a "meal of recovery." But how can a mourner, just returned from depositing a body of a loved one in a grave, come home and eat? The decision is again taken away from the bereaved, in order to prevent their over-identification with the deceased. The prescribed meal, prepared by neighbors, is rich in grief allusions and symbolism affirming life. Eggs, symbolic of life and rebirth, and other round foods like lentils are used because they are shaped without a mouth-like opening. This symbolizes the mourner who is left speechless by the loss. Bread must be included in connection with mourning practices mentioned in the Bible (Ezekiel, 24:17); bread is also a simple staple food that is "broken" between friends. In this stage spectators become participants, bringing the sustenance of life to the mourner, and so become involved with him or her. It is mandatory for the neighbors, not the mourner, to prepare this meal. The meal lets the mourner make a statement, symbolically, to choose life.

During the week of *shivah,* mourners are encouraged to talk about the deceased; photograph albums are often shared with family and friends. Freud writes about the dynamics of the mourning process, describing the great preoccupation with the "specific memories of the deceased, or love object" [2, p. xiv:245]. He regards this sharing as "the painful work of mourning essential for readjustment to the loss" [2, p. xiv:245].

The *shivah* has been described by Kidorf as a form of group psychotherapy [26]. The house in which the *shivah* takes place lends itself to a setting for psychodrama. Visitors often prompt role playing on the part of the mourner, and people who tend to be overcontrolled can act out in a socially approved manner. He writes: "mourners sitting together as a group . . . have an opportunity to project their feelings from themselves as individuals to the group as a whole" [26, p. 45]. Regression in the service of the ego can be easily facilitated because of the "in group" nature of the *shivah* participants. The *shivah* period affords an opportunity to cry, to express feelings, to attempt to resolve ambivalences, all in a leaderless group setting. There are of course dangers of withdrawal from the group, but the physical proximity and the time constraints force the members to look at the outside world toward the end of the week of mourning. Kidorf concludes:

> . . . with the end of the *shivah* . . . a kind of end spurt occurs. One sees this often in individual as well as in group therapy . . . members who have worked through the stages of catharsis, regression, and the return of ego functioning have now reached a new level of maturity [36, p. 46].

At the end of seven days, the second phase of mourning begins lasting for thirty days. The restrictions of the first phase are somewhat relaxed. Work resumes. The saying of the *Kaddish,* the memorial prayer, continues, bringing the mourner into the communal service twice a day to face and share the loss within a healing togetherness. This twice daily recitation of *Kaddish* for a dead parent continues for eleven months following the death, and can be seen as the third stage in the mourning process. Females are not obligated to recite the *Kaddish;* they are, however, encouraged to take this responsibility upon themselves if they so wish, especially when there is no son to do so.

Finally the continuing role of the *Halakha* in grief management leads to the annual lighting of a memorial candle, coupled with joining the congregation to recite *Kaddish,* creating an opportunity to reexamine any residual ambiguities related to the loss and to consolidate recent gains.

THE USE OF VISUAL IMAGES IN GRIEF THERAPY

Each individual faced with loss and death will conjure a mental image of events or objects, depending on his or her culture and past experience—perhaps a certain way of dress, a wreath on a door, an open grave, the interment, a wake, or a painful void. Pictorial representations of memories, personal symbols, and archetypal symbols related to unresolved grief are frequently found in the art work of people undergoing Art Therapy. Simon writes that since Art Therapy stimulates both the conscious and unconscious expression of conflicts, and provides a safe setting in which to work on their ultimate resolution, "unresolved bereavement needs often surface spontaneously in art works" [27, p. 136]. Ulman explains how Art Therapy may help permit the direct expression of dreams, fantasies, and other inner experiences to flow onto paper or to emerge in other plastic forms [28]. It creates a situation in which unconscious material escapes censorship more easily. The productions are durable, so their content cannot be erased by forgetting, and their authorship is hard to deny. The therapeutic process is thus speeded up, and "the resolution of transference is made easier" [28, p. 42].

Kohut, representing a psychoanalytic point of view, points out that artistic work functions as a means of dealing with pain and tension by transforming it into a form of imaging or allowing recall of an object when it is not there [29]. The introjection of the object and then identifying with it to the point where it becomes part of the person is the structure building or "transmuting internalization" referred to by Kohut [29]. Martin contends that grief must be shared [30]. In order to share the feelings of loss in therapy, we must risk trust before expressing inner rage at being abandoned. Martin writes: "Society has few areas where this degree of feeling can be expressed short of murder and violence" [30, p. 1]. Art can be seen as a substitute for violence since it encompasses the same impulses that drive a person to violence: "the hunger for meaning, ecstasy, risk, and the drive to create" [30, p. 12].

Grief resolution can be achieved in a multitude of ways, many of which lend themselves to the use of the visual image. The process of "Operational Mourning," a technique devised by Paul and Grosser, creates an environment in which they involve the family in a belated mourning exercise [31]; it can be enhanced by drawing. "Reliving, Revising, and Revisiting," a technique proposed by Melges and DeMasco, uses guided imagery to facilitate *reliving* the sequence of the loss in the "mind's eye," *revising* the scene to remove the grief barriers, and finally *revisiting* the revised scene as if it is happening in the present [11]. The use of art in guided imagery is widely accepted, rendering this technique especially adaptable for Art Therapy.

As already mentioned, clinical intervention in childhood bereavement is especially important as a preventative measure to forestall many adult psychiatric disorders [8]. The use of Art Therapy in hospitals to help children cope with terminal illness and grief is now spreading. The nonverbal activities may allow the children to express conflicts that they would be unable or afraid to discuss in traditional, insight-oriented therapy. Zambelli et al. state: "A creative arts approach enables bereaved children to transcend the intellectual and emotional limitations associated with understanding and conveying feelings about death" [32, p. 42]. The rationale for conducting a parallel parent support group rests with the assumption that anxiety about death creates a closed system of communication in a family. Such programs help the family achieve a better level of emotional functioning through facing the anxiety of death together.

Proposing another use of Art Therapy for grief resolution, Junge suggests that grieving family members create a "Book about Daddy Dying" as a vehicle for family ritual to aid in the transition from one life stage to another [33]. The book, which utilizes art therapy techniques based on a family systems approach, has as its goal "the openness and flexibility of the system at a time of great family crisis and change" [33, p. 4]. Junge has used this technique with children and their surviving parent. Drawings, paintings, photographs, and written reminiscences, good and bad feelings, were put together in this symbolic ritual act to become a permanent container of memories, feelings, and history. Junge concludes:

> It is a book made by those still living and is representative of the acknowledgement and permanency of important feelings and memories, and that those we love live on in our memories and feelings. This acknowledgement can be crucial in the process of saying goodbye, for it is the beginning of letting go and of going on [33, p. 9].

A qualitative investigation was undertaken by McIntyre trying to answer the question, "What is the experience of art therapy for bereaved children?" [34]. She concludes that in the art process, healing comes through creative transformation of pain and conflict. This is expressed also in the interpretation of the art by its young creators. She concludes, based on interviews with participating children and their parents: "the image created in art provides an opening to express grief issues. . . . The child uses this opening to gain understanding and control over the grief process" [34, p. 24].

Story-telling in words and pictures is a powerful tool. A group of children age eight to fourteen under my supervision used computers with a drawing program and a word processor. By writing animal or imaginary creature stories, they were able to express emotions previously blocked and to share them with the group. Many therapists using Art Therapy have probably developed other innovative techniques that are yet to be published. The field is still in its infancy, and the literature is by no means vast.

CONCLUSION

By investigating the role of the visual image in the psychodynamics of grief management, my hope was to show the potential hazards of unresolved grief, to understand the role visual images play in grief resolution within Jewish tradition, and to suggest potential uses of the visual image in treatment or intervention. I agree with Simos that given the proper external support and validation, the bereaved can experience normal grief as both a self-draining and a healing process [7].

Therapists do not come into a relationship without their own baggage, or as Strupp calls it, *weltanschauung* (view of the world, system of beliefs) [35]. This system of beliefs contains, besides theoretical orientations, personal experiences steeped in cultural background. Obviously these beliefs play an important role in determining what and how the client will learn. Concepts of mental health and moral and religious values are all communicated. Strupp comments: "Like it or not, there is no such thing as 'value free' psychotherapy, and the 'neutral stance' advocated by orthodox psychoanalysis is surely a myth" [34, p. 316]. The sound psychological dimensions employed in the *Halakhic* approach certainly influence my *weltanschauung*. Strupp emphasizes, however, the considerable difference between a therapist who openly indoctrinates a patient and one who is aware of the potential impact of his or her own value system on clients, and encourages them to find their own solutions. Faith, or a belief system, may help a mourner mourn, but it cannot be a substitute for mourning. Therefore, it is the therapist who must help the client with unresolved grief find a way to mourn.

From my experiences with people in grief, I have learned that a clinician has to listen (and bear to hear repetition), to support expression of feelings (and reassure about their normality), and above all to remain serene in the emergence of client dependency, in order to allow it to develop toward growth from within. Finally, in order to tolerate another's pain without prematurely cutting it off to relieve one's own discomfort, clinicians must, as Simos says, have studied their own grief and loss and worked them through to a healthy resolution [7, p. 341].

REFERENCES

1. A. M. Klein, *The Collected Poems of A. M. Klein,* M. Wadington (ed.), McGraw-Hill, Ryerson Ltd., Toronto, 1974.
2. S. Freud, Mourning and Melancholia, in *The Standard Edition of the Complete Psychological Works of Sigmund Freud,* J. Strachey (ed.), Hagan Press, New York, pp. 239-260, 1973.
3. C. G. Jung, *Man and His Symbols,* Dell, New York, 1964.
4. E. H. Volkhart and S. T. Michael, Bereavement and Mental Health, in *Explorers in Social Psychiatry,* A. H. Leighton, J. A. Clausen, and R. N. Wilson (eds.), Basic Books, New York, 1957.
5. E. Lindemann, Symptomatology and Management of Acute Grief, *American Journal of Psychiatry, 101,* pp. 141-148, 1944.
6. D. Peretz, *Loss and Grief: Psychological Management in Medical Practice,* B. Schoenberg et al. (eds.), Columbia University Press, New York, 1970.
7. B. G. Simos, Grief Therapy to Facilitate Healthy Resolution, in *Social Casework, June,* pp. 337-342, 1977.
8. V. M. Solomon, *Psychodynamics of Grief Management in Jewish Law and Tradition,* Ph.D. dissertation, New York University, 1981.
9. *Diagnostic and Statistical Manual of Mental Disorders,* American Psychiatric Association, Washington, D.C., p. 49, 1968.
10. *Diagnostic and Statistical Manual of Mental Disorders,* American Psychiatric Association, Washington, D.C., 1987.

11. F. T. Melges and D. R. DeMasco, Grief-Resolution Therapy: Reliving, Revising, and Revisiting, in *American Journal of Psychotherapy, XXXIV*:1, pp. 51-61, 1980.
12. T. Parson and V. Lidz, Death in America Society, in *Essays in Self-Destruction,* E. S. Schneidman (ed.), Science House, New York, pp. 133-140, 1967.
13. G. Gorer, The Pornography of Death, in *Modern Writing,* W. Phillips and P. Rahv (eds.), McGraw-Hill, New York, pp. 157-188, 1959.
14. G. Gorer, *Death, Grief and Mourning,* Doubleday, New York, 1965.
15. D. Feuchtwanger, Creative Inter-Personal Experience of Mourning in Psychotherapy, *Israel Journal of Psychiatry and Related Sciences,* 22:1-2, pp. 105-112, 1985.
16. M. J. Barry, The Prolonged Grief Reaction, *Mayo Clinic Proceedings, 48,* p. 331, 1973.
17. J. Bowlby, Grief and Mourning in Infancy and Early Childhood: Psychoanalytic Study of the Child, *American Journal of Psychiatry, 15,* pp. 9-52, 1960.
18. T. A. Rando, Creating Therapeutic Rituals in the Psychotherapy of the Bereaved, *Psychotherapy, 22*:2, pp. 236-240, 1985.
19. J. C. Coleman, *Abnormal Psychology and Modern Life* (4th Edition), Scott Foresman, Glenview, Illinois, 1972.
20. S. F. Moore and B. G. Myerhoff, *Secular Ritual,* Van Gorcum Asset, Amsterdam, The Netherlands, 1977.
21. M. Jastraw, *A Dictionary of the Targumim, The Talmud Babli and Yerushalmi, and the Midrashic Literature,* Title Publishing, New York, 1943.
22. M. Lamm, *The Jewish Way in Death and Mourning,* Jonathan David Publishers, New York, 1969.
23. A. Gordan, The Psychological Wisdom of the Law, in *Jewish Reflections on Death,* J. Rimer (ed.), Shocken Books, New York, pp. 95-104, 1974.
24. A. Adler, *Understanding Human Nature,* W. B. Wall (trans.), Permabooks, New York, 1949.
25. V. Frankel, *Man's Search for Meaning,* Beacon Press, Boston, 1962.
26. I. W. Kidorf, The Shiva: A Form of Group Psychotherapy, *Journal of Religion and Health, 5*:1, pp. 43-46, 1966.
27. R. Simon, Bereavement Art, *American Journal of Art Therapy, 20,* pp. 135-143, 1981.
28. E. Ulman, Art Therapy: Problems of Definition, in *Art Therapy in Theory and Practice,* E. Ulman and P. Duchinger (eds.), Shocken Books, New York, 1975.
29. H. Kohut, *How Does Analysis Cure?* University of Chicago Press, Chicago, 1984.
30. G. W. Martin, *A Pictorial Study of Grief and Loss in the Life Cycle,* The Union for Experimenting Colleges and Universities, Ph.D. dissertation, Cincinnati, Ohio, 1981.
31. N. L. Paul and G. H. Grosser, Operational Mourning and Its Roles in Conjoint Family Therapy, *Community Mental Health Journal, 1*:4, pp. 339-345, 1965.
32. G. C. Zambelli, E. Johns-Clark, L. Barile, and A. F. DeJong, An Interdisciplinary Approach to Clinical Intervention for Childhood Bereavement, *Death Studies, 12,* pp. 41-50, 1988.
33. M. Junge, "The Book About Daddy Dying": A Preventive Art Therapy Technique to Help Families Deal with the Death of a Family Member, *Art Therapy, March,* pp. 4-10, 1985.
34. B. B. McIntyre, Art Therapy with Bereaved Youth, *Journal of Palliative Care, 6*:1, pp. 16-25, 1990.
35. H. H. Strupp, The Therapist's Theoretical Orientation: An Overrated Variable, *Psychotherapy: Theory, Research & Practice, 12*:4, pp. 314-317, 1978.

Pathological Grief—
A Problem in Search of a Definition:
The Tragedy of Hamlet as a Model

Roberta Halporn

Picasso said, "Art is a lie which tells the truth." And the arts offer us one of the best ways to teach and to learn. Here we will use the work of a master storyteller and an insightful student of the human mind, William Shakespeare, who never heard of Freud, Lindemann, or Rando, yet who has given us a vivid picture of pathological grief—a label all too easily applied by mental health professionals but one for which we still lack a solid definition. We are taking *Hamlet* as a model because we are *sure* the drama represents pathology—by the end of the play, six of the main characters are dead, several strewn around the stage. I don't think you can get more toxic than that!

What does the word "pathological" mean? *Stedman's Medical Dictionary* says it is "a state caused by or involving disease—morbid, any deviation from the normal or efficient condition." Volkan, a psychiatrist, had the temerity to use this adjective in "The Recognition and Prevention of Pathological Grief" [1]. He said: "Pathological grief can be defined by the fact that the following symptoms have lasted over six months":

> The mourner is still hoping for the return of the deceased, or
> Has an obsession with the deceased's grave, or
> Has made a fetish of a physical remembrance, or
> Is drinking to excess, taking too many pills, driving poorly (what Schneidman
>   calls "subintentioned suicide" [2]), or
> Is unable to work or leave the house [1].

Several of these symptoms can be found in the behavior of Queen Victoria. She was only forty-three years old when her husband, Albert, died, and for the next forty years, until her death, his rooms were kept exactly as he left them, his clothes were laid out daily, and even five years after her widowhood began, she rarely wrote a note without mentioning the "terrible misfortune which laid . . . low the Queen's happiness." Yet during her reign Great Britain came to its apogee—the time when "the sun never set on the British Empire."

She certainly made a fetish of a physical remembrance, but was she pathological? She functioned well enough to lead a nation into world dominance. I have a sneaking suspicion that she was tired of sex and child-bearing and was beginning to feel her oats as an adult ruler around the time of Albert's death. Unable to admit these uncomfortable ideas to herself, she made a fetish, indeed, of her widowhood, which also served the purpose of successfully keeping other suitors away.

Another point sorely missing from Volkan's definition is the issue of the influence of cultural customs. Take, for example, the Chinese. For centuries they practiced the system of "double burial." When seven years had passed after a death, the bones of the dead were exhumed and stored in an urn, which was again buried. The soul tablet that represented the form of the deceased in the home was finally taken out and placed in an ancestral hall to stand for eternity. This exchange, therefore, between the living and the dead could stretch on for generations [3].

Thus, if we try to make decisions about what really constitutes pathological grief, we must come to a definition that transcends culture. I don't presume to know how to formulate such a definition, but in analyzing Shakespeare's masterpiece, perhaps we can begin to approach a solution.

I'm sure that every reader is nodding his or her head sagely and agreeing that the play is a masterwork. But because of the uninspired way the play is taught and the inability of many teachers to deal with its Elizabethan English, many readers will settle themselves in to doze. Yet the melody of the language is superb. Many readers will, on revisiting the play, discover in astonishment how many lines of the text have passed into our common speech. And the descriptions of the emotional states of the participants are timeless. The study of *Hamlet* can enrich the knowledge of the thanatology student in a way no textbook makes possible.

One of the first barriers to understanding Hamlet is that we have all been misled by our memories of forty-year-old Lawrence Olivier, or any number of other, far too mature actors. What is made perfectly clear by the author is that Hamlet is actually a scruffy college boy, with all the impulsive traits that characterize the average male adolescent to this day. He is certainly not an average student—he's the kind of kid who can get himself into serious trouble because he has such a vivid imagination. The second barrier, already mentioned, is the archaic language; a little translation can make what seem mysterious pronouncements much more comprehensible. In this chapter, my own "translations" are set off by brackets.

The Tragedy of Hamlet, published in 1601, is supposedly set in a medieval, militaristic court in Denmark [4]. Yet for his sources, Shakespeare was probably drawing on his knowledge of the cabal-ridden Elizabethan court. Hamlet is a college student at Wittenberg, probably a prestigious school like Harvard. He has been indulged by his parents. He is artistic, very bright, with a philosophical bent, and conscious of his destiny as the future king. Because his culture has demanded it, he is already a skilled and experienced soldier. In the warlike atmosphere of the times, all young men had to be taught early to bear arms and defend themselves.

Gertrude, his mother, was married as a young woman to a much older man (Hamlet's father), probably for dynastic reasons. When the play opens, she is possibly no older than thirty-eight, still full of vigor and sexual energy. She adores her son. But after her husband's death, she married Claudius, his brother, in what her son describes as indecent, impulsive haste.

Claudius is now the king. We learn that he has always desired the throne, and, unfortunately, has also always lusted after Gertrude. Other pivotal characters are

Polonius, an aging councillor to both kings, and his children—Ophelia, his adolescent daughter, and his son, Laertes, a student in France.

Hamlet has come home for his father's funeral and, to his distaste, has had to witness not only the coronation of the new king, but the almost simultaneous remarriage of his mother. Her rationale is that the throne must never be empty. (The saying, "The King Is Dead, Long Live the King" is still an honored practice.) But Gertrude has surely made one of those impulsive decisions that grief counselors are always warning new widows against, because they can lead to disaster. In this case, of course, it does.

The drama opens with Claudius playing psychiatrist—diagnosing Hamlet's grief as pathological. We learn that the old King, "is only two months dead," hardly enough time to recover from a close attachment to a father. Shakespeare is also building, by contrast, Claudius's negative image—he also should have mourned longer for a brother.

The King asks: "How is it that the clouds still hang on you?" and Gertrude chimes in:

> Good Hamlet, cast thy nighted colour off . . .
> Do not forever with thy veiled lids
> Seek for thy noble father in the dust.
> Thou know'st 'tis common—all that lives must die . . .

Shakespeare is also very conscious of fraudulent manifestations of bereavement put on for show. Hamlet replies:

> 'Tis not alone my inky cloak, good mother, . . .
> Nor windy suspiration of forc'd breath, [difficulty breathing]
> No, nor the fruitful river in the eye, [crying]
>   . . .
> Together with all forms, moods, shapes of grief,
> That can denote me truly. These, indeed, *seem*;
> For they are actions that a man might play; [simulate]
> But I have that within which passes show—
> These but the trappings [the appearance] and the suits of woe.

The King is impatient:

> 'Tis sweet and commendable in your nature, Hamlet,
> To give these mourning duties to your father;
> But you must know your father lost a father;
> That father lost, lost his; and the survivor bound, . . . for some term
> To do obsequious sorrow. But to persevere . . . is a course
> Of impious stubbornness . . .

And now he pulls out all the stops, first by accusing Hamlet of being a sissy and then a blasphemer:

> 'tis unmanly grief.
> It shows a will most incorrect to heaven,
> . . . Fie! 'tis a fault to heaven,

> A fault against the dead, a fault to nature,
> To reason most absurd; whose common theme
> Is death of fathers, and who still hath cried,
> From the first corpse till he that died to-day,
> 'This must be so.'

Hamlet idolized his father. He obviously wants to return to Wittenberg, to avoid contact with what repels him—his mother's swift rejection of his father, and his father's possible murderer ensconced on the throne. The whole tragedy devolves on the fact that the couple refuses to let him go.

Hamlet has already made it clear he loves Ophelia. But both Laertes and her father Polonius have warned her not to trust his affections, since she is a commoner. "For he, himself," they chide her, "is subject to his birth."

> He may not, as unvalued persons do, carve [choose a wife] for himself. For on his choice, depends the sanity [safety] and health of this whole state.

Polonius forbids Ophelia to allow Hamlet to court her again.

Although Ophelia is portrayed initially as a naive and innocent adolescent, Polonius's remarks indicate that this is far from the truth. He scolds her, saying: "You speak like a green girl, unsifted [inexperienced] in such perilous circumstances." We therefore realize that, to her father, she has lived long enough to watch out for the pitfalls of court life.

Hamlet wanders on stage, articulating a textbook picture of the emotional state of a depressed mourner. He says:

> How weary, stale, flat, and unprofitable,
> Seem to me all the uses of this world!
> . . . 'tis an unweeded garden,
> That grows to seed; things rank and gross in nature
> Possess it merely.

Then he evokes the common memorial impulse of the bereaved:

> That it should come to this!
> But two months dead! Nay, not so much, not two.
> So excellent a king that was to this [Claudius]
> Hyperion [a god] to a satyr [a beast];

And describes the relationship between his parents:

> so loving to my mother,
> That he might not beteem [permit] the winds of heaven
> Visit her face too roughly. Heaven and earth!
> Must I remember? Why, she would hang on him
> As if increase of appetite had grown
> By what it fed on; and yet, within a month . . .
> Frailty, thy name is woman!
>
> A little month, or ere [before] those shoes were old
> With which she followed my poor father's body,

> Like Niobe, all tears—why she, even she—
> O God! a beast that wants discourse of reason
> Would have mourn'd longer—married with my uncle . . .
> But break, my heart, for I must hold my tongue.

As young as he is, Hamlet is also wary of court intrigue.

In the play's opening scene, two soldiers announce some frightening news—they have seen the ghost of Hamlet's father. In one scene, Shakespeare lets us all see the Ghost, but in another, the Ghost appears to no one but Hamlet. It may be that Shakespeare was a crowd-pleaser, and since the Elizabethans did believe in ghosts, he gave them one for titillation, just as the horror movies do today.

The Ghost accuses Claudius of his murder, and asks his son to "Revenge thy father's foul and unnatural murder." Hamlet explodes. "My prophetic soul—my uncle!" Now we realize that he has already fantasized his uncle as the possible, though originally unthinkable, perpetrator.

"However," cautions the Ghost, "taint not thy mind against thy mother. Leave her to Heaven." Hamlet is not convinced he isn't hallucinating and devises a way of discovering if this murder actually took place, or is a product of his "fevered imagination." He also expresses his reluctance to deal with a problem of such magnitude: "The time is out of joint. O cursed spite that I was ever born to set it right."

It's fashionable of late to describe Hamlet as a procrastinator. It seems to me this charge derives from a misreading of the situation. As much as Hamlet has felt intimations that "something [was] rotten in the state of Denmark," what the Ghost is requesting places him in a dreadful dilemma. The assignment is, first, to kill a blood relative, second, to remove the man who is currently married to his mother, and third, to destroy the monarch whom he would succeed. His rule would be forever tainted by his people's suspicion of his motives.

As we know, he decides to act mad, to see if he can discover better evidence to back up the Ghost's tale. Our first report comes from Ophelia. She cries to her father: "O my lord, my lord, I have been so affrighted!" Polonius responds: "With what, i'th'name of God?"

She replies,

> as I was sewing in my closet, [sitting room]
> Lord Hamlet, with his doublet [tunic] all unbrac'd [untied],
> No hat upon his head, his stockings fouled . . .
> Pale as his shirt, his knees knocking each other,
> And with a look so piteous in purport
> As if he had been loosed out of hell
> . . . comes before me . . .
>
> He rais'd a sigh so piteous and profound
> As it did seem to shatter all his bulk
> And end his being.

Polonius, ever officious, decides to investigate this phenomenon for himself, and after a conversation with Hamlet concludes:

Though this be madness, yet there is method in't.
Will you walk out of the air, my lord?

Hamlet relies: "Into my grave." "Indeed," responds the councillor: "that's out of the air."

How pregnant [thought-provoking] sometimes his replies are!
a happiness that often madness hits on . . .
My lord, I will take my leave of you.

Hamlet retorts: "You cannot, sir, take from me anything that I will more willingly part withal," and in an aside, continues, "except my life, except my life, except my life." In this reply we see Hamlet's growing depression.

His odd behavior is soon noticed by everyone in the court. Polonius is of the opinion that Hamlet is "mad" because Ophelia, on her father's orders, has rejected his suit. Concerned about his health, the King and Queen send for Hamlet's school friends, Rosenkrantz and Guildenstern, to see if their company will stir him out of his doldrums.

In response to their question of why he seems so lethargic, Hamlet replies:

I will tell you why . . .
I have of late . . .
lost all my mirth, foregone all custom of exercises; [an example of the physical paralysis of the mourner]
and indeed it goes so heavily with my disposition that this goodly frame,
the earth, seems to me a sterile promontory; [a barren land] . . .

What a piece of work is a man!
How noble in reason . . . in form, how express and admirable!
. . . how like a god! . . .
And yet, to me, what is this quintessence of dust?
man delights not me . . .

And as his schoolmates smirk, in bawdy imagination, he quickly retorts, "Nay, nor woman either." Hamlet realizes very quickly that the two friends have not come to support him, but to spy on him for the King, and he dismisses them. He expresses his sense of impotence at his inability to carry out his dreadful assignment. He is filled with self-loathing.

Why, what an ass am I! This most brave,
That I, the son of a dear father murder'd,
Prompted to my revenge by heaven and hell,
Must, like a whore, unpack my heart with words,
And fall a-cursing . . . [All I am doing is talking about it]

He still feels the need for more concrete proof of the murder. Told by Polonius that wandering players [actors] have come to the castle, he decides to trap Claudius into an admission of guilt through a performance:

I have heard
That guilty creatures, sitting at a play,

Have, by the very cunning of the scene
Been struck so that presently
They have proclaim'd their malefactions; [misdeeds]
For murder, though it have no tongue, will speak . . .
I'll have these players
Play something like the murder of my father
Before mine uncle. I'll observe his looks . . .

And still afraid he may have been hallucinating, he comments:

The spirit that I have seen
May be a devil; and the devil hath power
T' assume a pleasing shape; yea, and perhaps
Out of my weakness and my melancholy,
As he is very potent with such spirits,
Abuses me to damn me. I'll have grounds
More relative than this. The play's the thing
Wherein I'll catch the conscience of the King.

In the following familiar soliloquy, his despair has deepened to the point of suicide:

To be, or not to be—that is the question;
Whether 'tis nobler in the mind to suffer
The slings and arrows of outrageous fortune,
Or to take arms against a sea of troubles, . . .
To die, to sleep—
No more; and by a sleep to say we end
The heart-ache and the thousand natural shocks
That flesh is heir to. 'Tis a consummation
Devoutly to be wish'd . . .
To sleep, perchance to dream. Ay, there's the rub;
For in that sleep of death what dreams may come,
When we have shuffled off this mortal coil . . .
Who would . . .
. . . grunt and sweat under a weary life,
But that the dread of something after death—
The undiscover'd country, from whose bourn
No traveller returns—puzzles the will,
And makes us rather bear those ills we have
Than fly to others that we know not of . . .

Polonius convinces the King to test his theory that Ophelia's rejection is the cause of Hamlet's insanity, since the experiment with the school friends has failed. Polonius contrives to bring Ophelia in contact with the Prince. Hamlet's behavior is so bizarre that she is heartbroken. (The pain of the protagonists is beginning to escalate.) Hamlet tells her, "I did love you once." "Indeed," she responds, "you made me believe so." He retorts, "You should not have believed me. I loved you not . . . Get thee to a nunnery . . ." And as he wanders off, she cries:

O, what a noble mind is here o'erthrown!
The courtier's, soldier's, scholar's, eye, tongue, sword . . .
And I, of ladies most deject and wretched,
That suck'd the honey of his music vows . . .
O, woe is me
To have seen what I have seen, see what I see!

Having hidden themselves to listen, the King and Polonius emerge. Claudius has now determined that something else lies at the root of Hamlet's behavior. He says:

Love! His affections do not that way tend;
Nor what he spake, though it lack'd form a little,
Was not like madness. There's something in his soul
O'er which his melancholy sits on brood . . .
[and continuing the image of a nesting fowl, he continues:]

I do doubt the hatch and the disclose
Will be some danger . . . which for to prevent
I have in quick determination thus set it down
He shall with speed to England.

Hamlet sets his trap for the King with the "Murder of Gonzago," a melodrama whose story resembles his father's killing, as the Ghost has reported it. The King becomes hysterical and outraged. Claudius knows that Hamlet has gotten too close to the truth, and he must destroy him before he reveals this outrageous deed to the world. But Claudius is also restrained by outside forces. He knows that if a second murder can be traced to his door, he will lose Gertrude forever. "The Queen," he muses, "lives almost by his [Hamlet's] looks."

Claudius makes one more desperate attempt to muzzle his nephew. He orders Gertrude to try to bring Hamlet in line, with Polonius again serving as a hidden witness.

As Polonius leaves on his errand, Shakespeare displays his deep insight into the human condition—of both saints and sinners. One could almost feel sorry for the murderer, Claudius, when he is left alone and tries to find comfort in prayer.

O, my offense is rank, it smells to heaven;
Pray can I not, though inclination be as sharp as will . . .
What if this cursed hand were thicker than itself with brother's blood.
Is there not rain enough in the sweet heavens to wash it white as snow? . . .
Help, angels, make assay! [try to reclaim me]

Commanded to visit his mother, Hamlet reminds himself: "I will speak daggers to her but use none . . ." The Queen asks, "Why, how now, Hamlet! Have you forgot me?" Hamlet replies,

No, by the rood, not so. You are the Queen, your husband's brother's wife;
And—would it were not so!—you are my mother . . .

She is very angry. "Nay then, I'll set those to you that can speak."

Hamlet restrains her so vehemently that she becomes frightened. It says a great deal about the atmosphere of the Court that her first thought about her son's behavior is:

> What wilt thou do? Thou will not murder me?
> Help, help, ho!

And Polonius chimes in from his hiding place:

> What, ho! help, help, help!

Hamlet is by now so enraged that he seizes the opportunity to kill the interloper, hoping it is Claudius.

> How now! a rat?
> Dead, for a ducat, dead!

and he stabs Polonius through the curtains.

Gertrude seems to calm down very quickly. On the death that Gertrude has just witnessed, she comments moderately: "O, what a rash and bloody deed is this." This gives Hamlet the opportunity to tell her what he came to reveal:

> Almost as bad, good mother,
> As kill a king and marry with his brother.

The Queen is astonished: "As kill a king!" Hamlet replies, "Ay, lady, it was my word."

Absorbed by their interaction, neither seems too upset about the corpse behind the curtain. Again a cultural difference. It's hard to imagine anyone today sitting quietly discussing the dear departed with someone's body lying a few yards away. But perhaps in Sarajevo today, this would not be so unlikely. Now Hamlet forces her to recall the man he has set up on a lofty pedestal, comparing him to the ancient deities:

> See what a grace was seated on this brow;
> Hyperion's curls; the front of Jove himself;
> An eye like Mars, to threaten and command;
> A combination and a form indeed
> Where every god did seem to set his seal . . .
> This was your husband. Look you now what follows:
> Here is your husband, like a mildew'd ear
> Blasting his wholesome brother. Have you eyes? . . .

and revealing his jealousy (perhaps close to an Oedipal attachment)

> What devil was't
> That thus hath cozen'd you . . .
> You cannot call it love
> For at your age, the blood is tame . . .
> And waits upon the judgement . . .
> Go not to my uncle's bed.

To this day, adolescents can only rarely conceive of their "old" parents having sexual attachments, and when they do, they are usually horrified.

But suddenly Hamlet, and only Hamlet, hears the voice of his ghostly father, chiding him for forgetting his vow. Gertrude sits astonished. Only a few moments ago, she was listening to an angry but sane scolding, and now her son is having a conversation with the air. She queries:

> Alas, how is't with you,
> That you bend your eye on vacancy,
> And with th' air do hold discourse? . . . [talk to the air]
> Whereon do you look?

Hamlet replies, "On him, on him! Look you how pale he glares . . ." Gertrude is bewildered. "To whom do you speak this?" Hamlet asks "Do you see nothing there?" and she responds: "Nothing at all; yet all that is I see." Sadly the Queen concludes, "This is the very coinage of your brain."

Back to his rational self, Hamlet remembers his silent victim: "this counselor is now most still," and still punning, "most grave." Reaching for the body, he tells her, "This shall send me packing." And so they separate, as he "lugs the guts into the neighbor room," knowing that the death cannot be concealed and that he will be punished by banishment. Indeed, shortly afterwards he is sent to England in the company of the traitorous Rosenkrantz and Guildenstern, who bear orders to have him killed in England. Yet mother and son have ventilated a great deal of their fury and estrangement, and have crossed the barrier that separated them emotionally.

Now we are introduced to true, clinical pathology. Ophelia cannot cope with the multiple traumas: Hamlet's rejection, her sorrow over his insanity, and the anguish of knowing that her lover has been the instrument of her father's death. She is now alone, abandoned, and unprotected in the hostile world of the court. She comes wandering into the throne room, singing and talking to imaginary companions. (The songs of this virginal girl are full of sexual metaphors. Perhaps Shakespeare was attempting to show how far she had traveled from her "true" self.)

> Quoth she, before you tumbled me [had intercourse], you promised me to wed . . .

> We must be patient; but I cannot choose but weep to think they would lay him i'
> th' cold ground. My brother shall know of it; . . . Come, my coach! Good night,
> ladies, [to imaginary companions]
> good night, sweet ladies, good night, good night . . .

Even the King is moved:

> O' this is the poison of deep grief; it springs
> All from her father's death.
> O Gertrude, Gertrude!
> When sorrows come, they come not in single spies,
> But in battalions! First, her father slain;
> Next, your son gone, and he most violent author [cause]
> Of his own just remove; [banishment]

and ever the politician:

> the people muddied,
> Thick and unwholesome in their thoughts and whispers.

Profoundly hostile, Laertes reaches Elsinore in secret. Since he's the kind who shoots first and asks questions later, he wants revenge against his father's killer and hatches a plot with the King. He is further outraged by Ophelia's state: "Oh heat dry up my brains. Is it possible that a young maid's wits be as mortal as an old man's life?" The King and Laertes are plotting Hamlet's death when Gertrude enters, announcing: "One woe doth tread upon another's heel, So fast they follow. Your sister's drown'd, Laertes." Ophelia fell into a brook, and her heavy garments pulled her down before she could be rescued, perhaps a subintentioned suicide [2].

Hamlet has escaped captivity, and returns to find the grave diggers opening a new grave. In the scene he overhears, we are presented with a picture of Gertrude's tender side. As she follows Ophelia's body to the cemetery, she shows herself as the compassionate parent we have not glimpsed before. "Sweets to the sweet: farewell!" she says, throwing flowers on the grave. ". . . I thought thy bride-bed to have decked, sweet maid, and not to have strew'd thy grave."

Hamlet doesn't know that this ceremony is for Ophelia until he gets his clue from Laertes' complaints to the priest conducting the funeral. Laertes demands: "What ceremonies else?" The priest indicates that, given the choice, he would have buried her in unsanctified ground as a suicide, but the King and Queen have overruled him.

Laertes protests: "I tell thee, churlish priest, a minist'ring angel shall my sister be, when thou lies howling [in Hell] . . ." In grief, and in fury at her defamation, he acts on impulse: "Hold off the earth awhile, till I have caught her once more in my arms," and he leaps into the grave. He is willing to die, as well, in his misery. He has lost his whole family within a few weeks.

> Now pile your dust upon the quick and dead, [the alive and dead]
> Till of this flat a mountain you have made

Hamlet is traumatized as well:

> I lov'd Ophelia: forty thousand brothers
> Could not, with all their quantity of love,
> Make up my sum. What wilt thou do for her?
> I'll do't. Dost come here to whine?
> To outface me with leaping in her grave?
> Be buried quick with her, and so will I . . .

and fighting over the coffin, they take out their raging grief upon one another.

All these poisoned choices bear fruit in the last scene. A fencing match has been arranged as an entertainment between Hamlet and Laertes, who battles unfairly with a poisoned sword. Discovering that he has been betrayed by Claudius, Laertes, mortally wounded, warns Hamlet that, having been pricked by the same weapon, he is dying as well. Finally Hamlet gains the courage to kill Claudius. Gertrude drinks a poisoned cup originally meant for her son.

Since he has outlived his uncle by a few minutes, Hamlet has achieved one of his ambitions—he is now the King. His final plea, to his best friend, is that of most dying patients: 'Don't forget me.'

> Horatio, I am dead:
> Thou livest; report me and my cause aright . . .
> O God! Horatio, what a wounded name, . . .
> shall live behind me!
> If thou didst ever hold me in thy heart,
> Absent thee from felicity awhile,
> And in this harsh world draw thy breath in pain,
> To tell my story.

His faithful friend pronounces his eulogy,

> Now cracks a noble heart. Good night, sweet prince,
> And flights of angels sing thee to thy rest!

The stage is covered with bodies—the King, the Queen, the Prince, and all their minister's offspring—two lines erased.

Have we come any closer to a definition of pathological grief? Perhaps we have. Some of the conditions include those of an "untimely" death, the absence of an acceptable support system, and deep guilt about some aspect of the mourner's relationships with the deceased. Some of the symptoms include an inability to assume normal life functions after a long period, suicide attempts (not just ideation), an obsession with the death rather than just the deceased, a continuing avoidance of heterosexual activities, and a rigidity of thought and behavior. Finally, unlike what many bereaved commonly report, "that I could actually sense him/her there," the existence of concrete hallucinations relating to the actual appearance of the deceased.

Pathological grief is a very difficult subject to define scientifically, because it is still a definition that lies in the eye of the beholder. But Shakespeare has intuitively revealed, I believe, some of its parameters.

REFERENCES

1. V. Volkan, The Recognition and Prevention of Pathological Grief, in *Normal and Pathological Responses to Bereavement,* J. Ellard et al. (eds.), MSS Information Corp., New York, 1974.
2. E. S. Schneidman, *On the Nature of Suicide,* Jossey-Bass, San Francisco, 1973.
3. R. G. Knapp, The Changing Landscape of the Chinese Cemetery, *The China Geographer, 8,* pp. 1-12, 1977.
4. W. Shakespeare, *The Tragedy of Hamlet. Prince of Denmark,* various editions, 1604.

Keeping Emotional Time:
Music and the Grief Process

Lesleigh Forsyth

They that sow in tears shall reap in songs of joy.

Psalm 126:5-6

When Antonie Brentano, Beethoven's dear friend and possibly his "Immortal Beloved," lay ill and desolate in Vienna, only one person was able to comfort her. During her long periods of illness, she withdrew completely from company and remained in her room, unfit to see anybody. Beethoven, however, used to come in regularly, and, as she described it, "seat himself in her antechamber without any further ado and improvise; when he had 'said everything and given solace' to the suffering one in his own language, he would depart as he had come, without taking further notice of anybody else" [1, p. 177].

What more could we ask during periods of illness and grief than having a dear friend "say everything and give solace." These are times when we seek answers to life's most profound questions, and need comfort almost beyond the human capacity to provide it. Music was Beethoven's language. In music he could answer questions we barely know how to ask and take care of his friend by giving her the profound solace of his musical vision.

During periods of suffering and grief, music can have a powerful effect on us. As we have distanced death from life and surrounded it with sanitized rituals, we have cut ourselves off from vivid experiences of grief. Although in mourning, we are expected to resume productive functioning very soon after the loss of a loved one and given little time or encouragement for the absorbing work of grieving. Friends are encouraged to distract us from pain as though we were children to be picked up after a fall.

We may have a natural inclination to turn away from the painful experience of grief, but its effects are inevitable. If we fail to acknowledge the feelings engendered by the loss of someone we love, those feelings may become masked as depression or physical illness, conditions difficult to diagnose and treat. Grief must be acknowledged rather than hidden, and experienced rather than repressed. Music can help us free our grief, release it and (paradoxically) by enhancing it and expressing it more deeply, enable us to begin the healing process.

The stages of grieving are well documented, although each grief experience is unique and proceeds according to its own timetable. In spite of our distance from the rituals of death and dying, we have become knowledgeable, linguistically at least, about the stages of grief. It is not only psychologists who use such terms as "denial" or "resignation" when describing parts of the grieving process. They are in fairly common use. But knowledge about the different stages of grieving, even in one's own experience, is very different from the experience itself. A friend had a vivid illustration of this when, thinking that she was coping very well with her mother's cancer and chemotherapy, she had a reaction of utter astonishment when told that her mother's hair was falling out. As she did not, at some level, fully acknowledge to herself that her mother was seriously ill, her reaction to a simple proof of that fact was one of shock. When possible, self-awareness about one's own grieving process, or that of a friend or patient, can be helpful when considering whether to use music for access to emotion. In my own experience, it was an intellectual understanding that my grief had been blocked that led to an eventual emotional release.

When my niece, Julia, was killed in a car accident at the age of thirteen, my shock and grief were intense. But because I live far away from my extended family, I was not faced with constant reminders of Julia. I was able to turn my attention away from the extremely painful fact of her death. However, I soon began to notice that I had developed an obsession with cars. Although they had never interested me in the slightest, I began to notice every car on the road: the year, the model, how the styles differed from year to year and model to model. Many months later, I experienced a serious depression, and was helped to understand that both the car obsession and the depression were related to Julia's death. Although the connection did not seem at all obvious to me at the time, my ability to understand it as "denial" was important in helping me to face my loss and experience it emotionally.

This raises the question of why one would be open to experiencing the pain of grief through music when one may have been working so hard in other ways to ignore it. My answer comes again from personal experience. When I did eventually begin to untie the emotional knot of grief, it was music that helped me do it. I listen frequently to music and didn't have to make a decision to do so. When I happened upon the music that enabled me to mourn (some songs by Schubert), it was after the mourning had begun that I understood what was taking place. I was not required to conceptualize or verbalize about my experience of loss—acts that I was clearly avoiding. Instead, through the music, I found myself in the midst of mourning. Although I would have turned away from thinking or talking about Julia, it was possible for me to have an experience of grief that did not originate in thoughts or words. Once the process had begun, the thoughts and words followed and I was able to face them.

There are many complex reactions to the loss of a loved one. They may include guilt, regret, anger, fear, pain, and sadness. Often these emotions are intermingled. If we think of grief as an illness of many stages, it is possible to think of music as a prescription appropriate in varying ways to its treatment. Music can soothe and comfort; it can distract; it can intensify emotion. Because of its immediacy, music can hasten experience and make feelings accessible.

Music is so supple a bearer of meanings that it can, like the most subtle uses of literary language, suggest attitudes not easily articulated, at times asserting contradictory poses simultaneously [2, p. 217].

Music affects emotions. We know this from our own experiences and find evidence for it in the social uses of music that we see around us. Music is used to kindle patriotism at political and sporting events, to signal and enhance dénouements in film and theater, to intensify religious devotion and celebrate rites of passage. We would find it very odd to view the presidential inauguration or the World Series without the national anthem, to watch a moving film without a musical score, or to see a bride walk down the aisle in a silent church.

We attest to the power of music but are mystified about how and why it affects us as it does. Scientific exploration into the way music works in the brain has grown in sophistication with the use of imaging techniques. Scientists have been able to map musical networks in different areas of the brain and to pinpoint the location of musical processes such as hearing, recognizing, remembering, and reacting to music. They have found that these networks extend into the limbic system, the part of the brain where the emotional circuits are located. This research begins to provide a scientific explanation for something many of us know from experience—the deep and direct emotional impact of music [3].

Music has personal meaning for us throughout our lives. We remember lullabies from childhood, chart busters from our teen idols, favorite songs that remind us of particular events or favorite people. And then there is "the food of love." There is never a time when we are so easily in touch with our emotions and so ready to have them enhanced and intensified by music as when we are in love. We relish hearing, in melody and lyrics, about the ways in which others have taken the measure of this experience. A musical experience shared with a loved one enters the history of a relationship. A few overheard strains of "our song" can bring an instant awareness of essential loving connection to a couple otherwise burdened with difficulties. In contrast, the feeling of grief is not one we seek to intensify, musically or any other way. We close ourselves to the pains of grief just as we open ourselves to the joys of love. The songs or poems that remind us of a lost love can bring a vivid awareness of that loss.

*   *   *

It is the immediacy of [the] marriage of mind and heart, this very fusion of musical cerebration directed toward an emotionally purposeful end, that typifies the art of music and makes it different from all other arts.—Aaron Copeland [4, p. 65]

Once we have decided that music might help us with the process of grieving, we face another decision. That is the decision to listen attentively. We live in an age of constant sound, and not only the ambient sounds of wind, traffic, and so forth. The more aggressive noises of television, radio, computers, and electronic games rarely cease. Some would describe those as the ambient sound of the younger generation. What I have described as listening "on purpose" may involve more than selecting the right music. Anyone who has tried to shut out unpleasant music in restaurants, department stores, supermarkets, telephones "on hold," recognizes that it's possible not to "hear" something regardless of its decibel level. The more we are assaulted with public noise, the better we become at shutting it out. We are following a prescription by listening for a purpose, and, as with other prescriptions, there are ways to make it more effective. We might begin with some respect for the rare commodity of silence, as described by Thomas Merton:

> Silence does not exist in our lives merely for its own sake. It is ordered to something else. Silence is the mother of speech . . . In silence we learn to make distinctions . . . How tragic it is that they who have nothing to express are continually expressing themselves, like nervous gunners firing burst after burst of ammunition into the dark, where there is no enemy. The reason for their talk is: death. Death is the enemy that seems to confront them at every moment in the deep darkness and silence of their own being. So they keep shouting at death. They confound their lives with noise. They stun their own ears with meaningless words, never discovering that their hearts are rooted in a silence that is not death, but life. They chatter themselves to death, fearing life as if it were death [5].

Considerations other than the need for silence are more obvious: we need privacy, some assurance that we will not be interrupted, physical surroundings that make us feel comfortable and secure. Most of all, we must be willing to have an emotional experience that might be painful.

* * *

> In our Western world, music speaks with a composer's voice, and half the pleasure we get comes from the fact that we are listening to a particular voice making an individual statement at a specific moment in history [4].

In a society which offers books, articles, and support groups for almost every conceivable problem, we are accustomed to considering the experiences of others as resources which we consult as they pertain to our own needs. Music is a similar resource because it is a communication about personal experience which a composer shares with a listener. In thinking about Beethoven playing the piano for Antonie Brentano, we do not imagine that she heard the music merely as pleasant sound emanating from her antechamber. She heard it as communication from a noble spirit who had grappled with the profundities of life and death. Beethoven was telling her what was in his heart, and, judging from her response, that is what she heard.

Many composers have written music about death and parting. We know through their choices of text, their biographies, letters, and writings about their own music much of what they wanted to convey in their music. What a composer seems to express in a particular piece of music may not be suitable for every person in mourning. For example, someone who is reacting to the death of a loved one with feelings of anger and resentment may not have a helpful response to music that expresses resignation or transcendence. Likewise, a person who is experiencing the deep pain of separation and fear of death will not be comforted by a tumultuous musical depiction of a wrathful day of judgment.

In exploring the music which was written, purposefully, about parting and death, we find expression of a range of emotions as wide as that which exists within each person and each parting. Just as we seek understanding friends to talk to, or books that comfort us with the assurance of shared experience, we may find, for ourselves and for others, music that can help us release the emotions of grief.

Grove's *Dictionary of Music* lists over one hundred composers who have written musical settings of the Requiem or Mass for the Dead [6]. In addition, there are hundreds of settings of liturgical and poetic texts dealing with death. In thousands of other works, pain and separation are part of the experience of love and loss. Comparison of a few of these works shows how we might expect them to differ in their emotional impact, thus guiding our choices for further exploration through listening.

THE REQUIEMS OF BERLIOZ, FAURÉ, AND BRAHMS

Although the Requiem of Hector Berlioz is filled with contemplative and prayerful moments, it is best known for its majestic treatment of the texts announcing the Day of Judgment and sounding of the trumpets of doom. The circumstances under which the work was commissioned, written, and performed were filled with political intrigue and professional competition. The original notion that the work would commemorate the anniversary of the July Revolution of 1830 was meaningful for Berlioz, as he had participated himself in this unsuccessful revolt against the Bourbon monarchy. The work was begun in 1837 and Berlioz speaks of it in his *Memoirs*: "For a long time the text of the Requiem had been to me an object of envious longing, on which I flung myself with a kind of fury when it was put within my grasp" [7]. Knowing of Berlioz's ambitions and frustrations in life, one is not surprised to hear the passion in Berlioz's depiction of the wrathful day when all wrongs would be punished and virtue would be rewarded. After the first performance, a poet and friend of Berlioz commented that "The music was beautiful and strange, wild, convulsed, and dolorous."

In contrast, the Requiem of Gabriel Fauré contains no musical setting of the *Dies Irae* and *Tuba Mirum* texts. According to his student and biographer, Charles Koechlin, Fauré rejected "the cruel anthropomorphism of divine justice modeled upon the sanctimonious prudery of human courts." Fauré said of his own Requiem, "Altogether it is as gentle as I am myself." The work was written between 1886 and 1888, not for a specific occasion but for use in regular services at the church where Fauré was organist and choirmaster. The emphasis of this work, which begins and ends with the word "rest" (requiem), is on the prayers that ask eternal rest and perpetual light. The music is tender and transcendent. In Fauré's words: "My Requiem . . . has been said to express no fear of death; it has been called a lullaby of death. But that is how I feel about death; a happy deliverance, a reaching for eternal happiness, rather than a mournful passing" [8].

Johannes Brahms began the *German Requiem* in 1856 while mourning the death of his close friend Robert Schumann, and completed it four years later shortly after the death of his mother. Listening to a work of this intimacy, we are not surprised to learn the circumstances that led to its composition. In the *German Requiem,* Brahms departed altogether from the text of the Latin mass and made his own choices of Biblical passages representing universal human response to problems of human existence. His intention is to address the living who grieve rather than those who have died ("Blessed are they that mourn, for they shall be comforted") and he says in a letter of explanation that "German" referred to the language in which the work was sung, and that, instead, he would gladly have called it "a *Human* Requiem" [9]. In music that is alternately somber and consoling, despairing and hopeful, Brahms underscores textual materials which express both the sorrow of loss and the joy of the eternal.

I have used these works to give an idea of how one might explore music about death by examining the circumstances of its composition and the composers' choice of text.[1] The following list was chosen from a vast amount of great music with some connection to death and separation. Outlining a journey of sorts, the lists include 1) works by Beethoven, Berlioz, and Mozart that express the gravity, tumult and anguish of loss; 2) music by Mahler and Strauss dealing with love and regret; 3) lullabies by Schubert and Strauss which resonate with poignancy and longing for comfort; 4) works by Brahms and Mendelssohn bringing messages of comfort and hope; 5) an aria by Bach expressing deep resignation; and 6) transcendent works by Schubert and Fauré. Countless other works could have been chosen, within the classical music literature and well beyond it. These are personal selections, but I have added notes and text where possible to suggest general emotional content and impact. Because I am limited to words in this essay, the list is weighted heavily in the direction of the song literature but there are many other works such as the Passions of J. S. Bach, the string quartets of Beethoven, Schubert, and Schumann, and symphonies by Mahler and Shostakovich which could be included.

Anguish, Tumult

Ludwig van Beethoven

Symphony No. 3 in E flat, Op. 55 ("Eroica"), second movement, *Marcia funebre*

Ernest Newman, commenting on whether the second movement, Funeral March, was written to lament the death of Napoleon, wrote that "such immensities of grief as Beethoven has expressed in his music do not gather about the shades of mere ordinary humanity" [11].

Hector Berlioz

Requiem Mass (Grande Messe des Morts, Op. 5)

Text of *Dies Irae, Tuba Mirum* movements:

---

[1] See [10] for a detailed examination of music by the following composers on the subject of death: Brahms, Mahler, Mussorgsky, Strauss, and Shostakovich.

Day of wrath, that day dismaying,
Shall fulfill the prophets' saying,
Earth in smoldering ashes laying.
Oh, how great the dread, the sighing,
When the Judge, the All-descrying,
Shall appear, all secrets trying!

Then shall the trump's weird knelling,
Through each tomb and charnel dwelling,
All before the Throne compelling.

Wolfgang Amadeus Mozart

Requiem, K. 626, *Lacrimosa*

Ah, that day of tears and mourning, from the dust of earth returning, man for judgement must prepare him. Spare, O God, in mercy spare him: Lord all-pitying, Jesu blest, grant them thine eternal rest.

Mozart died before completing this work and, in his illness, became convinced that he was writing it for himself. "On one occasion [Mozart] himself with Sussmayr and Madame Mozart tried over part of the Requiem together, but some of the passages so excited him that he could not refrain from tears, *and was unable to proceed.*"—from the diary of Vincent Novello, 1820.

Love, Regret

Gustav Mahler

Symphony No. 5 in C Sharp Minor, Part Four: *Adagietto*

This movement, which is often performed as a single work, was broadcast at the time of the death of John Kennedy. When the death of Leonard Bernstein coincided with a concert in New York by the Boston Symphony Orchestra, with which Bernstein had had a close association, it was this movement which the orchestra performed in his memory. It is thought to have been written as a love song to Alma Schindler whom Mahler had recently met and would soon marry. As with many love songs, it is interesting to note the seeming expression of sorrow and anticipation of parting that are inherent in many loving relationships.

Songs of a Wayfarer, No. 4
Text by Mahler, translated by Lionel Salter

My love's two eyes of blue
have sent me out into the wide world,
I had to bid farewell to the spot I cherish.

O eyes of blue, why did you look at me?
How grief and sorrow are forever my lot.
I went out in the still of night,
at dead of night across the gloomy heath.
No one said goodbye to me, goodbye;
my companions were love and grief.

By the road stands a linden-tree:
there at last I found rest in sleep.
Under the linden-tree,
which snowed its blossoms down on me,
I knew naught of life's pain;
all, all was well again—
all, all! Love and grief,
My world, my dreams.

Lullabies, the Longing for Comfort

Franz Schubert

Text of *Wiegenlied,* Anonymous

Sleep, dear, sweet boy,
Your mother's hand rocks you softly.
This swaying cradle strap
Brings you gentle peace and tender comfort.

Sleep in the sweet grave;
Your mother's arms still protect you.
All her wishes, all her possessions
Ah hold lovingly, with loving warmth.

Sleep in her lap, soft as down;
Bare notes of love still echo around you.
A lily, a rose
Shall be your reward after sleep.

This lullaby, addressed to a dead child, is moving for obvious reasons, but I find lullabies in general (as below) to be very poignant. Perhaps this is because they bring wistful thoughts of the strong but simple bond between mother and baby, or suggest the desire to be comforted oneself with this sort of straightforward tenderness.

Richard Strauss

Text of *Wiegenlied* (Op. 4, No. 1) by Richard Dehmel
Translation by Phillip L. Miller

Dream, dream, my sweet life,
of heaven, which brings the flowers;
blossoms glisten there; they quiver
to the song your mother sings.

Dream, dream, bud of my care,
of the day when the flowers sprouted,
of the bright blossoming morning
when your little soul came into the world.

Dream, dream, bloom of my love,
of the silent holy night
when the flowering of his love
made this world a heaven for me.

Comfort, Hope

Johannes Brahms

A German Requiem (Ein Deutsches Requiem), Op. 45
Text of Movement 5

Ye now have sorrow; but I will see you again, and your heart shall rejoice, and your joy no man taketh from You (John 16:22). I will comfort you as one whom his mother comforteth (Isaiah 66:13). Behold me with your eyes: a little while I have had tribulation and labor, and have found great comfort (Ecclesiasticus 51:35).

Felix Mendelssohn

Elijah, an Oratorio, text from the Old Testament, Op. 70

No. 28. Lift thine eyes to the mountains from whence thy help cometh. Psalm 121:1-3

No. 29. He, watching over Israel, slumbers not, nor sleeps. Shouldst thou, walking in grief, languish, He will quicken thee. Psalms 121:4, 137:7

No. 32. For the mountains shall depart and the hills be removed and pass away, but Thy kindness shall never depart from me; neither shall the covenant of Thy peace be broken. Isaiah 54:50

Resignation

Johann Sebastian Bach

Aria *"Es ist vollbracht"* from Cantata No. 159

It is completed. The song is over, We have been saved through God's righteousness from our fall into sin. And now I will hurry to thank my savior. World, good
night.

Transcendence

Franz Schubert

Du bist die Ruh (words by Friedrich Rückert)

You are repose
And gentle peace;
You are longing
And what stills it.

Full of joy and grief,
I consecrate to you
My eyes and my heart
As a dwelling place.

Come in to me,
And softly close
The gate behind you.

Drive all other grief
from my breast!
Let my heart
Be full of your joy.

The temple of my eyes
Is lit
By your radiance alone:
O, fill it wholly!

Gabriel Fauré

Requiem, Op. 48

In Paradisum

May the Angels lead you into Paradise; at your coming may the martyrs receive
you, and conduct you into the holy city, Jerusalem. May the chorus of Angels
receive you, and with Lazarus, once a pauper, eternally may you have rest.

REFERENCES

1. M. Solomon, *Beethoven Essays,* Harvard University Press, Cambridge, Massachusetts, 1988.
2. E. Rothstein, *Emblems of Mind,* Times Books, New York, 1995.
3. The Mystery of Music: How It Works in the Brain, *The New York Times,* May 16, 1996 (Section C, p. 1).
4. A. Copland, *Copland on Music,* Doubleday, Garden City, New York, 1960.
5. T. Merton, *No Man Is an Island,* Image Books, Garden City, New York, 1967, c.1955.
6. *Grove's Dictionary of Music & Musicians,* Macmillan, London; St. Martin's Press, New York, 1954.
7. H. Berlioz, *Memoirs,* Knopf, New York, 1932.
8. C. Koechlin, *Gabriel Faure,* Dennis Dobson Limited, London, 1946.
9. B. Jacobson, *The Music of Johannes Brahms,* The Tantivy Press, London, 1977.
10. S. Silverman, *Expressing Death and Loss Through Music,* Baywood Amityville, New York, forthcoming.
11. E. Newman, *On Beethoven's Symphonies,* by Ernest Newman–liner notes, Beethoven Nine Symphonies, The Philharmonic Orchestra, conducted by Otto Klemperer, Angel, 1961.

A Study in Grief:
The Life and Art of Kaethe Kollwitz

Louis A. Gamino

Few visual artists have portrayed the emotions of grief as authentically and as poignantly as Kaethe Kollwitz. Born out of suffering multiple personal losses, including those of her son and grandson in the great World Wars, Kollwitz's lithographs, woodcuts, and sculptures expose the anguished travail of the human psyche in mourning. In addition, Kollwitz left behind an extensive diary which mirrors, in prose, the powerful images of her artwork. Together they provide an unparalleled, first-person account of the vicissitudes of grief. When the tragedies of Kollwitz's private life are juxtaposed with the evolution of her art, a fascinating study of the phenomenology of grief emerges. This chapter traces the developmental history of Kaethe Kollwitz with a focus on how the major losses in her life shaped her bereavement and the message of her work.

CHILDHOOD AND ADOLESCENCE

Kaethe Kollwitz, née Schmidt, was born in 1867 in Koenigsberg, East Prussia, which is now part of the present-day Russian Republic. The Prussian kingdom was a militaristic, authoritarian entity which valued conformity and discipline among its citizens. Nonetheless, the late nineteenth century was an era of social unrest among the economically disadvantaged working class who powered the Industrial Revolution.

Kaethe's father, Karl Schmidt, had been educated as a lawyer, but his socialist views ran at cross-purposes with the prevailing Prussian autocracy. Rather than practice law within the confines of the arch-conservative state structure, he turned to masonry to support himself and eventually made a comfortable living as a master builder.

Kaethe's mother, Katharina (after whom Kaethe was named), was the daughter of Julius Rupp, a well-known social progressive and religious dissident who rejected the doctrinaire church establishment of East Prussia and founded an alternative Free Religious Congregation. Katharina shared her father's socialist views and, like him, was reserved emotionally with her family even while remaining attentive to the needs of her children. Katharina was also talented in drawing and spent some time copying works of the old masters.

Kaethe was the fifth of seven children born to Karl and Katharina but, due to less favorable infant mortality rates in the nineteenth century, only four of the Schmidt children survived the first year of life. Kaethe grew up with an older brother, Konrad, whom she especially admired, an older sister, Julie, and her younger sister, Lise, to whom she was always closest. Kaethe was a nervous child given to various psychosomatic aches and ailments.

Kaethe was old enough as a child to recall later the events of the birth and death of her youngest sibling, Benjamin, who died from meningitis at approximately one year of age. Her mother's painful but stoic suffering at the loss of her son was vividly imprinted on Kaethe's consciousness as evidenced by this recollection in her memoirs.

> It must have been shortly before the baby's death—we were sitting at table and Mother was just ladling the soup—when the old nurse wrenched open the door and called loudly, "He's throwing up again, he's throwing up again." Mother stood rigid for a moment and then went on ladling. I felt very keenly her agitation and her determination not to cry before all of us, for I could sense distinctly how she was suffering [1, p. 19].

Given her sensitive nature and then, at a young age, witnessing how her primary caregiver reacted so intensely to loss may have acutely attuned Kollwitz to emotions of grief that she later experienced as an adult. Bowlby has written convincingly of how such experiences with early attachment figures bias the individual's subsequent response to separation and loss [2]. Kollwitz clearly seemed to struggle with a heightened affective sensitivity to grief as evidence by her repeated depictions of mournful figures and the looming specter of death.

Kaethe's formal art lessons began privately at age fourteen because art education was segregated at that time and, being female, she could not be admitted to Koenigsberg's Academy of Art. Karl Schmidt was most interested in cultivating Kaethe's emerging talent and was ahead of the times in encouraging her to develop it. On the other hand, he was traditional in thinking that a young woman could not both pursue art and get married. These he saw as mutually exclusive. Therefore, Schmidt was alarmed by Kaethe's romantic interest in a pre-medical student, Karl Kollwitz, when she was seventeen. The following year Kaethe was sent to Berlin to study in the Women's School annex of the Berlin Academy of Art.

In Berlin, Kaethe was steered away from painting and guided toward the graphic arts of etching and lithography because of her exceptional drawing skill. Kaethe was already inclined toward "naturalistic" portrayals of laborers and ordinary people and she resisted more prosaic "genre" pieces, such as a cotillion, that her father tried to compel her to paint. The achromatic starkness of the graphic arts and Kollwitz's interest in exploring the barbary and pathos of the human condition were a well-suited match.

MARRIAGE AND EARLY ADULTHOOD

In 1888, Kaethe entered the School for Women Artists in Munich. She was inspired by the works of Prussian graphic artist Max Klinger, who asserted that drawings and prints were more powerful in presenting subjects that may be unseemly or repugnant. As Kaethe gained technical familiarity with the graphic media, she made the decision to forego painting in favor of drawing and etching. At the same time, Kollwitz's socialist conscience surfaced in her work as she chose for her first major drawing, *Germinal* (based on Emile Zola's novel by the same name), the subject of striking coal miners in northern France.

After two years of study in enchanting Munich with its permissive student subculture, Kaethe felt stymied back in Koenigsberg both because of limited training and employment opportunities in art and because of her father's tendency to try to direct her personal life and her professional activities. Conflicted by the societal double standard that limited a woman's advancement in the arts, Kaethe made the unorthodox decision to marry *and* continue her art career despite her father's stern admonition that she could not do both.

In 1891, Kaethe Schmidt married Karl Kollwitz who supported her dual aspirations. They moved to Berlin where Karl practiced as a physician with the Krankenkasse, a state-administered health insurance program for workers and their dependents, similar to Medicaid today. Both committed socialists, Karl used the healing arts to cure the sick and Kaethe used the graphic arts to portray the desperate plight of the social underclass.

Karl's office was downstairs from their modest flat and Kaethe's small studio was next to his office. Kaethe often studied and sketched Karl's patients from seeing them in the waiting room. And she became a sympathetic listener for many of them.

> When I became acquainted with the difficulties and tragedies underlying proletarian life, when I met the women who came to my husband for help and so, incidentally, came to me, I was gripped by the full force of the proletarian's fate. Unsolved problems such as prostitution and unemployment grieved and tormented me, and contributed to my feeling that I must keep on with my studies of the lower classes. And portraying them again and again opened a safety-valve for me: it made life bearable [1, p. 43].

In this passage, Kollwitz provided an uncannily eloquent description of the intrapsychic process of sublimation [3]. In essence, she dealt with her own distressing negative emotion by channeling it into her artwork, one hallmark of a psychologically healthy individual according to Valliant. Throughout her life, Kollwitz sought to express in her work the strong emotions she experienced and utilized this creative outlet to achieve an equilibrium within herself.

Coming into her own as a graphic artist, Kollwitz, in her first major series, explored the revolutionary themes of *The Weavers,* a dramatic play by Gerhart Hauptmann about a group of Silesian linen weavers who revolted in 1846 because, working with hand looms, they could not meet owners' impossible demands to compete with machine-woven fabric from England. The lithographs and etchings showed not only the indignant wrath of a workers' rebellion but also a deeply compassionate depiction of loss: a mother's loss of her sick child due to poverty and the loss of life as the ultimate consequence of violent insurrection.

Kaethe's completion of "The Weavers" in 1898 provided a vehicle for rapprochement with her terminally ill father. During her work on this series, the Kollwitz's second son, Peter, was born (their first son, Hans, was born in 1892), and Kaethe had demonstrated amply her ability to master simultaneously the triple roles of wife, mother, and artist. Of her father's reaction to seeing the work dedicated to him, Kaethe wrote:

> I had the pleasure of laying before him the complete *Weavers* cycle on his seventieth birthday in our peasant cottage at Rauschen. He was overjoyed. I can still remember how he ran through the house calling again and again to Mother to come and see what little Kaethe had done. In the spring of the following year he died. I was so depressed because I could no longer give him the pleasure of seeing the work publicly exhibited [1, p. 42].

Exhibition of "The Weavers" in 1898-99 brought Kollwitz critical acclaim and established her, at the age of thirty-two, as one of "the foremost artists of the country" [1, p. 43].

Hereafter, Kollwitz's artistic focus turned increasingly toward mothers and children, with death as an unwelcome wedge in this most primal of human bonds. Her own son, Hans, fell seriously ill with diphtheria one winter. After seeming to begin recovery, Hans had an alarming relapse and both parents maintained an anxious all-night vigil faced with the very real possibility of losing their first-born. Kaethe described her awful feelings in a letter recorded by her close friend, Beate Bonus-Jeep.

> During this night an unforgettable cold chill caught and held me: it was the terrible realization that any second this young child's life may be cut off, and the child gone forever . . . It was the worst fear I have ever known [4, p. 100].

Out of this brush with death came one of Kollwitz's most provocative lithographs, "Woman with Dead Child," inspired by the episode with Hans but, ironically, with her younger son Peter as the model. As if resolutely refusing to part with her progeny, the distraught mother figure strains to reclaim, even reabsorb, the life she once carried and nurtured.

Kollwitz's newfound notoriety as a "socialist artist" helped earn her a commission for her next major series entitled "The Peasants' War." Not only did she extol the virtue of armed uprising by the indentured proletariat, but also worked from a distinctly feminist viewpoint, which became a signature feature of Kollwitz's art [5]. Women are portrayed as protagonists in the rebellion. They also bear the brunt of the suffering that ensues. One plate, "Battlefield," shows a stooped mother, lantern in hand, searching among the fallen for her son. Both "Battlefield" and "Woman with Dead Child" appear, in retrospect, to be grim foretellings of the tragic loss Kollwitz herself was to sustain imminently.

MIDDLE AGE AND THE LOSS OF HER SON

As the winds of hostility were whipping into the World War in 1914, Kaethe was filled with gloomy foreboding, as evidenced by this journal entry in August 1914, chiding nationalistic calls for German women to sacrifice:

> . . . the joy of sacrificing—a phrase that struck me hard. Where do all the women who have watched so carefully over the lives of their beloved ones get the heroism to send them to face the cannon? I am afraid that this soaring of the spirit will be followed by the blackest despair and dejection. . . . For us, whose sons are going, the vital thread is snapped [1, p. 62].

What followed was the single most monumental event in Kaethe's life. Her younger son, Peter, swept up in the siren call of patriotic fervor, enlisted and was shortly thereafter killed on the Belgian front in October 1914. The most terrorizing fear imaginable to Kaethe, that of losing her son, was realized. Kaethe was abject with grief.

The fact that young Peter's death was so untimely and so arguably needless undoubtedly complicated Kaethe's bereavement process. Rando's review of the literature on mourning enumerates several circumstantial variables associated with a more difficult bereavement, including unexpected death, violent death, a death that is perceived by the mourner as preventable, and the death of a child [6]. Neugarten has posited that a death which occurs "off-time" in the lifecycle, at a moment or in a manner not anticipated, presents the griever with a more problematic adjustment challenge since the loss seems to defy assumptions about the natural order of events [7]. Thus, contemporary theories of bereavement would seem to predict exactly what happened next in Kaethe's life. Peter's death set into motion mourning so profound it permeated the soul of Kollwitz's self-portraits (Figure 1), which convey a sense of dejection, depersonalization, and despair from which she seemed to never recovery fully.

Kollwitz's revolutionary idealism, which had been cultivated since childhood, was shattered by Peter's death and replaced by angry disillusionment. Her sorrow and rage over Peter's annihilation became a weeping wellspring from which her work flowed. Kollwitz eventually transformed her grief into a campaign of pacifism using a line borrowed from her favorite poet, Goethe, as her mantra, "Seed for the planting must not be ground." Peter had been the seed corn, her future and the future of Germany.

Almost immediately after Peter's death, Kollwitz set to work on a memorial. As Kollwitz struggled to assimilate her loss, her creative quest to find a suitable sculptural expression of Peter's life and of her grief was blocked frequently by melancholic brooding. It was a full ten years, in 1924, before Kollwitz began to emerge sufficiently from her acute grief to design satisfactorily her memorial to Peter. Recent epidemiological evidence has indicated that the pain of bereavement, especially parental bereavement, lasts longer than many professionals have realized and may last a lifetime [8]. In this context, Kollwitz's ongoing struggle to accommodate her grief appears normative rather than pathologic.

Figure 1. "Self-Portrait," 1921. Etching touched with black ink and white.
Museum of Fine Arts, Boston, Frederick Brown Fund.

Within the first decade after Peter's death, Kollwitz completed perhaps her most formidable major series incriminating the lunacy of war. Borrowing from the methods of an artistic compatriot, Ernst Barlach, whom she greatly admired, Kollwitz chose the medium of woodcuts to accentuate the directness of her anti-war diatribe. Whereas her earlier series "The Weavers" and "The Peasants' War" were based on literary sources that moved her, "War" emanated from her own wrenching agony over losing Peter. It represents sublimation of emotion with only the thinnest layer of printers' ink separating the viewer from the ferocious tumult of her grief, raw horror, fear, despondency, and fury. As a grieving parent herself, the third print in the series, "The Parents" (Figure 2), has special autobiographical significance. It is also one plate which Kollwitz reworked repeatedly until it appropriately expressed "the totality of grief." In the process, her own pain was kneaded into the print and metamorphosed into an image of haunting beauty.

Because of Kollwitz's known sympathy for the downtrodden and for victims of social injustice, she voluntarily executed several posters to raise money for various causes during the post-war years: famine relief, aid for displaced workers, foreign aid to the fledgling socialist state in Russia, and pacifism. Like sublimation, Valliant has

Figure 2. "The Parents" (Die Eltern), 1923. Woodcut. Third print in the seven-print series *War* (Krieg). Hamburger Kuntshalle. Co Elke Walford, Hamburg.

identified altruism as another dimension of healthy coping [3]. Kollwitz's altruism through art is an important part of what enabled her to cope with the ravages of bereavement. Involving herself in service to others provided an avenue for transforming her vast psychic pain into a reservoir of energy for worthwhile social causes:

> When I know I am working with an international society opposed to war, I am filled with a warm sense of contentment . . . I am content that my art should have purposes outside itself. I would like to exert influence in these times when human beings are so perplexed and in need of help [1, p. 104].

Contemporaneous with the lifting of Kaethe's acute pall of grief was the introduction into her life of a rejuvenating element—grandchildren! Hans, now a physician, had married Ottilie Ehlers, a printmaker, and their first-born was a son they named Peter in memory of his slain uncle. Kaethe delighted in her grandchildren and yet at the same time fretted with worry over their well-being.

> My feeling of love for these five is often so strong as to be painful. And of the three children it is always Peter who is closest to our hearts. I do not know quite why it is that Karl and I often tremble with concern over the boy [1, p. 115].

It seems even the pure joy of grandparenthood could only be experienced in the long shadow of sorrow cast from the loss of her son Peter.

An incredibly productive decade of work for Kollwitz came to a close in 1932 when she finally finished the memorial to Peter. She and Karl traveled to Belgium to oversee its installation in the military cemetery where Peter was buried. It was the final phase of an eighteen-year labor, the same number of years Peter lived. Instead of a marker merely for Peter's grave, Kollwitz had settled on a sculptural embodiment of all grieving parents, "The Father" and "The Mother." The father, with folded arms, is trying stoically to hold in his bursting sorrow and the mother is bowed low by the crushing burden of burying her own child.

> I stood before the woman, looked at her—my own face—and I wept and stroked her cheeks. Karl stood close behind me—I did not even realize it. I heard him whisper, "Yes, yes." How close we were to one another then! [1, p. 122].

OLD AGE

As Hitler came to power in 1933, Kollwitz rapidly fell out of favor with the new Nazi regime because of her progressive socialist and feminist beliefs. Her work was no longer permitted to be displayed publicly and she became, along with other intellectuals and artists, a *persona non grata*.

Now in her middle sixties, Kollwitz's work focus appeared to take on a more introspective quality. Perhaps she was anticipating her own death. In part she may also have been reacting to the loss of her age peers: her brother, Konrad, in 1932 and her kindred graphic artist, Barlach, in 1938.

Kollwitz's final major series, entitled simply "Death," consists of eight plates which show a variety of affective responses on the part of those for whom death calls. Its visual range is strikingly presentient of what Kübler-Ross later described as five distinct affect states (shock, anger, bargaining, depression, and acceptance) observed in terminal patients [9]. The terrorizing death anxiety which Kollwitz portrayed so well is evident in swooping, clutching skeletons of death seizing their panicked prey. In other frames, despondent surrender to death is shown as well as scornful embrace of death, the relentless pursuer. The final frame, "Call of Death" (Figure 3), is a self-portrait suggesting calm acceptance of the inevitable. The serenity of the protagonist is complemented by the hand of death which, fleshy as opposed to skeletal, looks more providential than macabre.

During the 1930s, Kollwitz completed a bronze relief marker for Karl's and her gravesite entitled, after Goethe, "Rest in the Peace of His Hands." Visible is a vulnerable childlike figure safely cradled in the protective hands of the Almighty. Karl died in 1940, and that same year Kollwitz finished a touching sculptural tribute to him, "Farewell" (Figure 4). Karl's slumping figure succumbs to death while Kaethe's counterpart stretches to embrace his neck, reluctant to relinquish the attachment to her lifelong partner.

As a bellicose Hitler bullied the continent toward another war, Kollwitz reiterated her mantra militating against sacrificing young lives in the madness of war. Her 1938 sculpture entitled "The Tower of Mothers" has a maternal heroine in the

Figure 3. "Call of Death" (Ruf des Todes), 1934-35.
Courtesy Galerie St. Etienne, New York.

foreground who fiercely guards a group of children by placing herself, together with other mothers, squarely between the youngsters and the "threat": conscription of war, hunger, privation, or death itself. The same visual theme was the subject of Kollwitz's last lithograph completed in 1942 at the age of seventy-four, "Seed for the Planting Must Not Be Ground," a reprise of the *raison d'être* of Kollwitz's artistic life, irefully forged from the still smoldering anguish over Peter's death in World War I.

The ultimate irony occurred in October of that year when news came that her grandson, Peter, namesake of her own son, was killed fighting on the Russian front. Kaethe fatefully endured this cruel chapter of history repeating itself.

Finally in 1943, the incessant bombing of Berlin forced Kaethe to flee for the relative safety of a rural setting. She became ill with heart failure and was tended by her granddaughter, Jutta, in her last days. Kaethe Kollwitz died in Moritzburg in April 1945, four months before the war ended. She was buried in Berlin with Karl and her brother, Konrad, under the bronze relief she had made a decade before.

Figure 4. "Farewell" (Abschied), 1940. Bronze.
Courtesy Galerie St. Etienne, New York.

CONCLUSION

The life and work of this remarkable artist, Kaethe Kollwitz, have much to teach about adapting to loss. What her sister, Lise, termed Kaethe's lifelong "dialogue with death" began with her early-life, sensitizing experience of her mother reacting to Benjamin's death, continued through her own cataclysmic loss of her son, Peter, and beyond to the deaths of her husband, grandson, and herself.

From her own private Hades of grief, Kollwitz poured out her feelings through her evocative portrayals of suffering mourners. She laid bare the soul of the human organism in grief. This sublimation through art provided an emotional safety valve for her and left a legacy of incomparable images of mourning. In her artwork, Kollwitz offers catharsis for the bereaved and insight for those who, thus far, have escaped the ravages of mourning.

Her altruistic advocating for those oppressed by modern industrialization, such as underpaid workers, battered women, and vulnerable children, as well as for the "victims" of armed conflict, serves as a testament to Kollwitz's humanitarian heroism.

Kollwitz's life story seems to verify contemporary theories of bereavement. First, the process of grieving is an individualized experience whose course may be influenced by many potentially complicating factors. Second, grief probably lasts longer than thought and, indeed, may last a lifetime. Third, a parent's loss of a child is among the most profoundly devastating deaths that can be endured within the spectrum of human loss. Reviewing Kollwitz's life and work leaves the almost certain conclusion that she forged some measure of healing for her grief through her creativity in art.

REFERENCES

1. K. Kollwitz, *Diaries and Letters of Kaethe Kollwitz*, H. Kollwitz (ed.), R. Winston and C. Winston (trans.), Henry Regnery, Chicago, 1995.
2. J. Bowlby, *Attachment and Loss: Vol. 3. Loss: Sadness and Depression*, Basic, New York, 1980.
3. G. E. Valliant, *Adaptation to Life*, Little, Brown, Boston, 1977.
4. B. Bonus-Jeep, *Sechzig jahre freundschaft mit Kathe Kollwitz* (*Sixty Years of Friendship with Kaethe Kollwitz*), Karl Rauch, Verlag, Berlin, 1948.
5. M. Kearns, *Kathe Kollwitz: Woman and Artist*, Feminist Press at City University of New York, New York, 1976.
6. T. A. Rando, *Treatment of Complicated Mourning*, Research Press, Champaign, Illinois, 1993.
7. B. Neugarten, Time, Age, and the Life Cycle, *The American Journal of Psychiatry, 136*, pp. 887-894, 1979.
8. M. Osterweis, F. Solomon, and M. Green (eds.), *Bereavement: Reactions, Consequences, and Care*, National Academy Press, Washington, D.C., 1984.
9. E. Kübler-Ross, *On Death and Dying*, Macmillan, New York, 1969.

Death and Grief Made Visible:
The Life and Work of Edvard Munch

Judith M. Stillion

> What is Art? Art grows from joy and sorrow, but mostly from sorrow. It grows from man's life.—I do not believe in an art which has not forced its way out through man's need to open his heart. All art, literature as well as music must be brought out with one's heart blood.—Edvard Munch [1]

Art illuminates the human condition both in process and in product. In the process of creating, artists frequently act out their needs and expose their personal life histories. The products produced by artists, in turn, reach out to others, helping them to understand and participate in the reality of the artist. Great artists deal with universal issues and frequently expand the boundaries of both their art and their humanity by permitting their deepest feelings to become visible in their work. Viewers of great visual art often find that they are touched by the artist's vision and experience a sense of understanding bordering on empathy with the artist and his or her work. They also frequently find their own world expanded and come to a deeper understanding of the commonalities that they share with all other humans.

Too often, however, professionals in health-care fields compartmentalize their intellectual lives, failing to utilize the work of artists in either their teaching or clinical practice. This chapter has three purposes: first, to trace the effect of life experiences on the art of an individual by using Erikson's theory of the stages of healthy human development; second, to make visible the pain of separation, death, grief, and loss as revealed in the art of Edvard Munch; and third, to suggest ways in which an artist's work can be used to help others experience universality and healing in their own lives. To accomplish this, it will be necessary to summarize Erikson's theory.

ERIKSON'S THEORY OF PSYCHOSOCIAL DEVELOPMENT

Erik Erikson's most prolific work occurred in the mid-twentieth century [2, 3]. Erikson believed that human beings move through predictable stages of development across their lifetimes. His theory recognized the importance of psychological and physical development, but also emphasized the role of the social milieu in shaping the level of adjustment individuals would reach. Erikson believed that there were critical years in which humans incorporate basic attitudes about themselves and the world.

The attitudes learned by humans at the various stages of life either promote future positive mental health or set the stage for poor mental health. Erikson identified polar opposites of mental health at each stage, while indicating that most people would fall somewhere along the continuum that connected the polar opposites. Moreover, Erikson taught that even those children who are able to attain positive positions in any given period may experience reversals if their circumstances change drastically. Similarly, individuals of any age can move from the negative to the positive pole if their social environments permit and support such psychological growth.

Erikson suggested that during the crucial first two years of life, children must build a healthy sense of trust in the world if they are to grow up to be mentally healthy. Children who develop a basic sense of trust are more likely to see the world as a pleasant, at least moderately predictable place, to view themselves as having some control over life's circumstances, and to begin to develop individual independence and initiative. However, children who live in unpredictable environments or who experience traumatic, negative life events generally develop a sense of basic distrust that affects their future developmental and mental health, sometimes for life. The earliest years are especially critical because they are largely prelingual years; that is, they are years in which children do not yet have the ability to process their life experiences using words to understand and perhaps ameliorate their impact.

In the next stage, children who have established a basic sense of trust can begin to develop their own individuality or sense of autonomy. Parents may experience this period as "the terrible two's," but children who are psychologically healthy delight in the use of the words "no," and "mine," thereby establishing some sense of independence from their parents. Children who enter this stage at the negative pole of mistrust tend to be more reluctant to express their individuality and are likely to develop a sense of self-doubt accompanied by shame.

The third stage of psychosocial development, between the ages of four and six, finds well-adjusted children trying out their new sense of independence in ever-widening environmental circles, including neighborhoods and preschools. Those who have arrived at this stage with a sense of mistrust of the world and feelings of self-doubt are likely to be less adventurous and may experience a sense of guilt as they observe peers move more easily into the larger world.

The school-age period, between ages six and twelve, finds well-adjusted children actively engaged in mastering their environments. Their earlier healthy foundation permits them to try out new relationships, develop new skills, and seek out new activities. In contrast, children who do not trust their environments and who have integrated self-doubt and guilt in earlier stages may be less willing to explore these new areas. Their reluctance may be interpreted by others around them as lack of ability, which may lead to the development of a sense of inferiority.

As a result of a positive sense of independence and much industrious exploration, healthy children may enter adolescence prepared to develop a sense of identity, which includes a positive sense of self, including both strengths and weaknesses. This sense of identity often leads to tentative efforts to select career paths. Children at the opposite end of the pole are more likely to endure an adolescence in which their sense of themselves and their place in the world are indistinct, and may develop a lack of direction, which Erikson referred to as a sense of role diffusion.

During adolescence and young adulthood, healthy young people struggle to develop a positive sense of intimacy, leading to the formation of one or more ongoing relationships that become more meaningful with time. Those who are less healthy may reject intimacy altogether, choosing instead to live a life of psychological isolation, which is often accompanied by anxiety, loneliness, and depression.

Beginning in young adulthood and lasting until around age sixty-five, healthy adults become generative, finding ways to give back to the society that nurtured them. Parenting, volunteer work, and pursuing a career are all paths that require generativity. Those who arrive in adulthood with no clear sense of identity and no real intimate relationships may find themselves drifting through the adult years, accomplishing little. Erikson identified the negative end of the pole of generativity as psychological stagnation, a state in which people stop growing, lose their zest for living, and often turn inward in a futile attempt to nurture themselves.

The final hallmark of healthy psychosocial development, according to Erikson, is the development of a sense of ego integrity. Its polar opposite is the development of a sense of despair and disgust. Erikson believed that this stage could be reached only after a lifetime of experience. Healthy persons who have attained ego integrity show positive self-regard and appreciation for their own life histories, while those who arrive in old age on the negative end of the continuum view their lives as lacking any meaning and often question the very reason for existence. This short review of Erikson's eight stages of psychosocial development provides a structure for examining the life and work of Edvard Munch.

CHILDHOOD AND ADOLESCENCE OF EDVARD MUNCH

Born on December 12, 1863, in Loten, Norway, Edvard Munch was the second of five children born to a medical doctor and his tubercular wife. During the first five years of his life, he lived in a home marked by illness and the ever-present threat of death. Young Edvard probably sensed life-threatening illness in his mother very early in his life. For example, as an adult, Munch reflected that his mother "came of good strong farming stock, but her natural strength was gradually eaten away by the worm of consumption" [4, p. 31]. His mother had five children in spite of an active case of tuberculosis. She died when Edvard was five. That this death was traumatic for young Edvard is undeniable. One of Munch's most famous paintings depicts a small child standing a short distance away from a bed on which there is clearly a dead female figure. Other adults in the picture are obviously grieving in lonely silence, preoccupied with their own sorrow. The child, however, stands with hands clamped over his or her ears. The eyes of the child betray anxiety, even panic, and a loss of innocence so profound that it is irreversible. Munch returned to this theme in different guises, producing woodcuts and in 1893 a sketch that he entitled "Dead Mother." In each rendering of this theme, Munch captured in the eyes of the child the very essence of what we now call death anxiety.

Figure 1. "The Dead Mother and Child," 1897/99. Oil on canvas.
National Gallery, Oslo.

Although Edvard and his siblings were raised by a caring, if somewhat strict and overly religious, father and a loving aunt, it is clear from his work that he never outgrew the early loss of his mother and the accompanying anxiety and mistrust of the world that it generated. As an adult, he reflected upon his own birth, saying, "I arrived in the world on the point of death and my parents had to have me christened at home as quickly as possible" [4, p. 31]. Perhaps he captured some of the self-doubt and accompanying helpless feelings in a painting which he called "Heritage I" or "The Inheritance." The painting depicts an infant in its mother's lap. On its chest are droplets of what appear to be blood. Its eyes are huge and dark against a chalky, yellow-white body. About this picture, Munch wrote, "the child's big eyes peer into the world it has unintentionally entered. Sick and fearful and inquiring it stares ahead, surprised at the painful life it has entered upon, already asking, 'Why? Why?' " [5, p. 170].

It is clear that Munch believed that his physical health was threatened from birth onward; he wrote, "From birth they stood by my side. The angels of anxiety, sorrow, death followed me outside when I played; followed me in the spring sun; in the beauty of the summer. They stood by my side in the evening when I closed my eyes and threatened me with death, hell, and eternal punishment" [6, p. 50]. Munch revisited the themes of illness, insanity, and death often in his art. Using a variety of techniques, he turned out drawings, paintings, and woodcuts that depicted black-garbed figures hovering over the deathbed of a dimly seen individual as well as self-portraits with a skeletal arm beneath the figure.

In addition to doubt about his physical well-being, the young Edvard learned a deep sense of guilt from his very devout and rigid father. As an adult, he ruminated, "At an early age I was taught about the perils and miseries of life on this earth, about life after death, and also about the agonies of Hell that lay in store for children who sinned" [4]. He captured the essence of these thoughts in a self-portrait showing himself against a background of tortured crimson, which he entitled, "Self-portrait in Hell."

By the time Edvard was six, it is likely that he had learned a basic sense of distrust in a world that took away his mother as well as self-doubt because of ill health. He probably also had fundamental feelings of guilt absorbed from his fundamentalist Christian background. However, worse events lay in store as the young Edvard watched his sister attempt to cope with her own case of tuberculosis.

His sister Sophie died when she was fifteen and Edvard was nearly thirteen. The moments before her death were indelibly inscribed in his consciousness. He later wrote, "Sophie's eyes became red. I could not believe that death was inevitable, so near at hand. The priest arrived in his black robes and his white ruff collar. Was she really going to die? In the final half hour she felt much more comfortable, the pains had gone. She tried to get up and pointed to the armchair by the side of her bed. 'I would so like to sit up,' she whispered." Revealing the depth of his identification with his sister, he went on to write, "How strange she felt—the room was different—it was as though she was seeing it through a veil—her body seemed to be weighed down with lead—she was so tired" [4, p. 34].

He captured that scene again and again in his paintings, perhaps as a tribute to his lost sister or perhaps in an attempt to work through the trauma caused by his vivid memory of the scene. Among the series of pictures capturing Sophie's death was one of his most famous, "The Sick Child." The painting shows a young girl whose face is abnormally pale against her long red-brown hair. The child appears exhausted but still holds the hand of a woman who is bowed over with her grief. It was this painting of the sick child that propelled his work into national visibility and controversy. Critics condemned it as a sacrilege to art because its subject matter was not viewed as appropriate. Munch, however, considered it as a breakthrough in his art: "Most of what I later have done had its birth in that painting" [6, p. 65]. He returned to this theme throughout his lifetime, rendering a version of the sick child at least six different times [7].

Clearly, by the time Munch entered puberty, he had experienced a difficult life. Yet neither the loss of his mother nor the death of his sister was his greatest burden in childhood. At age thirteen, he himself experienced a tubercular crisis. He wrote of his memory of this time in a passage that surely must rate as one of the most eloquent passages on facing death ever written.

> One Christmas night I lay—the blood running out of my mouth, the fever raging in my veins, the anxiety screaming inside of me.—"Daddy it is so dark. The stuff I am spitting; it is blood, Daddy." He stroked my head. "Don't be afraid, my boy." I was going to die from consumption! [6, p. 55].

Switching to the third person, he described his ordeal in a slightly more objective manner:

> During the day he had to lay still, not talk. He stared quietly into space. He knew one could live several years with consumption, but he couldn't run down on the

Figure 2. "Fever," circa 1894. Sketch and gouache.
National Gallery, Oslo.

street, couldn't play with Thoralf.—Then he got a mouthful of blood which he spit into the handkerchief. It became dark red in color. He held it up in front of him and looked at it. Look, father! And he showed it to his sister. She rushed out, terrified, and brought back the aunt. Oh, there is more coming! They shouted for the doctor. He ordered ice. "Don't be afraid my boy," (his doctor/father said). But he was so afraid! He felt the blood rattle inside the chest. When he breathed it felt as if his whole chest was loose and as if all his blood would flush out of his mouth [6, p. 56].

He went on to describe the terror and guilt he had felt as an adolescent facing death:

"Daddy, I am dying! I cannot die! Jesus Christ—!" He was interrupted by a new fit of coughing—a new handerkerchief—the blood dyed almost the entire hand-kerchief! "Jesus, help me. I am dying!" Fear seized hold of him. In a few minutes he would be standing in front of God's judgment seat. He would be condemned forever. He would burn forever in sulfur, in hell! If only he believed wholly; but there was doubt. If only he had time, only one day, so he could prepare himself; but he was going to die now! He felt how his chest was boiling. Just the slightest breathing now filled his mouth with blood. His aunt put the handkerchief to his mouth and hid it quickly. Occasionally the blood was running onto the sheets. He lay whispering, "Jesus, Jesus, I dare not die now" [6, p. 57].

After the crisis had passed, he slept for many hours. As an adult, he recalled in detail the scene that greeted him when he awoke. He described the lamp by the table, his aunt in a nightdress, some greenish medicine bottles with red labels. He was to capture many of these images in his depictions of the sickroom. In one famous lithograph and india ink illustration that he entitled "At the Deathbed," but which is also called "Fever" and "The Son," he shows an anonymous figure in a coffin-like bed. At the right of the bed are five grieving figures, two of which are surely his father and his aunt. At the foot of the bed, depicted in wavy dark lines, are the spectral images of two other faces. This work captures the very essence of dying with its hallucinatory quality and its sense of hovering between two worlds.

About his own reaction to surviving this crisis, he said,

> He lay in the middle of the bed with his hands stretched out on the eiderdown and looked straight ahead. He was in pact with God now; he had promised to serve him if he got well and didn't get consumption. He could never have fun as he used to. He looked at his brother who ran around with Petra and Marie. Why then shouldn't he have fun like them? Was he any worse than they? It was a thought coming from the devil. He folded his hands and prayed for forgiveness [6, p. 58].

This passage clearly depicts the fear and bargaining we have come to expect from those facing death. It also shows the beginnings of ambivalence about the Christian faith of his father, ambivalence that grew as he entered adulthood. However, the fact that he could not be as active as his peers probably assured that young Edvard would have time for drawing and painting. Although he had entered his childhood years on the negative side of Erikson's three earliest stages, his ability to use art to express himself permitted him to attain a positive sense of industry and the beginning of a sense of identity that were to stand him in good stead throughout his long lifetime. His growing artistic ability also enabled him to work through negative emotions including grief, loneliness, and anxiety and to use the positive ego defense mechanisms of compensation and sublimation.

ADULTHOOD

Erikson suggests that during adolescence and young adulthood, humans must struggle with the task of developing a positive sense of intimacy or risk adopting an ongoing posture of isolation. As a young man, Munch wrestled with this task and explicitly rejected the thought of marrying and having a family: "Should we sick people establish a new home with the poison of consumption eating into the tree of life; a new home with doomed children?" He produced a painting that captured this sentiment. Entitled "Madonna in the Churchyard," it depicts a grieving mother standing amid gravestones while a small skeleton is partially visible at the left of the painting.

In addition to deciding that he should not procreate out of the fear of spreading sickness, Munch was highly ambivalent about women. In one painting entitled "Sin," Munch depicts a naked woman whose flowing red hair and bright green eyes should speak only of beauty; however, the expression on her face conveys a sense of corruption. He also captured his ambivalence in words, describing a woman as "at the same time a saint, a whore, and a hapless devotee" [4, p. 120]. Although he rejected traditional monogamy, Munch did have one love affair with a woman named Tulla who "set her cap" for him and would not be denied. His ambivalence about Tulla is observable in one of his best-known paintings, "The Dance." All three female figures in this painting are Tulla. The woman in the center, engaged in the dance, is dressed in scarlet. The younger woman on the left is dressed in virginal white, while the older one, clearly withdrawn from the dance of life, is in black. The central male figure is Munch himself [5]. Some biographers believe that it was Tulla's influence, coupled with his overuse of alcohol, that led to Munch's first "nervous breakdown" in 1908.

Munch believed that women might interfere with his art by draining his energies or directing his time and attention away from his work. He often portrayed women's hair as binding a man. His belief about women's interference became a kind of self-fulfilling prophecy. When he left the hospital after his first breakdown, he attempted to end the turbulent affair with Tulla. However, she feigned illness and threatened suicide in an attempt to gain his attention. In a final scene, he and Tulla struggled over a gun and it discharged, severing the top two joints of a finger on his left hand. After the incident, Munch produced at least three works that, on the surface, were intended to memorialize the death of Marat. However, the murderess in each of these works has the features of Tulla [5]. In each rendition, Munch has placed everyday objects, a still life of fruit, plate, and hat, in the foreground, and the emotionless woman stands between the objects of life and the slain, bloody figure of the man on the bed. The light in the paintings highlights the still life, while the figure of the murderess has stilled the male figure forever.

As an older man, Munch summed up the lack of intimacy in his life, saying, "I have never loved. I have experienced the passion that can move mountains and transform people—the passion that tears at the heart and drinks one's blood. But there has never been anyone to whom I could say, 'Woman, it is you I love. You are my all'" [4, p. 174].

In addition to struggling with intimacy, Munch must also have searched for a way to express his generativity and to avoid a sense of stagnation. After a false start at a career in architecture, he devoted himself totally to his art. As he experimented with style and media, he became for a time a fringe member of a bohemian sect whose intellectual discussions followed the writings of Emil Zola. One of the major precepts of this group was the injunction, "Thou shall write thy life." Munch took this to heart, believing that communication is the most important thing we do in life. His art became his writing and his major style of communication. One of his largest and best-known major works, "The Frieze of Life," was produced during his bohemian days. Given his life situation at the time and his difficult relationship with Tulla, perhaps it becomes clear why Munch portrayed what should be an enjoyable pastime, a male and female embracing while dancing, with the blackness of anxiety and depression. The painting also connotes a sense of loneliness even in the midst of other people, as do many of his other paintings. While Munch was an interested, even passionate observer of life, he never lost his sense of aloneness—not even during his bohemian period when he drank too much and experimented with drugs. His style of painting across his long lifetime has been referred to variously as impressionism, realism, naturalism, and symbolism. But always, it was a desire to "write his story" that propelled his painting, lithographs, and woodcuts.

As an adult, the backdrop of Munch's life and the underlying theme of most of his work was anxiety. Even his landscapes are unsettling, depicting desolate scenes in which trees, houses, even clouds exude a type of anxious depression. His best-known piece, "The Scream," graphically portrays the anxiety that characterized his life. He described the experience that lay behind his painting of "The Scream" as follows:

> I walked along the road with two friends. Then the sun went down. Suddenly the sky became bloody red, and I felt a breath of sadness—a sucking pain beneath the heart. I stopped, leaned against the railing, tired to death. Over the blue-black fjord and city lay blood and tongues of fire. My friends walked on and I was left trembling with fear—and I felt a big unending scream go through nature [6, p. 135].

Munch's painting speaks to the universal emotion of anxiety that motivates much of human behavior. There can be little doubt that Munch's anxiety stemmed from his experiences with death, and the fear and dread that they engendered within

Figure 3. "The Dance of Life," 1900. Woodcut.
National Gallery, Oslo.

him. For example, he produced a drypoint of a woman passionately embracing and kissing the figure of death, depicted as a skeleton, and another of an old man in a boat, seemingly unaware of the skeleton beside him, who is in control of the boat. Far from rejecting his own illness and accompanying anxiety, Munch embraced it as a key to his art, saying, "For as long as I can remember I have suffered from a deep feeling of anxiety which I have tried to express in my art. Without anxiety and illness I would have been like a ship without a rudder" [4, p. 22]. Can there by a clearer example of the use of the ego coping mechanism of sublimation?

As Munch moved into middle age, his father's death caused a crisis and a re-evaluation of his life, as fathers' deaths often do in their sons. Critics have said that the painting "Night in St. Cloud," an impressionist painting of a half-hidden figure sitting by a darkened window at twilight, captures the depression and melancholy of the period following his father's death. He also addressed the subject of depression directly with several paintings entitled "Melancholy" in which he showed an unhappy young man alone on a beach and a depressed young woman sitting immobile at an elongated table. He knew the face of depression well since his sister Laura was hospitalized for severe depression.

After the death of his father, he wrote extensively about death and what happens after death. He believed in transformation, rather than extinction of the human substance:

> Nothing perishes. One has no example of that in nature. The body which dies does not disappear. The human substances disintegrate, are transformed. But the spirit, where does it go? Where nobody can say; to claim that it does not exist after the death of the body is just as foolish as to decidedly want to point out what kind, or *where,* this spirit will exist [6, p. 66].

Two pieces from that period include "Metabolism I" and "Metabolism II," which depict buried human bodies becoming gradually absorbed into their natural surroundings.

From a psychological standpoint, Munch clearly was a victim of cumulative loss—his mother, his sister, his father, his own health and accompanying sense of well-being. Furthermore, because the first loss came at such a young age, he was unable to process it clearly and had to return again and again to death themes in his attempt to cope with grief. His major coping skill became sublimation as he sought to turn his death anxiety, essential loneliness, and depression into something valued by our culture.

It was his art that gave meaning to his life and sustained him. As long as he could work, he felt that his life mattered. When, at last, his health failed so much that he could no longer create, he lost the will to live and died soon thereafter. This complicated man, totally absorbed in art, reflected deeply upon the meaning of life. He could truly be called an existential artist. Although he was often depressed and always anxious, his long productive life attests to an underlying belief in the value of life and work.

For Erikson, the final positive stage of psychosocial development was that of ego integrity. Its polar opposite was a sense of despair and disgust. People of advanced age are healthy, according to Erikson, if they have developed an appreciation for their own life histories, have come to some understanding of the values by which they have lived, and feel that their lives have been spent in worthwhile and productive ways.

There is reason to believe that Munch reached the positive pole of ego integrity. The power of his art and his prodigious generativity across his long lifetime permitted him to achieve ego integrity in spite of disastrously negative early experiences. Munch knew that his art was the central value in his life; he appreciated the meaning he experienced in producing it as well as the meaning it might have for others. In his later life, he asserted, "I have exploited my riches; not the filthy lucre of commerce, but the riches of my soul. I have exploited them to advance my art and for the good of my country and my people" [4, p. 278].

Evidence of ego integrity can also be found in some of his paintings that contain an element of light and hope. His painting "Alma Mater" was intended to be the centerpiece of the *Frieze of Life*. Never fully satisfied with it, he described it as reflecting "a different side of the Norwegian landscape and spirit: the bountifulness of summer, the urge for discovery, the spirit of achievement and enquiry" [4, p. 242]. Perhaps the best example of ego integrity, however, is a painting that captures the essence of hope lying just beneath the anxious surface of his life. Called "The Sun," it depicts the radiance of pure sunlight and the colors it can generate as though through a prism. The painting, the antithesis of depression, exudes both life force and a sense of positive peace. The message of the painting is echoed in Munch's words:

> Nothing is tiny, nothing is huge. There are worlds within us! The small is part of the great as the great is part of the small—A drop of blood is a whole world, with a sun at its center and planets, and stars. The sea is a drop of blood, a tiny part of a body. God is within us and we are within God—primitive and original light is everywhere, shining out wherever life is found [4, p. 246].

USES OF MUNCH'S ART IN TEACHING PROSPECTIVE CAREGIVERS

Great art does not need to have practical uses. As one of the highest forms of human expression, it needs no explanations or reasons for existence beyond its own being. As one of Munch's critic stated, "I believe that his pictures will continue to be relevant for as long as painting relies on any feeling of immediacy for its expressive force. What he portrayed as a painter we are able to experience in our lives" (Misse Zetterberg, 1977, cited in [4, p. 293]).

However, in the case of Edvard Munch, it is easy to see multiple uses for his work. When used to teach death and dying to prospective caregivers, Munch's work forces students to confront essential truths. It illuminates the human condition, making visible fear of death, anxiety, and depression as well as the moment of death and the suffering of survivors. It promotes understanding of universality, a condition that Yalom feels is necessary to growth in therapy [8]. As students come to understand that all humans share a common set of experiences and will suffer a common

Figure 4. "The Sick Child," 1895-96. Oil on canvas.
National Gallery, Oslo.

fate, they become better prepared to reach out to all clients, seeing beyond superficial differences of sex, race, and socioeconomic status.

The use of Munch's art with such students also expands empathy, a skill Rogers believed was one of three necessary for effective counselors [9]. Simply asking students to identify what the people standing around the bed are feeling in the painting "The Sick Child" or "At the Deathbed" encourages the development of accurate empathy for those who must helplessly watch the death of a loved one. Reading the description of Munch's near-death experience while viewing his painting "The Son" brings students nearer to understanding the world view of terminally ill clients. Viewing paintings like "Melancholy I" and "Melancholy II" helps students conceptualize the depression inherent in the dying process, while viewing "The

Scream" and "The Dead Mother" promotes insight into anxiety better than all the words in the abnormal psychology texts.

Using slides of Munch's work also enables instructors to cut through the ego defense mechanisms of denial, rationalization, and intellectualization students use to guard themselves. The honesty of Munch's work evokes similar responses in viewers and promotes sharing of both ideas and feelings that are necessary to growth.

In addition to promoting feelings of universality, expanding empathy, and helping students understand specific emotional states, use of Munch's works also exposes students to a powerful tool that they can use with their clients and their clients' families. In their caregiving roles, students can share such art directly to let their clients know that they are not alone with their psychological suffering: others have experienced it and have triumphed over it.

Toward the end of his life, Munch remarked about his work: "In my art I have tried to explain to myself life and its meaning. I have also meant to help others to clarify their lives" [6, p. 141]. By making death and grief visible, Munch bestowed a gift to teachers of death and dying and to their students who aspire to be caregivers.

REFERENCES

1. B. Torjusen, *Words and Images of Edvard Munch,* Chelsea Green, Chelsea, Vermont, 1986.
2. E. H. Erikson, *Identity and the Life Cycle,* International Universities Press, New York, 1959.
3. E. H. Erikson, *Identity: Youth and Crisis,* Norton, New York, 1968.
4. R. Stang, *Edvard Munch: The Man and His Art,* Abbeville Press, New York, 1977.
5. A. Eggum, *Edvard Munch: Paintings, Sketches, and Studies,* Clarkson N. Potter, New York, 1983.
6. B. Torjusen, *Words and Images of Edvard Munch,* Chelsea Green, Chelsea, Vermont, 1986.
7. J. H. Langaard and R. Revold, *Edvard Munch: Masterpieces from the Artist's Collection in the Munch Museum in Oslo,* McGraw-Hill, New York, 1964.
8. I. Yalom, *The Theory and Practice of Group Psychotherapy* (2nd Edition), Basic Books, New York, 1975.
9. C. R. Rogers, *On Becoming a Person,* Houghton Mifflin, Boston, 1961.

Against Daily Insignificance: Writing Through Grief

Martha K. Davis

> The healing power of art is not a rhetorical fantasy. Fighting to keep language, language became my sanity and strength. . . . Poetry, whether found in poems or in prose, cuts through noise and hurt, opens the wound to clean it, and then gradually teaches it to heal itself.
>
> —Jeanette Winterson [1]

On a summer night in 1990, I came home to my apartment in San Francisco to the blinking light of my answering machine. It was a message from my mother asking me to call her immediately, whatever the time, even though it was three hours later in New York City—by then, one in the morning. When I called, she was still awake. She told me without preamble that Ned, my brother, had died.

I had been with my writing group earlier that evening. We had met regularly for about a year and a half to read and discuss one another's work. I was trying to give my writing higher priority in my life, trying to find the time to write my short stories when I wasn't at one of my three part-time jobs. That evening we had discussed a second draft of a story I had given them. I had chosen a subject—homelessness—that was already being covered in the papers every day. In the warm evening air of sunset, the five of us sat at a picnic table down by the piers overlooking the bay. They told me that the piece was sentimental. I had not made my characters three-dimensional or the story unique. They pointed out the interesting places and made suggestions about how I might refocus the story. I left the group feeling discouraged. At the same time I was already thinking of ways to rewrite it.

Then I came home and found out that my brother—my only sibling—had died, and writing dropped away from me. Everything fell away. Instead of living a daily life of work and play and love and rest, I was struggling, often moment to moment, to survive the surprisingly physical and emotional pain that my brother's death caused me. There was nothing more real than the fact of his death. There was nothing more important to me than the understanding that I would never see him again. My humorous, hardworking, gentle brother. Ever. It was as though even my skin had been stripped off, my internal organs incinerated, so that I was left as only bones, the bare skeleton of myself.

For weeks, I had no words, literally. Everything I said was repetitive or banal: I miss him; my heart is breaking. There was no way for words to help me. In New York for the memorial service and then back in San Francisco, I cried whenever I thought of him. Sometimes I forgot that he had died and my remembering made the anguish I felt that much worse. I felt as if I'd been punched in the stomach, then turned inside out, and every part of me hurt. I remember trying to describe how I felt, trying to locate the words to communicate with the people around me. I could only say it simply: I want him back. I could only use metaphor: I'm struggling not to drown in a sea with no land in sight.

I looked to other writers' words to help me. Surprisingly, I was unable to read fiction. It wasn't immediate enough; it couldn't plunge me to the depth of feeling I was constantly submerged in at that time. I turned to poetry, scouring my shelves and the bookstores for poets who spoke of death, of grief. At the burial of Ned's ashes three months later, I read aloud "Dirge Without Music" by Edna St. Vincent Millay. The third stanza especially spoke for me:

> The answers quick and keen, the honest look, the laughter, the love—
> They are gone. They are gone to feed the roses. Elegant and curled
> Is the blossom. Fragrant is the blossom. I know. But I do not approve.
> More precious was the light in your eyes than all the roses in the world [2].

It wasn't until three weeks after Ned's death that I began to write again, having begun scribbling notes to myself about the plane flight back home, my frequent dreams of him, the bizarre experience of attending a memorial service where he wasn't sitting there beside me because the service was for him. I bought a marbled-cover hardbound journal and wrote almost daily, obsessively, pages at a time.

At first I recorded everything I could find out about his death. He had died of heart failure brought on by an infection of the heart valve he had had replaced in an operation three years before. I wanted to know all the details of the last few days, the last few hours, gathering them to me like many of his clothes which I took back with me to San Francisco. I remember feeling—hoping—that having as many of the facts surrounding his death as possible might bring me closer to him at the time of his death. When he died I had been far away, across the country. I hadn't known that my proudly athletic brother had been having difficulty climbing stairs, though I did know that his two full-time jobs kept him overworked and exhausted. I wrote down everything I was told by the members of my family who had gone to the hospital that night, no matter how seemingly inconsequential, no matter how useless now that he was dead: that after having had a heart attack, his heart was functioning at one-third capacity when he reached the hospital; that he was pumped full of antibiotics; that after his heart stopped the doctors opened up his chest and physically massaged his heart to try to start it again. "I hate these details," I wrote, "they make me queasy, but I wanted to know everything that happened, and I want to record everything I remember."

I began each journal entry with a statement of how long it had been since Ned had died. Keeping track of time helped me. As much as I longed for and in fact occasionally expected him to return—because, after all, hadn't he always shown up before?—recording the days and weeks passing made me acknowledge that he was still dead. It helped me focus on adjusting to life without him. But the passage of time also made me feel I was losing him, if "having" him was only a matter of being close to the time he was alive. As weeks, then months went by, I wrote of feeling as if Ned had fallen into the sea, and I was on an ocean liner steaming away, leaving him in my wake, fixed in place, growing smaller with distance, until at some point I knew I wouldn't be able to see him anymore. Time was taking me from him. "Sometimes life seems so normal; I start to plan my day, or I've just parked my car for the night, and then the physical memory returns and I have to sit in my silent car, stunned, or stand over the oatmeal I'm stirring, trying to let the wave of pain pass through. It does bother me that at times I feel like I'm getting used to the idea, that I sometimes feel I can live the rest of my life without Neddy." As I went on with my life, and the date of his death drew farther away, I had to let him remain behind. I hated having to, but writing down feelings like that helped. At least there was a record of my struggle, my graceless fight against a truth I resented and couldn't change.

The journal was also a place to remember as much as I could about who he had been. I had become afraid of forgetting. I remembered him from our childhood and from the year before he died—how easily he had laughed, his stubbornness and rage, the effort he had put into getting good grades in school, his plans for his future. Writing my memories of him was a way to keep him close to me in some way, even though he himself was gone. I also learned later that it is natural for people mourning loved ones to go over their memories, sometimes repeatedly, becoming obsessed with them. Each memory must be unearthed and looked at in light of the death. In one entry I wrote, "On Sunday night I lit two candles before going to bed and watched them until they fizzled out, thinking of that last weekend with Neddy which neither of us imagined would be the last. It's odd to give significance to an event in retrospect simply because it was the last." Death changes the significance of the past. The future is no longer open-ended; the past cannot be remembered as if it were.

During that first year I also needed to explore in my journal, as well as with other people, our relationship as brother and sister. Ned's death devastated me, not only because it was sudden and he was only twenty-seven, but because I had always taken our being siblings for granted. In the midst of my grief I discovered that he was much more deeply embedded into my psyche than I had thought. Being his older sister was a large part of my identity. I had lived my entire childhood with him. As adults we were very close. I had expected that we would get old together too, reminding each other of memories from our shared background that the other had forgotten, that no one else remembered or knew about. Now I was no longer his sister, no longer his ally in our ongoing struggle with our parents, no longer a mentor and a friend, as he had also been for me. My journal provided a place to focus on this relationship, to turn it over and over as I tried to adjust to both the loss of being a sibling and the loss of having a little brother in my life. Often these entries took the form of letters I addressed to Ned. In those letters I wrote the things I would have shared with him if he were alive. I reported experiences he would have enjoyed and others I was glad he didn't have to take part in anymore. I described for him the first snowfall I saw that year on a visit to New York in December. I wrote him on his birthday, on Thanksgiving and Christmas. I couldn't give up my side of our relationship entirely. I still speak to him and write him letters, though not as often. I think I always will.

As I slowly moved through my grief, I clung to detail and description in my writing. I wanted to render even the rituals and experiences surrounding his death vivid, because they were connected to him too. For the first year I was afraid to let anything go, including my own mourning. Besides, I knew this was an extraordinary time, one that was changing me into a completely different person from the one I had been before Ned's death. I kept writing, writing, filling in what I hadn't said yet but that gnawed at me, needing expression, release. I described him the last time I saw him, in a casket at a funeral home in the Bronx. "I took in his eyelashes, the texture of his skin, his cropped balding hair, the pink of his scalp, the delicateness of his ears, the long line of his jaw. And then he'd become unrecognizable again. His short, stubby, chewed fingernails. His hands, his Neddy hands." In the same entry: "In some ways it was terrifying. I kept expecting him to wake up, tell us he'd been fooling. Partly I was afraid of that, of some movement, and partly I was desperately hoping for that. That I would wake up. Or he would. . . . Somehow the planes of his face had changed. The life was gone. There was no expression. No smile, no glint in his eye, no angry clenched jaw, nothing of what was characteristic of *Neddy*." I had gone to see my brother's dead body so that I could face the finality of it. I needed to describe it so that I could move on.

After the burial of his ashes in the fall, my mother and I took a trip, planned months before Ned died, to a small coastal town in Italy. I sketched the views from our hotel room patio. I wrote, "It smells of the ocean, of bougainvillea and trees whose names I don't know, of fish and lemon as we pass restaurants, of wood fires, of, simply, fresh air, the mountains by the sea." It was the first entry that acknowledged the reality of something outside my small, grief-filled world. Almost four months after Ned's death, I was finally able to see the brightness of yellow sunlight, to feel its warmth, to breathe the flowered scents in the air, to enjoy my surroundings again.

At about this time I began to write poetry, also as a way to address Ned's death, to find words to describe the incredible pain I felt. I had written poems on and off since grade school but had never taken myself seriously as a poet. Writing poetry had been, like keeping a journal, something I did that I showed no one. That began to change, as everything was changing for me: what remained important in my life, who my friends were, where I would and would not live, how open I was with others. The way I wrote began to change too, as my need to search for the rhythm of the line, the cleanest language, the most evocative image intensified.

Some of the poems I wrote during the first months after my brother's death were written to gain some kind of relief and never made it past a first draft.

Today
I might have been
running on the beach
rewriting my summer story
or at dinner with a friend.
But the fog covers the city

in a heavy gray shroud;
on the beach where I walk
I can't see the ocean
until it pulls, hissing,
at my feet, cold and colorless
and inexorable.
. . .
On my shelves
I keep shells, striped pebbles,
whole sand dollars harvested
from the sea one spring.
They hold the memory of the sun's glitter
and the breaking foam, the sand
warm between my toes.
But there is nothing
I can have to hold your memory,
my loss,
nothing huge enough
or horrified
except perhaps the roaring waves
dashing themselves
against the sand.

There was something satisfying about writing these poems. I managed to distill some part of what I was going through into a shape, a color, a single feeling. The sorrow itself eased only a little after writing a poem, but working with language again, trying to craft it, was healing; it began to give me another self.

Alone in bed
I put my arms
around this slight body
beginning to rock
again with sobs
and I wonder
how it is
that vigorous
hopeful
you died
while I
repeatedly
thrown down
and broken
open by
this crushing pain
still live.

Before Ned's death I had worked on second, third, and fourth drafts of stories, but I had rarely given my poetry such prolonged attention. In December of 1990 I finished a poem I had been working on since the fall, "The Planets Leave Their Orbits." I discovered that the discipline of rewriting was a pleasure I had missed. Up until then I had only occasionally rewritten a poem until I felt satisfied with it or ready to allow other people to read it. I showed "The Planets" to my parents, who showed it to friends and relatives. It was the first communication with the world since Ned had died that I felt worthy of. I was beginning to consider myself a poet as well as a short story writer.

The Planets Leave Their Orbits

Now I'm an only child, I thought
the night my brother died.
That, and I miss you,
as though the words themselves repeating in my head
could ease me, anesthetized,
into this brutal, undreamed trajectory of my life,
as though missing him as fiercely
as I did might bring him back
to comfort me. Returning to my parents'
homes, I kept waiting
for him to walk through the door,
late and unapologetic in the crush
of hugs. Even at his funeral reception,
welcoming cousins left behind
years ago, I looked for him among us wearing
his best Brooks Brothers suit, a small smile
curling the corners of his mouth
as he inclined his head to listen.
I stood bravely in my black silk
holding his absence inside me
like a blown-up balloon
burst into tatters.

Last night I dreamt the planets left their orbits,
shooting out beyond the reaches of space
into black oblivion,
the whole order of things disrupted.
On our orphan planet Earth, we wondered
how we would survive
with no natural light or warmth,
how our lives could continue without
our brother planets
orbiting nearby
as they had since galaxies were born.

A little over a year after Ned's death, I moved back to New York to be with my family and to attend graduate school in fiction writing. I had realized the fall before that the only interest that remained with me throughout the months of grief was my need to write. The constant question I kept asking was: what would I regret if I knew I were going to die? Every time there was only one answer. If I was going to live the rest of my life in a meaningful way now that my brother was dead, I knew I had to pursue my writing. There was nothing else that mattered more—that mattered at all—to me.

Although I was attending school to write fiction, I took a poetry workshop—my first ever—through an organization unaffiliated with my writing program. We continued to meet for several years as an informal group. It was the first time I was willing to show my poems to other poets and to hear them critiqued. My poetry at that point continued to focus primarily on Ned's death, and to reflect the stages of my grief, but I learned to experiment more, to risk and not be ashamed by failure, to accept praise. And I wrote more poems I was proud of.

In the summer of 1994 I took a poetry workshop at a retreat outside the city that immersed me in language. I wrote over ten poems in five days. Most of them had nothing to do with Ned. They had everything to do with my enjoyment of language as well as the life I had come to live by then. I was lighter, funnier, happier. I was in love again with words.

> It is not easy to plunge to the heart of truth.
> No one said it was.
> Easy is when coins glint
>   from a fountain basin
>   and you throw in one of your own.
> Everyone is looking at the waterfall.

I did not begin to write fiction again until over a year after Ned's death. That first year I felt incapable of writing short stories, the form I had chosen above all others as my own. Stories appeared to me then to be puzzles or mazes: too structured, too complex, too daunting. They required characterization, the creation of a world in which something might or might not happen. For the same reasons that I could not read fiction after Ned died, I couldn't write it. I didn't know yet how to use it to go to the heart of what I felt; I didn't have the tools or the control to mold it successfully. Most of all, I didn't have the patience. I was living very much in my skin, on the surface, and my feelings were all there too, accessible. For a long while I wasn't capable of dwelling in the still places inside me, taking the slow time required to learn from the writing and allow it to surprise me. This is an experience I have only when writing fiction; it's why I write it.

In the fall of 1990, about five months after my brother's death, I applied to graduate schools with stories I had written a year or two before; by the time I moved to New York and started the program I had chosen, I hadn't even attempted to begin a short story. I still felt too scattered, unfocused. In a way, I went to graduate school to force myself to write fiction again. I knew that on my own I didn't have the discipline or the motivation. I needed something outside of myself to inspire me, set up deadlines, create competition, and offer the kind of thoughtful, constructive criticism I had always craved but never found, even with my writing group back in San Francisco.

When I applied to writing programs, I expected to work on a project I had already started the year before: a collection of interwoven stories told by the four members of a family through a stretch of fifteen years. The characters were based on the members of my own family. All together, the stories would see the two children to adulthood. During my first semester at school, I wrote another story for that collection and discovered that I had lost interest in the project entirely. The family I had had in mind no longer existed. The situations I had wanted to illuminate no longer seemed compelling. I wanted instead to write about people and situations that did not reflect my own experience. I wanted to get out of my own skin for a while.

Required to bring something in to show to my workshops, I began writing rough first drafts of stories again, painstakingly, not very well at first. The class would discuss them, and I would go home and write some more. I had to relearn some things, discover others for the first time. How to use detail to reveal character. How to make elegant transitions. My brother was never far away. It was for him I wrote, to him I dedicated my thesis, a collection of stories. Death was never far away: of the seven stories I had finished when I left school, one was about a young man whose mother has died who tries to repair his relationship with his father; another concerned a girl who looks to the men employed in her apartment building for a substitute for her dead father; another told the story of a recent widow coping with old age alone; and another was about a woman whose lover's sister dies and how her lover's grief and her own attempts to assuage it affect their relationship. The death of a family member or spouse hovered in the background of many of my stories, providing the landscape against which the characters had to be viewed. I wrote these stories during a period when I felt I had to be seen in the same way. I was someone whose brother had died a year, two years, three years before. For a long time, this was the first truth about myself.

In January of 1995, on Ned's birthday, I began writing a novel. My short stories had been stretching to over twenty pages. One was forty-two pages long, and several people had suggested it could be expanded into a novel. Instead of producing the brief, condensed pieces that writing poetry and my initial reluctance to wade into the deeper waters of fiction suggested, I had become incapable of writing shorter work. I discovered a need to explore a feeling, an event, a situation between people by looking at it from every angle, all perspectives. Once I found a subject to investigate, I wanted to luxuriate in it, following where the writing led me instead of the other way around. I was more curious and less afraid of what I might discover. After my brother's death I had developed a new relationship to fear: one of acceptance, even gratitude. Dread was very informative, and I had learned to face some of my deepest fears head on.

As I write this, I am nearing the end of the first draft of the novel. It has essentially the same structure as the collection of connected stories I originally set out to write. It is told in alternating chapters by the three main protagonists, a mother, her daughter, and the daughter's best friend. Their stories reveal the texture and turning points of their lives together. This time their lives are very different from mine, and yet all three of them reflect some aspect of myself. Perhaps inevitably, there is a brother's death in the distant past. I recently wrote a chapter in which one of the characters recognizes and expresses her delayed grief. Yet the novel itself is much more cheerful, dynamic, and hopeful than any story I have written before.

Mourning my brother was a time of intense, painful work—and it *is* work. A full two years passed before I felt I had regained a life that I could call my own. By then it was completely different from the one I had been living two years before. I was transformed by my brother's death, in many ways, both positive and negative. In the midst of my grief, I wrote in an attempt to transform his death into something more than the end of his life. I wrote to make sense of it, to come to terms with it, to remember him. Writing helped me to move on. In the middle of the ocean in which I was drowning, writing became an island where I could swim ashore.

> Against daily insignificance art recalls to us possible sublimity. It cannot do this if it is merely a reflection of actual life. Our real lives are elsewhere. Art finds them.
>
> —Jeanette Winterson [1]

And this is also true: the sadness still takes me by surprise sometimes and is capable of making the rest of my life crumble, at least temporarily, in the strength of its grip. The grief will never fully go away. I will always miss Ned.

REFERENCES

1. J. Winterson, *Art Objects: Essays on Ecstasy and Effrontery,* Knopf, New York, 1996.
2. E. St. Vincent Millay, *Collected Poems,* Harper & Row, New York, 1928, 1955.

Sculpting Through Grief

Nancy Fried

My fifteen-year relationship with another woman is over. I fought for the last two years for her to love me. I feel like a part of me has been amputated. This is much more painful, much more consuming than when I had breast cancer and a mastectomy. But there are symptoms of grief that are the same.

That awful moment between sleep and consciousness. Even before opening my eyes, I remember that this is real. This is the nightmare and there is another long day to get through. The nightmare hangs on like a sticky fog. All day I have to fight to get to the other side for breath. Another symptom is that no matter what I'm doing I'm always aware of the loss, the sadness. It's like always having a low-grade infection.

I'm grieving the loss of the dream of the relationship, the loss of the fantasy of the future. I'm grieving the loss of trust, the shock of being betrayed by the person who I thought loved and wanted to protect me. I have good days and bad days. After feeling okay, not great, but okay for a few days, I'll be unprepared for how awful it feels when that powerful weight of grief comes over me. But it gets easier—the loss becomes more familiar, more a part of my reality.

One of the problems with any grieving period is how friends, out of love, want you to be better fast. I experienced this after my mastectomy. People would say how are you and either really didn't want to know (so I'd say "fine") or would ask but their expression of hurt for me was too much so I'd say fine. Sometimes I get very tired of being strong, especially if it is for other people. Being alone is often easier and more comforting than being with friends. Not having to put on that smile is such a relief. I spend hours madly trying to get my endorphin level up. I run and bike. I go for two-hour fast walks on the beach. I work for six hours on my sculpture. So the fog lifts; but that low-grade infection is always there.

After I had breast cancer and a mastectomy I made sculptures about loss, grief, anger, and regeneration. The work also was about redefining female beauty. These pieces helped me reclaim my sense of beauty, sensuality, and sexuality. They helped me throw out that awful prosthesis and believe that this one-breasted body is beautiful.[1]

Two years ago I knew something was very wrong. My friend Cee said everything was fine. But that amazing unconscious knowledge that appears in one's art created pieces about grieving—a torso carrying two grieving heads under her arms

---

[1] See images and discussion on Nancy Fried in the Introduction, pp. 9-12 [Ed.].

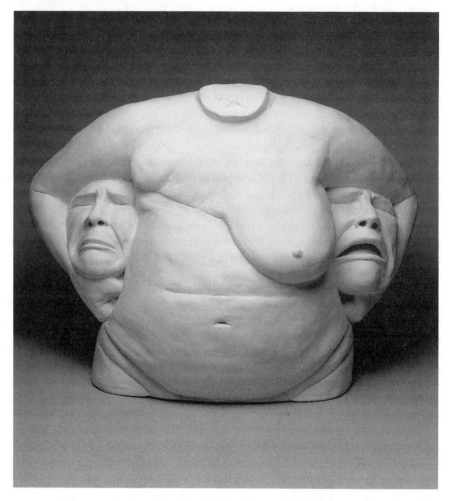

Figure 1. "Self-Portrait," 1994. Terra-cotta.

called "Self-Portrait" (see Figure 1); "Marking the Pain" (see Figure 2) has the figure marking with a nail different hurts on the body.

Last year when I learned Cee had been having an affair for a year, I made heads that were self-portraits. Blind-folded heads, heads tortured with ropes tightly digging into the skin (see Figures 3 and 4).

After two years of struggling to save our relationship, it is over. My new pieces deal with that struggle, with the feelings of helplessness and loss. One sculpture is of the figure hugging a house in her arms. In another she rips open her chest to expose a heart with broken arteries. In another a torso holds out and up her handless arm (see Figure 5).

I'm so used to having one breast, even thinking it's "cool," that I don't know what I would do with two. Will I feel like that about Cee one day?

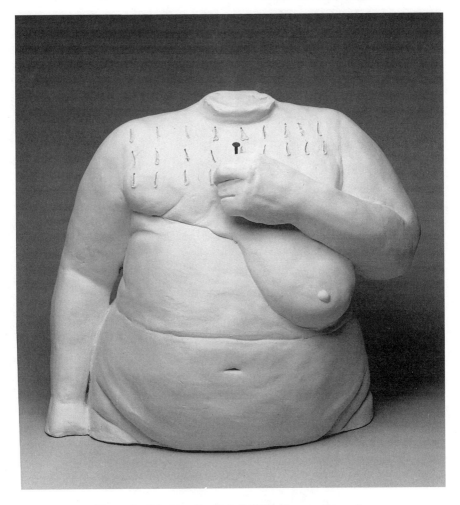

Figure 2. "Marking the Pain," 1995. Terra-cotta, nail.

Figure 3.

Figure 4.

Figure 5.

All Nancy Fried's sculpture, Courtesy of DC Moore Gallery, New York City, New York.

AIDS Time:
A Passage Through Cawthra Park

James Miller

The Cawthra Park AIDS Memorial in downtown Toronto is a good place to meditate on the therapeutic value of time-keeping in a time of catastrophic loss. With its curving series of boulders and menhir-like blocks, the site looks from a distance like an archaeological ruin—a Stonehenge for the Stonewall generation. Just as the rough-hewn monoliths at Stonehenge functioned as a giant dial to record the passage of solar time, so the smooth concrete columns of the memorial serve to measure and enclose and preserve—in a word, to "keep"—AIDS time.

To enter the time zone of the epidemic, take the walkway that winds through Cawthra Park to a paved path that curves up a small knoll through the Memorial (see Figure 1). As soon as you step into the paradoxical bend of AIDS time, you have to reckon with the cultural timing of the epidemic and its cruel untimeliness, the sudden imposition of a sharp divide between "Before" and "After," the fatal syncopation of thousands of lives. Though lifespans are perceptually shortened by AIDS, the prognostic contraction of time has the ironic effect of lengthening every waking moment for the diagnosed. Time here ceases to be valued in the usual terms, or ticked away in familiar clockable units. Years, for instance, are measured by the keepers of the Memorial in numbers of deaths rather than days, and each death is counted as untimely.

AIDS time begins abruptly in 1981, the unheeding year the epidemic was officially proclaimed. It was a very short year by the standards of the Memorial—marked by only one death. Year 2 was the same length. But come to Year 3, and suddenly you're looking at twelve untimely deaths. Year 4 extends the count to nineteen, and by 1995, hundreds of deaths attest to the bitter acceleration of AIDS time compared to the slow steady march of the solar years.

AIDS time is different from the media-trumpeted notion of the "Age of AIDS," which has a morally timely ring to it like the "Age of Innocence" or the "Age of Faith." AIDS time should never have happened. It is not a period of penitence that naturally follows a period of sensual excess, as Lent follows Mardi Gras. No calendar shows an Easter at the promised end of it.

To approach Cawthra Park as a site for questioning the moralizations of AIDS that commonly go unquestioned in public commentary is to turn your back on a whole world of images chosen by the media as emblems of the disease. Editorial cartoons of the Grim Reaper casting his shadow over the "African Hot Zone"; TV

Figure 1. The Cawthra Park AIDS Memorial (opened June 1993) records the
annual tides of the epidemic in Canada on a series of concrete columns
bearing the names of the dead. The Memorial is located in downtown
Toronto at the heart of the Church Street Gay District.

movies on the fate of "innocent victims" swept into the maelstrom of the "gay
plague"; tabloid photos of hookers, junkies, and other "guilty carriers" hellbent on
corrupting decent society; radio phone-ins on the fallout from the latest "tainted
blood scandal"—all such reflections on AIDS belong outside the hallowing precincts
of the Memorial.

The popular vision of the epidemic still promoted by the media after more than
a decade remains as it was in the first years of the crisis: an updated version of
Brueghel's macabre icon "The Triumph of Death" [1]. The invisible legions of the
Human Immunodeficiency Virus (HIV) have simply replaced Death's visible armies
of skeletons as the punitive force driving the innocent and the guilty into the trap of
eschatological terror. Like plague in the fourteenth century, AIDS currently haunts
the public as the most fateful of fatal illness—the black hole at the convergence of
our worst fears and desires. Despite critical efforts to release it from the protean grip
of metaphor, it constantly mutates as a figure of despair in full-blown allegories
of the Doom.

The old universalist conception of death as the fitting end for fallen humanity is
calmly challenged by the AIDS dead recollected in Cawthra Park. Removed from the
Doomsday battlegrounds where the televangelists like to set the tragic dénouement of
the epidemic, the Memorial simply celebrates the continuing value of thousands of

individual lives to the community that raised it against the moral panic of the AIDS apocalypse.

Beside the Memorial you'll find a children's playground that seems to mock the media's preoccupation with morbid solemnities. Though TV camera crews like to shoot the Memorial on rainy days so that the whole park looks like it's weeping, death can hardly triumph in such a setting. There's too much desire in the air. Ask any policeman on Yonge Street where Cawthra Park is, and you'll be directed east to the old cruising ground at the heart of Toronto's gay ghetto.

The memorial was officially unveiled in June 1993 at the twelfth annual celebration of Toronto's Gay and Lesbian Pride Day. Designed by architect Patrick Fahn and landscaper Alexander Wilson, it is the first of its kind in the world—a monument specifically devoted to the memory of a community's AIDS dead. Though its design clearly recalls the lists on the wall of the Vietnam War Memorial in Washington, D.C., the NAMES Project Quilt, and the Amsterdam Homomonument, these architectural allusions only serve to deepen the significance of the Memorial. By gesturing toward the world beyond the park, Fahn and Wilson have articulated a space for contemplating the international scope of the epidemic.

At the heart of the Memorial is a concrete plateau enclosed on two sides by a semicircular path along which columns are positioned at regular intervals of about four feet (see Figure 2). As an area set aside for quiet thought, it has clearly marked boundaries without closed borders. Its open design serves as the visual equivalent of something hard to pin down in exact terms, yet impossible to put out of your mind.

If definitions are primarily memory-aids for the doubtful mind, recalling what has already been carefully established about particular points in a field of knowledge, then memorials might act as defining-aids for the mournful eye. These visual patterns may reassure us that our tumultuous impressions, or badly fixed ideas, of death can be displaced by a field of orderly changes that are calmly knowable because they are memorably patterned.

The geometry of the Memorial alerts us at the very least to the gestalt of death. As we look hard at it, its design may surprise us by seeming to change before our very eyes into something different, even something opposite to what it initially seemed to be. Ultimately it provokes us to question the subjective basis of our perceptions. We may be deeply changed by such a design, by its unexpected gestalt-effects, when it is also constructed as a sacred place for the ritual undoing of Death. Here, as at Isenheim where Grünewald constructed his famous altarpiece, the despair of all who have borne witness to the plague may be miraculously converted into its opposite: a triumph of hope [2].

The space for remembrance in Cawthra Park is permeable and expansive without seeming vague or lost in the mazy geometries of the cityscape looming all around it. A stroll through the park will lead you right by the concrete plateau, yet its focal position in Cawthra's tiny pastoral enclave is far from obtrusive. Sheltered by a grove of young birches, it invites contemplative discovery.

If the Dantean crescendo of "sonic waves" in the finale of John Corigliano's AIDS symphony has a resonant counterpart in architecture, it is the concrete columns that measure the annual toll of the epidemic in Canada, since 1981, along the

Memorial's curving path. On the first column, a steel plaque inscribed with an elegy by Toronto poet Michael Lynch bids the viewer not to endure

> these waves of dying friends
> without a cry [3].

As if to answer the elegist's traditional outcry against personal oblivion and public indifference, the thirteen remaining columns record the names of the proud lives lost in the waves of infection and sorrow that swept Lynch himself to his untimely death from AIDS in 1991.

As the path curves around the central plateau, six lighting fixtures flush to the ground mark the sites where new columns will be raised to record the future waves of dying friends. This urban landscape, echoing the noisy traffic on nearby Church Street, provides the setting for reflections on time and timelessness in the midst of the AIDS tempest.

Lynch's elegy "Cry" evokes a timeless world, a world of pastoral pleasures forever at odds with the city's harsh realities and the plague's relentless toll. Lynch's voice does more than mourn the loss of his friends to AIDS: it also laments the fading of their pre-AIDS dream of changing the hostility of the city into the welcoming loveliness of a sanctuary garden:

> Morning through a city garden widens
> its swath. Shiny eyes of cinquefoil,
> azure eyes of myositis, bruised lobelia
> refuse to blink [3].

To counter AIDS depression, Lynch actually grew a garden of blue flowers in his backyard, and it is surely this tiny landscape that these lines celebrate as a paradisial sight for sore eyes. However bruised by the advance of time, his flowers—like his fellow activists with AIDS—refuse to blink at their imminent demise. He himself had been a tireless activist in the post-Stonewall movement to create a flourishing downtown environment where gay and lesbian refugees could form a vibrant community. Located behind the Community Centre Lynch helped to found, Cawthra Park provides an appropriate urban garden for the symbolic realization of this dream.

For outsiders who might think the park is reserved for mourners only, the middle section of "Cry" provides an insider's cheerful warning about its continuing pastoral uses:

> Some days we doze in the sun
> and dream we too are cinquefoil or lobelia,
> blowing and blanching without demur [3].

Long before the Memorial was erected, Cawthra Park had been hallowed by gay men and lesbians as a spot where they could sun, doze, show off, play ball, socialize, dance, cruise, kiss. It was a welcome erotic refuge in the seventies and early eighties, and the poet, speaking now for the dead, wishes it to remain so in the nineties. Its reputation as a lively nocturnal cruising ground for gays has not been lost in the epidemic.

Lynch's lyrical evocation of good old days in the park seems to exclude the rage of the activists, whose percussive militancy constantly interrupts the nostalgic solos in Corigliano's AIDS symphony [4]. At first glance nothing defiant or overtly political disrupts Lynch's retrospective vision of the garden:

> Then pneumocystis breaks [3].

And his idyll of aesthetic consolation ends in activist rage. Look again at the Memorial through Lynch's eyes, and a visible sign of his defiance will leap out at you. United with the haunting aestheticism of the landscape of loss is an apotropaic talisman of AIDS activism: the pink triangle from ACT UP's "Silence = Death" campaign [5]. It appears twice in the design (see Figure 2). The large concrete triangular plateau is mated with a small triangular stone placed between the seventh and eighth columns. While the base of the greater triangle ends in two shallow steps, its apex touches the lesser triangle in mid-path as if transmitting activist energy from the public domain into the elegiac privacy of the arc. A crescent-shaped hedge in two distinct sections separates the plateau from the path, broken only at the symbolic intersection of the two triangles. From the first column to the break, the hedge consists of low evergreens; after the break it changes to deciduous boxwood.

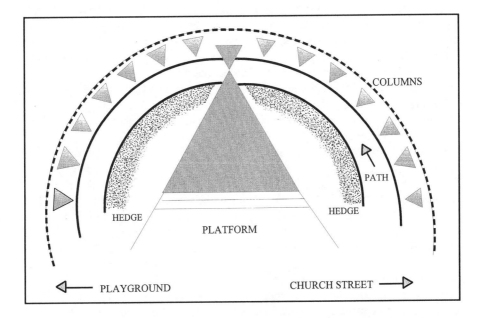

Figure 2. Schematic outline of the Cawthra Park AIDS Memorial (bird's-eye view). The large central triangle and the small triangle touching it are flush with the ground. The photograph in Figure 1 was taken near the arrow pointing to Church Street.

The break marks a dramatic change in the path—the transition from innocence to experience perhaps? At the very least the boldness of the horizontal "event" disturbs the quietly vertical concord of the columns with a rupturing reference to the familiar activist analogy between the AIDS crisis and the Holocaust. The infamous pink triangles, once marks of disgrace on the uniforms of homosexual inmates in Nazi death camps, were reclaimed as badges of pride by the Gay Liberation Movement in Toronto in the late seventies, and were refigured as logos of defiance by the AIDS Coalition to Unleash Power in New York in the late eighties.

The redemption of this once-dreaded symbol is signaled by its inversion. While the Nazi triangles pointed oppressively down, their post-Stonewall counterparts point optimistically up. No doubt this inversion is represented in the Memorial by the opposition of the lesser triangle to the greater. While the lesser has been placed among the columns because of its historical association with mass death, the greater spreads its life-affirming message of liberation and empowerment out into the park. If you walk through the break from the columns to the platform, you are figuratively passing out of fascist history into AIDS time, which is the present tense of gay history.

The triangular plateau has a practical function too—as a stage, a ritual space where the dead may be venerated by the actions of the living. Pride-Day parties, political rallies, speeches, benefit concerts, flower-layings, and ceremonial readings of the names will all happen here as the years add more columns to the Memorial.

Even at a short distance the names are hard to see, let alone read. To scan the roll call of the dead, you have to pass along its columned pathway, which turns out to be the arc of an unfinished cenotaph. This "empty tomb" (as *kenotaphion* originally meant in Greek) is not where any of the AIDS dead actually are buried. They lie elsewhere. Here only their memory is harbored, honored.

If you pass on to relatively lower things, like the bars on Church Street, you may experience a sense of relief that you've had to think about AIDS only in passing—not like the people named on the monument. They had to think about it all the time, in whatever time remained to them after their diagnoses.

"I've been positive for five years," confides Steve, a bartender with the kind of good looks called "drop-dead gorgeous" in the good old days before the plague set in. His name will definitely not appear on a column in the Memorial because he's only a character in *Jeffrey*, an AIDS play by Paul Rudnick (now also a sweetly larky film, with Michael T. Weiss as Steve). Though he doesn't die in the play, Steve's sexually energetic role as the Perfect Dreamdate is ironically defined by his experience of fatigue: "every once in a while, like fifty times a day—an hour—I get tired of being a person with AIDS" [6].

But even Steve has experienced the acceleration of AIDS time, the weariness of making every moment count in a suddenly contracted lifespan. Rudnick leaves him at the asymptomatic stage—frustrated but still feisty—because his audience of admirers would not care to imagine his disfigurement once the wasting syndrome hit him physically. Thank heavens, Steve isn't real.

There are many real Steves listed in Cawthra Park, all now released from AIDS time except for their names and dates:

Steven Flint 1950-1986
Steven G. Cypert 1957-1992
Steve Lyon 1958-1994
Steve Osborne 1955-1991 . . .

These small names bind us as readers to the enormous experience of their collective loss. Whoever they were in real life, their presence on the Memorial transforms them into actors in a vast unwritten drama of suspense and suffering. While the mere listing of names does not make a drama, it implicitly demands one, or many, as many as there are names—2,304 as of January 1998.

The Memorial defies anyone who would read its text as a murder mystery. You can skim the names of the dead but never reach a better part of their story, a part that explains everything, a finale where all the mysterious dying turns out to be worthwhile because it leads to the imprisonment of the killer or the discovery of his motives or some such morally stabilizing conclusion. Something about the ascetic presentation of the names forbids the luxury of conclusiveness. It's their visual crescendo along the path—their gradual build-up, numerically and architecturally, on column after column—that stops you and makes you wonder: what did all these people have in common?

Obviously it wasn't the sad fact that they all died; for then anyone and everyone would be eligible for immortalization under the Cawthra birches. Nor was it just an AIDS diagnosis that brought all these names together, for hundreds of people who've faced that particular trauma are not met with by name here. Though dying from "AIDS-related causes" is a necessary condition for accepting someone's name for the lists, it's still not a sufficient condition—any more than donating the hundred bucks to cover the fee for engraving a single name.

No ready cash? Don't grieve: the Memorial Committee carrying on the work of its founder, Michael Lynch, will make a donation for any eligible name and will not turn any Cawthra-worthy soul away from what they call a "Celebration of Life."

At a glance you can easily tell that most of the dead were men, and you can safely assume that most would have turned up now and then in the bars on Church Street to celebrate Life—or to cruise the perfect Steve—which may have amounted to the same thing.

Who would call it a gay monument—anymore? The names of women and children may be found here and there on the columns, especially toward the recent end of the path:

Baby Paula 1984
Baby Marie Christa 1983-1985
Shielagh Myra Casey 1948-1994
Claire Elizabeth Taylor 1964-1994
Pamela Lynn Pitblado 1959-1995

Unlike the guarded entrances to the bars and bathhouses in the Ghetto, admission to the Memorial is clearly not restricted by age or gender.

In stark contrast to the blazoning of ethnic pride on the NAMES Project Quilt, the racial identities of the named do not visibly figure in the design of the cenotaph. They can only be inferred from the names themselves—usually unreliably—always with the suspicion that the information is less important now than it once was. There are no privileged souls in the uniformly spaced and lettered names on the columns. Everyone has been an insider to one of the specific lives celebrated here. While becoming an insider in the exclusionary world outside the park is often determined by gender, sexuality, race, or age, none of these biographical factors determines the sufficient condition for being included on the Memorial.

For that condition is this: someone or other—a lover, a friend, a sibling, a parent, perhaps even a stranger—must care enough about a particular PWA (Person With AIDS) to make private grief at his or her loss a matter of public concern, of public record.

The death of any memorialized PWA must be valued for what it testifies to: a loving regard. Otherwise the Memorial would take us nowhere, lead us to nothing. As Lynch bids us posthumously in "Cry," we must

> . . . open our eyes to that skyline we incised
> and know as a jet cuts through cloud . . . [3].

that cities of the dead can be turned into gardens of reclaimed hope if we collectively resist the pressures and prejudices of the doom-mongers. . . . The columned cenotaph in Cawthra Park functions as a holy site where the living may commune with the dead, even as the dead symbolically congregate with the living [7]. As the genius of the park, its tutelary spirit, Lynch reveals to the readers of the names the anagogic objective of all the members of his community, past and present:

> We hoist our lives high over the drone
> of traffic. . . . [3].

Even as now the columns hoist up the memorialized lives of the dead, whose visibility in the park ensures them a continuing place in a community that refuses to be felled by the epidemic, or forced back into the closet by the social pressures of the city.

In 1995 the Memorial Committee added a second poem to the first column as an egalitarian corrective and inspirational complement to "Cry." While Lynch's elegy (first published in 1989) originally had nothing to do with the Memorial, Shoshanna Jey Addley's incantation "Circles of Stone: To Those Unnamed" was composed specifically for the site. "We stand at this place," it begins, as if the columns themselves were speaking to us like runic crosses in a medieval churchyard. By standing here as our surrogates, they will keep strong the memory of the martyrs even when we fail to honor them in person or in time forget their names. "Our strength," they proclaim, "though withered and sapped, regenerates here."

Suddenly the reference of the first-person pronouns shifts from the stones to the readers of the stones, who by the very act of standing beside the columns somehow magically recover the inner strength drained by the fatiguing demands of living in AIDS time. Where the Male Voice cries in the urban wilderness, the Female Voice must answer it with elemental challenges to its elegiac authority. While the Male Voice is plangent and nostalgic, the Female Voice is psalmic and oracular: "Each name on each standing stone remarks thousandfold upon those unmarked from sea to sea . . ." Why? Simply because "We exist"—as mourners, as memory-bearers. The global scope of the epidemic strains the capacity of the Memorial to contain our grief for the Unnamed. It must spill out beyond the park like a flood of tears, or rise up beyond the birches like one of the ghetto apartment blocks.

Assuming the dauntless tone of a Sybil, an ecstatic guardian of the grove, the Female Voice strives to call back the Arcadian dream of pastoral timelessness from the depths of AIDS time. Carefully the stony ground is sown, and new monoliths of memory spring up to sustain the fantasy of regeneration:

> Further stones planted, the last meets the first,
> A circle is formed.

Thus perfected in a geometrical and ethical sense, the Memorial becomes a magic circle—an AIDS-henge with Addley as its Druidical priestess. The new circle miraculously gains volume as its imagined dimensions swell to include the AIDS community of the globe, and from this healing ring no one who truly enters into the anti-discriminatory spirit of that community will be excluded. By remembering, we also "mark the day we have no further need for such Circles of Stone." Such a day, of course, exists outside of AIDS time.

When you reach the column for the year just past and consider the incompleteness of the circular path, it's hard not to feel the utter inadequacy of all our current definitions of AIDS.

Mortality is oddly absent from the definition of AIDS encoded in its blandly bureaucratic acronym: A for "Acquired"; I for "Immune"; D for "Deficiency"; and S for "Syndrome." The denotation of these terms is clear enough. AIDS is defined as "acquired" because it's not genetically transmitted like other kinds of immuno-deficiency. It's identified primarily as a "deficiency" of the immune system because various blood cells, crucial to the body's biochemical defenses against disease, are initially weakened or reduced in number so that invading pathogens meet with little natural resistance. It's accurately called a "syndrome" to distinguish it as a rather loose combination of wasting diseases and malaises (including viral infections, fungal rashes, fevers, and cancers) from the more familiar disease process that manifests a single clear set of symptoms or a predictable sequence of phases.

The acronym, first formulated in 1983 at an urgent meeting of public health officers in Washington, D.C., has stuck because of its apparent social neutrality and scientific objectivity. It makes AIDS sound official, manageable, even respectable—another problem for medical researchers to tackle along with Sudden Infant Death Syndrome (SIDS) and Toxic Shock Syndrome (TSS). Yet unlike these illnesses, which sound as deadly in their unabbreviated form as they actually are, Acquired Immune Deficiency Syndrome defines itself with a distinctly euphemistic muting of any reference to the shocking strangeness and untimeliness of the AIDS deaths reported in the medical press in the early 1980s. You would hardly know from the name, for instance, that gay men in Toronto had died of opportunistic infections hitherto treated by veterinarians, or that mundane ailments like psoriasis or diarrhea had suddenly turned into hellish agonies for PWAs in the final months of their lives.

For reasons not yet fully understood, the syndrome seems to develop in the body once the circulatory system has been infected by the retrovirus identified since 1987 as HIV. Though blood and lymph are the main conveyors of HIV, nerve tissue has also been found to harbor the virus. Diagnostic definitions of AIDS—as updated by the Centers for Disease Control (CDC), for instance—have accordingly started with a definition of HIV infection primarily as a blood disease, followed by a list of the symptoms indicative of severe immune suppression, and the various opportunistic infections and neurological conditions that typically occur in unpredictable combinations as indicators of the syndrome.

Such definitions have been criticized for favoring the theory that AIDS is directly caused by a single factor—exposure to HIV. Rival theories involving multiple factors (such as HIV in combination with syphilis and other sexually transmitted diseases) continue to be proposed and highlight the present lack of any definitive medical explanation of the syndrome. Diagnostic answers to the question "What is AIDS?" remain loose and provisional, if only because no two AIDS patients present precisely the same set of symptoms, or the same sequence of secondary illnesses. Despite the idiosyncratic ups-and-downs in the health of each PWA, diagnosticians working with clinical statistics have organized the continuum of AIDS into clearly discernible phases: from asymptomatic seropositivity through gradual immune suppression to the fulminant eruption of Kaposi's sarcoma lesions and other defining signs of the "full-blown" stage. Death, in their present understanding of AIDS, is the endpoint in this continuum, the apparently inevitable dénouement to the relentless immunological breakdown.

Where immunology and clinical medicine stress the impact of the syndrome on the human body, epidemiology defines AIDS in broad demographic terms as a public health crisis, a global catastrophe, a pandemic. Waves of sickness and dying are of great interest to epidemiologists, who study the fluctuations in the morbidity and mortality rates for various social classes and age groups in order to measure the spread of infectious diseases like HIV from one population to another and to assess the global progress of previously local epidemics like AIDS. Waves of dying friends are of even greater interest to the them, however, since the social and sexual links between the stricken have provided valuable evidence for charting the routes of viral transmission within communities and across nations.

By 1984, epidemiologists from the CDC had firmly established that infection with HIV can only occur when the semen, blood, or vaginal fluid of an infected person passes directly into the bloodstream of an uninfected person. Transmission of the virus *may* occur during such "high-risk" activities as the sharing of unclean hypodermic needles, the transfusion of untreated blood, and the exposure of genital tissue to ejaculate during sexual intercourse without latex protection. Pregnant women who test positive for HIV may also pass the virus on to their unborn children.

Armed with such knowledge, the Global Project on AIDS at the World Health Organization (WHO) has marshaled its data-collectors and computers to contain the unruly epidemic within the manageable domain of numbers. Epidemiological statistics trumpeted from the UN have come to define AIDS at a macro-level through the swift translation of cumulative totals and demographic projections into media facts. By the year 2000, there will be ten million reported cases of HIV disease worldwide, with Southeast Asia and sub-Saharan Africa reporting the highest rates of seroconversion.

Aside from the impersonality of long-range medical views of the crisis—friends tend to vanish in the tidal waves of statistics—the main problem with WHO efforts is that epidemiologists have not rested with the determination of risk behaviors in their cluster studies of HIV-transmission. They have also identified certain "high-risk" groups (e.g., sexually active homosexual men, heroin addicts and their sexual partners, prostitutes and their johns) who are supposedly more inclined to engage in reckless activities than members of the more cautious general public.

This dubious taxonomy of "infectious" social types has done much to stigmatize communities already reeling under the impact of the virus by encouraging the disidentification of the well from the sick. "AIDS is everyone's concern" and "AIDS doesn't discriminate!" became popular slogans at activist demonstrations in Toronto in 1988-1989 because many people by then—particularly young people—were mistakenly assuming that they couldn't contract HIV since they didn't move in any of the social hot zones charted by the WHO. Membership in a risk group seemed to imply not only that you were automatically eligible for HIV-infection, but that you inevitably posed a health risk *to* society at large.

HIV disease is not contagious: it can't be caught simply by touching or coming into daily contact with someone infected. It is (merely) infectious. Since the crucial distinction between contagion and infection is usually lost on the public, it tends to regard all high-risk types as potential AIDS pariahs, carriers of contagious death.

How is AIDS defined by PWAs who still rejoice in the erotic affirmation of life? Ask my friend Dave what AIDS is, and he'll point to himself with an exaggerated expression of alarm on his face, as if he had just touched a B-movie alien with his bare hands, before screaming "It's alive!" This is Dave's way of proving that several years after his HIV diagnosis he's very much alive and can be found at his usual desk in the university bookstore near the sci-fi section, which is about as close to deadly aliens as he cares to come.

AIDS is now so routinely identified with death that something of the shrugged-off inevitability of what we all must face at the end of our lives now adheres ironically, like a sad musty growth, to the once shocking unfamiliarity and catastrophic immediacy of the syndrome. Dave is, as he would say, "philosophical" about this. He's just lost another lover to AIDS, his second within three years. A pianist named Jean-Guy. A beaming "before" photo of Jean-Guy appears in a color Xerox on the cover of his memorial service program, which Dave hands me for admiring inspection. Jean-Guy in his prime, dressed in a smart black dinner jacket as if set for a gig at a summer wedding reception, smiles out at me from a baby grand posed on the unseen edge of the grave.

"This is how he wanted to be remembered," Dave smiles. What I admire after taking in Jean-Guy's dashing Québecois features is the look of unsentimental equanimity in Dave's steady gaze as he looks back at his permanently smiling lover across the landscape of loss.

That landscape, I notice, has been clearly mapped out for Jean-Guy's mourners in a helpful narrative inserted into the program as a kind of vade mecum, a Dantean mini-allegory of Life (specifically Jean-Guy's life with AIDS) as a Journey toward Death. "Imagine helping a friend on a journey to a remote monastery perched on top of a mountain," it begins:

> As you begin your trip, the path is fairly clearly marked and the goal easily seen in the distance. But as you approach, the monastery is often obscured by the tops of trees in the forests through which you pass. And you say, "if only we could get out of this woods, we would be able to see the monastery again and see where we're going."

Mists rise in this "selva oscura" to obscure the path [7]. Lost for a time, the faithful friends scramble through the terrors of the wood until they reach the foot of the distant mountain. As they start to scale its perilous heights, trying hard not to see the journey itself as their goal, one of them grows weak and fears that he will not reach the top. He faints from fatigue. No coureur de bois, he. But his friend keeps him going, eventually carrying him over rocky crags and through forbidding passes when his strength entirely gives out. Finally, at the summit, they reach the heavy cedar gates of the lonely monastery which open to admit only the dying man—by this time practically a ghost.

"Clearly it's not one of those progressive monasteries where same-sex unions were consecrated and consummated in the early Middle Ages," I observe to Dave, "Too bad John Boswell didn't write the ending." Dave had only recently sold me a copy of Boswell's long-awaited final work on homoerotic monasticism and martyrology. We were both aggrieved by the secrecy of the great historian's long and sorely unallegorical battle with AIDS [8].

"Jean-Guy couldn't finish it," Dave adds wistfully.

I'm sure he meant Boswell's book and not the journey up the mountain, which ends on a poignantly "philosophical" note. After death's door is figuratively slammed in his face, the surviving comrade stoically turns back down the slope like Virgil descending Purgatory, saddened yet relieved that he'd lost his Dante to higher things.

"Was Jean-Guy—religious?" I inquire, not wanting to sound too critical of the tactfully de-gayed forest through which he'd been dragged in "The Journey." Did his real life's journey ever take him through the bushes in Cawthra Park? If I'd asked whether he'd been a Catholic, my tone would have been reflexively polemical.

"Not especially," Dave shrugs.

Where, I want to ask him, does this traditional allegory acknowledge the queerness of Jean-Guy's last years, the unexpectedness of his coming out, the erotic joie-de-vivre in his eyes, the bitter bouleversement of his diagnosis, the mysterious workings of the syndrome under his skin, the continuing value of Dave's loving regard for him?

"We fought a lot towards the end," Dave confesses. He would be the last person to expect everyone to understand what only a relatively small number of people in Canada have had to experience at close hand, in the unpredictable day-to-day struggle to keep spirits up and temperatures down.

Those whom the syndrome has most deeply affected are usually quick to counter the fatalistic backgrounding of the epidemic in its sluggish second decade. Tom, a student council officer at my university and a friend of Dave's, has resolved not to be privately "philosophical" about the relentless tides of indifference washing over his little beachhead of AIDS activism. He proudly and publicly identifies himself as a "Person Living with AIDS," an epithet that foregrounds his activist resistance to the assumption that his illness is a Death Sentence handed out by Fate to the Human Condition. Too bad that the Human Condition seems to be concentrated in certain undesirable "risk groups," as well-meaning souls still tell him to his face. But there it is. Can't be helped. Loathing all such moralizing abstractions, Tom sets up display after display on AIDS prevention in the University Community Centre. It's his way of proclaiming not only the unnecessariness of the whole crisis (condoms are his talisman against fatalism) but also the urgent need to drive out the virus from the university community through what in palmier days used to be called consciousness-raising. You have to start somewhere, he insists.

"How's Tom doing?" I ask Dave.

"Holding in there."

"He's not the type to get sucked under," I go to say, but suddenly change the subject: "Tell me, Dave: are you going to have Jean-Guy's name engraved on the Memorial in Toronto?"

"I've been meaning to do it for some time now. Got the application form from the Memorial Committee last fall, but missed the deadline for this year I think. It's good therapy, you know—filling out the form, sending in the donation, visiting the park on Pride Day to see whether they spelled the name right. Helped me work through Danny's death, the mourning and all. They even spelled his name right! It was great to see it up there, in Toronto, in public. Some people, I've heard, have objected to the park as the setting for the Memorial. Doesn't bother me one bit. Did you ever meet Danny? My last lover but one: quite a guy. Now he's 'Danny Vanwyngaarden 1951-1992.' Jean-Guy was quite a different story, I tell you. Maybe I'll get him up there next year. Another year, another name, eh?"

AIDS time. . . .

REFERENCES

1. A. Wied, *Brueghel,* A Lloyd (trans.), Studio Vista, London, 1980.
2. W. Fraenger, *Matthias Grünewald's Isenheimer Altar,* Benna Schwabe, Basel, 1988.
3. M. Lynch, *These Waves of Dying Friends,* Contact II Publications, Bowling Green, New York City, 1989.
4. See Corigliano's notes on pp. 12-13 accompanying the 1991 Erato CD release of the Chicago Symphony Orchestra's performance of his *Symphony No. 1* (conducted by Daniel Barenboim).

5. D. Crimp and A. Rolstan, *AIDS Demo Graphics,* Bay Press, Seattle, 1990.
6. P. Rudnick, *Jeffrey,* New York, p. 47, 1994.
7. Dante, *Inferno,* C. Singleton (trans.), Princeton University Press, Princeton, New Jersey, 1970.
8. J. Boswell, *Same-Sex Unions in Premodern Europe,* Villard Books, New York, 1994.

Social Support "Internetworks," Caskets for Sale, and More: Thanatology and the Information Superhighway

Carla J. Sofka

Gone are the days when avenues for exploring issues of death, dying, grief, and bereavement were difficult to find. Forums for discussion among professionals and nonprofessionals abound as seminars, conferences, and support groups are commonplace. These formerly taboo topics now merit their own section heading among self-help titles in most book stores. More recently, thanatechnology—technological resources like videos, computer-assisted instruction programs such as one that simulates being diagnosed with a terminal illness [1], and interactive videodiscs useful for gaining information about topics in thanatology—brings these subjects into educational and service settings as well as the home. This chapter will explore a unique indicator of change in our openness to and interest in these topics by presenting an overview of society's most easily accessible type of thanatechnology, the World Wide Web and the Internet.

The World Wide Web, often referred to as the "Web" or "WWW," is a complex system that disseminates information through the Internet—a network of inter-connected computers. Individuals and organizations store information in computer files that are accessible via a connection to the Internet through the use of a computer modem. Just as businesses and residences have a unique mailing address, each site on the World Wide Web has a unique combination of letters and characters (a Uniform Resource Locator or URL) that informs your computer how to connect to the location where the information is stored.[1] This chapter will provide an introduction to the types of thanatology resources available on the Web, including social support resources for individuals and their families who are coping with life-threatening illness, the process of dying, and grief. Implications for clinical practice, death education, and thanatology research will also be discussed.

Reprinted with permission by Taylor & Francis, 1997.

---

[1] URLs reported in this chapter are subject to change. A Web browser or search engine may be used to locate any site whose URL has changed. URLs for sites referenced by superscripts 2-30 are available in the Appendix.

RESOURCES FOR SOCIAL SUPPORT

Opportunities to gain social support on the Internet and the Web are diverse, creating the potential for dynamic "social support Internetworks" among individuals who use these innovative resources. Three types of social support are available: informational or guidance support, emotional or affective support, and instrumental or material support.

Informational support [2] or guidance support [3] involves sharing advice, directives, or factual information that a person can use in coping with personal and environmental problems. Emotional or affective support consists of behaviors or acts that involve caring, love, empathy, and trust [4, 5]. Instrumental support or material aid involves tangible resources such as financial assistance or physical objects for use in care or the provision of services [4, 6, 7]. While these basic definitions of social support have been used in clinical work and research [8], the development of computer technology, and creative applications for this technology, lets us expand the mechanisms through which social support can be provided. Communications researchers have provided a theoretical framework that describes the role of technology in providing social support. A discussion of this framework and examples of thanatology-oriented social support resources on the Web follows.

Mediated Interpersonal Communication

Mediated interpersonal communication is used to describe any situation where a technological medium is introduced into interpersonal interaction [9]. Several specific types of mediated interactions that provide social support are represented on the Internet and the Web. These resources and the potential benefits of their use in clinical work with clients throughout the illness or bereavement process merit consideration.

Interpersonal Mediated Communication for Emotional Support

The first category, interpersonal mediated communication, "refers to any person-to-person interaction where a medium has been interposed to transcend the limitations of time and space" [9, p. 44]. In the following examples, the medium to facilitate interaction is a computer equipped with a modem. Participation in a chat group, discussion group, or newsgroup allows individuals with a common life experience or mutual interest to communicate through the use of electronic mail (e-mail) at any time of the day or night. Responses can be posted to all participants in the group or sent privately to a particular individual. Newsgroups or bulletin boards including the word "support" in the group name (i.e., alt.support.grief) are likely to incorporate a supportive component to the discussion. For example, "grief chat," sponsored by Rivendell Resources (http://rivendell.org) is a general discussion list for any topic related to death, dying, bereavement, or other major loss. There are also support groups for specific types of losses (i.e., spouses, parents, children, siblings, pets). Individuals simply follow the directions posted at this site to join the chat group and check their mailbox for responses from other members of the group.

Online support groups, also known as computer-mediated support groups [10], provide forums for communicating with other individuals to share experiences and coping strategies. These support groups can simulate a traditional support group by occurring in "real time"—at a regularly scheduled time during which conversations are interactive, with members typing responses to questions or comments made by others who have logged into the group via computer modem.

Several strategies are recommended to locate online support groups. First, well-known commercial providers (e.g., America Online, Prodigy, Compuserve) may offer online support groups related to thanatology topics. Check the menu of services available through your current provider or contact a customer service representative to inquire about the availability of online support groups. Second, publications or newsletters specific to a topic or issue may describe online resources.

Person-Computer Interpersonal Encounters for Informational Support

The second category of mediated interpersonal communication is a person-computer interpersonal encounter. This type of encounter includes situations in which computers serve as interpersonal proxies, with an individual interacting with a computer program that simulates dyadic communication [9]. For example, the Comprehensive Health Enhancement Support System (CHESS) is an interactive computer system that contains information, social support, and problem-solving tools [11]. Although this program was not available on the Internet or the Web when this chapter was written, some Web sites provide opportunities for a similar type of interaction.

Numerous sites for informational support are available. As individuals cope with the diagnosis of a life-threatening or terminal illness, they often have concerns about the limited time available for communication with doctors or the difficulties in finding current information about the illness and treatment options. Web sites containing frequently asked questions (FAQs) and medical information can serve as an adjunct resource used in conjunction with the advice of a physician. For example, clients coping with cancer can benefit from accessing CancerNet,[2] a product of the International Cancer Information Center, or OncoLink,[3] developed by the University of Pennsylvania Medical School. These sites offer information about cancer diagnoses, treatment options, psychosocial aspects of cancer, and resources for coping.

Opportunities are also available for computer-mediated discussion with professionals. At one such site, individuals can also participate in a live interactive chat to discuss mental health issues with Dr. John Grohol[4] at specified times. A "Question and Answer Board" to allow individuals to post queries via e-mail for response by experts in the field of death, dying, and bereavement is available through the Bereavement Education Center.[5] Clinicians and clients can access Web sites that provide descriptions of available services and resources. In addition to formal services such as medical treatment or hospice, these online directories may describe opportunities for informal emotional support through self-help or support groups. The information varies significantly, influenced by the purpose of the Web site as well as sponsorship of that particular site (e.g., national organization, local agency, provider, non-profit group, or an individual). Sites may also include automatic connections to other relevant sites ("hotlinks"), accessed by the click of a mouse. Several sites help individuals locate informational bereavement resources quickly. Both GriefNet[6] and the Bereavement Resources[7] site are excellent places to begin accessing these resources on the Internet and the Web.

Person-Computer Interpersonal Encounters for Instrumental Support

Web sites are also available to assist consumers with a variety of decisions related to the funeral process. In addition to help with planning a funeral and purchasing caskets online, sites offer information about cremation (the Internet Cremation Society[8]) and products to assist with memorialization available through the Memorial Gallery[9] such as cremation jewelry or memorial books.

Using a tone unlike the philosophy of most death professionals, Stral [12, p. 415] described the Web's first "virtual funeral home"[10]: "Visionaries who prophesy the benefits of the Information Superhighway touching everyone from cradle to grave can rest comfortable, knowing at least one end is now covered." Sites such as these may decrease the sense of mystery and taboo surrounding the funeral industry.

Narrative, Commemorative, Expressive, and Experiential Sites

While the following sites do not fall within the framework of mediated inter-personal communication, they contribute to the value of the Internet and the Web as a resource.

Narrative sites include stories or descriptions of a personal experience with illness or loss. Prior to his death on May 31, 1996, Timothy Leary's home page provided the most highly publicized example of a narrative site. In addition to mental and physical status reports, Dr. Leary described his activities to achieve "Hi-Tech Designer Dying" and his efforts at pain control, with his average daily input of neuro-active drugs. A similar site documented the struggle of Austin Bastable, a Canadian who fought to legalize physician-assisted suicide until his death by assisted suicide on May 6, 1996.[11] Sponsorship of this site by the Right to Die Society of Canada incorporates an advocacy component, sensitizing readers to the legal and policy-oriented issues involved.

Other sites include less controversial narratives about grief and loss, such as "A Place to Honor Grief."[12] At this site, sponsored by social worker Tom Golden, bereaved individuals can read about others who have experienced similar losses. This site may also be described as a *commemorative site,* one that includes personal stories but also incorporates memorialization and ritual. In addition to opportunities to describe the life and death of a significant other (human or pet) through the creation of a memorial, these sites allow an individual to participate in a variety of meaningful activities.

The World Wide Cemetery[13] is one of the most impressive sites to memorialize a loved one. Individuals can erect a permanent monument to a loved one for a nominal fee (less than $10.00 at the time of publication). These memorials can include images (photos, artwork) and sound, connecting visitors to the life of the deceased and allowing them to leave flowers at a particular gravesite.

The Pets Grief Support Page[14] allows those grieving the illness or death of a pet to commemorate their companion. Candle Ceremonies, held each Monday night, allow persons with a common loss to join in spirit for support.

Expressive sites are forums for the expression of thoughts, emotions, and experiences through the use of writing, poetry, art, photographs, and potentially music or sound. The use of creative artwork by children as a means of coping with illness can be seen in the gallery of pediatric oncology patients' art within the OncoLink site,[15] a unique collection sponsored by the University of Pennsylvania Cancer Center.

In response to a highly publicized tragedy, an Internet sympathy card was created for victims of the Oklahoma City bombing. Following the assassination of Yitzhak Rabin, a Web address to send condolences to Rabin's widow was publicized. Messages of sympathy can be expressed immediately: over 150,000 e-mail messages on Web sites were devoted to TWA Flight 800 victims within two weeks of the tragedy [13]. One example is a site devoted to victims from Montoursville, Pennsylvania.[16]

While most of us would not define impending death or the experience of grief as amusing or comical, the existence of "gallows humor" indicates the need for comic relief from the anxiety generated by these subjects. Brain supports this notion: "evidently we laugh at what we find most threatening" [14, p. 22]. Individuals searching for thanatology information on the Internet and the Web are likely to encounter sites that include examples of dark humor, which some may find offensive. A relatively innocuous site called "The Graveyard"[17] contains humorous epitaphs; however, other sites ("The Bones"[18]) can also be quite gruesome. Some sites include notices of potentially objectionable content, but one may stumble upon offensive material without warning.

Experiential sites explore one's own reactions to or attitudes about a thanatological issue. An individual can confront his or her own mortality by "The Death Clock."[19] This site uses figures on the average life span to estimate how many seconds a visitor has left to live. The creator, Raymond Camden, also notes: "the page will automatically update itself every 10 or so seconds, so you can keep a running meter on your desktop." While this type of site is relatively rare, experiential sites will become more common as individuals become more familiar with the programming skills required to create these sites.

For assistance in locating additional sites, a variety of publications (Internet or WWW "Yellow Pages," directories) are available in the computer section of bookstores or public libraries. Information about life-threatening illnesses such as cancer or AIDS is also found under the topics of health, medicine, diseases, and disorders. Resources on these topics may also be listed under social issues, sociology, and self-help/mental health.

Commercial search engines may have thanatology sites with multiple hotlinks. For example, Yahoo's Culture & Society category has a "Death" subsection[20] including hotlinks to sites on capital punishment, cemeteries, cremation, euthanasia, funeral companies, hospice, and suicide. Perhaps the most comprehensive collection of sites related to death is available through the WEBSTER site.[21] These two sites are excellent places to start.

IMPLICATIONS FOR CLINICAL PRACTICE AND DEATH EDUCATION

The rapid growth of the Web and the Internet is expected to continue. New multimedia (audio and video) capabilities will significantly increase the value of these resources for use in clinical practice and death education.

Information and Referral

Clinicians and death educators have traditionally presented resources for information and referral (I & R) to clients and students in the form of telephone numbers to call for additional assistance, brochures or directories, or bibliographic reference lists. Frustrations inherent in these methods of I & R include inaccurate or outdated information, printing and distribution costs, and the time lag between identification of bibliographic materials and receipt of these items.

Information on the Internet and Web is often "state of the art," updated frequently and rapidly, with no associated printing and mailing costs. Individuals can access information any time of the day or night, receiving responses in significantly less time and with potentially less expense than in traditional searches.

Benefits for the Bereaved

In addition to advantages in the I & R process, there are potential clinical benefits. The process of contributing to a commemorative site or including commemorative material in an individual home page may provide cathartic outlets for the expression of grief. Development of a commemorative site may be especially helpful in situations where a body was not recovered or distance to a gravesite hinders the process of mourning a death.

Feelings of isolation may be decreased by visiting narrative sites and reading the stories of others experiencing similar losses. Of particular interest is the use of online support groups as sources of affective support for those coping with disenfranchised grief, such as AIDS-related death, suicide, or pet bereavement.

Opportunities to learn about reactions to loss may provide reassurance during difficult times of adjustment. In addition, chat groups also eliminate one traditional barrier to participation in groups—schedule conflicts.

Participation in these types of groups is not affected by access to transportation or limitations in physical mobility. Another potential advantage includes the opportunity to remain anonymous [10].

Resources for Death Education

Although death education courses and community-based opportunities to learn about thanatology are increasingly available, the Web and the Internet provide information to individuals who live in communities without such resources. For example, students can consider the option of earning transfer credits through a course on grief as a family process developed by Kathleen Gilbert and offered by Indiana University.[22] Interactive bereavement courses for volunteers have also been designed.[23]

Several sites provide information on end-of-life issues. Choice in Dying's site[24] describes procedures to document advance directives and offers a mechanism to provide twenty-four-hour access to these wishes. DeathNet[25] contains a thanatology-specific online library related to physician-assisted suicide. Thanatology information is also available on Cultural Diversity.[26] Libraries such as Sociology Online[27] or other archival sites may contain similar resources.

At the present time, it is difficult to estimate how often the Internet and the Web are used as resources for death education. The development of strategies to evaluate the effectiveness of death education via this technology is a task that deserves attention.

Professional Resources

For professional growth, clinicians and death educators can turn to the Web to locate information about conferences, certification programs, and other resources available to members of the Association for Death Education and Counseling (ADEC), found on the ADEC home page.[28] Individuals seeking literature on suicide can visit the home page of the Suicide Information and Education Centre (SIEC).[29] In addition to information about the largest English-language suicide resource center and library in the world, SIEC caregiver workshop schedules are also available. The site developed by the Project on Death in America (PODA)[30] presents upcoming events and exhibits nationwide and funding opportunities for research.

Challenges and Cautions

While the advantages are significant, individuals utilizing these resources should note several challenges and cautions. Since the Internet and the Web are constantly changing, it is difficult to predict whether site addresses will remain the same or even if the site will exist over time. Uniform record locators may change if commercial providers make changes in their service network or if the owner of a site switches to a new commercial provider.

Technology used to construct sites on the Web is constantly improving. Although low-cost terminals to provide Internet access are becoming available, software and hardware are also being developed that allow sites to become more sophisticated. Consumers may have access through the availability of a low-cost terminal or "cyber cafes" (businesses that sell Internet and Web access by the hour), but may be restricted by the types of programs and hardware needed to take advantage of video or sound capabilities.

While the increasing availability of this technology and of thanatology sites is desirable, individuals purchasing products or services via the Internet and the Web should be familiar with consumer protection issues related to electronic sales methods, particularly when purchasing funeral-related items at the time of need. Consumers must ascertain the reliability of information. Since anyone can post absolutely anything on the Web, information should be assessed in relation to the integrity of its sponsor and used in consultation with a trusted professional.

Some practitioners may react negatively toward chat groups or discussions that are not moderated by professionals. Do these resources create an alternative solution for those who in the past have sought professional support, potentially creating a hesitancy on the part of professionals to refer to these resources? Does the possibility of receiving inaccurate information or "bad advice" pose a threat to the mental health of the dying or the bereaved? The potential occurrence of misunderstandings between individuals who do not meet face to face must also be considered [15].

Topics presented on the Internet and the Web may challenge the comfort levels of individuals as well as professionals. Issues of suicide and assisted suicide are openly discussed. Right-to-die organizations have posted much information online, including an address to contact Dr. Jack Kevorkian. First Amendment rights allow this content to be posted; death professionals may need to facilitate discussions addressing any concerns raised by the availability of this information.

IMPLICATIONS FOR RESEARCH

Other than anecdotal evidence, there is currently a dearth of empirical evidence on the benefits of these resources. Analysis of the content and frequency of postings could shed new light on events that prompt an individual to reach out for support. An increased understanding of coping strategies could emerge as individuals share their experiences. Their common concerns could highlight issues appropriate for inclusion in community death-education efforts.

Ethical Issues

Along with these opportunities, serious concerns may be raised by using this technological medium for research. Many of the ethical considerations for traditional bereavement research outlined by Parkes are relevant [16]. Participants in bereavement-related groups may feel that the private nature of the experiences should be respected. "Lurking" in a chat group—passive participation through the reading of postings without communicating with the other participants—appears to be acceptable according to current "nettiquette." However, a recent discussion about research using a bereavement chat group indicates different levels of comfort. While the value of research is recognized, its appropriateness is being challenged due to feelings of uneasiness and the perceived degree of intrusiveness. Potential respondents to formal requests to participate in traditional survey research have the right to informed consent prior to participation. Similarly, individuals must be informed of their rights and potential risks, including information about the confidentiality of their online responses, which may not be clear-cut with electronic media.

Due to the vulnerability of the bereaved, prevention of harm is important. When a computer serves as an "interviewer," obstacles that interfere with the recognition of distress (such as geographical distance or lack of awareness of the need for additional support) are present.

Limitations

Researchers must always consider the role of selection bias among respondents and the potential lack of representativeness within samples gained by traditional means [17]. This problematic tendency toward limited generalizability is further compounded by the fact that access to the Internet and the Web is not universal.

CONCLUSION

With the evolution of these innovative resources and how they are used both by the public and professionals in the field of thanatology, the potential for positive benefits is strong; the potential for unsettling consequences also exists. Researchers must develop safeguards to protect the rights of individuals participating in studies conducted via the Internet and the Web. Dialogue among clinicians, death educators, and researchers using this technological resource must be created. As the "Web of Death" [18] continues to grow, thanatologists should be watching.

APPENDIX
Thanatology Sites on the World Wide Web

Informational and Emotional Support

Cancer-Related

[2]CancerNet: http://cancernet.nci.nih.gov/icichome.htm
[3]OncoLink: http://oncolink.upenn.edu

Computer-Mediated Discussion with Professionals:

[4]Dr. John Grohol's Mental Health Page: http://www.grohol.com
[5]Bereavement Education Center: http://www.bereavement.org/index.html

Sites with Multiple Hotlinks:

[6]GriefNet: http://www.rivendell.org/index.html
[7]Bereavement Resources: http://www.funeral.net/info/brvres.html
[20]Yahoo's Death Page: http://www.yahoo.com/Society_and_Culture/Death/
[21]Webster's Death, Dying, and Grief Guide: http://www.katsden.com/death/index.html

Narrative Sites:

[11]Austin Bastable: http://www.rights.org/deathnet/HELP_AUSTIN.html
[12]A Place to Honor Grief: http://www.webhealing.com

Commemorative Sites:

[13]World Wide Cemetery: http://www.interlog.com/~cemetery
[14]Pet Grief Support Page: http://www.petloss.com

Expressive Sites:

[15]Pediatric Art Gallery: http://oncolink.upenn.edu/images/child/gallery3.html
[16]Flight 800 & Montoursville, PA: http://flight800.sunlink.net/

Advance Directives / End of Life:

[24]Choice in Dying: http://www.choices.org

Experiential Site:

[19]The Death Clock: http://www.deathclock.com

Instrumental / Material Aid

Funeralization / Memorialization:

[8]Internet Cremation Society: http://www.cremation.org
[9]Memorial Gallery Online Catalog: http://grief.com/index.htm
[10]Howard Funeral Home: http://www.shops.net/shops/Carlos_A_Howard_Funeral_
  Home/

Gallows Humor:

[17]The Graveyard: http://www.primenet.com/~trix/gyard.htm
[18]The Bones: http://www.thebones.com/

Death Education Opportunities:

[22]Grief as a Family Process Course: http://www.indiana.edu/~hperf558/
[23]Interactive Bereavement Courses: http://bereavement.org/index.html
[25]DeathNet: http://www.rights.org/~deathnet
[26]Cultural Diversity: http://www.execpc.com/~dboals/diversit.html
[27]Sociology Online Library: http:ixpress.com/lunatic/soc.html

Professional Resources:

[28]ADEC Home Page: http://www.adec.org
[29]SIEC Home Page: http://www.siec.ca
[30]PODA Home Page: http://www.soros.org/death.html

REFERENCES

1. M. E. Lambrecht, The Value of Computer-Assisted Instruction in Death Education, *Loss, Grief, & Care, 4*:1-2, pp. 67-69, 1990.
2. C. Schaefer, J. C. Coyne, and R. S. Lazarus, The Health-Related Functions of Social Support, *Journal of Behavioral Medicine, 4,* pp. 381-406, 1981.
3. M. Barrera, Jr. and S. L. Ainlay, The Structure of Social Support: A Conceptual and Empirical Analysis, *Journal of Community Psychology, 11,* pp. 133-143, 1983.
4. E. M. Pattison, A Theoretical-Empirical Base for Social System Therapy, in *Current Perspectives in Cultural Psychiatry,* E. F. Foulks, R. M. Wintrob, J. Westermeyer, and A. R. Favazza (eds.), Spectrum, New York, pp. 217-253, 1977.
5. S. Cobb, Social Support and Health Through the Life Course, in *Aging from Birth to Death: Interdisciplinary Perspectives,* M. W. Riley (ed.), American Association for the Advancement of Science, Washington, D.C., pp. 93-106, 1976.
6. B. H. Gottlieb, The Development and Application of a Classification Scheme of Informal Helping Behaviors, *Canadian Journal of Behavioral Science, 10*:2, pp. 105-115, 1978.
7. J. S. House, *Work Stress and Social Support,* Addison-Wesley, Reading, Massachusetts, 1981.
8. C. L. Streeter and C. Franklin, Defining and Measuring Social Support: Guidelines for Social Work Practitioners, *Research on Social Work Practice, 2*:1, pp. 81-98, 1992.
9. R. Cathgart and G. Gumpert, Mediated Interpersonal Communication: Toward a New Typology, in *Talking to Strangers: Mediated Therapeutic Communication,* G. Gumpert and S. L. Fish (eds.), Ablex Publishing, Norwood, New Jersey, pp. 40-53, 1990.
10. N. Weinberg, J. Schmale, J. Uken, and K. Wessel, Online Help: Cancer Patients Participate in a Computer-Mediated Support Group, *Health & Social Work, 21*:1, pp. 24-29, 1996.
11. F. M. McTavish, D. H. Gustafson, B. H. Owens, M. Wise, J. O. Taylor, F. M. Apantaku, H. Berhe, and B. Thorson, CHESS: An Interactive Computer System for Women with Breast Cancer Piloted with an Under-Served Population, *Proceedings of the Symposium on Computer Application in Medical Care,* pp. 559-603, 1994.
12. L. P. Stral, Web's First Virtual Funeral Home, in *What's on the Web,* E. Gagnon (ed.), Internet Media Corporation, Fairfax, Virginia, 1996.
13. R. Jerome, A. Duignan-Cabrera, R. Arias, and A. Longley, Beyond Sorrow, *People, 46*:6, August 5, 1996.
14. J. L. Brain, *The Last Taboo: Sex and the Fear of Death,* Anchor Press/Doubleday, Garden City, New York, 1979.
15. R. Slade and P. Bitar, *Misunderstandings in Messaging Systems,* original posting with response posted to the Computers and Society Digest, February 3, 1987.
16. C. M. Parkes, Guidelines for Conducting Ethical Bereavement Research, *Death Studies, 19*:2, pp. 171-181, 1995.
17. M. S. Stroebe and W. Stroebe, Who Participates in Bereavement Research? *Omega, 20*:1, pp. 1-29, 1989-90.
18. R. Wrenn, Personal communication via e-mail, April 10, 1996.

Healing and the Internet

Thomas R. Golden

My father died in November of 1994. He was a loving family man who had worked as a research scientist for NASA for many years. Near the end of his career he was "on loan" to a number of different cities through NASA's technology transfer program. He worked with city leaders in finding practical and everyday applications for the latest technology that NASA had discovered through the space program. The job was a perfect fit; he loved finding new ways in which science and technology could benefit people.

After his death I sought out a number of activities that would both honor his life and bring my grief for him into my awareness. My father and I both loved computers and had a definite respect for their potential. Our relationship included many happy hours sitting together at a computer keyboard attempting to solve a problem. Although our approaches to solving problems with the computer were vastly different, we got to know each other better through the process. There was usually great gnashing of teeth, but just as often mutual joy in successfully solving the problem. Given his history, it was no great surprise that one of the ways I found to honor him was through my work with computers.

I decided in January of 1995 to construct a World Wide Web site and dedicate it in honor of my father. It seemed a perfect fit: our mutual fascination and love of computers aligned with the growing graphical world of the Web. As I began to go about this, I connected with my grief for my father. I knew that the healing of grief comes in a long series of small "chunks." Now each chunk of experience—each time I read something new, each time I mastered a new level of competence in building the site—was connected with my grief. Each bit of effort I put into this project both honored my father and offered me the opportunity to feel a bit of my grief.

As I worked on building the Web site, I kept near the keyboard a photograph of my father, my brother, and myself. There we are, the three of us sitting on a couch. During those months, that photo, along with my work at the computer, kept bringing me back to my pain and grief over my father's death. I was aware of this process, and in some ways it empowered me in my task of building the Web page. A part of what I put up on the Web site were the writings I had done about my grief for my father. Placing them on this site was a powerful healing tool for me.

The Web page I built, "Crisis, Grief, and Healing" (http://www.webhealing. com), is meant to be a place on the Internet where people can feel comfortable in expressing their grief, finding support, and giving support to others. From my own experience over the past twenty years as a grief therapist, I knew there were precious few places in our culture where grief could be expressed publicly. Too often, people are forced to practice "guerrilla grief"—their grief hiding by day, coming out only at night, outnumbered by the opposition. My vision of this page was that it would be a public place where grief could be expressed openly and safely. I know that my father would have loved the use of technology to create a healing place. It is using technology to help people. Somehow the coolness of silicon doesn't usually bring to mind the warmth of the heart, but in this instance they are working together in a powerful way.

Why does this work? Why can the Internet and the World Wide Web function as a healing place? We need to first ask "What does it take to heal?" The anthropological literature tells us that all healing results from the practice of ritual, and that there are certain elements to all rituals, the first being safety. We must feel a certain level of safety before we can move into a ritual space and begin healing. As a simple example, consider the picture of my father, brother, and me next to my computer. I had chosen a place for it that was already a safe place. Next to my computer is a safe place, a place where I feel comfortable and at home. Interestingly, though, we don't want too much safety. Too much, and we become complacent. We need only enough safety to allow us to take a risk.

It is the risk that brings us to the second element, that of submission. Once we have a safe place, we need then to submit. In healing grief, this translates into needing a safe place to connect with the emotions of grief and then taking the risk of experiencing these emotions. When I choose to look at that photograph with an open stance—open to feeling what emotions may be present—that is submission. This activity of finding a safe place and then submitting to the emotions present is not a one-time activity. The healing of grief is dependent on our repeatedly following this process. Each time we find a safe place and then submit, and connect with the grief within, we are taking a small step toward healing. Many steps make a journey.

As another example of this process, a man helped himself heal from his wife's death by sculpting a bust of her out of a block of walnut. He first put the wood in a place that was safe for him. (We all tend to find safety in different places; the wide variety of paths to healing begin their diversity at this point.) Each time he worked on the piece he had the potential to connect with his grief. Each chunk he took from the block of wood honored his wife and allowed him the opportunity to submit to the emotions surrounding her death. It's easy to see how he was with his wife and with his grief each time he cut a sliver of wood.

Grief is not demanding about the type of behaviors to bring forth healing. It is very accepting of almost any type of behavior that allows the griever to connect with the grief. Endeavors such as music, sculpting, poetry, or practical actions like creating a trust fund are equally valid. The only "must" is that the action connect the griever with the pain.

So how does the Internet help facilitate this process? Doesn't a grand network of computers that encircles the world sound impersonal? Yes, but keep in mind that the end user, and therefore the Internet itself, often resides in a home or office. Consider my computer: it is located in a room devoted to my home office. It is surrounded by my "things" and is undoubtedly a safe place for me. Furthermore, I decide when to turn on my computer and log onto the Internet. Given my control of those two variables of place and time, the Internet can easily be a safe place for me.

With the potential for safety in place, we then need to find elements that will aid us in submitting to our grief. When I was planning the Web site, one of the elements I knew I wanted to include was a section that allowed other people to tell their stories of grief and healing. Telling our story is a powerful way to submit to our inner process. There is something very healing in bringing our personal story into the open for all to see. I decided to title this section "A Place to Honor Grief," and when the site opened, I alerted all visitors that this was my intent (see Figure 1).

At first people were slow to respond, and rightly so. This was one of the first pages on the World Wide Web devoted specifically to the topic of grief and healing. I offered to publish personal stories of one thousand words or less. As I began to get submissions I was moved by the depth and beauty of the writing, some of the most beautiful I had ever seen. As each person's story came in, I would post it on the "Place to Honor Grief" and at the end I would put a "mailto." This would allow anyone who visited the page and happened to read a person's entry to easily send the writer a message. For those who aren't familiar with the Internet, imagine a letter which has its text in black and the signature in blue. The blue indicates that you can "click" on the text with your mouse and the computer will "do" something. In the case of a "mailto," clicking on the blue signature brings up a screen addressed to that person. You simply type in a message, click a "send" icon, and your message will be e-mailed to the person.

The Honor page now has the writings of about 300 different people and gets about 1000 "hits" a day. This means that 1000 times each day someone reads one of the entries. Thus, thousands of people have had the opportunity to connect with others throughout the world who have experienced a similar loss. The majority of the entries are from the United States and Canada, but there are a number from other countries, including Australia, Sweden, Portugal, England, and Africa. A man from Sweden, who had written quite beautifully on the Honor page about the death of his son Mattias, wrote about the powerful effect of re-reading his own words on the Internet:

> It was a very special feeling. I felt as if I was entering a sanctuary. I've read the other stories before, often bursting into tears, feeling their grief and loss reflected in my own. Now reading about my experience with my own words, I feel affinity to a group of people scattered all over the world, linked, by the common human experience of the loss of someone related to them, with bonds stronger than death.

Since this Swedish father used the word "sanctuary" as a description of his experience, we can rightly assume that he felt safe when reading the Honor page. Many have offered similar reactions; the stories are personal, powerful, and moving. When we are moved to tears, we have found a safe place and have submitted to the emotions within. Each time we have this type of experience we are moving one step closer to healing.

http://www.webhealing.com/honor.html   A Place to Honor Grief—Crisis, Grief, and Healing—Tom Golden   Sunday, June 21, 1998

Tom Golden LCSW of the Crisis, Grief, and Healing Page brings you

A Place to Honor Grief

This page is a place that men or women can honor the person in their life who died by writing about a part of their own grief and healing. My vision is that it could serve not only as a memorial but as a place that any bereaved person on the www could come and read about others who have experienced a similar loss.

The following links are the writing of people on the net who have had the courage to send me a part of their experience with grief. The three categories are in chronological order each beginning in spring of 1995 when this page officially opened. Please note that when you see the "mail welcomed" sign at the end of these tributes this indicates that the writer is interested in corresponding and in many cases you can select the highlighted address to send them email. Also notice the "how to send me your experience" link at the bottom of the page which explains the process of contributing your writing. I hope to hear from you. Tom Golden LCSW of Crisis, Grief, and Healing

My special thanks to Dale Kelley for her loving persistence and tenacity in our work together of updating this page.

[how to send your experience]

NEW   Search the entries on the Honor Page with this Search Tool.

Children's Deaths

Bill Chadwick writes about the death of his son Michael.
Brian Wood writes of the death of his daughter Liana.
Sara Grimes writes of the grief from her daughter Haven's death in infancy.
Barbara, 39 years old, writes of her stepson Joe, 20, and shares a friends tribute to him.
Rae Ann Reichert - Organ Donation eases pain of Daughter's Death
Liisa Laine, 36, writes of the death of her nephew Christopher, 19.
Janie Gibbs 33, writes of her grief for her two sons and their brief lives.
Bo Jonsson of Sweden, writes about his grief for his son Mattias.
Stan Waisbrod of South Africa writes of his grief for his son Steven.
April Tilley writes of her grief for her infant son Tyler.
Lora Czarnowsky, writes of her grief and anger for the death of her infant son.
Gnetie Bossinga, of Australia, writes of the loss of her 19 year old son Damion.
Patti Etheridge, 43, writes of the death of her son 13 year old son Michael.
Marian Sinn, honors her sixteen year old daughter Rachel.
Cherie, 39, writes of living through the death of a child with faith in God as an anchor.
Ned Levitt, honors his daughter Stacey who died at 18 and includes some of her poetry.
M.M. McDonald, 29, writes of her grief for her infant daughter Emily Anne.
Vicki, 46, writes about honoring her son Jim and others on his birthday.
Carol, 47, writes in memory of her daughters Tracy and Toni.
Ruth, talks of her experiences at the loss of her infant daughter Simone Joy.
Kristine, 27, writes of the loss of her infant son, Jared.
Dody, 44, writes about her love for Honey.
John and Kim, write of their little angel Courtney.
Laura, 22, tells of the loss of her 2 sons.
Carol, 44, writes of the life and loss of her only child, Nicki.
Debbi Dickinson, shares her poetry for her father and her children who have died.
Judy Harper, 50, Jason's mom, writes, stop killing our children.
Tom and Mary, both 52, write of their daughter Roxanna... of their joy in her life and their grief at her passing.
Anne, 43, writes of her grief for her son John.
Jorge Oliveira, 54, of Portugal, writes about his daughter Rita,19.
Sharon, 47, writes of her son, John.
Mary Blando, 40, remembers her son and soul mate Tommy.
Connie Woznick, 47, writes "Kenny, My Son, Taken Too Soon: A Mother's Grief."

Page: 1

Figure 1. Crisis, Grief, and Healing Page.

With over two hundred entries, the Honor page contains a massive amount of text. Recently I put up a keyword search tool on the page, which allows visitors to search for particular entries. By typing in "AIDS," for instance, the search tool brings up all entries that mention AIDS. Typing in "mother" produces a list of all entries mentioning the word "mother." Many people who are newly bereaved find comfort in the writing of people with similar losses.

Like many other sites on the Web, "Crisis, Grief, and Healing" has a guestbook, a place where people who visit the site can leave a short message, usually saying thanks for having this resource or asking a question of some sort. Shortly after I put up my guestbook, people began using that space to tell a brief story, as in these examples:

> My baby David died in my arms on July 27, 1994. He died one day before his 4th month birthday. He was the oldest of two twin boys. I never knew what pain and agony were until David died. Then I experienced another type of "death" when I was surrounded by people who didn't understand what it was like to lose a baby. I find that I have to search, to find others like myself, who have lost children and need the comfort and the support of those in the same situation. If I can be of any help to anyone, just a shoulder to cry on, please e-mail me. I do understand, and we can help each other through this difficult time.
>
> Linda

> My father passed away just two weeks ago from coronary artery disease. None of the family, including him, knew he had it. It happened so suddenly and we all miss him very much. I have never had anything happen to anyone this close to me before and am having a very hard time dealing with just getting through each day. I don't know how to be supportive for my mother when I can't even be strong for myself. Where do I begin? Any advice would be very helpful for me and my family.
>
> Janice

Since the guestbook allows the writer to leave an e-mail address at the end of the message, people also use it as a means to connect with others, as in the following message:

> I am posting this in hopes that Dana H. will see it. I read your posting in the Guestbook put up on May 17. Dana, I want to respond to you, but am frustrated because you did not include an e-mail address. I would like to talk with you about your feelings and experience. If you see this, please respond at my e-mail address. My heart just ached when I read what you wrote. I will check the Guestbook frequently to see if you have added your e-mail address. I care, Dana.
>
> Maggie

This use of the guestbook for an intensely personal connection is a dramatic shift from the culture of the Web, which generally says that you stay pretty superficial in a guestbook. I am glad people are using it as they do, and I think it illustrates the dire need in our culture to find safe places to express and work with our grief. A good safe place is hard to find!

Shortly after I put up the guestbook, I started work on a Threaded Discussions page. This is like a bulletin board where someone places a message or query (called a "post" on the Net and Web). Someone else interested in the same topic then adds a response, another person responds to the response, and so on. In this way, you get long chains, called threads, of related messages about a similar topic, and thus the name Threaded Discussions. This page has become a very popular place for the discussion of specific topics about grief and as a place to tell one's story. It is called the Grief and Healing Discussions Page and is accessed about 2500 times a day.

Another section of "Crisis, Grief, and Healing" is called the Suggestion Page. Compiled by those who visit and use the site, it offers suggestions of what to do or not to do for someone who is bereaved.

All of the different resources I have mentioned are accessible via the "home page." A home page is usually the central point of any Web site. Generally, it will give you a condensed idea of the contents of the site and will have links to all of the various places on the site. You could liken it roughly to the table of contents in a book where the chapters are listed in blue text, or "hyper linked." When you click on a chapter heading, you then go to the beginning of that chapter. There you will find links back to the home page and also probably links to other places. The term "web" is appropriate, since you are able to move around in a circular manner.

"Crisis, Grief, and Healing" helps hundreds of people on a daily basis. It now gets about 350,000 hits a month from all over the world, meaning that about 350,000 different pages are read each month by about 25,000 different people. (These numbers are doubling every 3 to 4 months.) It provides the potential for a safe and healing place, and has become a public place for people to express their grief and to support others. I sometimes wish my father could see it. I know he would love it.

BASIC NEEDS OF GRIEVING PEOPLE

Therapeutic Touch:
For Those Who Accompany the Dying

Mary J. Simpson

In a society where dying is seen as failure on the part of the medical profession—or even worse on the part of the person who is dying—our relationship to those facing the end of their lives is fraught with anxiety and feelings of inadequacy. Never has that relationship been more important than it is today when the very act of dying is becoming difficult as medical intervention becomes more sophisticated, and families are faced with the horrifying act of signing a paper, which virtually sentences their loved one to death.

The question must be asked: "Am I prolonging this person's life, or am I prolonging this person's death?" Often the line between the two blurs, and as a result we have the ongoing conflict between those advocating euthanasia or assisted suicide and those who disapprove of them. Certainly medical intervention can manage pain remarkably well, but there is an actual "availability level" between big-city prowess and small-town knowledge and acceptance.

Families who have communicated poorly or never touched each other in health (although they may have a real need and desire to do so), are unlikely to be comfortable doing so in death. In addition, there may be a great deal family members want to say to the dying person, but now find themselves at a loss to express themselves—or are embarrassed by their attempts. Often it is simply too late, and the grieving family member is overcome with regrets and remorse.

Now we have a remarkable intervention technique that transcends conflict and allows anyone, whether a medical professional or a lay person, to assist in the needs of the dying person. Known as Therapeutic Touch (TT), it can be learned by anyone and is invaluable in promoting the comfort of the person "in transition."

> Andrew lies quietly in his hospital bed. His breath, which moments before had been rapid and shallow, slows and deepens as his pain subsides. With her hands, his nurse Susan makes gentle sweeping movements in the space about six inches over his body, moving from head to foot, occasionally focusing more intently in one area. After gently touching Andrew's feet for a few seconds, Susan stands quietly, eyes closed for a moment. She nods to his father, John, who is sitting nearby, and quietly leaves the room.
>
> John looks down on his resting, dying son. The thin pale man lying on the white sheets is a mere shadow of the robust youth he last saw five years ago.

"There is so much to be said," he says. Andrew's eyes open for a moment and linger on his father's face. His smiling lips form a silent "Yes."

John pulls a chair to the side of the bed on Andrew's left, and sits down. His hands reach for the emaciated hand of his son, and he gently massages the palm. Then he brings Andrew's hand up to his heart and lightly places his other hand on Andrew's chest. With closed eyes he holds that position for a short time, then sits back with Andrew's hand lying on his. Both appear to be resting, yet each has an occasional smile and at one point tears run down John's face. He wipes them away without embarrassment.

Susan peeks in the door, smiles and nods, and leaves father and son undisturbed.

Both the nurse's and John's actions are forms of Therapeutic Touch, and this scenario repeats itself many times a day all over the world in both hospitals and homes. The technique is having a worldwide impact in the caring professions—accepted because it works. This is an interesting phenomenon in the late twentieth century, where Western science has refused to acknowledge healing modalities that do not—perhaps because they cannot—fit into the mechanistic confines of empirical science [1].

HISTORY

In the early 1970s, Dolores Krieger, a professor of nursing at New York University, began teaching "Frontiers of Nursing" to her students. In that program she taught them her newly developed technique, one she called Therapeutic Touch (TT).[1]

Original experiments and research were carried out by Dr. Krieger in 1971 after she had become aware of the work of Bernard Grad of McGill University, who had investigated a "laying-on-of-hands healer," Oscar Estabany. Dr. Krieger joined the team of Otelia Bengssten, M.D., and Dora Kunz, a "clairvoyant healer," who were studying the healing process. Contrary to a number of well-known healers, Dora Kunz felt that people could be taught to heal, and she began a workshop to instruct others in the art of healing. Dolores Krieger was a participant and learned to use her hands to help and heal others, and began to develop a curriculum to instruct nurses in healing [1].

Krieger found a significant increase in the hemoglobin values in the healer-treated group of patients compared to the control group. She was thus able to obtain biochemical evidence that healers induce bioenergetic and physiologic changes in the patients they treated [2]. She found that her "nurse-healers" were able to increase the hemoglobin levels in patients as much as "gifted healers," and that the more time and effort students put into healing, the better they became. She concluded that Therapeutic Touch was a natural human potential and it could be a skill learned by individuals who had a strong intent to help or heal.

[1] The term *therapeutic touch,* when spelled with lower case t's can be considered a generic term implying physical touch with caring. The technique should therefore always be referred to as Therapeutic Touch, with upper case T's.

Twenty-five years after the original development of Therapeutic Touch, her technique is taught in eighty countries. An increasing number of hospitals are accepting it as a nursing intervention, some even requesting that all their nurses learn Therapeutic Touch, giving them time off to attend workshops.[2] In addition, non-medical people such as bereavement counselors, chaplains, and hospice volunteers are using the technique.

THE ASSUMPTIONS

During her investigations into healing, Krieger discovered the Yoga concept of *prana,* which is seen as a universal life force. In good health there is an abundance of *prana;* in illness, a deficit. Upon these teachings, and those of nursing theorist Martha Rogers (a colleague at New York University), she based her development of the assumptions of Therapeutic Touch. An understanding of these assumptions is essential to its practice:

- Each of us is an energy field, and these fields permeate space and interact with one another. This is validated by quantum physics, which tells us that the smallest particle of which an atom is composed is pure energy. Often called the *aura,* this oval-shaped field goes beyond our outstretched fingers.
- In a state of health, energy flows freely in, through, and out of our field in an organized, symmetrical, balanced way. The energy flows in through the top of the head (the crown chakra) and out the bottoms of the feet into the ground (referred to as "grounding"). Krieger describes this as being in a state of dynamic balance [1].
- In a state of illness, disease, or injury, the energy field is disorganized in some way and may be described as disordered, depleted, blocked, or in disharmony.
- All living things have the ability to heal themselves. This healing ability is affected by many things: nutrition, emotions, and state of our immune system.
- Therapeutic Touch practitioners learn to use their hands as a focus to sense areas of imbalance. Working with the intent of affecting the vital flow in the open energy system, practitioners attempt to restore order in a disorganized field by helping the flow of energy change in the direction of wholeness and health. *The intent is to enhance a person's natural healing ability.* The intent of the Therapeutic Touch practitioner and nature is the same.
- *Therapeutic Touch is not a miracle cure. Rather it attempts to assist nature in its efforts to enhance a person's natural healing ability* [3].

THE CONCEPT OF CURE VERSUS HEALING

In the Western medical model, *cure* is seen as the elimination of symptoms. The term "healing" comes from the Anglo-Saxon word *haelen* meaning "to make whole."

---

[2] Saint Joseph's Health Centre, Toronto, Ontario.

This understanding is crucial to the practice of Therapeutic Touch, which works at all levels of a person's reality, that is, mind, emotions, and spirit in relationship to his or her environment. Hence a person may be, for instance, *healed* emotionally without being *cured* of the physical disease, which may in fact cause his or her death.

> The leap from life, the last transition called death, may in fact be the healing of the dying; the becoming whole on another level not yet experienced by the living.—Cathleen Fanslow-Brunjes[3]

THERAPEUTIC TOUCH: HEALING WITHOUT A RELIGIOUS CONNOTATION

Throughout history, much of the healing act has happened within religious settings. Certainly the beginnings of Christianity were involved with the healings by Jesus and his disciples. Later it became "The King's Touch" and evolved into the laying-on-of-hands practice by "gifted healers."

Therapeutic Touch, however, does not have a religious context; its techniques do not require a particular belief system on the part of the patient, but simply that he or she is open to it (and has given consent for the session). Although Therapeutic Touch is not restricted to a gifted group, it does require that the practitioner come from a state of *focused intent* (called "Centering") and nonjudgmental love, with intent to help or heal.

Most medical treatments depend on the outcome or results as an indicator of perceived success or failure; hence, the concept that the TT practitioner is not attached to the outcome of the session is difficult for many to accept. The intent of the practitioner is to meet the need of the patient or client; therefore, the outcome rests solely with the receiver, who may in fact reject it—or use it to help his or her transition.

When practitioners are faced with developing these characteristics, their personal philosophy is challenged. If one considers that spirituality has to do with the sense of meaning and purpose in one's life, then because of these challenges, Therapeutic Touch may be seen as a "spiritual path."

EFFECTS OF THERAPEUTIC TOUCH

The Relaxation Response—The most consistent effect of TT is to quickly elicit a *relaxation response,* often within two minutes. When we look at the many effects of relaxation, we see that the heart rate slows, breathing deepens, blood pressure drops, muscles relax, and circulation improves.

---

[3] From a presentation by Cathleen Fanslow-Brunjes delivered to NH-PA Annual Conference, 1988. "Therapeutic Touch: Compassion awakened for dying persons and their families."

We constantly underestimate the benefits of relaxation in the recovery from illness. If we are in even a mild state of stress, the body cannot put its energies toward healing. As a relaxation technique, TT is remarkable. Often it takes people weeks of biofeedback training, progressive muscle relaxation, and so forth, to achieve some sort of relaxed state. When TT is used, the recipients actually experience the relaxation response in the first session . . . and they know what it *feels* like to relax. At home they are able to recall that feeling and achieve relaxation within a very short time.

Many clients report having the best sleep they have had for weeks. In fact, this is a consistent effect in the use of TT in fibromyalgia. A woman with this frustrating disease received weekly sessions of TT for one year. Using a variety of alternative therapies, she recovered during that time. "In retrospect," she commented, "my healing began when I started regular sessions of Therapeutic Touch. The sessions helped improve my sleep."

Reduction of Anxiety—Therapeutic Touch has the ability to reduce anxiety; hence a nurse in an intensive care unit can calm an agitated patient, often helping him or her to achieve restorative sleep. Research has shown that when Therapeutic Touch was used on premature infants, arousal states dropped significantly [4]. TT has a remarkable effect on panic attacks, and helps people understand that a panic attack is their response to stress and that they can actually calm it down. Tension headaches respond well, and TT seems to reduce the length of a typical migraine, stopping it completely if used at the first indication of a headache.

In the dying patient, anxiety, often sensed over the solar plexus area, can be reduced or calmed by the use of TT. The patient's family can also benefit from sessions, which may allow them to sleep without medication. Hospice volunteers report that a family member may observe the beneficial effects of TT on others, and tentatively ask, "Do you think it can help *me*?"

Changing The Perception of Pain—Anxiety may diminish the effect of an analgesia, hence a mild tranquilizer may be ordered. Therapeutic Touch acts in much the same way as a tranquilizer in the reduction of pain. Research on 168 patients in pain after major abdominal or pelvic surgery concluded that TT can significantly enhance the effect of analgesia, and thus decrease the need for post-operative pain medication [5]. The use of TT post-operatively means that the patient requires less pain medication—and for a shorter duration of time. In addition, TT has a remarkable ability to alleviate chronic pain, since much chronic pain, particularly in the lower back, is due to abnormal muscle tension. It appears to potentiate the effect of pain medications when used as a complementary therapy.

Currently in progress is an extensive one-year study on the effectiveness of TT in relieving pain and preventing infection of burn wounds. The researchers are hypothesizing that TT may stimulate endorphin production, the body's natural pain-killing chemical.

After an accident or surgery, the adverse effects of pain are a major contributor to complications and a prolonged recovery. From this perspective TT is remarkably cost effective.

PAIN IN THE TERMINALLY ILL

As we prolong the lives of those who are terminally ill, pain becomes one of the most feared outcomes, both for the patient and the caregiver, who feels helpless in the face of a loved one's agony. Good pain management is an essential aspect of palliative care. Prior to the development of pain management, the patient was either in pain or semi-comatose from the medication. Now with the development of new ways of measuring pain, such as the Visual Analog Scale (VAS) and the Facial Pain Scale, as well as the education of health professionals in the science of pain, patients are often able to live comfortably until death. Effective pain relief most often occurs in response to a variety of complementary measures (such as TT, hypnosis, and imagery), specifically developed for each individual. When the pain is so severe that the analgesic required to reduce it would put the patient into respiratory arrest, TT may make the difference. Terminal illness is not always terribly painful, and in these cases it can often be managed by regular TT administered by a family member or caregiver.

Enhancing Healing—The intent of TT is to enhance a person's natural healing ability. By changing the field in the direction of wholeness and health, and by eliminating blocks in the natural flow of energy, the practitioner is able to provide a healing environment so that nature may do its best.

California researcher Dan Wirth showed that daily use of TT significantly increased the rate of wound healing [6]. There is good evidence that fractures heal in 30 percent less time when TT is done daily.

HEALING OF THE GRIEVING

TT also benefits those who are grieving. A study at the University of Alabama used the Grief Experience Inventory (GEI) to measure the grief experience. Both those who had received TT and the control group (who received imitation TT) showed a similar decrease in despair, anger, guilt, depersonalization, and death anxiety over time. The experimental group, however, reported treatments had a positive effect on their grief more frequently than the control group.

Other research at the University of Colorado School of Nursing indicated that, following TT, grieving persons showed a decline in the OKT8 immune suppressor cells, indicating that TT may bolster the immune system by diminishing the immuno-suppressive effects of stress. The National Institute of Health is currently funding further research in immune response to stress [7].

VALIDATION OF GRIEVING

A common reaction for those witnessing the release of grieving is to commiserate with the person, pat them on the back, find the tissues, and try—with the best of intentions—to get them over their "crying fit." In actual fact witnesses may be so uncomfortable with the grieving process that they will do everything they can to stop it. This is often followed by a well-meant lecture, which includes such phrases as "I think you ought to . . ." or "You really should try . . . ," and so the griever pulls herself or himself together and "gets on with life," having capped the grief volcano yet again.

Practitioners find that the ability of TT to enhance their rapport with the client is invaluable. Patients may never have told another living soul of a devastating experience, yet they tell the practitioner who they sense is truly there for them, knowing that their confidence will be respected.

In TT, the compassionate interaction between the giver and the receiver may allow a person to cry perhaps for the first time in his or her delayed grieving process, because TT practitioners come from a state of unconditional love and nonjudgment, and do not act as therapists. Instead of attempting to stop the flow of tears, they reassure the person that it is safe to let go, and validate their need to do so—without offering lectures or initiating "therapy." Learning simply to "be with" a grieving person is a valuable aspect of Therapeutic Touch.

CONSCIOUSNESS AND THE HUMAN ENERGY FIELD

If we accept that we are an energy field, we can understand that the body is the physical manifestation that allows us to move around and communicate on planet earth. The state that we call "coma" means that the body has lost that ability to communicate. Similar states happen through anaesthetic experiences in the operating room. Post-operatively, patients may recall that their consciousness seemed to be hovering over the surgical team, aware of what was happening and what was being said. It now appears possible that we can interact at a level of consciousness that does not require verbal communication—in other words through our thoughts. There is some evidence that patients can name the nurse who gave them TT while they were in a coma, indicating that at some level of consciousness they were aware of what was happening to them.

Bereavement counselor and nurse Cathleen Fanslow-Brunjes, who works with patients dying of cancer and AIDS, states: "Therapeutic Touch facilitates the dying process. One of the things we see in the dying person is the bioenergetic field beginning to separate. This means that the field is much more open and fragile. Just as the field is open for energy to leave, it's also very open for energy to enter. The beauty of Therapeutic Touch is that the energy goes right where it's needed, and that is at the heart level. You're giving them the energy and strength they need to let go of life, of family, of relationships. It takes a tremendous amount of energy to let go. Therapeutic Touch eases the difficulties of resolving the life-death conflict within all of us" [3].

"THE HAND-HEART CONNECTION"

Through her work with the dying, Cathleen Fanslow-Brunjes developed a simple yet profound technique she calls the "Hand-Heart Connection." Through the many workshops on "The Hope System" she gives internationally to hospice volunteers, palliative care nurses, bereavement counselors and others, this way of being with the dying person is becoming widely known.

The Hand-Heart Connection can be easily taught to the patient's family. It allows the family to be "with" the patient in a comfortable nonintrusive way. There may be times when both are sleeping, yet the connection remains. As we move closer to another person, our energy fields (which can be considered our consciousness) blend and interact. In normal day-to-day activities we are not aware of this; but in the quiet intimacy of intentionally relating to the person who is dying, we can become aware of this interaction and the interrelationship of what might be termed our "sacred space" and theirs. The outcome can be a deep healing and letting go for both the family member and the patient.

> Robert had been out of the country for three years and was called home when his mother, Elizabeth, suffered a fatal illness. The doctor suggested that she was waiting for Robert to come before she died. She had opened her eyes and smiled at him, acknowledging his presence and then lapsed into a comatose state. Not wanting to leave his mother, Robert was upset and at a loss on how to behave in this difficult circumstance. The palliative care nurse sensed his discomfort and taught him the Hand-Heart Connection (Figures 1 and 2).
>
> 1. Sitting on his mother's left (heart) side, Robert gently takes Elizabeth's hand. He lightly strokes her palm with a sense of opening the hand center (chakra) as a connection, then places her hand on his left hand, so that the palms are connected. Robert completes that connection by placing his right hand on top of their clasped hands and rests for a time, sending her thoughts of peace and love.
> 2. Bringing Elizabeth's hand (still clasped in his hand) up to his 'heart center' (mid-chest), Robert lightly slides his right hand up his mother's arm to her shoulder, then moves down to her chest and gently rests his hand on his mother's mid-chest—her 'heart center.' Leaving his hand there he begins to

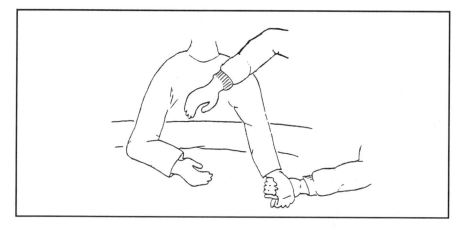

Figure 1. Making the connection.

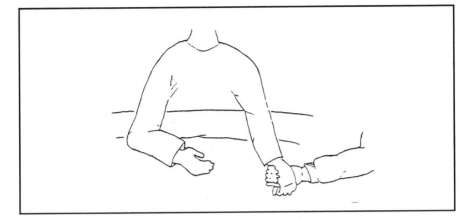

Figure 2. Maintaining the connection.

sense a loving connection of heart to heart, which intensifies through thoughts of love and peace.

3. When this connection is established, Robert slides his right hand back down Elizabeth's arm, moves the clasped left hands away from his heart, and places his right hand over them.

4. He then removes the right hand and, with the back of his hand on the bed, Elizabeth's hand resting in his, sits back comfortably with the Hand-Heart Connection established. He allows the communication to happen between his and Elizabeth's consciousness.

This simple yet profound exercise allows the family to stay in touch while "letting go" with love, and decreases their sense of helplessness at the end.

It is important that anyone using touch be comfortable with it. In this situation Robert was comfortable in touching his mother, but this may not be true for other children and caregivers. The Hand-Heart Connection could have been effective and powerful if Robert had only been able to hold his mother's hand between his hands, as family members may automatically do when they visit. Robert could also have simply rested his hand gently on his mother's shoulder or back while sending thoughts of peace and love to her. It is the *intent* of the person initiating the Hand-Heart Connection that is important.

The Hand-Heart Connection is "like holding the whole body in a warm, loving embrace and can be done for long periods of time . . . while sending thought messages of wholeness and peace and love" [8]. This is the time when thoughts can express words never spoken, words such as "I love you," "I forgive you," "please forgive me." Memories of times spent together can be recalled. It is important for the visitor not to "speak" all the time, but to allow an interchange of thoughts to happen . . . time to allow the patient's thoughts to be transmitted and absorbed.

Many people have reported a profound experience through the Hand-Heart Connection: "It was just like we were talking! He made me remember a time I had forgotten and I felt as though we were laughing together!" . . . "I was never really able to tell my son I loved him. It didn't seem the manly thing to do; but in the Hand-Heart Connection I was able to say 'I love you'—and it came to me as though I could actually hear his voice . . . he said he always knew and hoped I knew how much he loved me!" . . . "My mother and I were always disagreeing. We did not have a good relationship. I told her through 'The Connection' how much I had tried to please her and it was so clear that she said 'I know, and I am really proud of you.' It simply changed my relationship to her. My anger towards her was gone and after she died the grieving was with love."

THE PRACTICE OF THERAPEUTIC TOUCH

Therapeutic Touch can be learned by anyone who has a desire to do so. Some who learn feel as though they have been doing it all their lives. Although TT came out of a nursing model, a health-related background is not essential, and a simplified version can be learned by a patient's family.

Centering—The act of "Centering" is essential to the practice of Therapeutic Touch and is maintained through the entire session. This is quiet, inward-focused awareness without thought: "You relate to the extraordinary stillness of the personal, private world within you, and you bask in its profoundly quieting psychological and physical effects. In time you begin to realize you are your consciousness" [9]. The practitioner becomes aware of the flow of his or her own energy. Many practitioners view the act of Centering as being of great practical use in their lives. Those who suffer from attention deficit disorder, or who simply have trouble concentrating, appreciate how Centering ability quiets their "mind chatter." Experienced practitioners can center themselves by simple intent.

Assessment—In Therapeutic Touch we acknowledge that we do not stop at our skin. It is not difficult to sense our own field (Figure 3). The practitioner is able to move his or her hands around the client's body, about six inches from the surface, and sense areas of congestion or depletion (often initially sensed as hot or cold) in the flow of the energy field. In this step, the practitioner slowly but steadily moves his or her hands down the patient's body from head to foot, comparing one side of the body to the other.

The Energy Plan of Care—Once the differences in the field are noted, the practitioner begins to change the flow of energy. This is often done by using long, sweeping movements, called "unruffling," to establish the flow of energy in the whole field. The next phase of treatment focuses on a specific area noted in the assessment. Again, the flow of energy is primary, followed, if appropriate, by the direction and modulation of energy (called the "universal life force" or "healing energy") by the practitioner.

Completion of the Session—When practitioners decide that they have done enough, they may reevaluate the field and then consciously detach from their healing mode, reminding themselves that the outcome is in the hands of the client. The client is then expected to rest for at least ten minutes and may, in fact, go to sleep. The

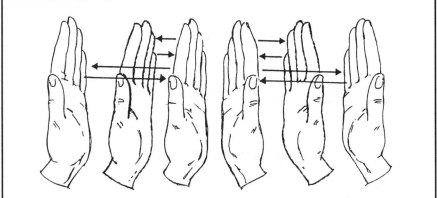

Start with the hands close together, but not touching. Move them apart 2 inches, then back together; then 4 inches and back together, etc., out to about 8 inches. Be aware of what is going on between your hands. It may seem bouncey or to have a magnetic push-pull sensation. Then try to sense the field of a friend's hands.

Figure 3. Sensing your own energy field.

effects of Therapeutic Touch continue even after the session has stopped, and rest is important in order to integrate the changes.

The fact that a full session in TT does not exceed twenty minutes is unusual since most healing methods take much longer—up to an hour and a half. Because TT is done in a state of focused intent, many practitioners say that they are not aware of time, and when the session is finished, they discover to their surprise that it may have taken only ten or twelve minutes. Patients are comfortable in knowing that they remain fully clothed during the treatment and may either sit up or lie down.

SPECIFIC USES OF THERAPEUTIC TOUCH

In *Spontaneous Healing,* Andrew Weil refers to Therapeutic Touch as a "learnable skill of great utility" [10]. Indeed, when we consider the effects of TT, and the difference in the concepts of "healing" and "curing," we realize that it can be used in a myriad of situations. It is used by practitioners from an amazing variety of work situations and professions such as addiction and detox work, dentistry, occupational and physiotherapy, sports medicine, veterinarian medicine, and animal training.

In Childbirth—The technique, when used by midwives and labor coaches, gives strength to the contractions and allows the laboring woman to rest between contractions. TT is taught to fathers in prenatal classes who then use it on their wives during labor, and with the newborn baby.

In Cancer Treatment—Sessions in TT benefit the nausea and discomfort of cancer patients during chemotherapy and radiation.

> Bruce took early retirement, and he and his wife, Peggy, looked forward to their lives together sharing many interests. Within a year Peggy was diagnosed with a rapidly growing cancer and was given less than a year to live. Devastated by the news, she accepted surgery, radiation, and chemotherapy and then, as she described it, "I got my act together and decided I wasn't just going to give up!" Peggy began to investigate complementary therapies, including TT. Bruce took her to a practitioner for sessions three times a week. Because of the chemotherapy, she had lost all her hair, and when she came for the treatments, her face and her scalp had a grayish color. As the first session progressed, Bruce observed with interest that normal pink skin color returned to her head and face.
>
> After the third week, the practitioner showed Bruce how to do TT so that Peggy could receive sessions at least once a day, as well as other times as needed. Follow-up by phone two weeks later revealed that Bruce was doing fine work with TT and that Peggy was very much involved in self-care with a variety of therapies. Six months later they resumed their traveling and interests.
>
> "I really feel that my healing began when I started Therapeutic Touch," Peggy commented. Markedly affected by his ability to do TT, Bruce said in a trembling voice, "I finally was able to do something for Peggy. I felt helpless— then we found Therapeutic Touch!"

First Aid When There's No Time—"First-aid" techniques in TT tend to focus on "the law of opposites." A practitioner envisions the impact of the injury and then proceeds to redirect the energy toward health. A blow to the shin or a burn would be treated by "pulling out" the congested field and reestablishing flow.

Nurses often feel that they cannot do TT because there just isn't enough time. With practice, however, they can bring their healing attitude to the person, as seen in Figure 4. Bob, in the center, is an injured person who is very anxious and in pain; his field may be seen as erratic. Linda, on the left, also has an erratic field and may be an upset family member or an overworked emergency room nurse. Linda does not help Bob's tension and agitation, and may, in fact, increase his anxiety or anger. Louise, on the right, has learned TT and brings a peaceful, compassionate attitude—that is, a calm field—into Bob's erratic field, calming him and being there, 100 percent, for him. Bob spoke later about "the nurse who was very kind and helped when nobody else cared!" It takes no more time to be like Louise than it does to be like Linda, but it does take practice to manifest a conscious intent to make your field peaceful and calm in the most trying of circumstances.

ACCEPTANCE OF THERAPEUTIC TOUCH IN THE NURSING FIELD

In the section of "Standards of Nursing Practice" dealing with promoting patient comfort, the College of Nurses in Ontario states that Therapeutic Touch can be

Linda   Bob   Louise

Energy Field Interactions

Figure 4. The healing attitude.

practiced by nurses. Within an institutional or agency setting where procedures exist, it is up to the individual institution to decide if TT should be included as a nursing intervention. A number of institutions in Ontario are dispensing with the Policies and Procedures and prefer to see nurses develop their own interventions. In such cases the hospital may issue a position paper but has no objection to any nursing procedure or intervention approved by the College of Nurses.

In 1993, the Toronto East General Hospital accepted TT as a nursing procedure and opened a TT Outpatient Clinic. This in effect broke the ice, and many hospitals began to accept TT as a nursing intervention and are actively encouraging their nurses to study the technique.

REDUCTION OF BURNOUT

The ability of TT to reduce burnout in health-care professionals is well documented. A recent study explored the effects of TT on practitioners themselves [11]. The five nurses interviewed felt that TT facilitated their personal and professional growth, improving their sense of inner strength and enhancing their self-esteem, self-confidence, and sensitivity to others.

Most nurses study TT on their own time and at their own expense, often because it brings them closer to the patient. As a loving, compassionate interaction between two human beings, it offsets the high-tech, often impersonal approach of the medicine of the 1990s.

RESEARCH

As with many aspects of "natural" healing or remedies where there is no potential for profit, research money is extremely scarce. Research in TT is not easy since it has to be qualitative rather than the scientifically accepted quantitative, double-blind studies. To date, most of the research has been done by nurses and includes at least fifteen doctoral dissertations and ten post-doctoral studies.

DETRACTORS

Despite the respect it has gained, TT is not without its detractors. "I think that there is a direct relationship between people who have been against TT and their ignorance about it. Some people are just afraid of new ideas," said Dolores Krieger in a TV interview. When confronted with the comment that it is "only a placebo effect," TT practitioners are likely to reply that if they can elicit a placebo effect on demand, that's fine with them.

An active group of skeptics and anti-fraud activists disparage the technique itself and imply that those who practice it are quacks. Some Christian fundamentalist persuasions are unable to accept TT outside the realm of their religious beliefs. They are offended by such terms as New Age (a derisive term they use to describe TT), paradigm, and quantum (as in physics). Practices such as meditation, centering, and imagery, essential to Therapeutic Touch, may be forbidden.

Therapeutic Touch practitioners understand, however, that they are on the leading edge of twenty-first century "vibrational medicine," and are not discouraged by negative comment and criticism. They believe that within a few years the equipment necessary to prove the existence of the human energy field will be developed. In the meantime, Therapeutic Touch will continue to gain credibility simply because it works.

LEARNING THERAPEUTIC TOUCH

Courses in TT are available through hospitals, colleges, and private workshops. The basic course takes twenty-four hours, usually done in three eight-hour workshops taken several months apart. The student is required to gain practice at each level before continuing on to the next. Therapeutic Touch support and practice groups are available in many communities in Ontario.

The Therapeutic Touch Network in Ontario, a nonprofit organization, is the professional association for TT and establishes guidelines for practitioners and curriculum for teachers. There is no "certification" in Therapeutic Touch, but those who meet the criteria established by the network are "recognized" practitioners and teachers. This network has members from all across Canada. Similar networks are forming elsewhere in Canada. In the United States, Dolores Krieger formed the Nurse Healers–Professional Associates, Inc., as the authoritative center for Therapeutic Touch throughout the world.

REFERENCES

1. D. Krieger, *Living the Therapeutic Touch: Healing as a Lifestyle,* Dodd, Mead, New York, 1987.
2. R. Gerber, *Vibrational Medicine: New Choices for Healing Ourselves,* Bear & Company, Santa Fe, New Mexico, 1988.
3. R. Weber, Philosophical Foundations and Frameworks for Healing, in *Spiritual Aspects of the Healing Arts,* D. Kunz (comp.), Theosophical Publishing House, Wheaton, Illinois, 1985.
4. R. Fedoruk, Transfer of the Relaxation Response: Therapeutic Touch as a Method for Reduction of Stress in Premature Neonates, *Disstertation Abstracts International,* 46.978B, 1985.
5. M. T. C. Meehan, The Effect of Therapeutic Touch on the Experience of Acute Pain in Post-Operative Patients, *Dissertation Abstracts International,* 46.795B (University Microfilms No. 8510765), 1985.
6. D. Wirth, The Effect of Non-Contact Therapeutic Touch on the Healing Rate of Full Thickness Dermal Wounds, *Subtle Energies, 1*:1, pp. 1-20, 1990.
7. R. Mackey, Discover the Healing Power of Therapeutic Touch, *American Journal of Nursing,* April 1995.
8. C. P. Ingerman, *Coming Home to Die,* Dinosaur Music Publishing, Brighton, Ontario, 1991.
9. D. Krieger, *Accepting Your Power to Heal: The Personal Practice of Therapeutic Touch,* Bear & Company, Santa Fe, New Mexico, 1993.
10. A. Weil, *Spontaneous Healing: How to Discover and Enhance Your Body's Natural Ability to Heal Itself,* Knopf, New York, 1995.
11. L. Cabico, *A Phenomenological Study of the Experiences of Nurses Practicing Therapeutic Touch,* unpublished master's thesis, D'Youville College, Buffalo, New York, 1992.

SUGGESTED READING

Chopra, D., *Quantum Healing: Exploring the Frontiers of Mind/Body Medicine,* Bantam, New York, 1989.

Gerber, Richard, *Vibrational Medicine: New Choices for Healing Ourselves,* Bear & Company, Santa Fe, New Mexico, 1988.

Krieger, D., The Timeless Concept of Healing, in *Healers on Healing,* R. Carson and B. Shield (eds.), Jeremy Tarcher, Los Angeles, 1989.

Harpur, T., *The Uncommon Touch: An Investigation of Spiritual Healing,* McClelland & Stewart, Toronto, Ontario, 1994.

Macrae, J., *Therapeutic Touch: A Practical Guide,* Knopf, New York, 1988.

Vietnam Women's Memorial

The Nurse and the Art Are One

CAROL PICARD

Meditation on the Vietnam Women's Memorial, 1994

Future

She stands, face uplifted, one hand resting on the arm of
her colleague, saying Help is coming. I see them.
If you step back you might think she is seeing the planes
taking off from National Airport,
one after the other, in slow aerial procession.
But no, not them.
How beautiful, her African face, bronzed
with mouth open—I see them.
Turning outward, body extended—an opening up to receive.

Past

You must crouch down to see her face under the hat.
She looks inward, backwards,
she is the face of memory and reflection,
of what she has witnessed, saved and lost,
both these men and her Ohio farm innocence
to blood and
sorrow and hope.
Her body is bent but in repose,
collecting and sorting memories.

Present

Like Czeslaw Milosz' angels, she looks ordinary.
Her thick brown hair is pulled up and away from her cheek.
Nothing hides her gaze as she looks into the face of
her patient, whose eyes are covered,
His body slack for all its muscular strength.
Michelangelo's *Pieta* here in the federal triangle.
There in the Meekong delta.
Pain around his mouth, teeth exposed.
She is pressing his chest to stay the wound using her hat.
The care in her face: I am here. I will help. You're not alone.

This time of whole time.
This place, grove away from grave,
These women are one.

This poem was first published in *Bay State Nurse News,* November 1996.

Hello, David

ANONYMOUS,
written by a nurse recalling her experiences in Vietnam

Hello, David—my name is Dusty.
I'm your night nurse.
I will stay with you.
I will check you vitals
    every fifteen minutes.
I will document
    inevitability.
I will hang more blood
    and give you something
    for your pain.
I will stay with you
    and I will touch your face.

Yes, of course,
I will write your mother
    and tell her you were brave.
I will write your mother
    and tell her how much you loved her.
I will write your mother
    and tell her to give your bratty kid sister
    a big kiss and hug.
What I will not tell her
    is that you were wasted.

I will stay with you
    and I will hold your hand.
I will stay with you
    and watch your life
    flow through my fingers
    into my soul.
I will stay with you
    until you stay with me.

Goodbye, David—my name is Dusty.
I am the last person
    you will see.
I am the last person
    you will touch.
I am the last person
    who will love you.

So long, David—my name is Dusty.
David—who will give me something
    for my pain?

Detail, Vietnam Women's Memorial, Washington, D.C.

My Mother's Hands

Elaine Freed Lindenblatt

They are fists now. Coiled in oblivion or defiance of all they were in life, they rest against her middle. Like her larger limbs, brittle, twiglike, they retreat more and more into an infantile posture. I take the right hand and set it on the tray attached to the wheelchair and, one by one, straighten each digit. Then those of the left. Before they can curl shut again, I slip a bean-bag against their underside, run its pebbly texture along the palms, anchor them open. The skin is close to transparent, a glove of exquisite sheerness. The balls of my own fingers knead the tiny wrinkles, the only parts of her that move effortlessly. The nails are safely clipped; the index fingers are bent inward in the old way. I look at these hands, my mother's hands, and I remember. . . .

They were large, supple, to a child's eyes the rough appendages dangling from a spare frame. That they were once the hands of a girl, the girl in the pictures with my father, her complexion redolent of roses, I was too late to know. By the time they had a fourth baby to hold, they were calloused and red. *Did* they hold me, I wonder, as much as dart over and around me, tending my physical needs? Each movement was emphatic—grating a washcloth back and forth on my loins, yanking my arms into a cardigan, pulling a comb through my tangles. If those fingers ever stopped to lace with mine, ever covered me in a moment of sweet repose, I have forgotten it.

Perhaps it had been the accident with the diaper pin of the firstborn, fifteen years earlier, which left one index finger shorter than the other, with rounded nail, an infection that, at levels beneath the apparent, never healed. Or perhaps it was simply that there was too much to do, too many tasks awaiting. They hung laundry in rows with clothespins. They scoured bathtubs. They showed lint no mercy. They sewed. Oh, how they sewed. Not a blouse or skirt from the store was deemed wearable until every button, hook or snap, loose or tight, was sewn over. Until those masters of prevention, their thumbs inured into sandpaper pincushions, left no play in the garment.

They were wary hands. On the way to the Christmas show at Radio City, they would clutch mine at each crossing and wait, as the crowds surged past, till the green light turned red, then green again. They took hold of the pile of orlon pullovers, outgrown, outdated, and quietly packed it away in a suitcase in the basement. A child or a sweater, they did not let go of anything easily. For all their nervous energy, they were scrupulously neat, hands that wrung at the sight of a mess. They taught me

371

to cry over spilt milk. Cry for too long, instead of wiping it up and getting on with things.

Most comfortable in solitary chores, they nonetheless delighted in social gestures. Opening every birthday card on the rack before choosing the nicest one. Wrapping a gift in once-used paper and ribbons. Breaking out the fruit bowl for a visitor. Affection was measured by length of handshake, from a cordial grasp to a spirited bobbing. And by food: slicing a fragrant Saturday morning challah into slabs that I might eat beyond satiety, while contenting themselves with a stale crust from the bread box. Hands that gave in excess to others practiced rigorous self-thrift, schooled through early privation in the science of making do.

Schooled, too, in the dutiful skills of penmanship and written expression, with a script that was both flowery and forceful, they wrote out their cards, their letters. But mostly their notes. Reminders not to forget the mail on the table, the lunches in the Frigidaire. Written on flaps of envelopes, scraps of brown bags, with a stub from our shoebox of stubs, the economy of pencil and paper was a stark contrast to the verbosity of the message.

They rode their highest tide of purpose, however, while submerged in water. Shampooing of hair or swabbing of tubs was merely prelude to their major vocation, enacted several times a day at the kitchen sink. There, abetted by neither sponge nor rag, they scrubbed each plate and cup, scrubbed until the pattern trickled into a faint wisp of color. Knuckles raw but unbowed were assuaged nightly in Jergen's lotion, sorely inadequate to its job, or in Boric Acid salve for the open cuts.

And so it was all the more amazing that from those fingers sprang music, glorious music, when they set themselves at the piano. They would venture a brief respite with the latest song, then linger for a few minutes over old favorites. They played with passion and authority, hands devoid of artifice embellishing the notes into trills. Time was to come, like a burglar in the night, and slowly steal cognizance and recall, yet the touch of the keys continued to evoke in each finger a memory of its own.

Serenity appeared in rare snatches, at instances of crisis. Palms lying upward in a lap, impotent to stem a parent's final illness. Wrists cradling a bag of groceries for twenty-two hours, stranded on a Short Line bus in a blizzard. Fingers splayed against the window pane, countering the stillbirth of a grandchild. Only then, while others clawed about for answers, did those wiser hands know that when there is nothing to be done, you do nothing. You do nothing. . . .

They have turned the calendar on ninety years, and their work is done. Incomprehensible, that never more will they tug and lug, seize and squeeze, mend and tend, feed and bleed, care and dare, forge a vibrant poetry of motion uniquely theirs. Whose are these hands, white with disuse, alien in their smoothness? Even as I watch, the bean-bags fall away, and my mother's hands turn into themselves.

The Sourdough Father

Lesleigh Forsyth

Sourdough is a leavening agent that is formed when a mixture of flour, sugar and water is acted upon by airborne yeast. Each time a dough or batter is made from sourdough, a portion of it is reserved to start the next batch. Sourdough starters were carried by settlers as they explored the Alaskan and Canadian wilderness or journeyed to the western United States during the Gold Rush. The daily trail diet was greatly enlivened by possession of one of these cultures since it could be used to bake bread, biscuits, pancakes, and cakes. A small portion of starter saved from each batch would ensure a succession of meals during the lengthiest journey. Crocks of sourdough were so important to these settlers and prospectors that they were often carried next to the body and even taken to bed to prevent freezing during the night.

Sourdough starters are also known as sourdough "mothers" (similar to vinegar "mothers," which also produce through a saved portion of each batch) because they give birth to future generations. There are starters in existence whose continuous use can be traced back as far as seventy years.

The story of the "Sourdough Father" arose from my desire to honor a friend on an important occasion. He uses a sourdough starter that comes from Alaska and that has been in use for fifteen years. He has given portions of it to many friends, myself included. An image of the many "bread children" that had come from his gift of the starter evolved into the main character of my story.

As I worked with the character, I thought about friends and the different kinds of nourishment they provide, often without knowing that they are doing so, and about the things we learn about ourselves from observing the qualities of our friends. These thoughts coalesced into the story of a sourdough starter during a day of self-discovery.

Working on the story was a process of self-discovery for me as well, answering a question that I had not previously asked myself, namely: "Why use art to say something?" The combination of evocative images and thoughts about my friend and his qualities started a subconscious process that grew into a story with a message I wanted to deliver. I couldn't have headed straight for that mark; the message came through the process of the writing, allowing me to tell more emotional truth than I would have otherwise. We do not generally say to our friends, "This is what I value about you." In telling and making a gift of a story, I was able to say what I would have said in a perfect world in which we know our thoughts and feelings without complications and express them without hesitation.

373

This story starts with a starter and is about things that never end.

The starter was a sourdough. He was called "mother" and lived in the home of a man who loved to bake.

Each week, the man took him out of the refrigerator, fed him flour and water, and left him to make the most of himself.

When the sourdough was big enough, the man took part of him away to bake bread and cakes for his family and friends. The rest of him went back to the fridge to cool off.

It was an old and comfortable ritual.

Living as he did, in the fridge, with only weekly trips to the countertop, the sourdough had a limited view of life. But enough trips anywhere can get you to wondering, and the sourdough got to wondering.

"Why did I get started and what am I doing here? All I know about myself is that I bubble and smell."

On his next trip to the countertop, he spent the day watching what was going on around him and trying to learn something about himself.

Some friends came to visit the man. They were musicians. They looked—well—unleavened. Their shoulders drooped, their eyelids drooped, their mouths drooped at the corners.

The man sat down at the piano and told his friends to take out their instruments. They began to play some beautiful music. Slowly, their shoulders started to rise. Their eyelids rose and fluttered. The corners of their mouths rose into smiles.

"It looks as though their spirits are rising," thought the sourdough. I am rising, too. It must be a good thing to do, because these people look very happy."

They were happy, but they were also tired and hungry. They sat down at the table and the man fed them a loaf of bread that he and the sourdough had made the week before. It was delicious. Soon the friends were full of energy and went off to play again.

"I did that!" thought the sourdough. "I turned into bread and gave them nourishment and energy. That is definitely a good thing because now they are playing again."

After all the music and excitement were over, the man went outside to work in his garden. The sourdough watched him from the kitchen window.

The man put lots of things into the ground: seeds, lime, peat moss, mulch, fertilizer, and the sweat of his brow. When he came back into the house, his arms were filled with vegetables and flowers.

"He puts things into the garden and takes things away," thought the sourdough, "and the garden goes on and on. He gives me flour and water and takes away part of me for baking. And I, too, go on and on."

At the end of the day, the sourdough thought he had learned some very important things about himself. He felt that his life was full of growth and a purpose that would endure. He went back to the fridge and thought the following:

I am called "mother" because mothers give us life. They feed us and help our spirits to rise. They help us make the most of ourselves. But I have learned about myself by watching a *father* do all of those same things. Now I must do something for him.

The next time he came out of the refrigerator, he had changed his name.

He was the Sourdough Father. And by some magic given only to bakers, the man knew it and was very pleased.

The M(ortality) Word and the L(ove) Word . . .

Elsa Dorfman

People take pictures when they are VERY alive, but half of their brain knows that the photograph will/might last longer than they will. That it will show people what they looked like, maybe WHO they were.

We accept the little death of the nanosecond the shutter opened and closed without thinking about it. We are even casual about the passing of the particular day. Indeed we don't think much beyond, "Did I look like THAT. What a good time. There we are in front of / doing / with."

It's the big death, the final picture that hurts. Then all the little pictures take on a new meaning. We who die become our shoebox of pictures to others.

In my work as a family portraitist, I have photographed eight people who knew they were dying and wanted to have a final portrait of themselves for and with their family. Of all the portraits I have made, these are the ones that mean the most to me. It's an honor to share the intimacy of the situation. I feel incredibly responsible to get a portrait that everyone in the family feels is just right. And my heart is always breaking. I am in awe of the bravery of the family members who are able to come to the studio and be themselves, mindful of the occasion.

Each person called me because he or she wanted a last family portrait of everyone together. They wanted the picture so the child would have a sense of the happiness and love that was shared within the family. That the child would have a sense of the specificity of the family. One family wanted the portrait "just in case" and to give the dad an incentive to heal. Sometimes it was the ill person who had the idea of the photograph and had to drag along the healthy partner and family members. Sometimes it was the healthy spouse who wanted one more image. Once it was a group of devoted friends. Each of these portraits was made with a sense of purpose and with a sense of what was to come. A sense that after death the portrait would really have its meaning.

Each session was full of bravado, bravery, and laughter. There is no other way to get through such a photo session. The whole idea is to make a portrait that is cocky, joyous, daring. There is also a sense of challenging death. How could death come when the photo is so real? How could the photo END? How could the photo become what once WAS?

I have also taken portraits of five families who wanted to come in front of the camera to commemorate their healing. To see for themselves that they have survived/prevailed/made themselves whole again. These pictures, too, are full of bravery and hope and love.

Figure 1. Jonathan and Kevin and Tobey together a month or so
before Kevin died.

Jonathan and Tobey. September 24, 1995.

Figure 2. And two years later, Jonathan and Tobey.
Jonathan, wearing Kevin's clothes, has said this portrait marked
the easing of his mourning.

Figure 3. Marge came to my studio with her five-year-old daughter Kathy.

Figure 4. These are the two families who would care for Kathy when Marge died.
Marge went right from my studio to the hospital to have her cells checked and
called to say that they were high. The photo session had energized her.
She could feel recovery. But a month later she was dead.

Figure 5. Jim Begin has written a wonderful essay about having a portrait made. He died April 20, 1997. His home page at http://www.tiac/net/users/newfound is being maintained by his friends.

COMMENTARY BY JIM BEGIN

What is it with me and not wanting to have my picture taken? At times I've taken my photophobia to the extreme, purging all family and extended family photo collections of even the faintest shadow of my likeness. Unable to understand my attacks on their family albums, relatives have taken drastic measures to safeguard pictures that I might confiscate and dispose of. When Elsa took my photo, I do believe it was the first time in my life I'd seen a photo of myself that I actually liked.

Why don't I like to look at old photos of myself? I think the answer to that question lies in the way I approach life. Much of my past has been filled with hardships. From growing up poor in a troubled home to learning at a young age that I had a serious illness, life never was all that easy. I learned the best way to see the future was to always have a better vision for tomorrow than memory of yesterday. Pictures, memories, even people were often too much of the harshness of worn-out times to carry into the future. Periodical purges of revealing photos, memories turned to nightmares, and old friends who were now acquaintances were all a part of moving on.

The body has withstood much, battered and worn down by years of illness. It becomes hard to think of having a picture done which makes you look "good" to observing eyes. The years of waging war to simply survive has changed so much of my physical appearance. Once a healthy adult my six-foot four-inch body weighed in at a solid 190 pounds. Battle after battle have taken their toll and now 145 pounds of a bony frame stand up against the strength of a strong wind.

Changes to the body, painful changes, make it difficult to still feel the same way about yourself as you once did. Photos often seem to capture moments of pain as well as higher times. In old photos I often see the pain of bad times or feel sorrow for better days that will never return. The body has changed much. Bones now stand out where well-developed muscles once made me proud of my body. Ribs covered with only a layer of flesh to define the wasting of a young body.

I once asked myself how attractive a body could appear that had an illness moving within it that would kill. A part of the vision is death, the image is one of a body fighting a slow losing battle. A part of the vision is life, a spirit hanging onto its only known way to stay connected to a fragile yet beautiful world. I have seen death in the eyes of people near the end; in the photo Elsa did I still see life in my own eyes.

I must explain the basketballs: the logical conclusion would be that basketball has somehow played an important role in my past. To a large extent basketball was once the center of my life, a skill I worked to develop, and learned well. For this photo the basketballs are less a reflection on the past and more an insight into an obtained faith in some future beyond illness and life.

During the early years of struggling with a serious illness, fear of death drove me to look for the answer to the hard question: "what is the meaning of life." I explored the traditional, investigated the nontraditional, and even considered the ridiculous philosophies of the world in a search for answers. There was an ongoing effort over several years to bring together some understanding of what life and death were all about. Working through the fears of my own death, I searched for a vision of peace beyond the world I knew.

I gave heavy consideration to several traditional religions, but in the end concluded that anyone who guaranteed me the perfect answer to all my questions was more confused than I was (but a confused I respected). Next I made an attempt to develop a vision of what is widely declared paradise or Valhalla or heaven. For me it would be a place of ultimate freedom, of perfect physical and mental health, where the company respected one another for being who they were. My paradise was a place where I could be me and be at peace.

As I examined my life, I worked to identify those moments when I had felt on top of the world and in total control of my life. Memories of playing basketball years ago brought back feelings of physical strength, innocence, hope, and a faith in the future. For me a sense of peace came from remembering back and concentrating on those good times: Running up and down the basketball court on solid muscular legs. Feeling the full use of my body and knowing I was very much alive. It was a time when getting a decent dunk down and working up a good sweat were the only cares I had in the world.

So my vision of heaven naturally had to incorporate a basketball court or basketball courts. Paradise is like any of the many courts I've played on over the years. You have to know the people here, playing this game, to know how different this is from any game that I could have ever played in my lifetime. The people who come to this place are the people you see suffering through life. The admittance to this game is based on hardships survived, courage, and a spirit that endures more than most.

People come to this basketball game to experience unfulfilled dreams, make up for years of lost independence, and to learn how free the spirit can be. We were the sick of the sick, those confined to wheelchairs, those that people had little hope for, those at the bottom of society. Those who wanted no pity but got labeled charity cases. Now the air is fresh, the time is new, and we are stronger than most. At a prime time in life we were forced to sit on the sidelines, or live as outcasts. In heaven we are the embodiment of courage and endurance. We stood up to the worst life could offer and emerged with our pride intact.

As I look at the photo Elsa took, I think of the next stage in my existence. I think about the place I will be going . . . and I am not afraid. The day will come that I am strong and free again, and in the dignified company of those who lived life as I did. We will know the burdens we each suffered, but our direction will be toward feeling freedom as no other group of people could. I would label the photo, "Heaven Is the Freedom You Never Had."

The body has changed so much over the years. Gone today are the shirt stretching biceps and chest muscles that I once took such great pride in. Those hours in the gym were spent on short-term vanity. Today I can look at myself and realize all the health issues I once took for granted. As with all people, those days were only meant to last a short time. The body is only meant to last so long before a journey is concluded.

I look at the "big photo" Elsa took and I can't help but think about what people think when they see me now. I hope they would see a spirit who fought one hell of a battle and lived the tough times with courage.

A FEW WORDS TO EXPLAIN
"JAMON. DAD. ELISE. NOVEMBER 23, 1996"
Commentary by Jeffrey A. Rahn

This photograph (next page) is a tribute to Clara, who unexpectedly died on November 23, 1995, while my family was on holiday in the Dominican Republic, leaving behind a relationship of seventeen years, a son of eight and a half years, and a fourteen-month-old daughter. To say her family was extremely important to Clara was an understatement.

Clara was a student of educational psychology and held many degrees in the field. Along the way she indirectly transferred to me a lot of her knowledge, and some of that helped me make it through the first year after her death. Running a business, keeping the vultures at bay, dealing with others' grief, keeping good- and bad-intentioned people in perspective, and more important trying to raise two young children alone (except for an elderly mother-in-law) was an experience that I would have preferred not to have experienced. I would not have been able to get through it all without trying to keep in logical perspective that the worst had already occurred.

Clara and I shared a love for art that was eclectic but based in modernism. One Saturday afternoon during July of 1995, we decided to go to Boston with the baby (we were experiencing our first prolonged separation from our son who was spending his first summer at overnight camp) and visit the Museum of Fine Arts. We were thrilled with a small exhibit of Elsa Dorfman's portraits.

I jotted down Elsa's name, only to lose it later to the lint collection in my bottomless pant pocket. I remember telling Clara that there was no way we could possibly afford this artist-photographer, but wouldn't it be fantastic to have her on our wall! Like Elsa's work, it was just a moment's thought, but documented in my memory somewhere.

Flash forward a year. The need to memorialize is overpowering, but how? Then I remember Elsa's work, but I can't remember her name. It is Yom Kippur, and the fasting and grieving is taking a toll on me; I visit an acquaintance's home, and lo and behold an Elsa Dorfman on the wall! Now I have the name (talk about divine intervention)!

The next step (in my mind) was to sell the artist on a concept I had. In my mind, having an artist that Clara admired help us pay tribute to Clara was important. Clara and I believed it was bad form to tell an artist how to do his or her work, but I wanted to push an idea in front of an artist I didn't know. Call to Elsa; long message left on her machine; expectation of two to three assistants blocking my entrance to the Oval Office. Quick live reply from Elsa; felt foolish to think she was a god-artist, and not a caring human being.

Concept: reverse the idea of posing with one's own objects. Instead I wanted the kids and myself to pose with the items that gave some impression of the person missing from the group portrait. I wanted it to be on the first anniversary of her passing. Sort of "Okay we survived this year, and here we are." Elsa agreed (I had no idea she had done "survivor photos" before).

The first-year anniversary date was important. Despite the necessity of trying to lead what appeared to be a "normal" life, I still had observed a full year of mourning.

Figure 6. Jamon. Dad. Elise. November 23, 1996.

I knew that the anniversary was a "hump" and that after I got over it, things would be more in cruise control.

Once the concept was in hand, the next idea step was to decide what objects should represent the life of a person. Symbolism can be everything and nothing, and I didn't want to have people read too much into what was visually offered. But if the portrait was to be a tribute to Clara (our presence together as a unit is in itself a tribute to her), it had to convey a certain style.

The first object is the purple Art-Deco-style chair we are sitting in. Clara would have had a fit if she knew I transported it out of the living room in western Massachusetts to the studio in Cambridge! She worked long and hard on designing her living room furniture, and had even sued the manufacturer over defects.

The stand to the left is nothing special but conveys her modernist leanings. The crystal lovebirds were an object I grabbed on my way out the door; only when I was pairing it on the table with the heart did I realize that the lovebirds were the first gift I ever gave her, and that the heart was the last gift. The heart is made out of unique shards of pottery, and had been an anniversary gift made by an artisan whose work she admired. The cracked nature of its surface did not seem to be prophetic at the time it was given. The glasses were hers (the shape and color were uniquely her own; she would spend whole days looking for the right frames as she preferred contact lenses and hated the look of glasses; while she would have hated the thought of being remembered by a pair of glasses, to me they symbolize her individuality).

The multicolored bag on the floor was Elise's diaper bag. Elsa suggested throwing it into the portrait for its color and uniqueness. She was right; it speaks of Clara's uniqueness.

The box to the right of us is a memory box that Jamon spent the winter building as a tribute to his mother to hold items belonging to Clara that he can share with his sister when she is older. Clara would have admired its beauty and the work he put into it, and she would have approved of its purpose. The photos were chosen because each one of them has Clara posing with each of us. Photos within photos were one way of exhibiting the missing person.

Elsa's coat rack holds a black cashmere dress of Clara's. It's meant to give an idea of her physical size, but also to exhibit her love of clothing (the hardest legacy Clara left me, other than raising her children without her, was emptying her sizable closet; a year and a half later I still don't have the heart to remove the last pieces of her wardrobe). The last item is her doctorate hood—to represent her hard-earned education.

Was it a happy day? The children didn't even know what day it was. I obviously did, but the logistics of gathering and transporting children and objects kept my mind off the significance. I felt relieved in some sense, and the smile I gave for the camera was to show that I was willing to go forward.

The finished portrait hangs in our family room to the left of the fireplace. I wanted to hang it in the living room with the bulk of our art, but Jamon reminded me that the *family room* was exactly what the name implied, "and that's where the portrait belongs." There is an equal space to the right of the fireplace that is empty, and someday we will add another Elsa portrait to it to complete the room.

THE WAYS WE REMEMBER CAROLINE:
EULOGY AND TWO POEMS
Margot Wizansky

We are Caroline's Women's Weekend group, Rita Daly, Carole Diamond, Caroline Graboys, Marilyn Hajer, Linda Hamlin, and Margot Wizansky. We came together in 1978, a bit haphazardly, at a Corner Coop Nursery School parents meeting. Our reason for being was to get away for a weekend when our children were tiny. Our two-day weekend grew to be three and then four days, culminating with an idyllic week last year on the island of Vieques in celebration of our twentieth year.

We are six women of strong opinions and talents, disparate in religion and roots. We have loved each other, laughed together, disagreed with each other, been angry with each other, gotten drunk together, supported each other, handed out copious measures of advice, and shared truths that resonated profoundly. We have faced illnesses together. We have provided each other with a safe place to utter our fears and wishes about our lives and our deaths and a respite from the demands of our lives. Now we face a break in our continuity.

Dear Caroline, these are some of the ways we'll remember you: On our first Women's Weekend, 1978, deliriously liberated from our toddling children, heading north in mud season on a two-mile uphill trek with all our gear to an unheated, unplumbed cabin in the woods. We slogged along in leaky boots with lumpy backpacks. And you, unruffled, without boots, golden in the cold misty air, from another place and time, with a straw hat on your long blond hair, a basket over your arm, holding baguettes and wine and a guitar, the bare necessities for a weekend picnic.

It was always that way; year after year you were the last to be picked up for Women's Weekend, looking fabulous, bringing something wonderful or difficult or important to share. A huge bag of scallops, a problem to solve, a book that had an impact on you. You were always the one who tried to move the discourse to a higher plane. So let's talk about the meaning of life. Is this all there is? Or, how will we get our children through adolescence? Let's take stock of our marriages. How is everybody doing? What did you accomplish in the last year that you're most proud of? Sometimes we resisted your efforts. Sometimes we didn't get serious until we were on our way home. We are grateful to you for pushing us to use those rare chances for connection and sharing.

On your birthday this past October you shared something quite wonderful with us. We gathered around the fire as your sister Nikila read the letters your grandmother wrote from England to your mother in the RAF, stationed in Washington, D.C., during World War II. In one letter Nikki read to us, your grandmother blessed you on the occasion of your birth:

> Well, your blessed Caroline Anne won't need that but I wonder if I could give her three fairy gifts, body, mind, and spirit, what I should choose. I think I will give her comeliness as being warmer and more workaday than beauty, and understanding as being more companionable than cleverness and I think might be stretched to include humour and lastly I think faith to keep her soul safe.

The Woman's Weekend. Twenty Years.

Dolman
11·20·97

Figure 7. The Women's Weekend.
For twenty years these women who met because each of them had a daughter in
the same school went away for a weekend together.

Those extraordinary letters deepened our understanding of your essence and your history, chronological and emotional, your literary sense, your pride and sense of style, the tradition of strong and elegant women that you came from, the tradition you imparted to your daughters.

You have shared so much of yourself, Caroline, in the last months. You have shared your strength, your good spirit, your love, your hopes and fears, and your soul. No matter how ill you were, you asked us, "Tell me about *your* life? How is *your* work going?" A visit with you was always a real conversation. You never stopped talking, making plans, and orchestrating events. And what a wonderful evening it was on New Year's Eve, gathered around you in your feather boa, laughing and reminiscing. For us, friends who love you, it was at times unbearable to watch death take you in front of our eyes as we feebly attempted to push it away with talk and soup and concern.

You, with your sense of history, were the one who started our group's journal, our archives. In Vieques you wrote, "I have just finished *The Spectator Bird* by Wallace Stegner. In it the writer refers to Goethe when he talks about the life of a person being nothing but the reflections we leave on others." Caroline, your reflection is indelible.

And this is our most perfect memory of you, an image of you that radiates pure and true. In Vieques, Puerto Rico, last March, the trip we almost didn't take except for your absolute determination. Nighttime on a little boat in the phosphorescent bay. Hale-Bopp and a trillion stars shimmering in the black sky. You were the first one to dive off the boat into the warm dark water. You swam and millions of tiny stars, the phosphorescent algae, trailed you. We all jumped in, held hands, bobbed in the shimmering water, an ecstatic experience. You climbed back into the boat and stood there, shining, your pale, nearly smooth head glowing, your white bathing suit sparkling, tiny stars falling all around you as the water dripped from your body.

This is the way we'll remember you.

Esperanza

Pale and spent
swaddled sleeping in a sheet
in the hot white island light
we barely see you.

On Good Friday you perch
on the sea wall in pain
watching Jesus of Vieques
drag his hand-hewn cross
through the streets of Esperanza.

But that night on the phosphorescent bay,
you are the first of us to dive
off the little boat we hired
into the dense dark water.
Millions of stars trail you.
We all jump in, bob in the shimmering water,
hold each other in wonder.
You're last to leave the water, and
you stand strong,
your smooth head and ivory swim suit shining.
Tiny stars tumble from you;
liquid diamonds slide off your skin.
We'll remember you like this, spilling stars.

My Life

She's prone on the sofa with no self-pity.
I watch in awe and think,
except for its shortened span,
this is an abundant life.

Unable to walk or eat or work
she still dwells in richness.
A procession of friends and sisters,
reading of psalms and letters,
celebrations planned or dreamed,
desks, closets, drawers of detritus and memory
pared down,
stories and lessons
to stow away till time is right.

And greater than all of this,
she gives blessings in extravagance,
holds her dear ones tight
for as long as time allows.

Dear Edith . . .

Jessie Kesson

The Warden of Anson House—a Home for Elderly Indigent Ladies—slammed the telephone down.

"We'd best get our skates on. A new resident's coming," she snapped to her trainee assistant. "Struth!" she grumbled, as she led the way upstairs. "They hardly give the old dears time to die before they pop another into their place!"

"This lot will take some clearing out," her assistant reflected as they stood staring round the recently vacated bed-sitting-room. "Books! Must be hundreds of them! Old Cresswell could never have read all this lot!"

"She reckoned she did." The Warden automatically flicked her hand across the bookshelves in her compulsive search for dust. "Nothing better to do, I suppose. And time to do it in."

"She wasn't a bad old stick," the assistant ventured.

"We've had worse," the Warden conceded.

"No next of kin, had she?"

"Not that I know of. And there was no mention on her admission sheet. There was"—the Warden straightened herself up from stripping the bed—"some woman she'd shared a flat with for years . . . what was her name again? *I* ought to know, didn't I? It'll come to me . . . it always does when you're not thinking about it . . . *Edith*! I knew it would come! It was when Edith died that old Cresswell came here. Same year as myself. And that's ten years since! 'My friend Edith,' on and on, as if Edith was still alive! Gave me a bit of a turn at first, being new to the work . . . 'I must write to my friend Edith.' "

"And did she? Write, I mean."

"If she did," the Warden said, "*I* never saw a letter go out from old Cresswell. Nor come in for her either."

"I suppose they get like that, muddled . . ."

"Confused." The Warden supplied the correct 'medical' term before bending again to strip the bed.

*　　　*　　　*

Reprinted from *Where the Apple Ripens* by Jessie Kesson published by Virago Press Ltd., 1993. Copyright © The Estate of Jessie Kesson, 1985.

"Dear Edith,

The horse chestnut tree in front of my window is in full bloom now. It set me thinking about you, took me back, back to that Sunday. We had just come out from the cemetery, our usual afternoon visit. Not that we had either kith or kin buried there, but as you always said since we would be longer there than anywhere else on earth, we might as well get accustomed to the place. Maybe, I don't know, maybe that was still on your mind when we sat in our usual seat in the park. The wind must have been beginning to rise, the red petals of the horse chestnut trees were fluttering down all round us, I started to play a little game—closing my eyes then opening them to see if any of the petals had landed on my shoes. 'Don't be so childish!' you said. 'Pay attention to what I am saying! When we come to be a burden to others, we will find our *own* way out . . .' That was when we put our plan into operation. Setting aside a few of our Seconal pills out of each monthly prescription. Better, you explained, to go sleepless for a few nights, than to be unprepared *if . . .*"

"Didn't you hear me knocking, Miss Cresswell! Forgot to put your hearing aid in *again . . .*"

"Sorry, Miss Ainslie, I was just finishing off a letter to –"

"Not feeling poorly again are you, dear?"

"No—thank you—I was just . . ."

"Anyhow, Miss Creswell, I just popped in to tell you the Committee Ladies have arrived to take us out for a little 'run.' I thought you might like –"

"Thank you, Miss Ainslie. Kind of you to bother, but I . . ."

"Don't feel *up* to it? Between *ourselves,* Miss Cresswell, neither do *I*. Thing is, thing is dear, the Ladies *expect* us to go. To show willing. They get a bit tetchy if –"

"Yes, I see. Very well. I'll just finish off my letter."

"Oh, Edith, I have forgotten what privacy is like. The Committee Ladies have swooped down on us again . . ."

"Ah! Miss Cresswell! Come to join us for a little 'spin.' That's a girl! Just the day for it. How about you, Miss Miller-Browne. Won't you join us today? Do you a world of good!"

"No, thank you! If *I* could go anywhere at all, with one foot in a caliper, and the other in a grave, I would gather up my skirts and get myself out of here—in a very rapid manner!"

"I know, Edith, I know I should be grateful for all that the Committee Ladies try to do for us, it's just, I get so tired of *having* to feel grateful. I was cajoled into going for a run. Helped and heaved into the car, we got stuck in a traffic jam on the way back, I found it so hard to contain myself. As you know, I always did suffer from a weak bladder . . .

"Miss Miller-Browne refused as usual, to be cajoled. She always reminds me of you. She has such courage."

*   *   *

"*Bloody-minded!* That's what *I* call Miller-Browne," the Warden confided to her assistant, as they stood unwiring the flowers sent in from the crematorium. "Uncooperative! Never leaves the house. Scared we get a minute to ourselves—anti-social!"

"To put our feet up," the assistant agreed. "This lot" she reflected, stripping the bottom leaves from the chrysanthemums, "must have cost a bomb!"

"*Waste!*" the Warden agreed. "Even the *dead* don't get the good of them. Not at the crematorium!"

"A rose tree now," her assistant said. "That's a different thing! You can plant that in the Vale of Rest. That's what *we* did when our Aunt Freda got cremated . . . we didn't bother with *flowers!*"

"Flowers from the dead to the dying. According to Miss Ainslie, who overheard as usual . . . I wondered what *you* would make of that, Edith . . .

"I tried to imagine, to hear you, 'a natural and thoughtful gesture on the part of the dead,' something like that, maybe? I chose some freesias. They seemed less death-like than the other flowers. I put them into that small green vase you gave me on a birthday . . .

" 'Green,' you said, 'will never clash with flowers of any hue. Which is why nature is so prodigal of its use.' "

"What are your beads?"

" 'Green glass, goblin . . .'

"Remember? Strange isn't it? I can remember long ago things, they just pop into my head of their *own* accord.

"They are brighter than stars
Brighter than water
Better than voices of winds that sing
Better than any man's fair daughter
. . . your green glass beads . . .

"It's the little every day things which I *ought* to remember, that sometimes elude me. And makes the Warden annoyed with me . . ."

"*Laundry!* Miss Cresswell. Don't forget your laundry again! Bring it down when you come to supper. Van collects first thing in the morning—*laundry,* I said!"

"Yes, yes, Warden. It's my hearing-aid. The battery's finished and I . . . forgot."

"Struth!" The Warden grumbled to her assistant as they prepared supper. "They do go on and on. Demanding. Always demanding. Nothing ever seems to be enough for them. Almost as if"—she paused, struggling to find words to fit her thought, "as if old age entitled them to everything . . . owed them. 'I need a new hearing aid, Warden!' 'I need a new bottom set. My lower dentures are slipping!' 'I need a new Zimmer. This one's too high for me now!' And you can't tell them that their gums are shrinking. Their bodies are shrinking. They don't want to know! They don't even listen to Dr. Crombie when he tells them that he hasn't got a cure for old age! You'll learn!" she assured her assistant. "If you stick to this job long enough!"

*   *   *

"It'll come to us all, I suppose," the assistant said, "if we live that long!"

"God forbid we should!" the Warden snapped. "And don't forget to put out the mustard pot tonight!"

"*Mustard!* With *fish,* warden? It's fish tonight!"

"With *everything!*" the Warden confirmed. "Mustard with everything! Just goes to show," she reflected. " 'A *bland* diet, Warden.' Committee always insisting on a 'bland diet.' They want to cook *here* for a week! You keep your ears cocked to the serving hatch," she advised her assistant, "and you'll hear what the old ones think of blancmange, tapioca, semolina. *No!*" she asserted. "They like a good old fry-up. And I don't blame them for *that!* A bit of 'taste.' I reckon it don't matter much what you eat when you're on the last lap. It's just the *mustard* I can't get over!"

"Maybe," her assistant suggested "they were used to it when they were young."

"I don't know about *that!*" the Warden admitted. "I'd just like a word in the geriatric dietician's ears!"

". . . I had intended to look through my book shelves in the hope of coming across one book that I haven't yet read. The mobile library comes, of course. But the choice is limited. That was *before* supper. *After* supper, Edith, I seldom feel in the mood to do anything at all. I, thankfully, cannot grumble about my health, it is reasonably good, but when we all gather together at meals, the main topic of conversation is aches and pains. By the time the meal is over, I feel that I suffer from every ill that afflicts man, as if the symptoms of the others have invaded me. What affects me, Edith, what frightens me most, is the anticipation with which what I can only describe as "medical days" are looked forward to. And when the unexpected happens, as it sometimes does—"repeat prescriptions" a day late in arriving, chiropodist's visit postponed, ambulance arriving half an hour late for the checkups—the blank that falls down on the day is filled with complaint. For the "medical days" have become the highlights of our weeks, of our existence.

"The seasons are brought in to us. Miss Ainslie told me that she heard the Warden discussing the Harvest Festival . . ."

"Miss Cresswell! The Vicar!"

". . . He's arrived, dear. *And* Church Sister—thought I'd better let you know. We're all getting together in the dining-room . . ."

". . . And we look forward," the Vicar was saying, "to having those amongst you who are able to do so, joining us in our Harvest Home Service on Sunday morning."

"We will, of course," Church Sister reminded the Vicar, "provide transport for those who are not quite so able. I have the list here. Miss Brecon, Miss Harris, Mrs. Wade, Miss Miller-Browne . . ."

"Wait for it!" the Warden whispered to her assistant, as they stood together, peeping through the half-closed serving hatch. "Miss Miller-Browne won't. She never does!"

". . . Miss Miller-Browne," the Church Sister was persuading, "you'll try to make the effort this year, won't you?"

"I have told you *before!* I have no truck with the Church since I was a child, and *then* under compulsion. But I *do* know the Bible! 'Remember thy Creator in the days of thy Youth . . .' I didn't do so then! And am most unlikely to do so in my old age."

"I knew it," the Warden triumphed. "She is an old so-and-so, Miller-Browne. Just the same," the Warden admitted reluctantly, "she sticks to her guns. Look at her! Calliper or no calliper! She can't half move herself out of it when something annoys her."

". . . The altar looked beautiful this morning, surrounded by autumn. Sheaves of corn intertwined with tea roses. We used to think, you and I, Edith, that tea roses looked old. Older than other roses. Because you said, they had their roots in a civilisation far older than ours—India? China? Persia? I forget.

"The Girl Guides sang—did I tell you? We have been 'adopted' by a Girl Guide. A nice child, mine. She came to have tea with me in my room. We talked and talked, but didn't communicate. The gap was too wide to be bridged by words . . . and yet today it seemed to be bridged in an almost miraculous way. The Vicar didn't announce this hymn, you see. The Girl Guides simply stood up, and the music seemed to swell out from nowhere . . . *your* hymn, Edith.

"Choose me in my golden time
In my dear joys . . .
Have part . . .
For Thee the . . .
Fullness of my prime
The gladness . . ."

"*Singing!* Miss Cresswell! You *are* in good spirits! I just popped up, dear, to let you know—tip you the *wink!* They've just brought in the Harvest Festival Offerings from the church, and remember what happened to *you* last Harvest Festival, Miss Cresswell! Only a few russets left by the time you came down to collect your share. Miss Brecon took the lion's share of the grapes! Said apples went for her dentures!"

"I don't mind, Miss Ainslie. *Truly,* I don't."

"You *should* mind, Miss Cresswell. We're all entitled. Warden ought to supervise the share-out. I daresay after she gets her pick, it's devil take the hindmost!"

"I doubt that. Now Miss Ainslie, if you'll excuse me . . ."

". . . And so, Edith, autumn was brought into us and piled high on the sideboard, a pyramid of colour. We could only stand looking at it, arrested by the intensity of the colour that confronted us. Apprehensive of putting out a hand towards it, lest it should tumble down at our touch. That moment and that mood passed, and *then* . . .!"

"*Ladies!* See what I mean?" the Warden flung over her shoulder to her assistant, as she flounced out of the kitchen into the dining room.

"Ladies! There's surely enough here for all of you! The others like grapes, too, Miss Brecon!"

"Ladies?" the Warden sniffed, perching herself up on her stool beside the serving hatch again. "I don't know . . . Better take your pick of what's left," she suggested to her assistant. "And there's not much of *that* now. Not after *that* lot's had a go.

"When I first came here," she reflected, "ten long years since, the secretary who interviewed me for the job—a Miss Fenwick she was. Dead now—went on and on about 'putting me fully in the picture.' She said, 'We don't accept "God Blimmees" here,' she told me. For a minute, I thought she meant *me*! And that I'd *had* the job! Till she went on to explain that they cared for women who had 'seen better days,' had 'come down in the world.' Sometimes," the Warden sighed, "I wish she wasn't dead. Fenwick, I mean. *I* could have told *her* something! There are ladies—and—*ladies*! And Brecon's not one. Nor Ainslie—"

"Miss Cresswell?" her assistant prompted.

"Cresswell?" the Warden considered the matter. "She's not with us half the time, but she'll pass."

"Miller-Browne?"

"She's the *real* thing. You can always tell!" the Warden claimed. "She didn't go to their Harvest Service, but she didn't barge in here and grab all the grapes either!"

". . . Christmas is almost upon us. How I dread it, Edith. Cards that come. Cards that go. A contest of cards. To see which of us can lay claim to the largest number of cards received, to prove something to ourselves? That we still have friends? Are still in touch with the world outside? That we still exist? Cards which will not herald the advent of this Christmas but testify to Christmas long past from well-wishers long dead. I realised this when Miss Ainslie invited me to her room to see 'all her cards.' I recognised the names of residents now gone from us, I made no mention of my discovery to Miss Ainslie. Then gifts, no longer personal, from friend to friend, but public tokens of our continued existence. Without the small surprise that sharpened and sweetened our Christmas tides, Edith, or so I feel. You see, Edith . . ."

"*Yes! Yes!* Miss Ainslie, I heard you knocking . . . I'm just trying to . . ."

"An artificial tree this year, Miss Cresswell. I've just seen the Council men bring it in by the back door. Not the same as a *real* treat. Not the same thing at all! To save the Warden I suppose. Always complaining about the fir needles on the carpet! *Anything* to save herself work! I thought I'd pop up to remind you that we've got to go into the sitting-room before tea. The Committee Ladies are coming."

". . . to put you *all* in the picture!" Miss Sherwood, the Secretary, announced, flicking through the lists of her Christmas agenda.

"You must," Miss Ainslie invited her, "pop in for a minute to see all my cards. More than last year!"

"Yes, yes. They do seem to mount up, don't they?" The Secretary acknowledged the invitation without accepting it, or lifting her eyes from her agenda.

"First of all," she proclaimed, handing her lists over to her assistant and trusting to memory, "The Ladies of St. Saviour's have once again risen nobly to the occasion. And will provide *and* serve tea on Christmas Eve, as usual. Then our Girl Guides, carols on Christmas morning. The Vicar himself will be along after Morning Service."

The applause which greeted this announcement, although appreciative, was modulated. For the old ladies knew the rote. They also knew what was what, and who was who.

"Then!" the Secretary continued, "the Rotarians"—the applause which greeted this announcement put her slightly off her stroke—"yes the Rotarians—always so generous in their giving—will be along." Forgetful of when exactly the Rotarians would 'be along,' the Secretary, grabbing the agenda out of her assistant's hand, began to flick wildly through its pages. "So many bits and pieces," she complained. "Where *did* I put the Rotarians?"

"In your handbag?" her assistant suggested.

"Of course! The Rotarians," she announced, "will be with us to hand out their gifts, just after lunch on Christmas Day."

"You will pop in to see my cards?" Miss Ainslee reminded her.

"Another time, dear," the Secretary assured her, before turning to assure the Warden. "That's everything, Miss Watson, everything under control!"

"Everything under control!" the Warden snorted, when herself and her assistant reached the safety of their kitchen again. "She forgets how they all collapse like burst balloons *after* Christmas. You won't see hair or hide of madam then! Not when all the viruses start going around. It's you and me that have to cope then! Strange thing," she reflected, "how the old dears always seem to be able to hang on like grim death till Christmas. After that"—the Warden shrugged—"they just seem to let go."

"Nothing to look forward to?" the assistant suggested.

"Could be," the Warden agreed. "Could be. Or that they think they mightn't reach another Christmas."

". . . And everything was laid on, Edith. Christmas got smothered and wept to get out. But, again, the Girl Guides sang beautifully. Echoing for me, Christmas remembered. *Our* hymn. Always my favourite. Though I could never tell why. Not until you discovered the reason. 'A poem,' you said, 'Christina Rossetti.' I sang it silently. From beginning to end, with the Girl Guides. Yet, now, I cannot remember one word of it. That happens to me, sometimes. And it vexes me. Things that tremble on the edge of my mind. Eluding capture. Battering against my brain, for outlet. Tormenting me. As if I could never find release, till I find the words . . . in the bleak

> "*Midwinter!*
> Frosty winds made moan
> Earth . . .
> Lay hard as iron
> Water . . .
> *Like*
> . . . a stone . . .

"A ghost? No. Ghosts walk at midnight . . ."

"Miss Brecon! It's Miss Brecon, dear—ambulance has just come for her. Different when it comes for a check-up, but when it's for hospital . . ."

"That's the first of them," the Warden announced to her assistant. "And there's Ainslie, creeping around, spreading the Glad Tidings! Miss Ainslie!" she demanded. "What are you hovering up there for! Keeping Miss Cresswell's door open. As if it isn't cold enough!

"Hospital always 'gets' them," she confided to her assistant. "Frightened they never come out. But," she admitted, "better to happen in hospital. When it happens here, it really does affect them."

"Wondering whose turn next!" her assistant supposed.

". . . Miss Brecon was admitted to hospital three weeks ago. We have just heard from Warden that she died yesterday. It's when death occurs *here* that Warden doesn't discuss it with us. We are taken out by the back door then. As if that could conceal a fact. A virus, Warden said. It seems to be catching. Dr. Crombie came this morning to Miss Miller-Browne and Miss Hardwick. I haven't been feeling too well myself. In spirit. I used to like my room, my books, and all the small momentoes of our life together, but now, Edith, now the walls of my room seem to crowd in on me, the momentoes to mock me. I feel like crashing them through the window. And pounding at the walls with my hands. I find myself wishing that I could dissolve with no trace left. I couldn't say so to the others, but I envied Miss Brecon her escape. I'm not afraid to die. But sometimes, Edith, sometimes I feel frightened to death . . ."

"That's that, then!" The Warden surveyed the empty bed-sitting-room.

"This junk," her assistant asked, "where does it go?"

"Basement still," the Warden considered. "Some of it might 'come in' one day. You never know."

"I didn't expect old Cresswell to go. Not sudden like that," the assistant said. "She wasn't ill. Not *properly* ill, I mean."

"Heart! Her heart was always sickly! And old age. We all die of *that* through time." The Warden stood considering a philosophy that had just struck her. "Another thing!" she remembered resentfully. "When Dr. Crombie came to sign the death certificate—going for midnight, it was. And he doesn't like late calls. But what about *me*! I don't like late calls either! And I had to be there too! I was jittery, I always am when they go off, sudden. Nervous. You know what I mean. You open your mouth and let anything come out of it. 'Old people are living longer now Doctor,' I said. Just for something to say, when he was signing the death certificate. STRUTH! You would think that *I* had killed old Cresswell! 'Old people are *lingering* longer!' he snapped, flung down the pen, and shot out the door. I felt as if my nose had bled! That's *it* then! Have you finished clearing out the chest of drawers?"

"Just about."

"Good, I'll see to this lot."

*　　　*　　　*

"Warden! Warden!" the assistant's voice halted the Warden at the door. "Look at this!" she urged. "Just take a look! Writing paper. Pages and pages! 'Dear Edith . . .' Nothing else. Just 'Dear Edith.' What a waste of paper!"

"No wonder they're always crying out for writing paper," the Warden snapped. "Just to waste it!"

"I could," her assistant suggested, "I could just cut off the tops and the others could use up the rest of the paper."

"You're welcome to the job! If you can find time to do it."

"Warden! She *has* written something! On this page—'Dear Edith I have changed my mind. Not about my going. The reason for it has changed, other people have become a burden to me . . .' "

Silent Conversations

Leigh Westerfield

I used to come to your office every week or so to talk. You'd look down at your hands in your lap, or occasionally file a fingernail while you listened to me. At some point, I became a listener for you. I meet up with you nowadays in another place. No one ever put a marker at the grave site where your ashes were buried, but it's here I find myself still talking and listening.

In her late forties when I met her, she was short and round, with one of those perms of tight little curls. Cigarettes, I imagine, had roughened the edges of her voice. Her deep belly laugh amused me, so I'd often try to say something funny just to hear the laughter that softly rumbled out of her.

What astonished me again and again when I was first getting to know her was that she appeared so delighted to see me at each therapy appointment. As she shut the door to her office, she'd look down at me sitting on her couch and grin. She charmed me. Once, I mentioned my wonderment to a friend, who replied in exasperation, "Well, if you had a chance to talk to someone like you, wouldn't you be glad?"

For a long time I try to avoid driving past the hospital, or if I have to go by, I won't let myself look at the building where I saw you last. One day, I'm drawn to the cemetery, though I dread what going there will feel like. I've recently returned from living abroad, but neither the distance of several thousand miles, nor two years' time, nor new relationships have helped me understand that you're really gone.

A friend nudges me by going with me to buy some flowers. Another friend comes along to the cemetery. Together we scrutinize the shaded, empty space next to your parents' headstone. We try to guess where your ashes were placed, and I lay the flowers on the bare grass. My friend leaves me standing there alone for a few moments. When he walks back over to me, he asks, "Did she have a sense of humor?" I nod, remembering what had once felt so warmly embracing. "Because I thought I heard someone laugh, or at least say 'Hello,'" he notes quietly.

She was "famous" in this college town. Her notoriety reached from the "townies," where she had her roots, to university people, to the women's community. At public events, people thronged around her like fans. She was naturally gregarious, and her broad face beamed as she drank in all the attention. I had occasionally run across other people with the same sort of charisma. My inclination in these situations was always to hang back, thinking I couldn't really compete with those vying for a few words or a smile.

These days, I find you on a hill that overlooks a busy street. The cemetery is located on a stretch of road that leads out of town to the rolling, rural landscape a few miles distant. Several blocks in the other direction is the Courthouse Square, ringed by restaurants, bookstores, and specialty shops. Cars speed past the cemetery before slowing down for the endless four-way stops downtown. The loudness of the car engines ruptures the stillness in the place where you are.

She usually stripped almost everything down to the essentials in just a few well-chosen words. I'd laugh as her irreverence punched through other people's pretentiousness. The blunt words lofted my way, on the other hand, left me gasping as if the wind had been knocked out of me. Whenever I'd repeat my conviction that what I needed was to be "normal," to be like everyone else, she'd declare flatly, "Don't talk to me about normal. I don't know what normal is." Or when I'd describe my feelings of confusion, she'd state point blank, " 'Confused' isn't an emotion. Are you happy, sad, angry, scared . . .?" Startled as I was by her straightforward-ness—and unable to cleverly dodge her truths—I nevertheless admired her for being her own person.

Your corner of the cemetery rises up several feet on a little hill that marks off this area from its surroundings.

"I think you trust me," she observed once in that soft low voice after I'd been seeing her for a while.

"I was desperate," I replied offhandedly, meaning it had been agonizing, terrify-ing, for me literally to walk in off the street and tell a stranger about my life.

"Well, you could have kept coming here and not ever trusted me. I think you do trust me," she responded with a calm self-assurance.

The edge of the cemetery, where I find you, stops abruptly at a cement wall that starts at ground level and drops down about five feet to the sidewalk. Across the street is a row of modest, nondescript frame houses.

We'd worked together for about a year and a half. I waited in the foyer one day before an appointment while she spoke to someone on the phone. The door to her office stood partly open, and I overheard her saying something about her concern for the "quality of life." As I gathered my things to leave at the end of the hour, I shuffled around in the doorway and asked reluctantly if she was all right. For all that she knew about me, she'd told me very little about herself. I hesitated to barge into her life.

She said she'd talk to me about her health the next time we met. I went numb for an entire week. I wanted to know the truth, but when I thought about something happening to her my mind would instantly blot out the thought, leaving only a disorienting black emptiness.

After she told me she'd been diagnosed with lymphoma, she mentioned how much it had meant to her that I'd asked. Her vulnerability caught me off guard. In my image of her she was always surrounded by admiring crowds. I'd assumed she had lots of friends and other people to talk to. What kind of a connection was this between the two of us?

Some time later, as we tried to iron out a misunderstanding between us, she revealed with some regret that, because her life was rather public, people often talked to each other about her, rather than relating to her as friends.

I've always thought you have a good view from this plot in the cemetery: the passersby on the sidewalk, the folks driving past, the families in their homes.

I couldn't shake the feeling that my personal problems were meaningless, really, in comparison with the situation she faced. Sitting in her office furnished in blues and purples and greens, I tried to tell her this. I said the issues about my family just didn't seem very significant anymore. In the back of my mind, I thought, "because you might die, and how do the ramblings about my life that I continually bring to you measure up against that?" As urgent and vaguely meaningful as my own circumstances had often seemed while I talked to her for so many months, now they suddenly appeared mundane, even trivial.

She told me she understood what I was saying and that part of her wanted to give up. She knew she wouldn't be happy, though, if she didn't go right on living her life as she always had, and that included seeing clients.

An old fir tree stands near your grave, its trunk some three feet wide. The branches span a broad radius, wrapping this entire corner in a dark and cool seclusion. Long tendrils of needles hang down from the drooping branches like fingers and surround this shady area so set apart from everything else—the crowded-together tombstones in the distance and the liveliness of the neighboring street.

During an appointment shortly after she told me about her illness, she showed me photos she'd taken of wildflowers at a festival in Tennessee and shared how much she loved these flowers. I listened to her for the entire session. The thought flickered through my mind while I sat there, and again after I left, that I should have been the one doing the talking. I felt guilty, though, for even thinking the hour should have been mine. At the same time, I found myself casting about for a way to help her.

A magnolia tree takes up right where the fir leaves off. Its gnarled trunk and crooked branches belie its gracefulness. While the fir exudes a sense of peace, the sturdiness and resiliency of the smaller tree remind me of your solid, compact frame and inner strength.

She said to me, "I always knew I'd get cancer. My father and grandfather died of it, and my mother has had it three times. I just didn't want to get it now because there are still so many things I want to do."

She was fifty-one when she died.

The cemetery owns a deep stillness. The traffic rushes by in sporadic, loud fits, but these breaks in the silence fall away instantly as the calm and the quiet take up again.

I came to her office one day after she had started chemotherapy and found her wearing a wig. Perfectly coiffed, frosted waves had replaced the sensible and practical perm. I looked at her, trying to decide whether I should say something but wanting more to pretend I didn't notice anything different. Her head bent partly downward, she only half looked at me as she said, ruefully, "It's wig day." She described how her hair had begun falling out in the shower that morning. I thought to myself, "You're still the same person, even if you're wearing a wig." But any words I might have said stuck inside me, as they often had since I was a child.

Just before I'm to leave town for a teaching position, having completed my Ph.D., I go to the cemetery, intending to tell you good-bye and how much you meant in my life. I'm frustrated and irritated at having to listen to several roaring lawn mowers as the grounds keepers, out o, view, tend the grass. The tranquility has been shattered and it can't be retrieved, I feel sure. Then the disruptive sound evaporates with such swiftness and deliberateness that it is, disconcertingly, as if the quiet has a will of its own as it retrieves its place in these surroundings.

Occasionally she'd recount conversations with her doctor. The dry, factual information about her illness never adequately hid the disbelief behind her words. She'd inquired how much a bone marrow transplant would cost, and the doctor had said, without blinking an eye, between $150,000 and $200,000. She'd asked what were the chances of the cancer recurring after chemotherapy, if she didn't have the transplant, and he'd told her 90 to 100 percent.

Eleven years have passed since your death. I find myself at the cemetery on a chilly day in December, a few days shy of Christmas. Several inches of pristine snow cover the ground; there are no footprints anywhere to mar the smooth white surface beneath the fir tree. What catches my eye as I look around is a single brown oak leaf standing on its stem in the snow, propped slightly against a smoky pint jar beside a gravestone.

Just before she left for the hospital in Lexington, Kentucky, where she'd have a bone marrow transplant, I lingered after a group session so I could tell her good-bye. She hugged me, and said, "You're special. You know that, don't you? Yeah, you do. You know you're special."

The silence in the cemetery enfolds me. On a cold December day, the only sound is the wind rustling the needles of the fir. Yet this noise doesn't disturb the stillness as much as it gives a texture to the quiet.

We never talked about the fact that she might die. She never seemed to believe it really might happen.

No matter what the season, the sky is often overcast when I'm at the cemetery. It never feels dreary or mournful, though. More often than not, the clouds suddenly part for a moment to reveal the sun's brilliance.

She returned to town after the transplant, and I heard through the grapevine that she wasn't doing very well. Soon she was admitted to the local hospital while the doctors tried to treat her. Complications from the transplant had damaged nerve endings and caused her to lose feeling in her legs and feet.

I felt at loose ends all day, wandering around town, thinking about who I'd find when I visited her.

As I approached the doorway of her room, it dawned on me why I was there: She was going to die, and I had come to say good-bye.

She smiled with surprise and said my name when she saw me, although she spoke slowly, thickly, and was disoriented. She thought she was in Lexington and that I'd driven a ways to see her.

Her bald head startled me at first, but that didn't bother me as much as other changes I noticed. She glanced at the bright floral arrangements in the room and remarked how nice it was to receive flowers in the springtime. She'd always loved the outdoors and wildflowers and people. Now, suddenly, it was fine with her to have these artfully designed bouquets in her hospital room. She didn't even mention that she'd rather be outside, surrounded by nature.

I wanted to tell her it was all right to die. But her son was sitting there, trying to lift her spirits by making the same kind of off-beat jokes I used to hear from her. He wanted to believe she'd get better. The three of us made small talk. I thought that behind the banter she knew why I'd come, what I wanted to say.

The physical therapist came in to work with her and help her stand up. It was a futile effort because she couldn't feel her legs and feet, but her son and the therapist tried to hold her upright for a minute or so as she held on with her arms slung around their shoulders. She grimaced as she went through the motions of trying to stand. The therapist reassured her that with continued practice she'd soon walk again. The woman's cheering words barely disguised the sad truth.

As she settled back into bed, she suggested it was time for me to leave. She took my hand. I said I'd come back to see her again, although I believe we both understood it would never happen.

A few more weeks went by and then she was gone. They'd taken her back to Lexington so the doctors who'd performed the transplant could treat her. Some friends called one night to say she'd passed away. I later heard that at the end she couldn't move at all, only blink her eyes.

*   *   *

She has stayed a part of my life. When I came to the end of my dissertation, several years after she'd died, I began to miss her again. I wanted badly to tell her I'd completed the project that had absorbed me for four years. When I'd first thought up the topic I'd write about, she'd said it sounded like "a treasure hunt" because it involved so much digging into the lives of obscure women writers. She knew my idea. Now I wanted her to know I'd finished. I went out into the darkness one night, found a star, and pretended it was her as I described the journey that had been my life since she was gone.

These days, we talk and listen in the stillness.

List of Contributors

Sally S. Bailey, an ordained minister in the Christian Church (Disciples of Christ), currently works in Branford, Connecticut, as a private consultant in spiritual care and the arts. She previously served eighteen years at the Connecticut Hospice where she designed a model program in the arts. She is a founding board member of the Society for the Arts in Healthcare and is coauthor of *Creativity and the Close of Life.*

Sandra Bertman, Ph.D., a professor of Humanities in Medicine at the University of Massachusetts Medical and Graduate Nursing Schools and founding director of the Medical Humanities Program, has pioneered the use of the arts and humanities in grief counseling and in the training of healthcare practitioners in clinical and academic settings. She lectures internationally on the psychology of loss, end-of-life care, clinician burnout, and the interface of suffering and spirituality. Author of *Facing Death: Images, Insights and Interventions,* she co-created the film *Dying,* is a member of the core team currently producing *Handbook for Mortals: Guidance for People Facing Serious Illness,* and is completing her book *The Language of Grief and the Art of Consolation.*

Lynn Cummings, M.N., has extensive experience in the field of palliative care as direct caregiver, educator, and administrator. She is a sessional lecturer at the University of Victoria School of Nursing where she teaches a palliative care nursing elective, and she has been a contributing author to resource materials developed by Victoria Hospice Society.

Cortney Davis is a nurse practitioner and poet. Her poetry collections are *The Body Flute* (Adastra Press, 1994) and *Details of Flesh* (Calyx Books, 1997); she is coeditor of *Between the Heartbeats: Poetry and Prose by Nurses* (University Press, 1995). *Hudson Review, Crazyhorse, Ms., JAMA, Lancet,* and *Annals of Internal Medicine,* and other journals have published her poetry. She lives in Redding, Connecticut, and works in women's health.

Martha K. Davis is a writer, teacher, and massage practitioner living in Ithaca, New York. Her fiction has appeared in *Story Quarterly, In the Family,* and the anthology *Hers2.* She is currently working on a novel.

Elsa Dorfman is a widely known portrait photographer with a studio in Cambridge, Massachusetts. Her works have appeared in major museums across the country. She has been using a Polaroid [20 × 24] camera since 1980. Because her work is mostly about families and family life, she has made several portraits capturing both the dying and healing process. Her home page is at <http://elsa.photo.net>.

Brenda Eng, M.N., is founder of and presently clinical nurse specialist at Canuck Place located in Vancouver, British Columbia. Canuck Place is North America's first free-standing hospice for children with progressive life-threatening illness, providing respite, palliative, and bereavement care. Since 1984, she has integrated puppet play in her care of children with chronic or terminal conditions.

Lesleigh Forsyth has worked as a concert and book publicist and as executive director of a public school violin-teaching program in East Harlem, New York. She is a cellist who has a long-standing interest in music and emotion. She is currently living in Larchmont, New York, writing a book on the connection between music and grief.

Nancy Fried is a sculptor who lives and works in New York City. Her sculpture is in the permanent collections of the Metropolitan Museum of Art and the Brooklyn Museum of Art. She is represented by DC Moore Gallery in New York City.

Louis A. Gamino, Ph.D., a diplomat in clinical psychology, is on the staff of the Scott and White Clinic in Temple, Texas. In addition to a clinical specialty in bereavement-related problems, Dr. Gamino teaches about death and dying at the Texas A&M Health Science Center College of Medicine. He also conducts empirical research on the phenomenology of grieving and has a long-standing interest in the interface between psychology and art.

Tomas R. Golden, L.C.S.W., has worked in the field of death and dying for more than twenty years as an author (*Swallowed by a Snake: The Gift of the Masculine Side of Healing*), speaker, and psychotherapist. His Web site *Crisis, Grief, and Healing* <http://www.webhealing.com> has won numerous awards.

Mindy L. K. Gough is a social worker currently completing her certificate in thanatology and palliative care at the University of Western Ontario. She draws upon play, art, photography, movement, music, and other creative techniques to enhance her counseling skills. A bereaved child herself, she feels her personal experience makes her well suited to help other bereaved children in their quest for healing.

Roberta Halporn, M.A. (in Arts Education), is the director of the Center for Thanatology Research and Education Inc., a non-profit resource center, library, and small press specializing in works on dying, death, loss, and bereavement. She is consultant to the Foundation of Thanatology in New York, and editor of its archives and abstract publications.

David Hatem, M.D., is a practicing internist at the University of Massachusetts Medical Center, devoting part of his practice to the care of those with HIV infection. He also teaches "Medicine and Literature: The Human Experience" to undergraduates at Boston College.

J. Havelka, Ph.D. (1922-1997), was a psychologist, philosopher, painter, novelist, essayist, and dramatist, and most important to many, a teacher. He taught psychology at the University of Western Ontario and King's College, both in London, Ontario. His interests included creative and cognitive processes, psychology of artistic functions, neuropsychology, and Eastern psychology. He wrote *The Nature of the Creative Process in Art, Reflections and Preoccupations,* and *Variations,* as well as publications in his native Czech.

C. Regina Kelley, now Ani Konchok Drolma, is an ordained Buddhist nun, currently dean of Buddhist Studies at Sunray Meditation Society. She holds an M.F.A in sculpture from the University of Pennsylvania and has exhibited internationally. She currently teaches workshops on cancer and creativity and hospice as well as Buddhist meditation and philosophy.

Jessie Kesson, (1916-1994), is known for her stories, poems, newspaper features, dramas, and novels. Her story "Dear Edith" is included here. She is author of *The White Bird Passes* (1958), *Glitter of Mica* (1963), *Another Time, Another Place,* (1983), and *Where the Apple Ripens* (1985). She was also the proud owner of a "scarlet goon," conferred by Dundee University in 1984.

Kevin Kirkland, an accredited music therapist from Vancouver, British Columbia, currently works at the University of British Columbia Hospital and at Yaletown House. He is past president of the Canadian Association for Music Therapy and coauthor of *Full Circle Spiritual Therapy for the Elderly* (currently in press).

Melvin J. Krant, M.D., is a retired professor of medicine and psychiatry at the University of Massachusetts Medical Center. He is also the founding director of the Pain Clinic at Deaconess Hospital, Boston. He continues to work in international health in the former Soviet Union and among Latinos.

William M. Lamers, Jr., M.D., established one of the earliest hospice programs in the United States during the early 1970s, called the Hospice of Marin. With over twenty-five years of clinical experience in the field of psychiatry, Dr. Lamers has written and coauthored a number of books and papers in the fields of medicine, psychiatry, and hospice care, and has received many honorary awards. Currently living in Malibu, California, he works as a consultant in the areas of hospice, palliative care, and pain management.

Aaron Lazare, M.D., is the author of the first book on outpatient psychiatry, *Outpatient Psychiatry: Diagnosis and Treatment* (1979), now in its second printing. During the mid-1970s he conducted pioneering research on the importance of understanding the patient's perspective, funded by the National Institute of Mental Health over a period of eight years. Dr. Lazare has been, successively, a professor of psychiatry, chair of psychiatry, and is currently Chancellor/Dean at the University of Massachusetts Medical Center.

Elaine Freed Lindenblatt of Tappan, New York, is a freelance writer whose essays have appeared in the Middletown, New York, *Times Herald Record* and the Rockland, New York, *Journal News*. Her mother, in a nursing home for twelve years with organic brain syndrome, died in April 1993, two months after Elaine wrote "My Mother's Hands."

Suzanne Lister, A.T.R., is the coordinator of the pediatric oncology Art Therapy Program at Children's Hospital of Western Ontario, London, Ontario. She also teaches art therapy at the University of Western Ontario. Her major areas of research include illness, grief, and death and dying.

Lynne Martins, M.S.W., is a clinical social worker and a grief therapist in private practice in Tacoma, Washington, where she specializes in delayed and complicated grief issues resulting from sudden death. The author of numerous publications and video productions, she has been counseling and teaching for more than a decade throughout the United States, Canada, and Australia.

Judith McDowell is a theatre artist and professional writer, living in Victoria, British Columbia. A former teacher and community development worker, she has written extensively about community health and health promotion issues for magazines and government publications.

James Miller, Ph.D., is the Faculty of Arts Professor at the University of Western Ontario, London, Ontario, and the founding director of the University's Research Facility for Gay and Lesbian Studies. He is editor of *Fluid Exchanges: Artists and Critics in the AIDS Crisis* (1992) and author of *Measures of Wisdom: The Cosmic Dance in Classical and Christian Antiquity* (1985). He is currently completing a collection of transgressive essays entitled *Dante & the Unorthodox.*

Linda G. Nicholas, A.T.R., is the coordinator of the Art Therapy Program at the University of Western Ontario. She is a registered art therapist with the American Art Therapy Association and the Ontario Art Therapy Association. Currently Nicholas is writing a textbook on art therapy entitled *A Nest of Dolls* with coauthor Irene Dewdney, one of the founding art therapists in Canada.

Carol Picard, R.N., M.S., C.S., is an associate professor at Fitchburg (Mass.) State College and a doctoral fellow at Boston College. Her areas of interest (and publications) are in poetry, the healing power of the arts and humanities (for both patients and nurses), and international nursing.

Christina Schlesinger, an artist and mural painter, began exhibiting in 1986. She has worked on murals with senior citizens, children, and the homeless since the 1970s. In 1976, with Judy Baca, she founded SPARC (Social and Public Art Resource Center), a still thriving public art center in Los Angeles. In New York City, she has created over one hundred murals with public school children including the "Yusuf Hawkins" mural discussed in her essay. She has received major public art commissions in New York City, Los Angeles, Kansas City, and New Hampshire. Schlesinger now lives in Sag Harbor, New York.

L. J. Schneiderman, M.D., is a professor of family and preventive medicine in the department of medicine at the University of California San Diego Medical Center. Author of more than one hundred medical and scientific articles and books, he is very active at both clinical and national-policy levels in dealing with controversial issues in medical ethics. His short stories have been published in literary journals, and his plays have been performed in San Francisco and New York.

Hannah Sherebrin, R.N., A.T.R, has worked as an art therapist with children with disabilities in Haifa, Israel, and London, Ontario. In addition to acting as a clinical practicum supervisor for students of the Art Therapy Program at the University of Western Ontario, in London, Ontario, Sherebrin is currently in private practice. Her main areas of interest are trauma, PTSD, and bereavement. She is currently planning to open an art studio for consumers of the mental health system, similar to the Art Craft Studio of the University of Western Ontario that she managed and helped establish.

Wilma Bulkin Siegel, M.D., spent nearly twenty years as an oncologist and educator at Montefiore Hospital and Albert Einstein College of Medicine in New York City. She later served as medical director of hospice at Beth Abraham Hospital in the Bronx. She also studied sculpture with Bruno Lucchesi at the New School and art at the National Academy of Design, both in New York City.

Mary J. Simpson, R.N., I.C.A.D.C., is the founder and director of the Positive Alternatives Wellness Center in Brampton, Ontario. She is a holistic-wellness consultant and addiction counselor. She has been involved in Therapeutic Touch since 1980 and was the cofounder of the Therapeutic Touch Network of Ontario.

Carla J. Sofka, Ph.D., is an assistant professor of social work at Skidmore College in Saratoga Springs, New York. She has a wide range of clinical experience in hospice, psychiatric and medical social work, and aftercare. Her research includes social support as a factor in coping with loss, grief issues related to mental illness, and the use of the Internet and World Wide Web as a clinical and supportive resource.

Barbara M. Sourkes, Ph.D., is a staff psychologist within the departments of psychology and home care at the Montreal Children's Hospital. She is also the clinical supervisor at the department of psychology at McGill University, Montreal, Quebec, and author of *The Deepening Shade* and *Armfuls of Time.*

Kurt Stasiak, O.S.B., is a Benedictine monk and priest at Saint Meinrad Archabbey, Saint Meinrad, Indiana. In addition to serving as the monastic community's vocation director, he is associate professor of sacraments and liturgy at Saint Meinrad School of Theology.

Judith M. Stillion, Ph.D., is a professor of psychology and Associate Vice President for Academic Affairs at the University of North Carolina. A past president and current board member of the Association for Death Education and Counseling, she is the author, coauthor, or editor of three books and nearly one hundred articles and chapters on such diverse subjects as gender differences in death, dying, and grief; suicide across the life span; and attitudes toward suicide.

Maria Trozzi, M.Ed., is the director of the Good Grief Program of Boston Medical Center and Judge Baker Children's Center in Boston. She is a clinical assistant professor of developmental pediatrics at Boston University School of Medicine. As a faculty member of the T. Berry Brazelton National Seminar Series, she lectures regularly on issues of bereavement throughout the United States.

Leigh Westerfield, Ph.D., currently teaches English composition and literature at Manchester College, Fort Wayne, Indiana. In addition to her teaching, she helps at-risk youth use the arts to curb the problem of violence. She has started a writing project for young people in Fort Wayne, in which they "publish" a magazine of their writings that they then distribute to other youth centers.

Kate Wilkinson has been a producer, arts animator, and administrator for over twenty years, mostly in the theater, opera, and the visual arts. She has also performed over twenty-five lead roles and has directed as well as taught drama to seniors and young people. She has been the artistic director of Target Actors with whom she has developed and directed seven productions. Frequently using the techniques of the Theatre of the Oppressed, these works explore predominantly seniors' issues.

Index

Abnormal Psychology and Modern Life (Colman), 242

Accidental death, 163, 167

Accidental Tourist, 152, 155-156

Acute grief, 16, 240

Adjustments to impending death, asking how the dying person made, 35

Adlerian theory of individual psychology, 242

Adolescent grief, 152, 161, 167, 187-199, 199-203

Affective support, 332-334, 339-340

African Americans, 54, 199-203

African sculpture, 13, 15f

After Surgery (Davis), 77

"Against Daily Insignificance" (Davis), 12, 303-312

AIDS (acquired immune deficiency syndrome)
Cawthra Park AIDS Memorial, 12, 317-329, 318f, 321f
films as catharsis in grief therapy, 153, 165-166
Quilt, AIDS, 4, 12, 95, 319

"AIDS Time: A Passage through Cawthra Park (Miller), 12, 317-329

Alfred Hitchcock Presents, 151

Altruism through art, 282-283

Amputation of a body part, 8-9, 71-84
breast, 8-12, 75, 77, 81
Cancer Ward, The (Solzhenitsyn), 76-77
Disabled (Owen), 74
Does It Matter (Sassoon), 73-74
Infirmity (Roethke), 82
Leg, The (Shapiro), 81
Out, Out— (Frost), 71-72
Semi-Private (Yglesias), 77
Sunshine (Klein), 76
Tell Me that You Love Me, Junie Moon (Kellogg), 77-81

[Amputation of a body part]
timing, 75-76
Virginia (Swenson), 75, 81

Ancient cultures and death, 7, 222

Anger, 25-26, 108, 109f, 240

Anguish and music, 270-271

Anointing of the sick, 227, 231
See also Ritual in the pastoral care of the sick and dying

Anticipatory grief, 141-142, 151-152, 156, 168, 170

Anxiety, 223, 355

Appassionata (Beethoven), 56

Approaches to Art Therapy (Rubin), 102

Arioso, in G (Bach), 55

Ars Moriendi, 241

"Art Techniques for Children with Cancer" (Sourkes), 5, 119-126

Arts, grief and the
balancing act between personal and professional involvement, 3-5, 11, 21-96
cultures old and new, lessons from, 7-9, 10f-11f, 12, 217-343
Five Stages of Grief (Pastan), 1-2
partnership, chemistry of, 13-15
re-inspiration, periodic, 1
See also individual subject headings

Art therapy, 5-6, 99-118, 237, 249-250
pediatrics, with, 99-118
See also cancer

Artwork
Alma Mater (Munch), 299
Call of Death (Kollwitz), 285f
Dance of Life, The (Munch), 297f
Dead Mother (Munch), 291, 292f, 301
Farewell (Kollwitz), 286f
Fever (Munch), 294f
Germinal (Kollwitz), 279
memorials, 12, 317-329, 318f, 321f, 360

[Artwork]
Parents, The (Kollwitz), 283f
Scream, The (Munch), 8f, 297, 301
Self-Portrait (Kollwitz), 282f
Sick Child, The (Munch), 300, 300f
See also Sculpture
Association for Death Education and
Counseling (ADEC), 337
Attachment, creating/transforming bonds
of, 15
Auden, W. H., 72-73
Authenticity and openness when dealing
with a suicide, 191, 194
Autonomy, a sense of, 290
Aztecs, 222

Bach, Johann S., 273-274
Bailey, Sally, 4, 53-58, 226
Balancing act between personal and
professional involvement, 3-5
Baptism, 230, 232
Barlach, Ernst, 282
Bastable, Austin, 334
Beaches, 156-157
Becoming the Patient (Davis), 51-52
Beethoven, Ludwig van, 265, 268,
270-271
Bengssten, Otelia, 352
Bereavement Resources, 16, 334
Berlioz, Hector, 269, 270-271
Black-and-white portraits, 210-211
Blood tests, 106, 107f
Bluebond-Langner, Myra, 16, 128
Boal, Augusto, 173
Body Flute, The (Davis), 85-87
Bowlby, John, 3, 16, 22, 252, 278, 287
Bonny, Helen, 53, 146
Boston Medical Center, 196-197
Brahms, Johannes, 269-270, 273
Brentano, Antonie, 265, 268
Bridgeman, Melinda, 143, 144f
Brody, Howard, 1, 14, 17
Brueghel, P., 73
Buddhism, 222
Bulletin boards on the Internet, 332
Burial service, 36, 246-247, 334
Burnout, reduction of, 1, 14-15, 39-41,
61-70, 393-402

Call of Death (Kollwitz), 285f
Cancer, 61-70, 71-84, 99-118, 119-126,
127-138, 139-144
Children's Hospital of Western Ontario,
102-103
choice, offering, 108-111
defining art therapy, 101-102
dying child, the, 112-113, 113f-115f
family drawings, 122, 123f
history and theory of art therapy, 102
introduction, 99-100
mandala, the, 119-120, 121f, 122
scariest image, 122, 124, 124f-125f
therapist, how this work affects the art,
113-115
treatment, cancer, 103-105
waiting game, the, 105-108
See also Art therapy/techniques
Cancer and Therapeutic Touch, 362
CancerNet, 333
Cancer Ward, The (Solzhenitsyn), 76-77
Caregivers needing care, 1, 65-69
Caroline's Women's Weekend group
(Wizansky), 388, 389f, 390-391
Cassell, Eric, 3, 16
Catechism of the Catholic Church, 228
Catholic Church, 225
See also Religion; Ritual in the pastoral
care of the sick and dying
Cawthra Park AIDS Memorial, 317-329,
318f, 321f
Centering, 354, 360
Centering Corporation, 209
Centers for Disease Control (CDC), 326
Childbirth and Therapeutic Touch, 361-362
Children, bereaved, 36-37
See also Cancer, art therapy/techniques
and children with
Children's Hospital of Western Ontario,
99-100, 102-103
China, 254
Chiochio, Julian, 61-69
Choice in Dying site, 337
Choices, the need for having, 108-111
Chronic grief, 241
Client/therapist relationship as a
partnership, 1, 13-15
Coconut Grove nightclub fire in Boston,
21, 22
Collective unconscious, Jungian, 222

College of Nurses in Ontario, 362-363
"Comfort Care" (Schneiderman), 5, 61-69
Commemorations
    Cawthra Park AIDS Memorial, 16-17,
        317-329, 318f, 321f
    creative, 6
    healing and the Internet, 343-345, 346f,
        347-348
    Internet, the, 334-336
    suicide, 195-196
Commissioning of a vocation, 232-234
Communication, 127-128
Community, sense of, 7, 143
Community resources, 6, 7
Community response to suicide, 191-195
Competent therapist, 14
Composers, musical, 268-269
    See also Music
Compounded loss, 238
Comprehensive Health Enhancement
    Support System (CHESS), 333
Computer technology, 332
    See also Internet, the
Confidentiality, 338
Connecting and companioning, music as a
    bridge to, 149
Consciousness and the human energy field,
    357
Consecration of a valued possession, 230-232
Containment/safety and intensity of
    emotions, 154
Contemporary art ignoring manifestations
    and meaning of death, 219
Corigliano, John, 319
Cosmocentric creativity, 217
Courage to be, 218, 219
Cradling Her Sorrow (Fried), 9, 9f
Creativity-culture-and death, 8, 217-224
Crimes of the Heart, 152, 157-158
"Crisis in the Cafeteria" (Trozzi), 6,
    187-198
Crow and Weasel (Lopez), 7
Crying, 25, 26, 55
"Culture-Creativity-and Death," (Havelka)
    8, 217-224
Cultures old and new, lessons from, 7-9,
    10f-11f, 12
Cummings, Lynn, 4, 43-50
Cure vs. healing, the concept of, 353-354
    See also Pain, suffering

Dance of Life, The (Munch), 297f
Darkness, image of, 229
Davies, Betty, 16, 47, 49
Davis, Cortney, 5, 39, 51, 59, 85
Davis, Martha, 303-312
Dead Mother (Munch), 291, 292f, 301
Dead Poet's Society, 152
"Dear Edith" (Kesson), 13, 393-401
"Death and Grief: Life of Edvard Munch"
    (Stillion), 8, 289-302
Death education, 151-153, 336-338
DeathNet, 337
Death of Ivan Ilych, The (Tolstoy), 72,
    79-80
Delayed grief, 241-242
Denial, 25-26, 217
Depersonalization of the patient, 48
Depression, 25, 241
Despair, 26
Detachment, 27
Developmental considerations for puppet
    play, 134t
Diagnostic and Statistical Manual, 239
Dialogue groups, 7
Dictionary of Music, 269
Disabilities and puppet play, children with,
    135
Disabled (Owen), 74
Disillusionment of nurses, 48
Divine Comedy, The (Dante), 99
Does It Matter (Sassoon), 73-74
Doka, Kenneth, 16
Dorfman, Elsa, 13-14, 14f, 377-392,
    378f-382f, 385, 386f, 389f
Dramatic play, 128-129
    See also Puppet play
Drugs used to escape from feeling, 23

Education, death, 151-153, 336-338
Education, medical, 71
Ego-anxiety, 223
Ego integrity, 291
Electronic groups, 7
Eliot, T. S., 225-226
Elliott, Willis, 57
Emblematic mourning, 247
Emotions
    bankruptcy of, 14
    clarification of, 153-154

[Emotions]
containment/safety, 154
music releasing, 6, 267
support, the Internet and emotional, 332-334, 339-340
Empathy, 13-15, 46, 72-73, 79-80, 89-92
See also Amputation of a body part, suffering
Energy field, each of us is an, 353, 357, 360, 361f
Eng, Brenda, 6, 127-138
Erikson's theory of psychosocial development, 289-291
Escapism during grief, 154-155
Estabany, Oscar, 352
Ethical issues, 5, 43-50, 61-70, 68, 338-339
Ethnicity affecting the resolution of loss, 36
Existential psychology, 246
Experiential sites on the Internet, 335
Expressive sites on the Internet, 335

Fahn, Patrick, 319
Family drawings, 5, 122, 123f
Fanslow-Brunjes, Cathleen, 357
Farewell (Kollwitz), 286f
Fauré, Gabriel, 269, 274
Fear, 99, 100f, 108, 109f, 218
Feifel, Herman, 21
Fever (Munch), 294f
Field of Dreams, 152, 158-159
Figley, Charles, 16
Films as catharsis in grief therapy, 6
    Accidental Tourist, 152, 155-156
    Brian's Song, 151
    Beaches, 156-157
    containment/safety, 154
    Crimes of the Heart, 152, 157-158
    Dead Poet's Society, 152
    death education in media, evolution of, 151-153
    emotions, clarification of, 153-154
    escapism during grief, 154-155
    Field of Dreams, 152, 158-159
    Love Story, 151
    Men Don't Leave, 153, 159-161
    My Body Guard, 152, 161-162
    My Girl, 153, 162-163

[Films as catharsis in grief therapy]
    Occurrence at Owl Creek Bridge, An, 151
    Ordinary People, 163-164
    permission to grieve, giving, 153
    Philadelphia, 153, 164-166
    Sophie's Choice, 152, 166-167
    Stand By Me, 152, 167-168
    Steel Magnolias, 152, 168-169
    Terms of Endearment, 170-171
Financial and legal picture, asking what is the, 32-33
Finger puppets, 133
First-aid techniques in Therapeutic Touch, 362
"Five Stages of Grief" (Pastan), 1-2
Focused intent, state of, 354
Forsyth, Lesleigh, 6, 265-276, 373-376
Forum theatre, 6, 173-185
Fox, Sandra, 197
Freeing, creative, 220-221
Freud, Sigmund, 3, 7, 16, 21
Fried, Nancy, 9-12, 313-316
Frontiers of Nursing program, 352
Funeral process, 36, 246-247, 334

Gamino, Louis, 8, 277-288
German Requiem, 269-270
Geriatrics, 13, 17f, 393-402
Gilbert, Kathleen, 337
Glen, Victor, 234
Global Project on AIDS, 326-327
Going on to familiar activities after the suicide, 196
Golden, Tom, 12, 343-350
Good Grief Program of Boston Medical Center and Judge Baker Children's Center, 196-197
Gough, Mindy, 6, 205-214
Grad, Bernard, 352
Gravestone rubbing, 203, 204f
Greatness, fear of, 218
Grief cycles, trajectories, 1-15, 26f, 239-240
Grief Experience Inventory (GEI), 356
Grief research, 16
GriefNet, 334
Grohol, John, 333
Grollman, Earl, 136, 197
Groups as a valuable resource, 7

Guided Imagery and Music (GIM), 146-147
Guided visualization, 119-120
Guilt, needless, 24, 166, 223-224

Halakhic components of mourning, 243-244
Halporn, Roberta, 6, 203, 253-264
Hamlet and pathological grief, 253-264
Hand-Heart Connection, 357-360
Hand puppets, 133
Harlem Book of the Dead (VanDerZee),
    211
Harling, Robert, 152
Harling, Susan, 152
Hateful actions by caregivers, 47-48
Havelka, J., 7, 217-224
Hatem, David, 4, 93-94
Hawkins, life and death of Yusuf, 6,
    199-202, 200f-201f, 203f
Healing ability, 353
    See also Therapeutic Touch (TT)
"Healing and the Internet (Golden),
    343-345, 346f, 347-348
Hearing impaired children and puppet play,
    135
Henteleff, Dr., 47
History and theory of art therapy, 102
HIV (human immunodeficiency virus), 4,
    12, 93-94, 318, 327
"Hope and Millie" (Hatem), 93-94
Hope System, The, 357
Hopkins, G. M., 22-23
Hospice care, 61-69, 91-92, 139-148
    Comfort Care Group, 61-69
    visual arts, application of participatory,
        6, 139-143, 144f
Hospital arrivals and the waiting game,
    106-107
How did the death occur, asking, 29-30
Humanistic psychology, 246
Hunger, 105f

I know what's best syndrome, 47
Immune response to stress, 358
Impact of this loss, asking about the,
    33-34
Inclusiveness, creating an environment of,
    189
Indiana University, 337

Individual variables in loss, 28
Infants. *See* Photographs, remembrance
Informational support, 332, 333-334,
    339-340
Information and referral on the Internet,
    336
Instrumental support, 334, 340
Internet, the, 7, 12, 331
    benefits for the bereaved, 336
    challenges and cautions, 337-338
    clinical practice and death education,
        336-338
    conclusions, 339
    death education, 336-337
    "Healing and the Internet" (Golden),
        343-345, 346f, 347-348
    information and referral, 336
    mediated interpersonal communication,
        332-334
    narrative/commemorative/expressive/
        experiential sites, 334-336
    professional resources, 337
    research, implications for, 338-339
    sites on the World Wide Web,
        thanatology, 339-340
    "Social Support, resources for," (Sofka),
        12, 332-336
Interpersonal communication, mediated,
    332-334
Intravenous treatment, 103, 104f
It's the Closure Fairy (Lorenz), 4f

Jean-Guy, 327-328
Jesu, Joy of Man's Desiring, 55
Jesus Christ. *See* Ritual in the pastoral care
    of the sick and dying
Jonah syndrome, 218
Journal, keeping a, 25
Journal of Palliative Care, 47
Joy at being released, 108, 110f
Judaism
    burial, the, 246-247
    Halakhic components of mourning,
        243-244
    keriah (rendering of garments), 244-246,
        244f
    seriated mourning process, 247-248
Jung, Carl G., 3, 102, 222, 237, 252
Juvenile delinquency, 242

Kaddish (Jewish memorial prayer), 247, 248
Kastenbaum, Robert, 16
Kelley, Regina, 6, 139-144
Kesson, Jessie, 13, 17, 393-402
Keriah (rendering of garments), 244-246, 244f
Kevorkian, Jack, 338
Kindertotenlieder (Mahler), 54-55
Kinetic Family Drawing, 122, 123f
Kings College Conference on Death, Dying and Bereavement (1995), 209
Kirkland, Kevin, 6, 145-148
Klass, Dennis, 16
Kollwitz, Kaethe, 8
Kollwitz, Karl, 279
"Kollwitz, life and art of Kaethe" (Gamino), 8-9, 277-288
    childhood and adolescence, 277-278
    conclusions, 286-287
    marriage and early adulthood, 279-280
    middle age and the loss of her son, 281-284
    old age, 284-285
Kollwitz, Peter, 281
Kol Nidrei (Bruch), 55
Koocher, Gerald, 16
Krant, Melvin, 71-84
Krieger, Dolores, 352, 364
Kübler-Ross, Elisabeth, 171, 287
Kunz, Dora, 352

Lamers, William, 4, 21-38
Languages used to communicate knowledge of impending death, 128
Latimer, E., 46
Laying on of hands, 231-232, 352
Lazare, Aaron, 4, 16, 89-92
Leary, Timothy, 334
Leg, The (Shapiro), 81
Legal and financial picture, asking what is the, 32-33
Lester, Suzanne, 5, 99-118
Libraries on the Internet, 337
Life force, universal, 360
Life review through music, 147-148
Lindemann, E., 3, 16, 22, 26, 171, 251
Lindenblatt, Elaine, 13, 371-372

Literature, creative, 71
    See also Amputation of a body part; Poetry
Longing, phases of recurrent, 25
Long-term impact of loss, 34
Loss, on the psychology of
    basic ideas of grief and loss, 1-3, 14-16, 238-239
    child's loss of a parent, 158, 159
    despair, 26
    detachment, 27
    dynamics of loss, 24-28
    grief reactions, 23-24
    guilt, needless, 24
    hospice care and visual arts, 140
    Internet, the, 332
    literature, professional, 21
    parent's loss of a child, 155
    poetry, 22-23
    prognosis, variables in, 28
    protest, 25-26
    questions to ask when working with grieving persons, 28-36
    recovery, 27-28, 36-37
    summary, 37
Love, nonjudgmental, 354
Love and music, 271-272
Lourde, A., 1
Lullabies, 267, 272-273
Lynch, Michael, 320-321

Maher, Gustav, 271-272
Man and His Symbols (Jung), 102
Mandala, the, 119-120, 121f, 122
Marionettes, 133
Martins, Lynne, 6, 151-172
Martinson, Ida, 16
Maslow, Abraham, 246
Material aid sites on the Internet, 340
McDowell, Judith, 6, 173-186
Meaning, search for, 3
Meaning of Death, The (Feifel), 21
Mediated interpersonal communication, 332-334
Medical education, 71
Memoirs (Berlioz), 269
Memorials, 12, 317-329, 318f, 321f
    See also Commemorations
Mendelssohn, Felix, 273

Men Don't Leave, 153, 159-161

Mental health community linkage and suicide, 193-195

Mental health problems, an increase in, 242-243

Merton, Thomas, 268

Miller, James, 12, 317-330

Mitzvah (divine commandment), 243-244, 246

Modern art ignoring manifestations and meaning of death, 219

Monuments, large-scale architectural, 12

Most Important Picture, A: A Very Tender Manual for Taking Pictures of Stillborn Babies and Infants Who Die (Johnson), 209

Mount, Balfour, 46

M(ortality) Word and L(ove) Word (Dorfman), 13-14, 377-391

Mourning and Melancholia (Freud), 21, 237, 245

Mourning to morning, the journey from, 53-57

See also individual subject headings

Movies. *See* Films as catharsis in grief therapy

Mozart, Wolfgang A., 271

Munch, "The Life and Work of Edvard," (Stillion), 8, 289-302

adulthood, 295-299

childhood and adolescence of, 291-295

teaching prospective caregivers using Munch's art, 299-301

Mural on the life and death of Yusuf Hawkins, 199-202, 200f-201f, 203f

Murder, 199-202, 200f-201f, 203f

Musée des Beaux Arts (Auden), 72

"Music—A Companion" (Bailey), 4, 53-58

"Music and Grief Process" (Forsyth), 6, 265-276

"Music Therapy" (Kirkland), 6, 145-148

Music

anguish and tumult, 270-271

Beethoven, 265

comfort and hope, 273

composers, 268-269

connecting and companioning, music as a bridge to, 149

emotions, releasing, 6

[Music]

feelings made accessible through, 266-267

Guided Imagery and Music (GIM), 146-147

life review through, 147-148

listening on purpose, 267-268

love and regret, 271-272

lullabies and the longing for comfort, 272-273

mourning to morning, journey from, 53-57

pain management, 147

religion, 145

repetition, 145

requiems of Berlioz/Fauré/Brahms, 269-270

resignation, 273-274

transcendence, 274

My Body Guard, 152, 161-162

My Girl, 153, 162-163

"My Mother's Hands" (Lindenblatt), 13, 371-372

Mysterium tremendum, 222

Narrative sites on the Internet, 334, 336

National Cancer Centre Institute of Canada, 99

Native Americans, 213

Needs of grieving people, basic, 13

Negative nursing behaviors, 45

Neimeyer, Robert, 16

New Age music, 145

Newman, Ernest, 270

Newsgroups on the Internet, 332

Nicholas, Linda, 5

Nickman, Stephen, 16

Night Nurse (Davis), 59-60

Non-creative person, 220

Nonjudgmental love, 354

Nonmaleficence, 43

Normal grief patterns, 1, 3, 16, 26f, 239-240

Numbness, a feeling of, 239

Numinosity, 221-222

Nurse Healers-Professional Associates, Inc., 364

Nurses caring for dying patients

conclusion, 49

discussion, 46-49

[Nurses caring for dying patients]
disillusionment, 48
literature review, 44-46
negative nursing behaviors, 45
patient-centered care, 43, 47
self-care, 1, 43
See also Burnout
shared power model, 13-15, 17
supportive care model, 44
Therapeutic Touch, 362-363

Occurrence at Owl Creek Bridge, An,
151
Oklahoma City bombing, 335
OncoLink site, 333, 335
Oncology. *See* Cancer, art therapy/
techniques and children with
Online support groups, 333, 336
See also Internet, the
Openness to client's creative acts, 3
Ordinary People, 163-164
Out, Out— (Frost), 71-72
Over-involvement, 48
Owen, Wilfred, 73

Pain, 1-17
music, 147
Therapeutic Touch, 355-356
See also Grief, suffering
Palliative care, 43
See also Cancer, art therapy/techniques
and children with; Nurses caring for
dying patients; Hospice
Parental loss, 158, 159
Parents, The (Kollwitz), 283f
Parent's loss of a child, 155
Parents of the friends of the suicide victim,
192-193
Parkes, Colin, Murray, 16, 348-351
Partnership, chemistry of, 13-15
*Pastoral Care of the Sick and Dying: Rites
of Anointing and Viaticum,* 227, 231,
233
Pathological grief, 240-242, 253-264
Patient-centered care, 43, 47
Permission to grieve losses, 153

Personal and professional involvement,
balancing act
between, 3-5
Personal relationships and creativity,
219
Person-computer interpersonal encounters
for informational
support, 333-334
Person-computer interpersonal encounters
for instrumental
support, 334
Personhoods, 3
Pets Grief Support Page, 335
Philadelphia, 153, 164-166
Photographs, remembrance, 6, 13, 14f
current practice, 206-208
families healing, 377, 378f-382f, 385,
386f, 387
historical perspective, 205-206
illness, 383-384
parents and professionals, perspectives
of, 208-209
photographs, the, 209-211
presenting, 211-213
Picard, Carol, 4, 96, 149, 367
Picasso, Pablo, 7, 253
Play, play therapy and therapeutic,
128-129, 129t
See also Puppet play
Plays (theater)
Wake for Dying, A, 6, 173-185
Plays (theatre)
Hamlet, 253-264
Weavers (Hauptmann), 279-280
Plush toys converted into puppets, 133
Poetry
After Surgery (Davis), 77
Becoming the Patient (Davis), 51-52
Body Flute, The (Davis), 85-87
Davis, Martha, 306-309
Disabled (Owen), 74
Does It Matter (Sassoon), 73
Esperanza, 290-391
Five Stages of Grief (Pastan), 1-2
Hello, David, 369-370
Infirmity (Roethke), 82
loss, on the psychology of, 22-23
My Life, 391
Night Nurse (Davis), 59-60

[Poetry]

Nurse and the Art Are One, The (Picard), 367

Out, Out— (Frost), 71-72

Seeing Fred on a Respirator (Picard), 96

Songlines (Picard), 149

Spring and Fall: To A Young Child (Hopkins), 22-23

truth and symbol, relationship between, 226

Virginia (Swenson), 75

What the Nurse Likes (Davis), 5, 39-41

Pornography of Death, The (Gorer), 241

Pragmatic stance toward life, 25

Preserving own integrity, concept of, 43, 45, 46, 49

See also Nurses caring for dying patients, Comfort care, Ethical issues, Poetry

"Preventing Harm" (Cummings), 43-50

Principals at schools dealing with suicide, 192

Prior loses, asking if the survivor has experienced, 34-35

Professional and personal involvement, balancing act between, 1, 3-5

Professional resources on the Internet, 337

Project on Death in America (PODA), 337

Protest, 25-26

Psychological roots and creativity, 221

Psychological support, 36

"Psychology of Loss" (Lamers), 21-38

Psychosocial development, Erikson's theory of, 289-291

Psychotherapy, art, 102

"Puppets" (Eng), 6, 127-138

Puppet play, 6

background rationale, 128-129

beginning where you are, 133

defining, 129, 131

developmental considerations, 134t

interpretation, caution against, 131

skills, enlisting your, 133, 135

summary, 135

types of puppets, 132-133

what is a puppet, 131-132

Quality of the relationship, asking what was the, 31-32

Questions to ask when working with grieving persons

approach impending death, how did the dying person, 35

basic, the, 28-29

financial and legal picture, what is the, 32-33

funeral, what was the impact of the, 36

how did the death occur, 29-30

impact of this loss, what is the, 33-34

prior loses, has the survivor experienced, 34-35

quality of the relationship, what was the, 31-32

sanctioned loss, was this a, 32

strengths of the survivor, what are the, 35

supports are present, what external, 35-36

survivor identification, are there symptoms of, 31

survivor involved in the care of the deceased, was the, 33

unfinished business remains, what, 32

when did the death occur, 30

where did the death occur, 30

who died, 29

Quill, T., 17

Quilt, an AIDS, 4, 95, 319

Rabin, Yitzhak, 335

Rando, Teresa, 16, 38, 171, 207, 213, 252, 287

Raphael, Beverly, 16

Reardon, Jack, 187-188

Recovery from loss, 27-28, 36-37

Redmond, Lula, 16

Regret and music, 271-272

Re-inspiration, periodic, 1

Relationships, creativity and personal, 219

healing, 13-15

Relaxation response and Therapeutic Touch, 354-355

Reliability of information on the Internet, 338
Religion
    Judaism, 7, 237-252, 243-248
    melancholy, getting beyond, 55-56
    music, 54, 145
    questions, spiritual, 1-2
    ritual in the pastoral care of the sick and dying, 7, 225-236
    rituals, 1-2
    Therapeutic Touch, 354, 364
Remembrance portraits, 205
    See also Photographs, remembrance
Remorse, feelings of, 25
Requiems of Berlioz/Fauré/Brahms, 269-270
Rescuer fantasy, 48
Resignation and music, 273-274
Resolution, grief, 237
    basic ideas of grief and loss, 238-239
    conclusions, 250-251
    defining, 238
    Judaism, 243-248
    normal grief patterns, 1-3, 16f, 239-240
    pathological grief reactions, 240-242
    rituals facilitating the mourning process, 242-243
    visual images, the use of, 249-250
    See also Grief research
Revisits of grief, periodic, 15
Right-to-die organizations, 334, 337, 338
Ritual in the pastoral care of the sick and dying, 8, 13, 225-235
    anointing of the sick, the sacrament of the, 227
    commissioning of a vocation, 232-234
    consecration of a valued possession, 230-232
    spoken words of the sacrament, 227-230
    truth, sacramental ritual as the incarnation of the, 225-227
Rituals facilitating the mourning process, 242-243
    See also Grief
Rodman, Flicka, 89
Rodman, Jane, 89
Rogers, Carl, 246

Roman Catholic Church, 225
    See also Religion; Ritual in the pastoral care of the sick and dying
Roy, David, 46, 47

Sacrament. See Ritual in the pastoral care of the sick and dying
Sacred texts, 1-2
Sanctioned loss, asking if this was this a, 32
Sassoon, Siegfried, 73
Scariest image as an art therapy technique, 122, 124, 124f-125f
Schlesinger, Christina, 6, 199-202
Schneiderman, Laurence, 5, 16-17, 61-70
Schubert, Franz, 272, 274
Schweitzer, Albert, 53
Scream, The (Munch), 8f, 297, 301
Sculpture, 313-314, 316f
    African, 13, 15f
    Annie and Medicine Shield (Fried), 142f
    Annie and the Owl (Kelley), 142, 143f
    Breast Flap (Fried), 11f
    Cradling Her Sorrow (Fried), 9f
    Flirt, The (Fried), 12f
    Hanging Out (Fried), 11f
    Making the Pain (Fried), 315f
    Nightmare, The (Fried), 9, 10f
    "Sculpting Through Grief" (Fried), 12, 313-316
    Self-Portrait (Fried), 314f
Search engines, Internet, 335
Searching, extended and undirected, 25
Seeing Fred on a Respirator (Picard), 96
Self-actualization, 218, 246
Self-appraisal, 47
Self-esteem, 108, 110-111, 111f
Self-knowledge, 47
Self-respect, 108, 110-111, 111f
Self-worth, 140
Selzer, R., 13, 17
Semi-Private (Yglesias), 77
Shallow mourning, 247
Sherebrin, Hannah, 8, 237, 252
Shivah (Jewish mourning period), 247, 248
Shloshim (Jewish mourning period), 247
Short-term impact of loss, 33
Shroeder-Sheker, Therese, 145

Sibling grief, 12, 71-72, 91-92, 161, 163-165, 167, 303-312

Sick Child, The (Munch), 300, 300f

Sickness. *See* Ritual in the pastoral care of the sick and dying

Side effects, 106f

Siegel, Wilma B., 4, 95, 95f

Silence, 268

"Silent Conversations" (Westerfield), 13, 403-407

Silverman, Phyllis, 16

Simpson, Mary, 351-365

Sleeping Beauty: Memorial Photography in America, 211

Socialist artist, 280

Social support, the Internet and resources for, 332-336

Sofka, Carla, 12

Somatic symptoms of grief, 239

Sometimes I Feel Like a Motherless Child, 54

Songlines (Picard), 149

Son's grief over death of father, 158

Sophie's Choice, 152, 166-167

"Sourdough Father, The" (Forsyth), 13, 373-375

Sourkes, Barbara, 5, 50, 116, 119-126

Spirituality, *see also* Introduction, Buddhism, Culture-Creativity-and Death, Healing, Religion, Suffering

Spoken words of the sacrament, 227-230

Spontaneous Healing (Weil), 361

Spousal loss, 159

Stand By Me, 152, 167-168

Stasiak, Kurt, 13

Status quo, negotiating a truce with the, 3

Steel Magnolias, 152, 168-169

Stick puppets, 132, 135

Stillion, Judith, 8, 89-304

Story aprons/totes, 135

Storytelling, 7, 250

Strauss, Richard, 272-273

Strobe, Margaret, 16

Strengths of the survivor, asking about the, 35

Stress of day-to-day encounters with death, 45, 356

String puppets, 133

Sudden death, 163, 199-202, 200f-201f, 203f, 303-312
See also Suicide

"Suffering, reflections on" (Lazare), 8, 89-92

"Suffering, to know of" (Bertman, Krant), 71-84

Suicide
authenticity and openness when dealing with, 191
commemoration, 195-196
community response to, 191-192
films, 152, 157, 161, 163, 167
going on to familiar activities, 196
inclusiveness, creating and environment of, 189
Internet, the, 334
mental health community linkage, 193-195
parents of the friends of the victim, 192-193
principals at schools dealing with, 192
requesting help to deal with, 187-188
Suicide Information And Education Centre (SIEC), 337
understanding why, 189-191

Summarizing of one's life, art leading to a, 141, 147-148

Sunshine (Klein), 76

Sunyata (objectless cosmic void), 222

Supportive care model, 44

Supports are present, asking what external, 35-36

Supports on the Internet, social, 332-336

Surrogate family member, becoming a, 48

Survivor identification, asking are there symptoms of, 31

Survivor involved in the care of the deceased, asking if, 33

Survivor's guilt, 166

Symbol and truth, relationship between, 226

Symbolic verbal/nonverbal language, 128

Symbolization, 223

Symptomatology and Management of Acute Grief (Lindemann), 21

Talmud, the, 245
Teaching prospective caregivers using Munch's art, 299-301
Teenage Pregnancy, 23
Tell Me that You Love Me, Junie Moon (Kellogg), 77-81
Terminally ill, pain in the, 356
Terms of Endearment, 170-171
Thanatechnology, 331
  See also Internet, the
Theatre, forum, 6, 173-185
"The Patient Examines the Doctor" (Broyard), 3
Therapeutic play, 128, 129t
  See also Puppet play
Therapeutic Touch Network in Ontario, 364
Therapeutic Touch (TT)
  assumptions, 353
  burnout, reduction of, 363
  comfort of person in transition, promoting the, 351-352
  consciousness and the human energy field, 357
  cure *vs.* healing, the concept of, 1, 13-16, 353-354
  detractors, 364
  effects of, 354-355
  grieving, healing of the, 356
  Hand-Heart Connection, 357-360
  history behind, 352-353
  learning, 364
  nursing field, 362-363
  pain in the terminally ill, 356
  practice of, 360-361
  religion, 354
  research, 364
  uses of, specific, 361-362
  validation of grieving, 356-357
Therapist/client relationship as a partnership, 1, 13-16
Therapists and stresses of working with the dying child, 1, 113-115
Time and timelessness, grief existing in both, 15
Timing and body-part sacrifice, 75-76
Torah, the, 243
Toronto East General Hospital, 363

Toys converted into puppets, plush, 133
Transcendence and music, 274
Transformational theatre, 173
Traps into which caregivers fall in the process of helping, 48
Trozzi, Maria, 6, 187-198
Trust, 290
Truth and ritual in the pastoral care of the sick and dying, 225-227
Tumult and music, 270-271
Twilight Zone, 151
Unconscious, Jungian collective, 222
Under-involvement, 48
Understanding the why when dealing with a suicide, 189-191
Unfinished business remains, asking what, 32
Universal life force, 360
University of Pennsylvania, 333, 335
Unresolved grief, 23-24, 152, 157, 158, 162
"Using Art Therapy with Pediatrics" (Nicholas, Lister), 99-118

Validation of grieving, 356-357
Victoria, Queen, 253
Victorian photography albums, 206, 206f
Virginia (Swenson), 75, 81
Visible words of the sacrament. *See* Ritual in the pastoral care of the sick and dying
"Visible Words" (Stasiak), 8, 13, 225-235
Visual Analog Scale (VAS), 356
"Visual Arts and Hospice Care" (Kelley), 6, 139-143, 144f
Visualization, guided, 119-120
Visually impaired children and puppet play, 135
Vocation of the sick and dying, 232-234
Volkan, V., 253-264

Waiting game, the, 105-108
Wake for Dying, A, 173-185

War heroes and amputation, 73
War memorials, 12
Weavers (Hauptmann), 279-280
WEBSTER site, 336
Westerfield, Leigh, 13, 403-407
What the Nurse Likes (Davis), 39-41
When did the death occur, asking, 30
Where did the death occur, asking, 30
Who died, asking, 29
Wilkinson, Kate, 6, 173-186
Wilson, Alexander, 319
Winterson, Jeanette, 303, 311
Wirth, Dan, 356
Wizansky, Margot, 388-392
Women's Weekend group, 388, 389f, 390-391

Worden, J. W., 1, 16, 38
World Health Organization (WHO), 326-327
World Wide Cemetery site, 334
World Wide Web (WWW), 331
See also Internet, the

Writing through grief, 303-311
See also Poetry; "My Mother's Hands"; "Dear Edith"

Yahoo, 335
Yellow Pages on the Internet, 335
Yoga, 353